DOS 5—
Everything You Need to Know

How to Order:

Quantity discounts are available from the publisher, Prima Publishing, P.O. Box 1260DOS, Rocklin, CA 95677; telephone (916) 786-0426. On your letterhead include information concerning the intended use of the books and the number of books you wish to purchase.

U.S. Bookstores and Libraries: Please submit all orders to St. Martin's Press, 175 Fifth Avenue, New York, NY 10010; telephone (212) 674-5151.

DOS 5—
Everything You Need to Know

Jonathan Kamin

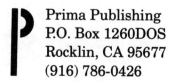

Prima Publishing
P.O. Box 1260DOS
Rocklin, CA 95677
(916) 786-0426

Typography by Futura Graphics
Production by Carol Dondrea, Bookman Productions
Copyediting by Candace Demeduc
Interior Design by Renee Deprey
Cover Design by Kirschner-Caroff Design

Prima Publishing
Rocklin, CA

Library of Congress Cataloging-in-Publication Data

Kamin, Jonathan.
    DOS 5—everything you need to know : a clear, simple, easy-to-use guide—from getting started to customizing your system / Jonathan Kamin.
      p. cm.
    Includes index.
    ISBN 1-55958-123-9
    1. MS-DOS (Computer operating system) 2. PC DOS (Computer operating system) I. Title.
    QA76.76.O63K328 1991
    005.4′46—dc20   91-3843
                                    CIP

91 92 93 94 RRD 10 9 8 7 6 5 4 3 2

Printed in the United States of America

To
NANCY, JARON, and JORDAN
with love, and thanks for your patience

Perseverance furthers.
The I Ching

Acknowledgments

This book would not be in your hands without the contributions of many besides the author. Frances Grimble did her utmost to give the manuscript a coherent shape. Mary Lyn Sorensen assisted with the word processing and prepared illustrations meticulously. I also owe a debt of thanks to Brent Krell and Eric Hoff of the Microsoft beta test program, and Christie Gersich of Microsoft's marketing department. They went out of their way to find the answers to many questions, to ensure that the information before you is correct. Special thanks also to Gary Sinclair of Modular Software and Philip Potasik of Toshiba, who kindly offered assistance on obscure points.

Many hands were involved in getting the manuscript into the form you see before you. Ben Dominitz of Prima Publishing helped to conceive the book. Jennifer Basye and Laura Glassover, also of Prima, kept the work moving, offering encouragement and assistance. Robin Lockwood, Carol Dondrea, and Candace Demeduc of Bookman Productions saw to the design, copyediting, proofreading, and printing.

Trademark Acknowledgments

Contents at a Glance

Contents

11   *Using the DOS Editor*   237

12   *Fine-Tuning Your Configuration*   257

Introduction

Who This Book Is For

DOS 5—Everything You Need to Know is intended for:

- The beginning user of an IBM-compatible computer that uses MS-DOS 5.0
- The more experienced user who wants to expand his or her knowledge of DOS in general and MS-DOS 5.0 in particular
- The experienced user who wants a quick guide to MS-DOS 5.0's new features

If you're a newcomer to computers, you will find detailed information, in plain language, about how to get your computer up and running, how to install DOS 5 if necessary, and how to interact with the computer using DOS 5's two modes of accepting instructions. As you become more experienced, you'll learn how to perform all the essential operations that DOS makes available to you.

If you're already somewhat experienced, you'll be able to use the more advanced material in this book to customize and enhance your system using the new facilities available in DOS 5.

If you are interested primarily in what's new, you'll find new features clearly indicated.

How This Book Is Organized

DOS 5—Everything You Need to Know is designed to be both a tutorial and a reference. You need not start at the beginning and work your way to the end. Just use the parts you need. At many points, the text clearly indicates parts you should skip if they don't apply to you, your equipment, or your software.

Chapter 1, "If You're New to Computers or Vice Versa," gives you an overview of your computer system. It explains the parts of the system and what they do and introduces DOS—the *operating system* that tells your computer how to perform its tasks. Many terms are introduced and defined.

Chapter 2, "Installing DOS 5," explains how to install DOS 5 on a computer with a hard disk that's already using another version, how to install DOS 5 on a computer whose hard disk does not yet have DOS, and how to install DOS 5 on diskettes. You can safely skip this chapter if your computer is already running DOS 5. You can refer to it later if you need to reinstall DOS.

You can interact with DOS 5 in two different ways—through the *command prompt* and the *Shell*. Chapter 3, "Getting Started," tells you how to start your computer. It then introduces the basics of entering and editing commands at the prompt. You'll also find out how to get help. Chapter 4, "Introducing the DOS Shell," presents the second way of interacting with your computer: through a system of menus from which you can choose commands. Even if you prefer the Shell, however, you should become familiar with the material in Chapter 3 because it will help you understand what you're doing.

A great deal of what you do in DOS consists of managing your system and the information in it. Chapters 5 through 9 present all the basic tools you'll need. Chapter 5, "Dealing with Disks," explains the commands for dealing with disks as such. You'll be working with the prompt because the Shell doesn't give you as much help with disks.

Chapter 6, "Managing Files and Directories in the Shell," and Chapter 7, "Managing Files and Directories at the Command Prompt," introduce the commands and procedures that affect *files* and *directories*. You'll learn that a file is the basic unit in which information is stored, and that a directory is a system of classification that lets you keep track of your files. As you've probably guessed, you'll learn how to manage your system from the Shell, then from the prompt. With this experience you'll be able to decide which method you prefer.

Chapter 8, "Organizing Your Directory Tree," presents principles for setting up a sensible filing system that will help you keep track of your data. When you've reached this point, you've mastered the essentials. And even if you go no further, you'll be able to manage your system adequately. If you proceed, however, you'll learn everything you need to know to make DOS your reliable servant, instead of "that thing you have to put up with."

Once you've gained an understanding of disks, files, and directories, you'll be ready for Chapter 9, "Advanced File Management." You'll learn how to use the Shell's advanced features for managing your files, how to change a file's attributes (and why you'd want to), how to compare files, and how to copy files selectively using several criteria at once.

In Chapter 10, "Safeguarding Your Data," you'll learn to prepare for (and recover from) the inevitable disaster: how to back up your files, arm yourself against unintended erasures, check for unusable areas on a disk, and recover data that has been written to such areas.

Chapter 11, "Using the DOS Editor," introduces a feature new to MS-DOS 5.0. You'll learn all the commands you need to use the *MS-DOS Editor* effectively. You may want to use this Editor to create the files you'll use in Chapter 12, "Fine-Tuning Your Configuration." This chapter explains the AUTOEXEC.BAT and CONFIG.SYS files, two files you can edit to control many aspects of the way your computer behaves and presents itself to you. You'll also learn about the specialized DOS functions controlled by these files. Chapter 13, "Batch Files," continues the work of customization. You'll learn how to create these simple files that streamline repetitive tasks, help you run programs with a single command, and simplify commands.

In Chapter 14, "Running Your Applications from the DOS Shell," you'll learn how to use the Shell to create a menu system for your software, enabling you to run programs just by pressing a few keys.

Chapter 15, "Controlling the Flow of Information," presents a variety of topics pertaining to getting information to a destination other than its usual one. You'll learn how to address your printer and other ports, and how to get information from a command to a file, and from a file to a peripheral device.

Chapter 16, "DOS and Windows," addresses the relationship between DOS and one of the hottest software products on the market. Windows is a program that can transform the way your computer presents itself to you and the way you work. If you find that your hardware isn't powerful enough to run this program, you'll be interested to learn about two others, *GeoWorks Ensemble* and *DESQview,* which can accomplish many of the same things.

Finally, you'll find five appendices. The first two are on the specialized topics of using MS-DOS 5.0 to prepare a hard disk and to manage memory. The final three include a reference to the most important DOS commands, descriptions of common error messages, and a glossary of the computer terms introduced in the book.

Conventions Used in This Book

To help you find what you need, several typographic conventions have been used to set apart various types of information. Text you are expected to type at the keyboard looks like this:

```
command
```

Messages and other text you'll read on the screen appear like this:

```
┌─────────────────────────────────────────────┐
│                                               │
│   Please enter your command:                  │
│                                               │
└─────────────────────────────────────────────┘
```

When you are asked to press a series of keys in sequence, their names are separated by spaces—for example, T A ↓ Enter. Sometimes you'll be asked to hold down one key while pressing a second. Such keystroke combinations are hyphenated: Ctrl-C, Alt-F. If you're not familiar with the keyboard, you'll find diagrams in Chapter 1.

DOS commands, file names, and path names all appear in uppercase text, to set them apart. When you type them at the keyboard, you can use any combination of upper- and lowercase.

Command Syntax

Every once in a while, you'll see a command expressed in a general form called a *syntax diagram.* This is what one looks like.

DIR [*d:*][*filename.ext*] [*/switches*]

The elements of a syntax diagram have specific functions. DOS commands, as noted, appear in uppercase text. Anything in brackets is optional. In the syntax diagram above, the only essential element is the command DIR.

The symbol *d:* or *d1:* represents the name of a disk drive. When entering the command, you substitute the name of a real disk drive.

The name *filename.ext* stands for any file name. Substitute a real one when you type the command. If instead you see the name *filename.txt,* you need to use only the name of a text file.

The symbol */switches* represents one or more *command switches.* These change the effect of a command. They usually take the form of a virgule followed by a single letter—for example, /C, or /A. Sometimes, they require additional information. When a switch contains a symbol such as *nn* or *nnn*, substitute a number in the indicated acceptable range. Whenever a syntax diagram appears, a list of acceptable switches, their form, and their effect also appears.

Items Worth Noting

Throughout the book, you'll see symbols in the margins indicating items to which special attention should be paid:

 HINT

This symbol indicates a helpful hint or tip.

! WARNING

Indicates a potential danger in misusing a command, or using it in an inappropriate situation. Pay special attention to these.

✳ NOTE

This symbol indicates an unusual or unexpected feature of which you should be aware.

✔ NEW FEATURE

This symbol indicates a discussion of a command, program, or modification that's new in MS-DOS 5.0.

How to Use This Book

DOS 5—Everything You Need to Know is a book that is meant to be used. You'll get the most out of it if you're at the computer while you read, so you can try out the commands and procedures described. What you read will make a great deal more sense this way than it would otherwise.

Good luck, and happy computing.

If You're New to Computers or Vice Versa

Chapter **1**

What You Will Learn

- The components of your computer system
- The parts of the keyboard
- Types of disks and how to use them
- What an operating system does
- The components of DOS 5

If you have computer experience and some understanding of DOS, you can go straight to Chapter 2. But if you're just starting out with your first computer, read this chapter. It explains briefly what a computer is and does. You might think of this chapter as equivalent to the small manual that comes with any appliance. You can certainly learn to use, say, a new microwave oven without reading the instructions. But you feel a lot more secure if you know what the various controls are supposed to do.

You'll learn many new terms in this chapter. You needn't memorize them; just get some basic familiarity with the vocabulary. When you come across a term whose meaning you can't quite remember later in the book, you can return here, or go to the glossary, to refresh your memory.

DOS, strictly speaking, stands for any *d*isk *o*perating *system*. In the world of desktop and laptop computers, however, the term refers to the set of instructions used to run

1

the IBM PC, the IBM PS/2, and *IBM-* or *PC-compatible* computers (so called because they closely match the IBM's design, which has become an industry standard). If you tell other computer users that you have an IBM clone or a DOS computer, they'll understand what you mean. Whenever you use one of these computers, you use DOS—often without being aware of it. In order to gain control of your computer, therefore, you need to gain control of DOS. To do so, you need to know something about the computer's machinery, because DOS tells this machinery what to do.

Your Computer Hardware

A computer system consists of two broad categories: hardware and software. *Hardware* is the actual machinery—nuts, bolts, printed circuits, and silicon chips—that makes up the computer. *Software* comprises the instructions on which the computer acts. DOS is your most important piece of software, since it controls the way all other software operates.

The hardware in a PC-compatible system has at least three parts: a *system unit*—the box with the switches and the disk drives and such—a *keyboard*, and a *screen* (see Figure 1.1).

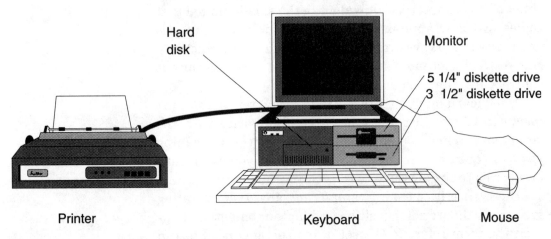

Figure 1.1   The parts of a computer system

The System Unit

The system unit contains many vital components. First and foremost is the *central processing unit*, or *CPU:* a silicon chip that makes up the "brains" of the computer. This is where all the actual processing takes place. From the point of view of the CPU, all other parts of the computer system are peripherals—that is, external components. In popular parlance, however, the term *peripherals* refers to other accessories that are plugged into the system unit via cables.

The CPU has three functions: reading information from one location, acting on it, and sending the results to another location. In computer talk, these processes are called *input, processing,* and *output.* Virtually every other component of your computer is used for input or output.

The system unit also contains *memory.* There are two kinds. *Read-only memory,* or *ROM,* contains basic instructions that tell the computer how to operate, even before DOS is present. (Without these instructions, the computer wouldn't even know how to load DOS.) *Random-access memory,* or *RAM,* is where information is stored while the computer is actually using it. Anything in RAM disappears whenever the power is turned off—even for a split second.

The system unit also contains one or more *disk drives.* Disks store information when the computer is not actively using it. They are the main source from which the computer reads information into memory. Thus they serve as *input devices.* However, since the computer also writes information to the disks, when appropriate, they are *output devices* as well.

You certainly have at least one diskette drive and may have two or even more. Diskette drives come in five varieties and two sizes in modern PC-compatibles. If you have only one, it's called drive A. If you have two, either the upper or the left-hand drive is drive A. The lower or the right-hand drive is drive B. You may also have a *hard disk*, which would be drive C. (If you have more than one hard disk, subsequent disks would be designated drive D, drive E, and so on). You can't see the hard disk from the outside of the system unit, but there's usually some indication that it is present. Most probably a light will come on when it's active. You'll learn all you need to know about disks and disk drives in Chapter 5.

The system unit also contains *expansion slots*. Printed-circuit cards are placed into them to give your computer additional capabilities. In most computers you'll already have two such cards: a video card, to send information to the screen, and a disk-controller card, to manage communications between the CPU and the disk drives. Some modern computers (including most laptops) have built-in electronic components that perform these functions instead.

The Keyboard

The keyboard is your most important input device. On it you type instructions that tell the computer what to do and you enter data that will be processed by your software. In this section you'll learn the general keyboard layout. In later chapters you'll learn how to use the specialized keys.

Keyboards for PC-compatibles come in several designs. At present two are relatively common, whereas laptop and notebook computers offer variations on these standards to cram more keys into a smaller space. Figure 1.2 shows the keyboard for the original IBM PC-AT, which has 84 keys. Figure 1.3 shows the "enhanced" keyboard, which has 101 keys. Your keyboard may not look exactly like either model. The important point is to locate the various types of keys and to understand what they do.

The Typewriter Keys. All PC-compatible keyboards are divided into several sections. At the center, usually in white or putty color, are the *typewriter keys*. These include all the *characters* found on a typewriter, which you can type directly from the keyboard. There are, however, a few additional characters not normally found on a typewriter, and there are still others that you can enter from the keyboard using various combinations of keys. We won't worry about those for now. Suffice it to say that if you're familiar with a

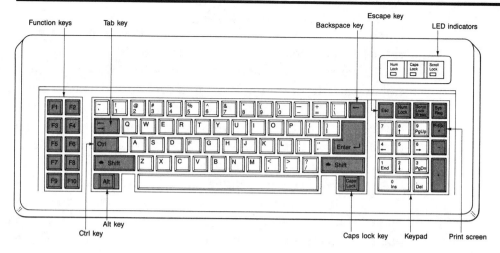

Figure 1.2   The IBM PC-AT keyboard

typewriter keyboard, you're familiar with the typewriter keys on the computer keyboard.

The Keyboard Control Keys.   To the left and right of the typewriter keys (but still in the same central area) are keys that control keyboard actions. You'll recognize the Tab key, which is marked by a pair of arrows, to the left of the Q key. You'll also find Shift keys, marked by hollow arrows, to the left of the Z and the right of the question

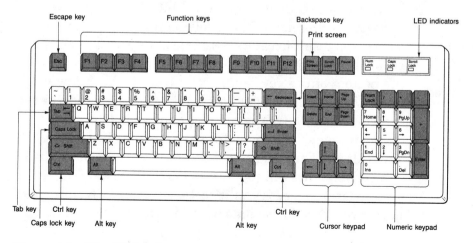

Figure 1.3   The IBM enhanced keyboard

mark, as you'd expect. The Backspace key is at the upper right-hand corner.

Above the right-hand Shift key is the Enter key, also called the Return key. It is marked by a broken-arrow symbol, ⏎. This key is more or less equivalent to the carriage-return key on a typewriter, except that there's no carriage. When you press the Enter key on a computer, it enters the *carriage-return character*. In many programs (including DOS), this signals the computer that you have finished entering a command. Often this character also moves the cursor—and therefore the point where you can begin entering characters—back to the beginning of the next line, at the left edge of the screen.

Similarly a space is a character entered by the space bar. As a rule you do not use the space bar to move the cursor unless you specifically want a space to appear. You use the cursor keys instead, which are described below.

You also seldom use the Backspace key to move the cursor. Instead you use it to delete the character to the left of the cursor.

The other keys in the central area may be unfamiliar or may behave in unfamiliar ways. These keys are distinguished (as are most of the special computer keys) by their color—a color usually referred to as gray, although it's more of a muddy gray-green-brown. You'll find a key marked Caps Lock. This is equivalent to the Shift Lock key, with two important differences. When you depress Caps Lock, all the letter keys result in capital letters. However, the symbol and number keys still issue the unshifted characters shown on the bottom of the key cap. If you press the Shift key while Caps Lock is on, you can enter the lowercase letters or the symbols at the top of the number and symbol keys.

Additionally the computer keyboard has two other shift keys, Alt and Ctrl. These stand for "alternate" and "control," respectively. (You will sometimes see the Ctrl key referred to with a caret mark, ^.) As with the standard Shift key, you hold Alt or Ctrl down while pressing another key.

 HINT

On most modern key-boards, a light comes on to let you know that the Caps Lock key is locked.

The Function Keys. At the left side of the PC-AT keyboard, and along the top of the enhanced keyboard, are *function keys*. The PC-AT keyboard has 10 keys, and the enhanced keyboard has 12. You'll recognize a function key by its name, the letter *F* followed by a number. When you are told to press, say, F2, you should press the key with F2 on it, not the F key followed by the 2 key.

The function keys are usually used as shortcuts to enter commands. They have different functions in different programs. Some have important effects in DOS. Any function key may be combined with the Shift, Alt, and Ctrl keys to produce additional commands.

The Keypad(s). On the right side of the computer are either one or two *keypads*. The PC-AT keyboard has one, the enhanced keyboard two. The rightmost set of keys on the enhanced keyboard duplicates the keypad on the PC-AT keyboard and is made up of white keys and gray keys. This keypad has two different functions.

The top of the keypad includes a key called Num Lock. Like Caps Lock, it changes a shift state and is indicated by a light. When it is depressed, the white keys duplicate the numbers at the top of the keyboard in the form of a 10-key numeric keypad. The gray keys perform arithmetic functions. (On computers the asterisk key, *, replaces the multiplication sign, and Enter calculates the result.)

When Num Lock is unlocked, the keys on this keypad move the cursor. The direction of movement is indicated by the arrows and by the notations Home, End, PgUp, and PgDn. The exact way these keys move the cursor depends on the program you're using. Some have functions in DOS, which you'll learn later in this book.

The two keys at the bottom of the keypad are marked Ins and Del, which stand for "insert" and "delete." Again their exact functions depend on the program you're using.

When there are two keypads, the second keypad, to the left of the one just described, contains only the cursor keys and the Insert and Delete keys. On keyboards with two keypads, the Num Lock key is automatically on when you

 HINT

You can override the effect of the Num Lock key by pressing a Shift key while you use the keypad keys. Thus if Num Lock is locked, you can use the keypad keys to move the cursor by holding down the Shift key. If Num Lock is unlocked, you can enter a number by first holding down the Shift key.

start the computer. On those with one, it's not. The keys on such a keypad have longer names. In place of PgUp and PgDn, you'll find Page Up and Page Down. In most cases these keys have the same functions as the equivalent keys on the numeric keypad. In this book you'll see the shorter names, but unless otherwise noted you can use the keys in either keypad if Num Lock is off.

Miscellaneous Keys. There a few other special keys. The Scroll Lock key, found at the top of the keypad on the PC-AT keyboard, or above the cursor keypad on the enhanced keyboard, is another locking key with an indicator light. In DOS it doesn't do anything, but in some programs it may change the way the cursor behaves. The Print Screen key (above the cursor keypad on the enhanced keyboard) or the PrtSc key (sharing space with the * on the PC-AT key-pad) copies whatever is on your screen to your printer. (If it is also the * key, you must press the Shift key at the same time you press PrtSc.) The Pause key on the enhanced keyboard will temporarily stop text from being displayed on the screen until you press another key. The SysRq (or Sys Req) key, found only on the PC-AT keyboard, doesn't do anything at all.

The Escape key is found in different locations on different keyboards. This important key is usually used to cancel whatever you're doing or to "back out of" an operation or menu.

The Screen

The screen, or *monitor*, is your principal output device. It is also known as a VDT (video display terminal) or CRT (cathode ray tube). The computer communicates with it through the video card installed in one of your expansion slots in the system unit.

What you type at the keyboard may or may not appear on the screen. Some keys may be interpreted as commands and acted upon instead. Some programs convert lowercase characters to uppercase. Programs may also display information on the screen: menus from which to choose commands, instructions on what to do next, warnings, error messages, and so on.

Several types of video displays are available for PC-compatible computers. Your monitor may display in *monochrome*—one color against a black or white background—or in color. Most systems can display graphics as well as text, but some types of monochrome systems cannot.

Beyond that, the various types of monitors differ in their resolution and, for color systems, in the number of colors they can produce. *Resolution* is the "grain" of the image. The screen actually displays everything in a pattern of dots. The more dots your video card and monitor can display, the higher the resolution. The most common types of displays at present are the Hercules-type, which displays monochrome text and graphics, and the VGA (video graphics array), which displays high-resolution color text and graphics.

Types of Disks

As noted, anything in the computer's random-access memory disappears when power to the computer is stopped. Therefore you need disks to store both the instructions the computer uses and the results of its work. When you load a program, the computer reads it from a disk into its memory. When you create a document, a picture, or a spreadsheet, you save it by telling the computer to write it to a disk. There are two main types of disks: *floppy disks*, or *diskettes*, and *hard disks*.

Diskettes. Diskettes store information in much the same way that audio or video cassettes do. Inside the diskette's square outer shell is a thin, flexible sheet of plastic (hence the term *floppy*) coated with a magnetic medium. When the computer writes to the diskette, it simply rearranges the magnetic charge of the molecules on the surface.

The earliest IBM PCs used only single-sided 5¼-inch diskettes. Today, there are five standard disk capacities: double-sided, double-density and double-sided, and high-density in both 5¼-inch and 3½-inch sizes, plus super-high-density 3½-inch diskettes. (See Figures 1.4 and 1.5.) Some modern PC-compatible computers can use only the double-density diskettes of the appropriate physical size, but most can use both. You will not be able to use the higher capacity high-density diskettes in drives designed for double-density diskettes. As of this writing, super-high-density diskettes were not yet available, so no illustration is included. However, they should be on the market by the time you read this.

You can usually tell the difference between a double-density and a high-density diskette by the manufacturer's label. If you have unlabeled diskettes, note that a high-density 5¼-inch diskette is marked by the absence of the *hub ring* shown in Figure 1.4. A high-density 3½-inch diskette is distinguished by the symbol shown in Figure 1.6 and by an extra hole opposite the write-protect window, which is a hole with a sliding latch. When it's open, nothing can be written to the disk. If you're still not sure what type of diskettes to use, consult your hardware manual or your dealer.

Diskettes are easily damaged. The flexible 5¼-inch variety is susceptible to more types of damage than the 3½-inch

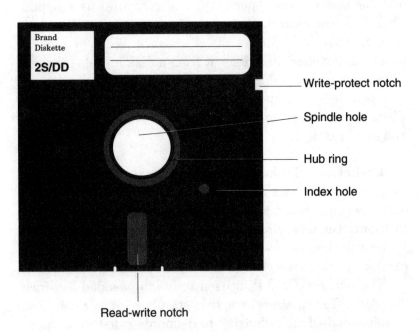

Figure 1.4   A 5¼-inch diskette

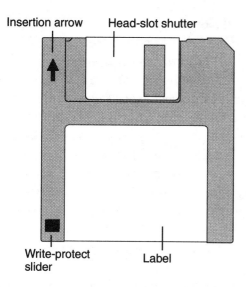

Insertion arrow · Head-slot shutter

Write-protect slider · Label

Figure 1.5   A 3½-inch diskette

type, which has a hard shell. Exposure to heat, cold, magnetic fields, creasing, bending, liquids, and grease can all render diskettes unreadable. Be especially careful with the parts of the case through which the actual recording medium is exposed.

To use a diskette, you must insert it into the appropriate type of diskette drive, holding the diskette by the edge that contains the label, with the label facing up (or toward you, if the diskette drive is vertical). Figure 1.7 shows how to insert a 5¼-inch diskette. When the diskette is fully inserted, rotate the latch on the drive so that it crosses the slot into which you inserted the diskette. The computer won't know the diskette is there until you do this. To remove the diskette, rotate the latch counterclockwise. The diskette pops out so you can grab it.

Figure 1.8 shows how to insert a 3½-inch diskette. There is no latch on a 3½-inch drive. Just push the diskette in gently until it clicks. To pop out the diskette, press the button on the drive.

Figure 1.6   The high-density symbol

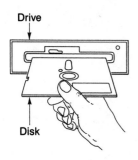

Figure 1.7 Inserting a 5¼-inch diskette in a drive

Hard Disks. Hard disks are so called because, unlike diskettes, their recording medium is on an inflexible surface. Most hard disks are entirely internal to the system unit.

While a hard disk isn't essential, the very significant advantages it offers make it the most cost-effective improvement to your computer. First, it holds considerably more information than diskettes. The most capacious diskette currently available holds about 3 million characters. The smallest hard disk holds over 20 million characters, and many hold considerably more. Second, the computer reads and writes even the slowest hard disks more quickly than a diskette. If you've never used a hard disk, you'll be amazed at the increase in speed. Third, hard disks are much more rugged than diskettes.

And fourth, it's not uncommon for today's software packages to require 10 or more diskettes. Setting up such a program to work only with diskette drives is often tedious. You have to keep track of several diskettes at all times and swap them constantly in and out of your drive(s) just to complete a single job. This drudgery is eliminated when you put the program on a hard disk.

Indeed, once you have a hard disk, you may find yourself using diskettes only to put new programs on it, to make backup copies of your work, and to share data files with your coworkers.

Other Components

Your computer system may have other hardware components. Let's look at several of the most common ones.

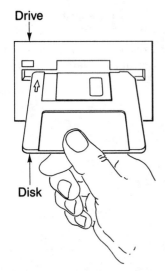

Figure 1.8 Inserting a 3½-inch diskette in a drive

The Serial and Parallel Ports. Ports are places where you can attach other components, such as a mouse or printer. Most PCs have at least one *serial port* and at least one *parallel port*. Both are trapezoid-shaped objects protruding from the back of the system unit, filled with a double row of either pins or small holes. *Serial* and *parallel* refer to two different styles of communication between the computer and the components. You'll learn about using the ports in Chapter 15.

The Mouse. A mouse is an input device that supplements the keyboard. It's a hand-sized object, usually with two or three buttons, that moves a pointer on the screen as you move the mouse across your desk. It is either attached to a serial port or to a special expansion card of its own. (Some mice are wireless, using a radio beam to communicate with the system unit.)

You can use a mouse only with programs that are designed to take advantage of it. Mice are generally used to select items from menus, to select text on the screen, and to move things around on the screen. Many contemporary programs have what is called a *graphical user interface*. This simply means a system of menus and small pictures called *icons*—similar to the symbols in the margins of this book—that you can select and manipulate with a mouse.

Few programs, except for some drawing and painting programs, absolutely require a mouse. However, you may want one anyway. Some programs are much easier to learn and use with a mouse. The mouse's main disadvantage is that it forces you to take one hand off the keyboard. If you're a touch typist who works primarily with text, you may find a mouse something of a nuisance.

DOS includes one component, the Shell program (about which you will learn in Chapters 4 and 6), which makes use of a mouse. The Shell helps you manage the information in your computer and run programs from a menu. If you find that you prefer using the Shell, you will probably want a mouse to go with it.

And if you give a mouse a menu, he'll probably want to order some cheese. And after he eats the cheese, he'll want a napkin. Then he'll get tired and want a place to curl up on your desk. Since he'll also need room to move around, you'd better reserve an area about 7 inches deep and 9 inches wide. He may also want a nice bed—a mouse pad. Unless, of course, you're one of those people who refuse to lead a hand-to-mouse existence.

One alternative to a mouse is a *trackball,* which you might think of as an upside-down mouse. Most mice work by rolling a ball across your desktop as you move the mouse, but a trackball remains stationary, while you move the ball itself with the palm of your hand.

The Printer.   You'll need some kind of printer to make paper copies of the work you do. (You will attach the printer to a port at the back of the computer, as you do a mouse.) Four types of printers are available for DOS computers: *dot-matrix, ink-jet, daisy-wheel,* and *laser,* in order of increasing price.

Dot-matrix printers can generally print a variety of sizes and styles of text as well as graphics. They are relatively inexpensive and some can produce quite handsome printed documents. However, text quality depends somewhat on how well your applications take advantage of your particular printer's features.

Daisy-wheel printers can print only text. Their type quality is comparable to that of a typewriter; but unlike other printers, you have to remove the print element and insert another one to change from one type style to another, say, from roman to italics. This is time-consuming and annoying. In addition, both dot-matrix and daisy-wheel printers tend to be noisy.

Laser printers can print extremely high-quality text and graphics, in a variety of sizes, styles, and orientations. They are virtually silent. They are also comparatively expensive to purchase and maintain. But for many purposes, what you gain in quality is worth the price.

Ink-jet printers might be considered poor relations to laser printers. They use the same basic means of receiving information from the computer as laser printers do and are as quiet. However, they print using a matrix of tiny tubes that squirt ink on the page. Although they cost considerably less than laser printers, they are quite a bit messier. They also share the laser printer's high maintenance costs. You'll learn how to deal with your printer in Chapter 15.

The Modem. A modem is a device that hooks up to a telephone so that you can send information to and receive it from other computers. Some modems are attached to one of the external ports, whereas others are installed in one of the expansion slots inside the system unit. You'll learn more about modems in Chapter 15.

What DOS Is

As was mentioned earlier, DOS is an acronym for *disk operating system*. You may wonder why specifically a *disk* operating system—obviously, there are other parts to the computer. But the disk operating system is fundamental for two reasons. First, most computers actually read the disk operating system from a disk and must do so before they can do anything else. (Some newer models—especially portable or laptop computers—may be able to read at least some of this information from elsewhere.) Second, one of DOS's most important functions is to help you organize the information on your disks.

There are many versions of DOS. Two companies—IBM and Microsoft—participated in its development. As a result, the two principal flavors of DOS are MS-DOS, the *M*icrosoft *D*isk *O*perating *S*ystem, and PC DOS, the IBM *P*ersonal *C*omputer *D*isk *O*perating *S*ystem. (Later versions are simply known as IBM DOS.) Other manufacturers of IBM-compatibles buy the rights to DOS from Microsoft and may or may not alter the software to fit the specifics of their hardware. But fundamentally all versions of DOS bearing the same version number are substantially similar. I've used IBM DOS and several different manufacturers' versions of MS-DOS on an assortment of compatibles and have never encountered any problems.

Now about those version numbers. As you've noticed from its title, this book is about DOS 5. What does the "5" mean?

Software manufacturers indicate software revisions through a generally accepted numbering system. Any release of a software package will have a number indicating its relationship to earlier releases. Generally, the number consists of a whole number followed by a decimal fraction of up to three places. The whole number is similar to the number for an edition of a book. If a software box says "Version 2.0" on it, you can think of it as equivalent to a second edition.

So what do the decimal numbers mean? Generally a change in the whole number signifies a major revision—new features, a new way of using the product, a completely new design for the screen, and so on. The decimal numbers indicate less far-reaching changes. A change in the first decimal place may mean that significant new features have been added without changing the overall design—sort of like changing the arrangement of the taillights and dashboard instruments on a car for a new model year. A change in the second or third decimal place signifies a "maintenance upgrade" or, less politely, a "bug-fix." Thus although DOS 4.01, for example, has exactly the same commands and features as DOS 4.0, some of them didn't work correctly in DOS 4.0 but do in DOS 4.01.

DOS 5, as you'd expect, is a major revision. Many new features have been added that make DOS 5 easier to use, allow you to manage your computer more efficiently, and allow you to access your system through a graphically designed menu.

The Parts of DOS

Now that you know the parts that make up your computer system, let's begin exploring your most important piece of software—DOS. DOS is a collection of programs and other files. On a computer, *file* is the term given to a collection of data that's stored as a single unit with a specific name. All programs are files, but there are many other types of files as well.

The System Files

The most important part of DOS consists of three files that the computer loads into memory when you start it. Two invisible, or *hidden,* files, contain the instructions that tell your computer how to manage the flow of information between its components. The third file, called COM-MAND.COM, is the *command processor.* It includes an important group of commands you can issue and displays error messages when the computer cannot complete a command you give. The commands contained in COM-MAND.COM are called *internal* commands because they are internal to the system files. Once a prompt has appeared, you don't need any additional software to execute these commands.

The External Commands

In addition to the system files, there is a collection of *external* commands. These commands often complete more complex procedures. Each command resides in a separate program on disk. If you have a hard disk, these programs are automatically copied onto it when you install DOS 5. If you have a diskette-based system, they are copied onto a series of diskettes.

DOS also contains many other files. It includes special files for changing the way the screen appears and the way the keyboard operates, files for changing the characters displayed on the screen and on certain printers for different languages, and a group of files that let you communicate information to the computer about the way it is set up, or to change the way it is set up. (The computer isn't always smart enough to figure these things out for itself.) These latter files are called *device drivers.* Each one gives the computer vital information about how to talk to a specific component (such as your mouse—or even your hard disk). Some components that you install may come with their own device drivers.

The Control Files

When you install DOS 5, it creates two *control files,* which tell the computer how you want it to behave when you start it. The first control file, called CONFIG.SYS, tells the computer how much memory to reserve for keeping track of various things. As soon as the first parts of DOS are in memory, the computer looks for this file and attempts to carry out the instructions in it. CONFIG.SYS is a simple text file that you can edit yourself.

It is also through the CONFIG.SYS file that you install device drivers. You'll be modifying this file several times as you work your way through the book.

The second control file is called AUTOEXEC.BAT. This too is a simple text file. If a file by this name is present, DOS executes the instructions in it as soon as it has finished installing itself. You can use it to have your computer automatically issue any command you want it to carry out when you first start up. You'll be developing an AUTOEXEC.BAT file throughout this book.

Installing DOS 5

Chapter 2

What You Will Learn

- How to tell if DOS 5 is installed
- How to install DOS 5 on a hard disk
- How to install DOS 5 on diskettes
- How to install DOS 5 on a new computer

You may already have DOS 5 installed on your computer. If so, skip this chapter. If you're not sure whether DOS 5 is installed, read the first section.

The way you install DOS 5 depends on whether you already have a version of DOS or are starting out with a new computer that was packaged with DOS 5. Indeed, the DOS disks you receive will be quite different depending on whether you purchased them as part of an upgrade package or as a component of a new computer system.

If you're upgrading from an earlier version of DOS, read "An Overview of the Upgrade Procedure" to get a general understanding of the process. If you have a hard disk, proceed from there to "Upgrading a Computer with a Hard Disk." If you don't have a hard disk, skip from the overview to the section called "Upgrading a Computer Without a Hard Disk." If you have a new computer on which you're installing DOS for the first time, go directly to the section called "Installing DOS 5 on a New Computer."

Using the Setup Program

NEW FEATURE

The Setup program replaces the Select program introduced in some versions of DOS 3 and all versions of DOS 4.

Regardless of which procedure you follow, you'll be employing an easy-to-use program called Setup to complete the installation. During Setup, a line at the bottom of the screen tells you what steps are currently available and which keys to press to access them. At almost any point, you can terminate installation by pressing the F3 function key. You can also get help on any procedure by pressing F1. As a general rule, the Enter key takes you to the next step and the Escape key to the previous step.

When you are asked to choose from among several items, you do so by moving a *selection bar*—an inverse video highlight—to your choice with the up-arrow (↑) and down-arrow (↓) keys on the cursor keypad and then pressing Enter.

Is DOS 5 Already Installed?

If your system has a hard disk, just turn on the system unit. After a bit of whirring and beeping, you should reach a point where you see a *prompt* (a symbol followed by a blinking line, at which you can enter commands) or some sort of menu. If you see a prompt, type

```
ver
```

and press Enter. If you see the message

```
MS-DOS Version 5.00
```

then you know DOS 5 is installed. Go on to the next chapter.

! **WARNING**

When you turn on the computer you may see the message

```
Disk boot failure
```

This means one of the following things:
- *There is no hard disk in your computer.*
- *Your hard disk doesn't have DOS on it.*
- *Your hard disk hasn't been properly prepared to hold data.*

If you know you have a hard disk, check with your dealer to find out whether it has been low-level formatted. *(You don't need to know what this means, just whether it's been done.) If it has, ask whether it has been* partitioned *and* formatted. *If the answer to all these questions is yes, you should be able to install DOS. If it has not been partitioned and formatted, see Appendix A, or return the computer to your dealer to have it done.*

An Overview of the Upgrade Procedure

Installing DOS 5 is a simple but not trivial procedure, which takes at least 20 minutes. You'll be asked to make several decisions along the way. Before we go into the procedure step-by-step, I'll give you an overview, so you'll know what to expect.

The DOS 5 files on the diskettes you receive cannot be used in the form in which you receive them. You *must* complete the installation procedure to "expand" the files into their usable form. However, simple instructions on the screen will guide you through every step of the process.

You begin by inserting disk 1 of the DOS 5 diskettes in one of your drives and running the Setup program. You'll be asked to prepare one or two diskettes to be placed in drive A. These can be used to undo the installation, if you find that for some reason your computer doesn't work correctly with DOS 5, and you want to revert to an earlier version. If you want to use double-density diskettes and your drive A is a high-density drive, you must use formatted diskettes. (If you don't know how to format a diskette, and you're not sure if yours are formatted, see Chapter 5.) However, you can also use old diskettes containing data that you don't mind erasing (you know these diskettes have already been formatted because otherwise they couldn't hold the data).

Setup will ascertain what kind of hardware you have and tailor the installation to it to some extent. You'll be asked whether you have a network installed. If you have, you'll need to exit the program and take several other steps before you proceed.

Next you'll be asked whether to back up the hard disk(s), if you have any. A bit later in this section, I'll explain the considerations involved.

After you've decided whether to back up the hard disk, you'll be asked to confirm the Setup program's assessment of your hardware. At this point you can make corrections and decide whether you want the DOS Shell to appear on your screen automatically when you start your computer. Having made these decisions, you'll begin installation.

Setup finds your current DOS directory, renames it to OLD_DOS.1, and, if you're on a network, creates a subdirectory of that directory called NETS. (If you don't know what a subdirectory is, rest assured that you will after you read Chapter 7.)

DOS 5 may make extensive changes to the structure of your hard disk. For this reason the next step provides you with an opportunity to undo the installation later. You'll be asked to create one or two Uninstall diskettes (the number depends on whether your diskette drive can handle high-density diskettes). These diskettes *must* go in drive A. You can use them to undo the DOS 5 installation and return to your previous version of DOS. The Uninstall diskettes contain all the information about the original structure of your hard disk and a program to write that information back to its original location. This ensures that your disk will appear to your previous version of DOS as it did before, and will behave as it did before.

Finally, you'll feed the diskettes into the drive as requested. When all the files have been copied onto the hard disk (or onto other diskettes) and expanded, you restart your system by pressing the Enter key. You are now running in DOS 5.

Should You Back Up Your Hard Disk?

As noted you are given an opportunity to back up your hard disk(s) during installation. I've tried DOS 5 on several quite different computers. Installing and using it appears to pose no risk of damage to your files. However, you should back up your hard disk if:

- You do not have a recent backup of all the data.
- You have a recent backup, but you made it using the BACKUP program included in a version of DOS earlier than 3.3.
- Your hard disk is larger than 32 megabytes, and you think it might be useful to set it up as a single, very large drive.

If you have more than one hard disk and you use the DOS backup system (rather than another program, such as Fastback Plus or PC Tools Deluxe), I'd urge you to back up at least drive C. In fact, you should back up drive C by your usual procedure even if you do use a non-DOS backup system. You can always back up the other drives after you've installed DOS 5.

! WARNING

Note to experienced DOS users: If you want to make a large hard disk into a single, logical drive and you're not sure how to proceed, see Appendix A, which explains how to repartition a hard disk. If you're not sure whether to change the organization of your hard disk, I suggest you leave it alone. You'll find some discussion on the pros and cons in Chapter 8.

Should You Install the DOS Shell?

Whether you install the DOS Shell is very much a matter of personal preference. In Chapter 3 you'll learn how to use the DOS command prompt. The Shell is an alternative *interface,* or point of interaction, between you and the computer. You'll explore it in Chapter 4.

Much of what you do with the Shell consists of putting together the details of a command line so that you can select the entire command from a menu, rather than type it in. If you're new to computers and you have a hard disk, I'd suggest you install the Shell as your main interface, at least until you feel secure in your knowledge of DOS commands. If you are comfortable with the command-line interface, don't install the Shell. Skip Chapters 4, 6, and 14 and those parts of other chapters that deal with it.

Upgrading a Computer with a Hard Disk

To install DOS 5 on a computer that has a hard disk with another version of DOS already installed, follow the steps below.

1. Place disk 1 of your DOS 5 diskettes in one of your drives. If you have a 3½-inch drive, use it, because it makes things go faster.
2. Type the name of the drive (the letter *A* or *B*), and a colon. Press Enter.
3. Type

   ```
   setup
   ```

   and press Enter. You'll see the welcoming screen shown in Figure 2.1. Press Enter to continue.
4. You'll be asked whether you use a network. If you do, press Y. You'll be told how to upgrade your network software, and then you'll be returned to the DOS prompt to take the necessary steps. When you've

completed these, return to step 1. If you don't use a
network, press N.

5. You'll see the screen in Figure 2.2, asking whether
   you want to back up your hard disk(s). If you don't,
   press the ↓ key to select

```
Do not back up hard disk(s).
```

and press Enter. Go on to step 10. If you want to
back up your hard disk(s), press Enter and go to
step 6.

6. You'll see the screen in Figure 2.3. If you have only
   one diskette drive, or both of your diskette drives are
   the same type, press Enter. If you have two drives of
   different types, I'd suggest choosing the drive (and
   diskettes) of the highest capacity your computer can
   handle—unless you have a plethora of unwanted

```
Microsoft(R) MS-DOS(R) Version 5.00
==================================

        Welcome to Setup

        Setup installs Microsoft MS-DOS version 5.0 on your hard
        disk. During Setup, some of your current system files will
        be saved on one high-density or two low-density floppy disks
        that you provide and label as shown below:

            UNINSTALL #1
            UNINSTALL #Z (if needed )

        The disk(s), which can be unformatted or newly formatted,
        must be used in drive A.

        Setup copies some files onto the Uninstall disk(s), and
        others to a directory on your hard disk called OLD_DOS.
        Using these files, you can remove MS-DOS from your hard
        disk and reinstall your old DOS if you need to._


 ENTER=Continue  F1=Help  F3=Exit  F5=Remove Color
```

Figure 2.1   The Setup program welcoming screen

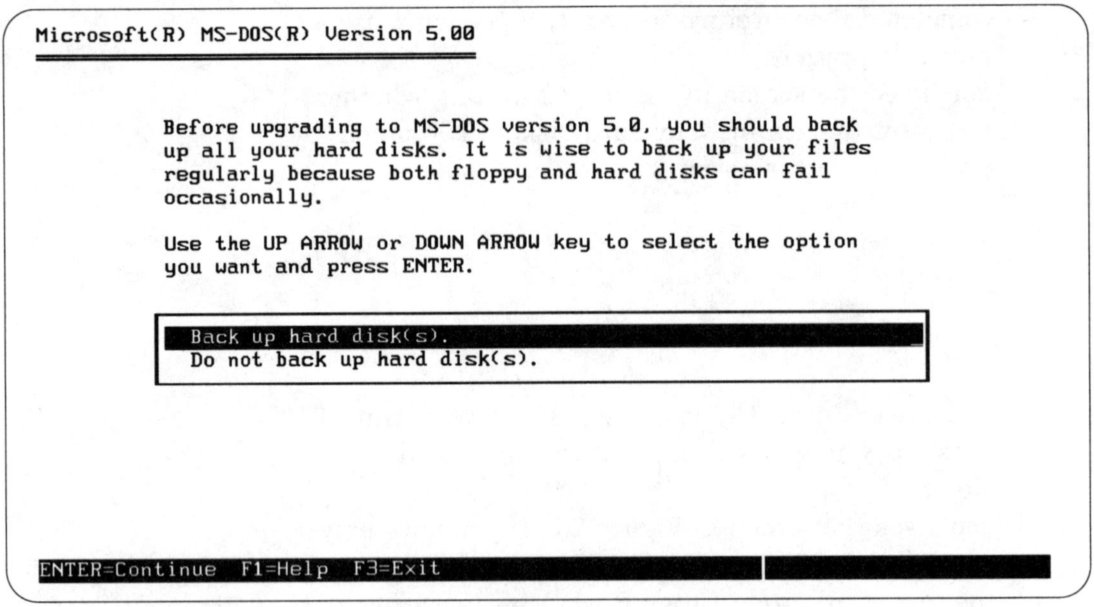

```
Microsoft(R) MS-DOS(R) Version 5.00
═══════════════════════════════════

          Before upgrading to MS-DOS version 5.0, you should back
          up all your hard disks. It is wise to back up your files
          regularly because both floppy and hard disks can fail
          occasionally.

          Use the UP ARROW or DOWN ARROW key to select the option
          you want and press ENTER.

          ┌──────────────────────────────────────────────────┐
          │  Back up hard disk(s).                             │
          │  Do not back up hard disk(s).                      │
          └──────────────────────────────────────────────────┘




ENTER=Continue  F1=Help  F3=Exit
```

Figure 2.2   Choosing whether to back up your hard disk(s)

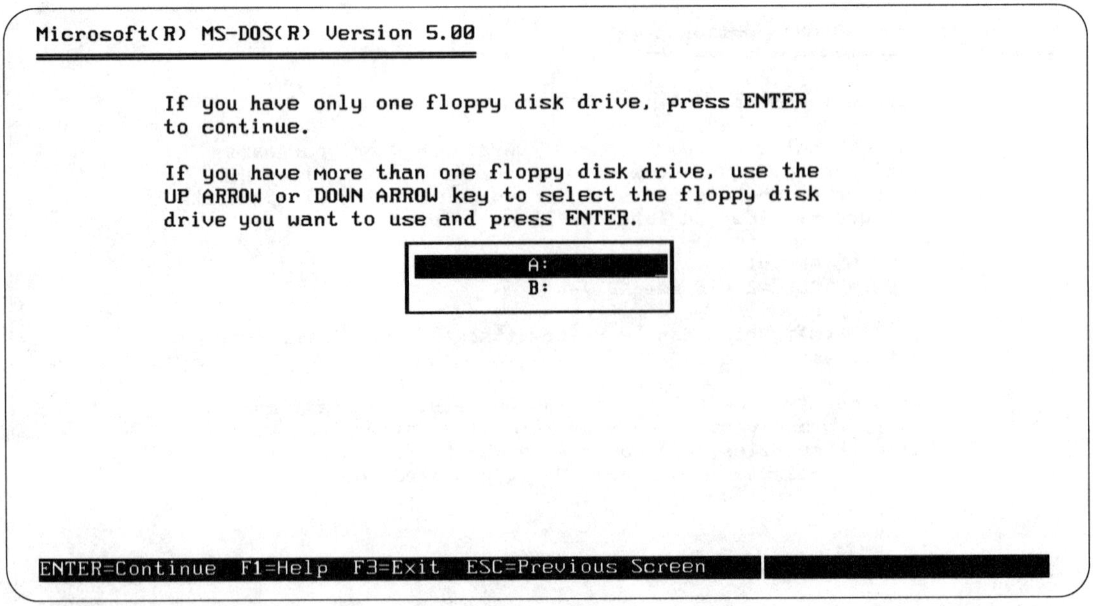

```
Microsoft(R) MS-DOS(R) Version 5.00
═══════════════════════════════════

          If you have only one floppy disk drive, press ENTER
          to continue.

          If you have more than one floppy disk drive, use the
          UP ARROW or DOWN ARROW key to select the floppy disk
          drive you want to use and press ENTER.
                    ┌──────────────────────────┐
                    │             A:            │
                    │             B:            │
                    └──────────────────────────┘




ENTER=Continue  F1=Help  F3=Exit  ESC=Previous Screen
```

Figure 2.3   Choosing a target drive for the backup

diskettes of another type. In that case choose the drive that writes to the type of diskettes you want to use up.

7. Choose the drive to back up. If you have only one hard disk, your screen will look like Figure 2.4. If you have more, you'll see a list of drive names in the box, similar to the one in Figure 2.3. Drive C will be highlighted with the selection bar. Press Enter to select the disk.

8. Choose the type of diskette to use for your backup. As you can see in Figure 2.5, Setup has scanned your disks to find out how much data you have to back up. It has figured out how many diskettes you'll need of each type to complete the job for each hard disk. Make sure you have enough diskettes of the type you choose.

9. Follow the instructions on the screen to complete the backup. You'll be told when to insert a new diskette and what label to put on it. A bar graph

```
Microsoft(R) MS-DOS(R) Version 5.00
═══════════════════════════════════

        If only one hard disk is displayed, press ENTER to back it up.

        If more than one hard disk is displayed, use the UP ARROW or
        DOWN ARROW key to select a disk to back up and press ENTER.
        Setup estimates approximately how many floppy disks you will
        need. After Setup backs up a disk, a check mark appears next
        to the drive letter. To back up another disk, select it and
        press ENTER.

                    ┌───────────────────┐
                    │         C:         │
                    │         D:         │
                    └───────────────────┘




 ENTER=Continue  F1=Help  F3=Exit  ESC=Previous Screen
```

Figure 2.4   Choosing the hard disk to back up

HINT

Number the diskettes as you are told to during the backup procedure. But don't worry that you might accidentally reuse one. Setup will recognize a diskette from this series and let you know when you insert one.

will show the progress of the backup and the percentage that has been completed. At the right-hand end of the bottom line, the name of the file being read or written will be displayed. When the backup is complete, if you have more than one hard disk you'll be returned to the screen in Figure 2.4. The drive you backed up will have a check mark next to its name, and the selection bar will be on the next drive name. Repeat steps 7 through 9 if you want to back up other drives. If you have only one hard disk, or you don't want to back up any others, go on to step 10.

10. Setup now shows you what it has found out about your system. It gives you a chance to make corrections, on a screen similar to the one in Figure 2.6. If everything is correct and you don't want to use the DOS Shell as your primary interface, just press Enter. If you want to use the DOS Shell, press the ↑ key twice to move to the line that reads

```
Microsoft(R) MS-DOS(R) Version 5.00
═══════════════════════════

        The estimated number of floppy disks needed to back up the
        selected hard disk are shown below.

        To begin backing up the disk, press ENTER. If you decide not
        to back up the selected hard disk, press ESC.

        Total 360K disks needed is --›      26
        Total 720K disks needed is --›      13
        Total 1.2M disks needed is --›       8
        Total 1.4M disks needed is --›       7_




 ENTER=Continue  F1=Help  F3=Exit  ESC=Previous Screen
```

Figure 2.5   Choosing the type of diskettes to use

```
Do not run MS-DOS Shell on startup.
```

Press Enter. You'll see the screen in Figure 2.7.
Press the ↑ key to move the selection bar to

```
Run MS-DOS Shell on startup.
```

Press Enter. You'll return to the screen shown in
Figure 2.6, ready to proceed. If the information
about your system is correct, press Enter to skip to
step 12.

11. If Setup has made any mistakes when scanning
    your system, use the ↑ or ↓ key to move the selec-
    tion bar to the erroneous information and press
    Enter. The only alternative to your manufacturer of

```
Microsoft(R) MS-DOS(R) Version 5.00

        Setup has determined that your system includes the
        following hardware and software components.

        ┌──────────────────────────────────────────────────┐
        │ Manufacturer   :MS-DOS                             │
        │ DOS Path       :C:\DOS                             │
        │ MS-DOS Shell   :Do not run MS-DOS Shell on startup.│
        │ Display Type   :VGA                                │
        │ Continue Setup: The information above is correct.  │
        └──────────────────────────────────────────────────┘

        If all the items in the list are correct, press ENTER.
        If you want to change an item in the list, use the UP
        ARROW or DOWN ARROW key to select it.  Then press ENTER
        to see alternatives for that item.



 ENTER=Continue  F1=Help  F3=Exit
```

Figure 2.6   The Setup program's assessment of your system

DOS is OTHER. If you select the Display Type, you'll
see a list of alternative display types from which to
choose. If your old version of DOS is in a different
directory, move the selection bar to DOS Path.
Press Enter and type in the correct directory name.
When you finish making any change, press Enter.
When you do, the selection bar moves back to Continue Setup. If you're not sure, accept Setup's
determinations.

12. You are now ready to install DOS 5. A box on the
screen displays the message

```
Setup is ready to install MS-DOS version
5.0. If you choose to continue, you may not
be able to interrupt Setup until it has
completed installing MS-DOS on your system.

To install MS-DOS now, press Y.
```

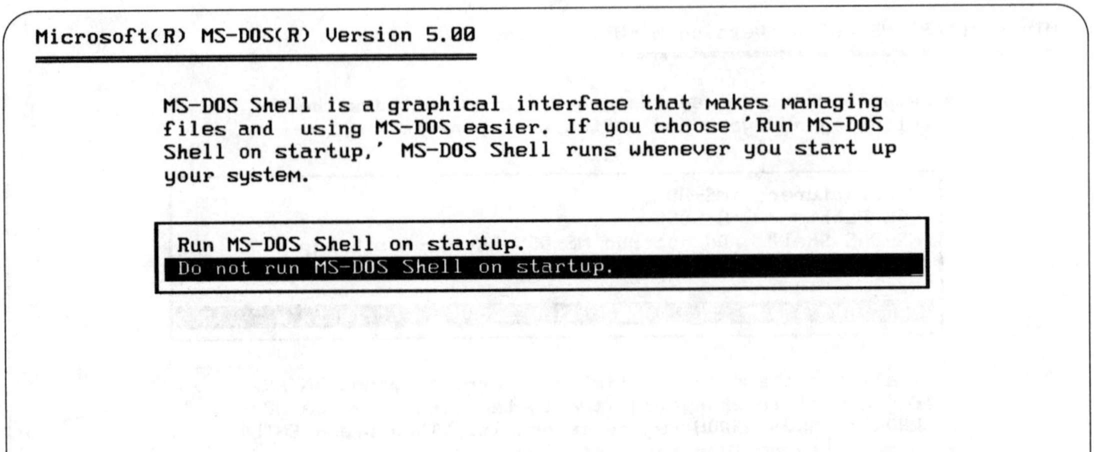

```
Microsoft(R) MS-DOS(R) Version 5.00

    MS-DOS Shell is a graphical interface that makes managing
    files and  using MS-DOS easier. If you choose 'Run MS-DOS
    Shell on startup,' MS-DOS Shell runs whenever you start up
    your system.

    Run MS-DOS Shell on startup.
    Do not run MS-DOS Shell on startup.




ENTER=Continue  F1=Help  F3=Exit  ESC=Previous Screen
```

Figure 2.7   Choosing to install the DOS Shell

```
To exit Setup without installing MS-DOS,
press F3.

To review your configuration selections,
press any other key.
```

13. Press Y to install DOS 5. You'll see the screen in Figure 2.8. Again, as in the backup procedure, a bar graph shows your progress, and the lower right-hand corner tells you exactly what Setup is doing. It begins by creating the OLD_DOS.1 directory.

14. After a few minutes, you'll see the message in Figure 2.9. Place an appropriate diskette in drive A. Press Enter. You'll see a similar screen asking you for a second diskette if one is needed. When Setup finishes creating the Uninstall diskettes, it moves your old DOS files to the OLD_DOS.1 directory. It asks you to reinsert disk 1 of DOS 5 in the drive you were using. It then proceeds to copy the files from

NEW FEATURE
Uninstall

```
Microsoft(R) MS-DOS(R) Version 5.00
═══════════════════════════════════════

        MS-DOS version 5.0 is now being set up.

        Setup installs a basic MS-DOS system. See the 'MS-DOS User's
        Guide and Reference' to learn about additional features.

        You may want to read the chapter on optimizing your system
        in the manual. This chapter describes how to fine-tune
        MS-DOS to achieve maximum performance.



        14% complete

        ┌──────────────────────────────────────────────────┐
        │██████████                                        │
        └──────────────────────────────────────────────────┘


                                          Writing  GLOBAL.DAT
```

Figure 2.8   The installation progress screen

```
        Label a floppy disk
             UNINSTALL #1
        and insert it into drive
                 A:

    When ready, press ENTER.

    WARNING:  All existing files
    on this disk will be deleted.
```

Figure 2.9   Creating the Uninstall diskette(s)

that diskette to the directory whose name you saw on the screen in Figure 2.6 (C:\DOS).

15. Insert each of the DOS 5 diskettes in turn when asked to do so. Press Enter after each one. When the bar graph shows that the procedure is 100 percent complete, take the diskette out of drive A. Press Enter to restart your computer using DOS 5.

16. To make sure you have diskette copies of the installed DOS 5 files to use in case something goes wrong with the files on your hard disk, follow the steps below.

Upgrading a Computer Without a Hard Disk

To install DOS 5 on a computer that doesn't have a hard disk, follow the steps below.

! WARNING

If you're creating a set of diskettes with usable files to supplement your hard disk installation, type setup /f *instead of* setup. *The* /f *stands for "floppy disks." If you don't add these characters, Setup will scan your hardware, find your hard disk, and prepare to install DOS 5 on it a second time.*

1. Place disk 1 of your DOS 5 diskettes in drive A.

2. Type

   a:

   and press Enter.
3. Type

   setup

   and press Enter.
4. If drive A is a 5¼-inch drive, you'll see the welcoming screen in Figure 2.10. If it's a 3½-inch drive, you'll see the screen shown in Figure 2.11. Prepare a group of diskettes as instructed. Press Enter to continue.
5. Press Enter to begin the installation. You'll see the screen in Figure 2.8. A bar graph shows your progress, and the lower right-hand corner tells you what Setup is doing. You'll periodically be asked to insert each diskette you've prepared and each DOS 5 diskette. Change diskettes when asked to do so and

```
Microsoft(R) MS-DOS(R) Version 5.00
═══════════════════════════════════════════════════════════════

           Welcome to Setup

           Setup will help you create a set of working disks of MS-DOS
           version 5.0. During Setup, MS-DOS files will be copied onto
           floppy disks that you provide and label as shown below.
           These disks can be formatted or unformatted.

           STARTUP
           SUPPORT
           SHELL
           HELP
           BASIC/EDIT
           UTILITY
           SUPPLEMENTAL

           If you want additional information or instructions about a
           screen or option during Setup, press the Help key, F1. To
           continue Setup, press ENTER. To exit Setup without creating
           a set of MS-DOS working disks, press F3.

ENTER=Continue  F1=Help  F3=Exit  F5=Remove Color
```

Figure 2.10   Beginning to install DOS 5 on 5¼-inch diskettes

```
Microsoft(R) MS-DOS(R) Version 5.00
═══════════════════════════════════════════════════════════════

       Welcome to Setup

       Setup will help you create a set of working disks of MS-DOS
       version 5.0. During Setup, MS-DOS files will be copied onto
       floppy disks that you provide and label as shown below.
       These disks can be formatted or unformatted.

       STARTUP/SUPPORT
       SHELL/HELP
       BASIC/EDIT/UTILITY
       SUPPLEMENTAL

       If you want additional information or instructions about a
       screen or option during Setup, press the Help key, F1. To
       continue Setup, press ENTER. To exit Setup without creating
       a set of MS-DOS working disks, press F3.



ENTER=Continue   F1=Help   F3=Exit   F5=Remove Color
```

Figure 2.11   Beginning to install DOS 5 on 3½-inch diskettes

press Enter. If your diskettes have never been used, you'll see the screen shown in Figure 2.12 if you're using 5¼-inch diskettes. You'll see a similar screen with different diskette sizes if you're using 3½-inch diskettes. If the appropriate type of diskette is highlighted, press Enter. If not, move the selection bar with the ↓ key on the cursor keypad. Press Enter.

6. When the bar graph on the screen shows that the procedure is 100 percent complete, take the diskette

```
┌─────────────────────────────────────────────────┐
│                                                   │
│   Please select the proper format for your disk.  │
│                                                   │
│              ┌─────────────────┐                  │
│              │      360K        │                  │
│              │     1.2MB        │                  │
│              └─────────────────┘                  │
│                                                   │
└─────────────────────────────────────────────────┘
```

Figure 2.12   Choosing your diskette format

```
Microsoft(R) MS-DOS(R) Version 5.0

        Welcome to Setup.

        Setup prepares MS-DOS version 5.0 to run on your system.
        Each screen has basic instructions for completing a step
        of the installation. If you want additional information
        and instructions about a screen or option, press the Help
        key, F1.

        To continue Setup, press ENTER.
```

```
ENTER=Continue  F1=Help  F3=Exit  F5=Remove Color
```

Figure 2.13   The Setup program welcoming screen for a new system

out of drive A. Insert the diskette called Startup and press Enter to restart your computer using DOS 5.

Installing DOS 5 on a New Computer

To install DOS 5 on the hard disk of a computer that does not have another version of DOS installed, follow the steps below.

1. Place disk 1 of your DOS 5 diskettes in drive A. Simultaneously press and hold down the Ctrl and Alt keys while also pressing the Del key. This reboots the computer and loads DOS 5 from the diskette. You'll see the welcoming screen shown in Figure 2.13. Press Enter to continue.

2. You'll be asked whether you use a network. If you do, press Y. You'll be told how to upgrade your network software, and then you'll be returned to the DOS prompt to take the necessary steps. When you've com-

pleted them, return to step 1. If you don't use a network, press N.

3. DOS is "nationalized" for the country in which you bought it. That is, it uses the keyboard layout, alphabet (including accented characters), decimal separator, and currency symbol for that country. When you continue, the next screen will ask you to confirm that you want to use the settings for your country. In the United States, you'll see a screen similar to Figure 2.14. Setup has surveyed your hardware and will present the choice INSTALL TO : Hard disk if a hard disk is present.

4. If you are satisfied with the selections, just press Enter and go on to step 5. If you want to use a different character set most of the time, move the selection bar to the COUNTRY selection and press Enter. You'll see the screen shown in Figure 2.15. Select a country using the selection bar and press

```
Microsoft(R) MS-DOS(R) Version 5.0

    Setup has determined the following default settings
    for MS-DOS version 5.0.

    If all the items in the list are correct, press ENTER.
    If you want to change an item, use the ARROW keys to
    select it.  Then press ENTER to see alternatives for
    that item.

             DATE/TIME   : 03-13-91  10:52
             COUNTRY     : United States
             KEYBOARD    : US Default
             INSTALL TO  : Hard disk

             The settings are correct.

ENTER=Continue  F1=Help  F3=Exit
```

Figure 2.14 Choosing country defaults and a destination for your installation

```
Microsoft(R) MS-DOS(R) Version 5.0
================================================

        MS-DOS version 5.0 supports international character sets.

        If the correct country is selected, press ENTER.

        To choose a different country, use the ARROW keys to select
        it, and then press ENTER.

        +-----------------------------------------------------------+
        |  Belgium            Hungary          Spain                |
        |  Brazil             Int'l English    Sweden               |
        |  Canada (French)    Italy            Switzerland          |
        |  Czechoslovakia     Latin America    United Kingdom       |
        |  Denmark            Netherlands      [United States]      |
        |  Finland            Norway           Yugoslavia           |
        |  France             Poland                                |
        |  Germany            Portugal                              |
        +-----------------------------------------------------------+

ENTER=Continue  F1=Help  F3=Exit  ESC=Previous Screen
```

Figure 2.15   Choosing a national character set

```
Microsoft(R) MS-DOS(R) Version 5.0
================================================

        MS-DOS version 5.0 supports international keyboards.

        If the correct keyboard is selected, press ENTER.

        To choose a different keyboard, use the ARROW keys
        to select it, and then press ENTER.

        +-----------------------------------------------------------+
        |  Belgian           German           Spanish              |
        |  Brazilian         Hungarian        Swedish              |
        |  Canadian French   Italian          Swiss (French)       |
        |  Czech             Latin American   Swiss (German)       |
        |  Danish            Norwegian        UK English           |
        |  Dutch             Polish           [US Default]         |
        |  Finnish           Portuguese       US English           |
        |  French            Slovak           Yugoslavian          |
        +-----------------------------------------------------------+

ENTER=Continue  F1=Help  F3=Exit  ESC=Previous Screen
```

Figure 2.16   Choosing a national keyboard layout

Enter. Then go on to select a keyboard layout as
shown in Figure 2.16.

5. Setup now prepares to install DOS 5 in a directory
called C:\DOS, with the Shell program as your main
interface to the computer, as Figure 2.17 shows. If
you're not sure that you want to use the Shell, see
the section above called "Should You Install the
DOS Shell?" If you prefer not to use it, move the
selection bar with the ↑ key to highlight Run Shell
on startup, and press Enter. You'll see a box with
the text

```
YES
NO
```

Select NO and press Enter again. It's best if you use
the directory that Setup wants to use for installing

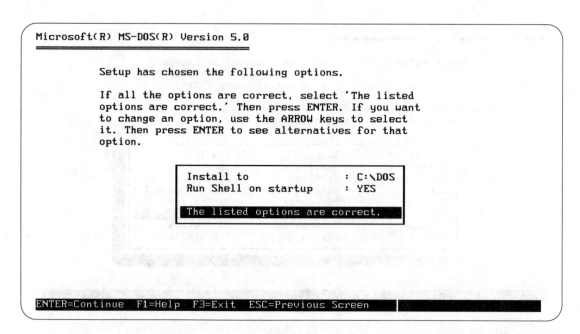

```
Microsoft(R) MS-DOS(R) Version 5.0

      Setup has chosen the following options.

      If all the options are correct, select 'The listed
      options are correct.' Then press ENTER. If you want
      to change an option, use the ARROW keys to select
      it. Then press ENTER to see alternatives for that
      option.

                ┌─────────────────────────────────────┐
                │ Install to            : C:\DOS       │
                │ Run Shell on startup  : YES          │
                │ ┌─────────────────────────────────┐ │
                │ │ The listed options are correct. │ │
                │ └─────────────────────────────────┘ │
                └─────────────────────────────────────┘




ENTER=Continue  F1=Help  F3=Exit  ESC=Previous Screen
```

Figure 2.17 Confirming or changing the Setup options

DOS 5. If you're happy with the selections Setup has made, just press Enter.

6. You are now ready to install DOS 5. A box on the screen displays the message

```
Setup is ready to install MS-DOS version
5.0. If you choose to continue, you may
not be able to interrupt Setup until it
has completed installing MS-DOS on your
system.

To install MS-DOS now, press Y.

To exit Setup without installing MS-DOS,
press F3.

To review your configuration selections,
press any other key.
```

If you press F3, you'll exit the Startup program, and you'll have to start all over again.

7. Press Y to install DOS 5. You'll see the screen in Figure 2.8. A bar graph shows your progress, and the lower right-hand corner tells you exactly what Setup is doing. Insert each of the DOS 5 diskettes in turn when asked to do so. Press Enter after each one. When the bar graph shows that the procedure is 100 percent complete, take the diskette out of drive A. Press Enter to restart your computer using DOS 5. You will now be running your computer from the hard disk.

8. Although you can start your computer with disk 1 from the manufacturer, most of the files on this and the other diskettes are not in usable form. To make sure you have usable diskette copies of the DOS 5 files installed on your hard disk in case something goes wrong with those files, repeat the procedure you've just completed, choosing INSTALL TO : and selecting Floppy disks in step 3. Be sure to

use diskettes that will work in drive A, so you can start your system with them if something goes wrong. At this point you can turn to the section called "Upgrading a Computer Without a Hard Disk" and begin with step 4 if you need more guidance than the present screen provides.

Now that your system is up and running with DOS 5, let's start exploring. Chapter 3 tells you how to start your system and introduces you to DOS commands, and Chapter 4 introduces the Shell program.

Getting Started

What You Will Learn

- How to start your system
- How to enter a command
- How to set the date and time
- How to get help with DOS commands
- How to edit commands
- How to modify commands
- How DOS executes commands

Starting Your System

When you turn on your computer, everything is cleared from memory and the hardware tests itself. This process is called the *power-on self-test,* or *POST.* You may see a series of diagnostic messages. You may also see a number changing quickly at the upper left-hand corner of the screen. This indicates that the computer is checking its memory. If everything is OK, the computer looks in drive A for a diskette, and if one is present, for a small piece of code called the *bootstrap program.* This program tells the computer to load DOS, which is why turning on your computer is called *booting.* If there is no diskette in drive A, the computer looks for a hard disk and attempts to read the bootstrap program from it.

If your computer has no hard disk, start your system by inserting the diskette labeled "Startup" in drive A and turning on your computer and monitor. If you have a hard disk, just turn on the computer and monitor. No diskette is required because your computer will read DOS from your hard disk.

! WARNING

When you turn on the computer you may see the message Disk boot failure *or* Drive not ready. *If you didn't put a diskette in drive A this means one of the following:*

- *There is no hard disk in your computer.*
- *Your hard disk doesn't have DOS on it.*
- *Your hard disk hasn't been properly prepared to hold data.*

If you did put a diskette in drive A, it means one of the following:

- *The diskette doesn't have DOS on it.*
- *You didn't close the drive door properly.*

If you have a true IBM computer with no hard disk, you won't see any of these messages. Instead, an abbreviated form of the BASIC programming language is loaded into memory. Don't worry about this. Just place the Startup diskette in drive A and follow the instructions below for performing a warm boot.

Once DOS is present in the computer, it takes charge of the flow of information. You'll know that it's present when you've reached a point where you can give the computer instructions.

When all the whirring and beeping stops, you'll see the *DOS command prompt*. If you started up with a diskette, it looks like this:

```
A:\>
```

If you started from a hard disk, and you installed the DOS Shell with the Setup program, you'll see the DOS

Shell screen, which should resemble Figure 3.1. Later in this chapter, when you use a command prompt, it will look like this:

```
C:\>
```

This prompt was installed in the AUTOEXEC.BAT file by the Setup program. You'll find out in Chapter 12 how to change the prompt if you wish.

The Warm Boot: Restarting Your Computer

You may sometimes need to reset your computer after you have been using it for a while. There may be something you have placed in memory that you must remove to run another

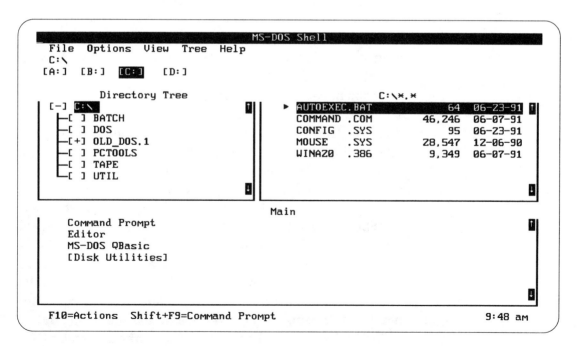

Figure 3.1   The opening DOS Shell screen

program. Or sometimes, sad to say, the computer may unpredictably lock up, making it impossible to continue your work.

You can reset the computer to its starting condition by pressing Ctrl-Alt-Del. (Hold down the Ctrl and Alt keys, then press the Del key. Whenever you see key names separated by a hyphen, it means you should hold down the first key(s) and then press the second.) This procedure is called a *warm boot*. In contrast, starting over by turning the power off and on (or by pressing a Reset button on your system unit) is called a *cold boot*.

When you do a warm boot, the computer doesn't reset itself or perform the self-test. It just reloads DOS from whichever source is available, executes the commands in the control files, and displays the prompt or the Shell.

HINT

Even if your system has a hard disk, you should know how to boot it from a diskette. There may be times when you want to bypass your normal startup routines, or times when something has gone wrong with your startup procedure.

Entering DOS Commands

In this section you'll learn how to enter DOS commands and a bit about how they work. Even if you prefer using the Shell to execute commands, a better knowledge of the DOS command structure will make the Shell easier to use, since a great deal of what it does is put together commands from the information you give it.

If you have a hard disk, press Alt-F4. You have exited the Shell and will see the command prompt.

If you don't have a hard disk, the screen will already display the command prompt. You need to learn how to work with this prompt, because most of your software will require a special diskette in order to start, which in turn will require you to enter commands at the command prompt.

When you see the prompt and the cursor, DOS is ready to accept commands. The space to the right of the prompt is called the *command line*. You enter a DOS command by typing it on this line. When you finish, press Enter. This tells the computer to execute your command. Typing the command and pressing Enter is called *entering* the command.

When typing a command, you may make a mistake. Use the Backspace key to move back to the error, then retype the rest of the command. If you've made a hopeless mess, cancel the entire command by pressing the Escape key. You can then start over.

The command line can hold up to 128 characters. When you reach this limit, the computer refuses to accept any more. It beeps until you press Enter or Escape.

The DOS Editing Keys

Some keys and key combinations have special meaning to DOS when you're working on the command line. Some may affect the way the computer behaves or the way the command line appears. Others allow you to edit the command line.

When you enter a command, DOS not only executes the command but stores it in a special memory area called a *buffer*. You can use the command in the buffer as a *template* for typing others. Each time you execute a new command, it replaces the previous one in the buffer. To see the current contents of the buffer, press F3. You should see the last command you typed. The cursor waits at the end of the command line, so you can edit the text on it. Only when you press Enter is the command executed, either in its original or its edited form. Table 3.1 summarizes the effects of the editing keys.

Trying Out Some DOS Commands

Let's try a few internal commands to see how they work. (As you may remember, the internal commands are those you can execute with nothing loaded into the computer except DOS itself.) Then we'll look at the general structure of a DOS command.

Most of what you see when you enter a DOS command will appear in uppercase letters. DOS, however, rarely cares whether you use uppercase, lowercase, or a combination. It simply translates what you type to uppercase for its own purposes.

Table 3.1 The DOS editing keys

Key	Effect
F1, →	Either of these enters one character from the previous command line.
F2 *c*	Copies all characters from the previous command up to the character *c* (where *c* represents the first instance of any character in the command) to the new command line.
F3	Copies all remaining characters from the current cursor position in the previous command to the end.
F4 *c*	Copies all characters from the previous command after the character *c* to the current command line.
F5	Copies whatever you enter on the command line to the buffer, but the command itself is not executed.
F6, Ctrl-Z	Either of these inserts an end-of-file marker; this allows you to create text files on the command line.
Ins	Allows you to add characters at any point in a command you've just issued (which is still in the buffer and appears on the screen above the DOS prompt). Use the → and ← to place the cursor where you want the new characters to appear, press Ins, and type. When finished, press F1 or F3 to place a portion or the rest of the command from the buffer on the command line.
Del	Allows you to delete characters at any point in a command you've just issued (which is still in the buffer and appears on the screen above the DOS prompt). Use the → or ← to place the cursor where you want to remove characters, press Del for each character you want to delete, then press F3 to complete the command.
Esc	Cancels the current command line without affecting the buffer.
Ctrl-C, Ctrl-Break	If you haven't pressed Enter yet, either key combination cancels the command on the command line without affecting the buffer, returning you to the prompt.
Backspace, ←, Ctrl-H	Any of these deletes the last character on the command line, moving the cursor to the left.
Tab, Ctrl-I	Either of these moves the cursor to the next tab stop on the current line (tab stops are every eight screen columns).
Ctrl-P, Ctrl-PrtSc	Either of these duplicates what appears on the screen on the printer, character by character. Characters will appear on the printer as soon as they are typed.
Ctrl-Num Lock, Ctrl-S, Pause	Any of these stops text from rolling off the top of your screen, pausing until you press any other key.
Shift-PrtSc	Copies everything on the screen to the printer if the printer is turned on. If the printer is off or none is connected, the computer may lock up. Press Ctrl-Alt-Del (a warm boot) to restart it.

Setting the Date and Time. When you create or change files, DOS stamps them with the date and time they were written. For this information to be useful, however, the computer has to know the current date and time. To find out if it does, enter the command

```
date
```

If you have a computer with an 80286, 80386, or 80486 chip, or one with what's called a *real-time clock,* you'll see something like this:

```
Current date is Mon 02-25-1991
Enter new date (mm-dd-yy):
```

If the computer's date is the current date, just press Enter to return to the command line. If the date isn't current, you can change it by entering it in the form suggested. You need not include zeros that appear before a significant digit, however, and you may use slashes instead of dashes. Thus any of the following would be acceptable ways of entering June 1, 1991:

```
6/1/91
6-1-91
06/01/91
06-01-91
```

If you enter the date in an unacceptable form, the prompt will reappear, giving you a second chance.

If you see the message

```
Current Date is Tue 01-01-1980
```

then you don't have any kind of internal clock. In this case you should always set the date before you start work.

The TIME command works just like the DATE command. Enter

```
time
```

and you'll see something like:

```
Current time is   5:40:34.69p
Enter new time:
```

Again, if the time is correct, just press Enter. If it's not, enter the time in the form shown. You need not include hundredths of seconds. If it's 5:00 P.M., you can just type 5p, or 17.

If the time shows a few minutes past midnight, but that's not the current time, it's another indication that your computer doesn't have an internal clock. Use TIME to set the correct time right after you set the date.

Viewing a List of Files.   DOS keeps track of files by storing information about them in *directories*. To view a directory, you type the DIR command. This command has many options, which we'll explore at some length in Chapter 7. For now, just enter the command

```
dir
```

If you booted your system from a diskette in drive A, the screen will show something like Figure 3.2. If you're using a hard disk, the result will be more like Figure 3.3.

Right now you might find the screen display rather confusing. Don't worry. I'll explain what all the parts mean in later chapters. For now just notice that the display is arranged in columns. The first two give you the file names. (If a file is a program, you execute it by typing the name in

```
A:\>dir

 Volume in drive A is STARTUP
 Volume Serial Number is 164C-6CD0
 Directory of A:\

COMMAND  COM    46246 06-07-91   5:00a
EGA      SYS     4885 06-07-91   5:00a
DISPLAY  SYS    15682 06-07-91   5:00a
FORMAT   COM    32285 06-07-91   5:00a
PACKING  LST     3610 06-07-91   5:00a
WINA20   386     9349 06-07-91   5:00a
ANSI     SYS     8868 06-07-91   5:00a
COUNTRY  SYS    13496 06-07-91   5:00a
HIMEM    SYS    11120 06-07-91   5:00a
KEYB     COM    14699 06-07-91   5:00a
KEYBOARD SYS    24336 06-07-91   5:00a
MODE     COM    23313 06-07-91   5:00a
SETVER   EXE     9162 06-07-91   5:00a
SYS      COM    13200 06-07-91   5:00a
UNFORMAT COM    17680 06-07-91   5:00a
AUTOEXEC BAT       24 06-15-91   1:39p
CONFIG   SYS       53 06-15-91   1:39p
        17 file(s)      248008 bytes
                         33792 bytes free

A:\>_
```

Figure 3.2   A directory of the Startup diskette

the *first* column.) The third column tells you how big the file is in bytes (roughly, how many characters it contains). The last two, rather more obviously, tell you the date and time the file was created.

At the bottom of the display are two lines telling you the number of bytes (characters) comprising all the files listed and the amount of unoccupied storage space remaining on the disk.

In Figure 3.3, you'll notice that some entries show the symbol <DIR> instead of showing the file's size. This indi-

```
C:\>dir

 Volume in drive C is MS-DOS_5
 Volume Serial Number is 2E01-5D8F
 Directory of C:\

COMMAND   COM     46246 06-07-91    5:00a
AUTOEXEC  BAT        64 06-15-91    1:39p
TAPE          <DIR>     01-11-91    3:10p
TOOLS         <DIR>     12-15-90    5:10a
UTIL          <DIR>     12-15-90    5:12a
CONFIG    SYS        94 06-15-91    1:39p
MOUSE     SYS     28547 12-06-90    5:01a
OLD_DOS  1    <DIR>     10-20-90   10:54a
WINA20  386       9349 06-07-91    5:00a
BATCH         <DIR>     12-15-90   11:13a
DOS           <DIR>     05-15-91    1:15p
       11 file(s)        39600 bytes
                      28040448 bytes free

C:\>_
```

Figure 3.3   A directory of a hard disk

cates that the file is really another directory. Again, you'll learn all about what this means in Chapter 7. Notice the DOS directory created by DOS 5 and the OLD_DOS.1 directory containing the previous version. Notice also that the screen shows

```
OLD_DOS   1
```

without a period. This is another way of representing the same name. Although DOS sometimes separates the two parts of file names with spaces to keep the columns neat, you must always enter a period between the two parts.

Creating a File. You can use the command prompt to create simple text files. Let's try it out. Enter the command

```
copy con myfile
```

Now enter a line of text, for example:

```
This is a new file that I have just created!
```

Press Enter, then press the F6 function key. You'll see the symbol ^Z appear on a new line. This symbol is the *end-of-file mark*. It tells DOS not to read past the point where it occurs. Press Enter again. In a few moments you'll see the message

```
1 File(s) copied
```

and the command prompt will return.

What you've just done deserves an explanation. CON is a special DOS name—a *reserved name*—for the *console,* or the combination of the keyboard and screen. The COPY CON command tells DOS to copy what you type on the console to the file you name (in this instance, MYFILE). There are actually four steps to this command:

1. You enter the COPY CON command to gain access to the console for creating the file.
2. Next, you type the text you want to place in the file, pressing Enter after each line.
3. When your file is complete, you press F6 (or Ctrl-Z) to enter the end-of-file mark.
4. Finally, you press Enter to complete the COPY CON command and tell DOS to copy the contents of the console to the file.

This is a very limited way of creating files. The only way to edit a line you have entered is to backspace over it, erasing characters as you go, and retype the text. You can't even edit the text on a line once you press Enter. You are limited to the *current line*—the line that begins after you most recently pressed Enter. A bit later in this chapter you'll learn how to gain access to the DOS Editor, a much more efficient and sophisticated tool for creating text files.

Viewing a File. Now that you've created a file, you might want to reassure yourself that you can view its contents. The command for viewing a file on the screen is TYPE, followed by the file name. To view the file you just created, enter

```
type myfile
```

You'll see the file on the screen. For now it's enough to know you can use TYPE to view any text file.

The TYPE command has a few annoying characteristics. For one, if the file is longer than the screen, the text will just keep rolling up too fast for you to read. (As you learned earlier, you can halt such a display by pressing Ctrl-S or Pause.) For another, if you view a program file rather than a text file, all you will see is a lot of peculiar graphics characters, accompanied by a mess of beeps. You'll learn another way to view a file in Chapter 4.

Clearing the Screen. By now assorted messages and prompts (output) from the previous commands are all over your screen. To wipe the slate clean, enter the command

```
cls
```

which stands for "clear screen." You'll see the screen go blank and the prompt reappear near the upper left-hand corner.

▶ **HINT**
If you have a hard disk, all the external programs are always available. Setup copied them to your disk.

Running a Program

As you may remember from Chapter 1, the DOS *external commands* are actually separate programs. You run a program by typing its name on the command line. You already ran one program when you installed DOS—the Setup program. Let's try another one now.

Bringing Up the DOS Editor. DOS includes a relatively complete text editor. You'll learn how to use it in Chapter 11. Let's take a brief look at it now. To run the Editor, enter the command

NEW FEATURE
DOS Editor

```
edit
```

In a few moments, you'll see the Editor screen in Figure 3.4. Press Enter and you'll see the "Survival Guide" shown in Figure 3.5. This tutorial and help system gives you some basic instructions on using the Editor. You can browse through it now by using the PgUp and PgDn keys, or simply press Escape to go to the editing screen.

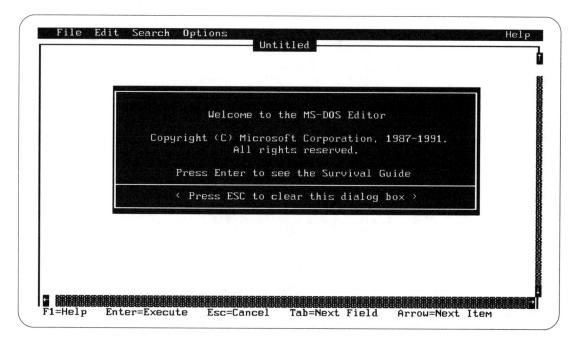

Figure 3.4   The DOS Editor opening screen

HINT

If you're using diskettes, you'll first have to put the BASIC/EDIT disk in drive A. You'll see the Editor opening screen. If you press Enter, you'll see the Survival Guide. If you use 5¼-inch diskettes, instead of the Survival Guide you'll see the message

```
              File EDIT.HLP not found.
Put the floppy disk with this file into
the drive and Retry, or change your Help
path in the Options+Help Path.
```

Put the HELP diskette in drive A and press Enter. Or just press Escape to get to the editing screen.

The DOS Editor uses a screen design similar to many programs that you run on a DOS computer, including the DOS Shell (which you'll use in Chapter 4). As the status line

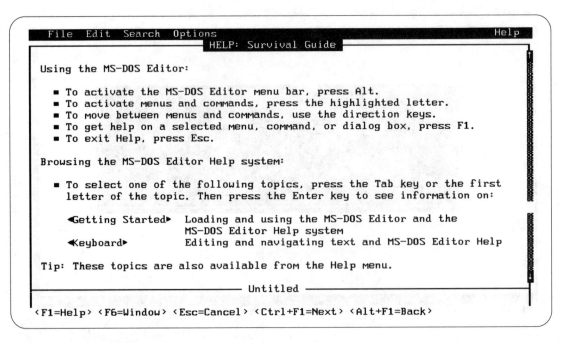

Figure 3.5   The DOS Editor Survival Guide

indicates, you press the Alt key to access the menu. For now, press Alt and then press F (or press the Alt-F combination), and you'll see the File menu that appears in Figure 3.6. Press X to invoke the Exit command and return to the DOS prompt.

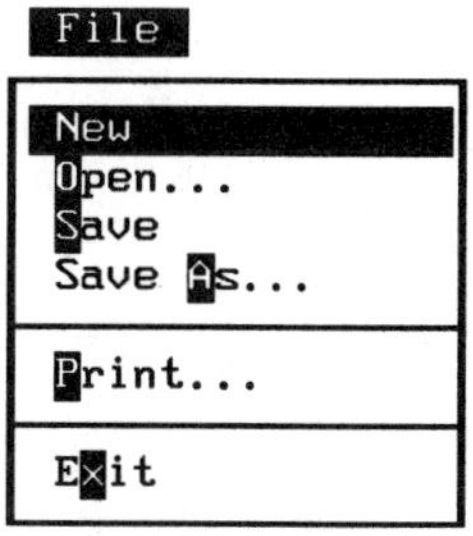

```
┌ File ────────┐
│ New          │
│ Open...      │
│ Save         │
│ Save As...   │
├──────────────┤
│ Print...     │
├──────────────┤
│ Exit         │
└──────────────┘
```

Figure 3.6 The Editor's File menu

The Structure of a DOS Command

Many DOS commands have several forms. So far in this chapter, we've looked at simple, one-word commands. But you can change the effect of many DOS commands by adding information on the command line. This information is of two types: parameters and switches. A *parameter* tells DOS exactly what object you want the command to affect. Usually it's the name of a file or a disk drive. A *switch* changes the way the command works. When you used the COPY CON and TYPE commands, you used the file name MYFILE as a parameter.

DOS commands follow a strict form, which is usually expressed in manuals as a *syntax diagram.* A syntax diagram shows you a generic form that any parameters for the command must take and lists all the possible switches. For example, you might see a syntax diagram such as

DIR [d̲:][*path*\\][*filename.ext*] [/P] [/W]
[/O[:*order*]] [/A[:*attr*]] [/S] [/B] [/L]**

In this diagram, everything in brackets is optional. The generic portions are shown in italics. Syntax diagrams can be confusing, because sometimes you can't use all the options at once. More often, you must pick one, or a few, from the list. And some options are mutually exclusive.

Let's pick this apart one piece at a time. First comes the command name itself, DIR. This is an abbreviation for "directory," the command you just used to examine a list of file names. Since everything else is in brackets, all the parameters and switches are optional. Therefore you can type this command with no parameters or switches.

If you want to use any of the options, you must separate them from the command itself with a *separator,* or *delimiter.* You create this separator by pressing the space bar, thereby inserting a space character. The optional parameters come next. The *d* followed by a colon represents a drive name. Next comes the optional *path.* This is an instruction that tells DOS where to look for a file. This is followed by the form *filename.ext,* which represents any file. It means you can ask DIR to tell you something about a particular file.

Notice that there is no space between the drive name, the path, and the file name. This means you don't insert a delimiter if you use more than one of these items.

At the end of the command, following the parameters, are the switches. Switches can sometimes completely change what a command does. If you're using a hard disk, you've already seen this effect. When you ran Setup for the second time, you added a switch: /F. This made Setup act as though you didn't have a hard disk in your computer.

NOTE

Together, the drive, path, and file name make up a path name—*a complete set of instructions on how to find a file. You'll learn more about path names in later chapters.*

▶ **HINT**

The commands that run any program—not just DOS commands— follow the same structure. You always type the name of the program, optionally followed by a separator and any parameters that might be appropriate, optionally followed by switches. For most programs, switches are preceded by the virgule (/). For a very few programs, switches are preceded by a minus sign. For fewer still, switches precede parameters. But with these exceptions, anything you type on the command line follows the same structure.

Table 3.2 shows the effects of some parameters for DIR. Try typing

```
dir command.com
```

You'll see the directory listing header (the volume label and serial number), the listing for the file COMMAND.COM, and the closing information about the amount of storage space used by the file and the amount of free space remain-

Table 3.2 Parameters for the DIR command

Parameter	Effect
d:	Tells DOS which drive to list
path	Tells DOS where to look for the file(s)
filename.ext	Tells DOS which file(s) to look for
/P	Pauses the display after each screenful of information
/O	Lists the files in sorted order, using a criterion you specify
/W	Displays only the file names, in a multicolumn list that takes half the width of the screen
/B	Displays only the file names, in a single-column list that uses periods instead of spaces
/L	Displays the directory in lowercase

ing. All other files will be skipped. If you see the message

```
File not found
```

instead of the directory listing for COMMAND.COM, it means that this file is not on the disk you're using.

If you type

```
dir command.com /l /b
```

and COMMAND.COM is on the disk, you'll just see

```
command.com
```

 HINT

You'll find the /P switch extremely helpful when your directories start filling up.

In the DIR command, some options cancel each other out. For example, you cannot display a list in both the vertical format (/B, for "bare") and the wide format (/W).

57

However, if you type

```
dir /b /w
```

you'll see the bare list, not the wide list.

Getting Help

DOS provides two types of *on-line help*—that is, you can get help in two different ways while at the keyboard. (The DOS Shell and the Editor also provide quite a bit of information on every one of their functions.) First, if you're not sure which command to use to complete a specific task, you can enter the HELP command to get an overview. HELP produces a brief explanation of the purpose of every command, a portion of which appears in Figure 3.7. When the screen is full, press any key to see more entries. (If you're using diskettes, this external program is on the HELP diskette.)

Obviously at this point, most of this information will seem like gibberish. You can't actually *learn* DOS using its HELP command (although you may be able to learn to use the Shell and the Editor in this manner, once you get started). However, as you become more proficient, you may find HELP a useful way of remembering what you're looking for.

```
For more information on a specific command, type HELP command-name.
APPEND   Allows applications to open data files in specified directories
as if they were in the current directory.
ASSIGN   Assigns a different drive letter to an existing drive.
ATTRIB   Displays or changes file attributes.
BACKUP   Backs up one or more files from one disk to another.
BREAK    Turns extra CTRL+C checking on or off.
```

Figure 3.7   Using the HELP command

When you need more extensive help with a specific command, just type it followed by a slash and a question mark. This help switch works with every DOS command, although many other switches have different effects with different commands. To look at an example, enter

```
dir /?
```

You'll see the display in Figure 3.8. Notice that the information is quite similar to that presented above in the section on

```
C:\>dir /?
Displays a list of files in a directory.

DIR [pathname] [/P] [/W] [/O[:sortorder]] [/A[:attributes]]
[/S] [/B] [/L]

pathname    The directory and/or files to list.
/P          Pause after each screenful of information.
/W          Use wide list format.
/S          Display files in the specified directory and all
            subdirectories.
/B          Use bare format (filenames only).
/L          Use lower case.
/O          List files in sorted order.
sortorder   N  name                   S  size
            E  extension              D  date and time
            G  group subdirectories   -  prefix to reverse order
/A          Display files with specified attributes.
attributes  D  subdirectories         R  read-only files
            H  hidden files           A  files ready for archive
            S  system files           -  prefix meaning "not"

Switches may be preset in DIRCMD environment variable. Over-
ride preset options by prefixing any switch with -, e.g., /-W.

C:>_
```

Figure 3.8   Getting help with a specific command

the structure of a command. Again, it probably tells you more than you want to know at present. However, if you're patient, you'll find the information you need.

How DOS Finds a Program

Let's look a little more closely at what the messages Bad command or file name and File not found mean. As you may remember, when you type a command, DOS first looks in the command processor, COMMAND.COM, to see whether the command is internal. If it is, DOS executes it.

If what you typed isn't an internal command, DOS looks in the disk directory for a program to execute—an external command—whose name matches the command you typed. So in simplest terms, the former message means that DOS couldn't find either an internal or external command by that name.

If what you've typed is the name of a file, DOS checks to see whether the file is a program file. (You'll learn how DOS knows this in Chapter 4.) If so, it executes the program. If not, it gives you the Bad command message.

DOS follows a similar procedure when looking for a file entered as a parameter. If it can't find any file in the directory of the disk you're using that matches what you typed, it tells you so.

Changing the Default Drive

The disk you're using is often referred to as the *current,* or *default,* disk. Its name appears as part of the prompt. The C:\> prompt tells you that the current drive is C and that DOS should look on drive C for file names. If your prompt says A:\>, DOS looks on drive A.

To make a different drive the default, type its name, followed by a colon, on the command line. Press Enter. (Strictly speaking, the drive's name *includes* the colon—the colon tells DOS that you're referring to a drive, not a file.)

If you're using diskettes, your BASIC/EDIT diskette should be in drive A. Put your Startup diskette in drive B. Enter

```
b:
```

If you're using a hard disk, put your BASIC/EDIT diskette in drive A and enter

```
a:
```

Now enter the DIR command. You'll see the directory of the diskette in drive B or A, respectively.

Running Programs on Other Drives

Unless you tell DOS otherwise, it looks *only* on the current drive for a program to execute. But you can tell it to look on other drives by including the drive name as part of the file name. If you're using a hard disk, make that the current drive by entering

```
c:
```

Now enter the command

```
a:edit
```

You'll see the Editor opening screen once again. However, this time you're actually reading the program from drive A rather than from drive C.

Finding Files on Other Drives

As noted you can also tell DOS to look on noncurrent drives for files named as parameters to commands. To verify this, enter

```
dir a:edit
```

You should see a display similar to Figure 3.9.

```
C:\>dir a:edit

 Volume in drive A is BASIC
 Volume Serial Number is 12D8-2549
 Directory of A:\

EDIT      COM       413 12-13-90    4:09a
         1 file(s)          413 bytes
                          45056 bytes free

C:\>_
```

Figure 3.9   Using a noncurrent drive in a command

Introducing the DOS Shell

Chapter 4

What You Will Learn

- What the DOS Shell is
- How to get around in the Shell with a mouse
- How to get around in the Shell with the keyboard
- How to use menus
- How to use dialog boxes
- How to run programs from the Shell

Now that you've grasped the fundamentals of the command line, let's explore the alternative: the DOS Shell. If you have a hard disk, to run the Shell just enter the command

```
dosshell
```

If you're using diskettes, first place the Shell diskette in one of your drives and make that the current drive. Then enter the command.

The Shell is most useful for locating and running programs from a hard disk. However, if you don't have a hard disk, you may still want to use the Shell as a file manager, to keep the files on your diskettes in order. (You'll learn how in Chapter 6.) As we mentioned in Chapter 3, the Shell isn't helpful for running programs on a diskette-based system. The special diskette required to start most programs means you can't use the Shell, only the command prompt.

The Shell Screen

You've already gotten a glimpse of the Shell screen in Figure 3.1. Figure 4.1 gives you a more complete view. As you can see, the screen is divided into several areas. There's a great deal of redundant information, which makes it especially easy to keep track of where you are and what you're doing.

At the top is the *title bar*. This tells you the name of the program. It's a common feature of many programs using a similar screen design.

Below the title bar is the *menu bar*. You'll see five commands on it:

File
Options
View
Tree
Help

All are the names of *submenus*. When you "pull down" a submenu—which you'll learn how to do in a little while—you'll see a list of additional commands. You can execute them by selecting them either with the keyboard or a mouse.

Below the menu bar, a line indicates the name of the currently selected drive and the *current directory*. (Directories as well as drives can be current when you have more than one.) You'll learn more about directories in later chapters.

Below this line is a series of *disk drive icons*. On the present screen they indicate a drive by its name in brackets. (Remember, a disk drive name includes a colon.) As you can see, the current drive, drive C, is highlighted. Monochrome screens use *inverse video* (a color the reverse of the screen's) to highlight items. Color screens use a different color.

Below these areas at the top of the screen are three *windows* in which you initiate different types of activities. Each window has a title bar. The upper left-hand window, called the `Directory Tree`, displays a list of directories on the current disk. (If you're using a diskette, you'll see only the drive name followed by a backslash, exactly as on the

Title bar

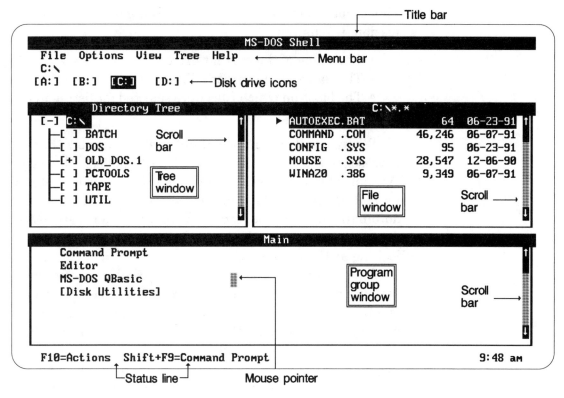

```
                           MS-DOS Shell
   File   Options   View   Tree   Help    ←——————— Menu bar
   C:\
   [A:]   [B:]   [C:]   [D:]   ←——— Disk drive icons

┌─────Directory Tree─────────────────┐┌──────C:\*.*─────────────┐
│  [-] C:\                          ↑││  ► AUTOEXEC.BAT      64  06-23-91 ↑│
│   ├─[ ] BATCH      Scroll         ││    COMMAND .COM  46,246  06-07-91  │
│   ├─[ ] DOS        bar        ——→ ││    CONFIG  .SYS      95  06-23-91  │
│   ├─[+] OLD_DOS.1                 ││    MOUSE   .SYS  28,547  12-06-90  │
│   ├─[ ] PCTOOLS   ┌──────┐        ││    WINA20  .386   9,349  06-07-91  │
│   ├─[ ] TAPE      │Tree  │        ││          ┌──────┐      Scroll ——→  │
│   └─[ ] UTIL      │window│        ││          │File  │      bar         │
│                   └──────┘       ↓││          │window│                 ↓│
└─────────────────────────────────────┘└─────────────────────────────────┘
┌──────────────────────Main──────────────────────────────────────────────┐
│   Command Prompt                                                       ↑│
│   Editor                                                               │
│   MS-DOS QBasic                ▓        ┌───────┐                      │
│   [Disk Utilities]             ◄───────┤│Program│      Scroll          │
│                                         │group  │      bar   ——→        │
│                                         │window │                      │
│                                         └───────┘                      ↓│
└────────────────────────────────────────────────────────────────────────┘
   F10=Actions  Shift+F9=Command Prompt                      9:48 am
```

└Status line┘   Mouse pointer

Figure 4.1   Areas of the DOS Shell screen

line above the disk drive icons.) You'll learn more about the items in this window and why it is called a directory tree in Chapter 6.

Turn your attention to the window to the right of the Directory Tree window, called the *file window*. It gives you more or less the same information as the DIR command, except that it doesn't show the time a file was created and it uses an inverse video (or different-colored) highlight bar.

Notice the title at the top of this window:

```
C:\*.*
```

This cryptic remark actually contains a great deal of information. It tells you:

- The name of the current drive
- The name of the current directory
- The basis on which files were selected for listing in the window

Where is all this information? Well, you know that C: represents the name of a drive. The backslash character (\) that follows always refers to the primary, or *root*, directory. If there are no other directories on a disk, you'll automatically see the root directory. If there are other directories, the backslash symbol lets you know you're looking at the main one.

Finally, there's that pair of asterisks separated by a period. This is known as a *wild-card pattern*. The basic form of a DOS file name contains up to eight characters, followed by a period, followed by a three-character *extension*. The extension usually, but not always, tells you something about the nature of the file. Programs, for example, always have the extensions COM, EXE, or BAT. The asterisk is a "wild card" because it can stand for any other characters, including no characters. The combination

```
*.*
```

thus stands for all file names. You'll learn a great deal more about wild-card characters and how to use them in Chapter 6.

The lower half of the screen is occupied by the *program group window,* titled Main, indicating that you're looking at the Main program group. You can run programs by selecting them from this window. You can also add other programs or groups of programs to it. You'll learn how in Chapter 14.

Once again, the issue of currency raises its head. Notice the item at the end of the list in this window:

```
[Disk Utilities]
```

The brackets indicate that this is another program group. (It's a group of external DOS commands that perform actions on disks.) At present the Main program group is current. When you select Disk Utilities from the Main program group, the window title becomes Disk Utilities. You see a whole new list of commands you can execute or programs you can run. You'll use programs in the Disk Utilities group in Chapter 5, and you'll learn how to add programs to the Shell in Chapter 14.

At the very bottom of the screen is the *status line*. This tells what actions are available at any given time and what keys to use to take them. It also shows the current time.

Moving Around the Shell Screen

Before you can do anything useful with the Shell, you have to know how to get around in it. You can move through the Shell either with the keyboard or with a mouse. The basic principle is that you select items upon which to act, then select the action. (This set of steps is sometimes called "pointing and shooting.")

Special Shell Keys

Table 4.1 lists keys that have special functions in the DOS Shell. You'll become acquainted with quite a few keys in the following sections. In later chapters you'll learn about other, more specialized keys.

KEYBOARD

Mouse Basics

If you have a mouse, it's especially easy to use the Shell. There are four basic mouse actions:

MOUSE

Table 4.1 Special Shell Keys

Key	Effect
Tab, Shift-Tab	Moves between screen areas
Ctrl-n	Selects drive n
Alt	Activates the menu bar
Alt-n	Pulls down the menu in which the character n is highlighted
Enter, space bar	Selects an item or executes a command
Escape	Moves back one level, to the previous activity; closes dialog boxes and menus
↑	Moves the selection bar up one item
↓	Moves the selection bar down one item; pulls down a menu if its name is highlighted
←	Selects the item to the left of the currently selected item; on an entry line, moves the cursor to the left
→	Selects the item to the right of the currently selected item; on an entry line, moves the cursor to the right
Home	Moves the selection bar to the first item in a list or menu; on an entry line, moves the cursor to the beginning
End	Moves the selection bar to the last item in a list or menu; on an entry line, moves the cursor to the end
PgUp	By scrolling up, replaces the items in an area with the same number of items immediately preceding those shown
PgDn	By scrolling down, replaces the items in an area with the same number of items immediately following those shown
F1	Displays information on your current activity
F3, Alt-F4	Removes the Shell from memory, returning to the DOS prompt
Shift-F9	Displays a DOS prompt, leaving part of the Shell in memory; type `exit` to return to the Shell

- *Pointing:* You'll notice a shaded rectangle on the screen in Figure 4.1. This is the *mouse pointer.* As you move the mouse around the desktop, the pointer moves around the screen.
- *Clicking:* To select an item on which the pointer rests, or an area within which it rests, depress the left mouse button. This is called *clicking* the mouse. In keyboard terms it's equivalent to pressing the space

bar, as you'll learn shortly. Pressing the right button is equivalent to pressing the Escape key, which in the Shell cancels a selected action. (If you have a three-button mouse, the third button doesn't do anything in the Shell, but it may have uses in other programs.)

- *Double-clicking:* When you click the left button twice in rapid succession, it has a different effect from clicking once. The effect depends on what is currently selected (i.e., on where the mouse pointer rests).

- *Clicking and dragging:* In some circumstances you can select several items at once by clicking at one point on a list, holding the left button down, and dragging the mouse pointer upward or downward through the list. When you release the button, the mouse selects everything it passed while you had the button depressed.

Selecting a Drive

When you first start the Shell, it automatically highlights the disk drive icons. You can select the drive you want either with the keyboard or with the mouse.

There are two ways to select a drive with the keyboard. **KEYBOARD** You can use the arrow keys to move the highlight to the desired drive icon and then press the space bar. If the drive is not an empty diskette drive, the contents of the tree and file windows will change to reflect the contents of the selected disk.

The second way to select a disk drive is to hold down the Ctrl key and press the letter key corresponding to the drive. Thus to select drive C, you'd press Ctrl-C.

To select a disk drive with the mouse, just place the **MOUSE** pointer on the disk drive icon and click once with the left button. The tree and file windows display information about the selected drive.

Dialog Boxes

If by chance you've selected a diskette drive that doesn't have a diskette in it (or has the latch open), you'll see the *dialog box* in Figure 4.2. Dialog boxes give you information and allow you to make choices. This particular dialog box displays an error message and gives you two choices of how to deal with the error:

```
1. Try to read this disk again
2. Do not try to read disk again
```

At the top of the dialog box is a title. Within the box, information about your choices appears. Some dialog boxes ask you to type in certain types of information, although this one doesn't. This is a *list box:* it contains a list of items from which you can choose one. At the bottom are three *buttons.* Each button represents an action. You thus have several ways to make a choice.

■ **KEYBOARD**

To select one option listed in the dialog box, press the key with the number corresponding to your choice. Then press the space bar. If you've got a diskette in the drive but the latch is open, you might close the latch and press 1. If you press 1 and in fact there is no diskette, the dialog box will reappear after a few moments.

Figure 4.2   A dialog box

The three buttons will read

```
OK
Cancel
Help
```

Almost all dialog boxes have these three buttons. Some have several more. You move among the buttons with the ← and → keys and then select one by pressing Enter or space bar. Select OK to confirm your choice. This is equivalent to pressing the space bar. Select Cancel to close the dialog box and return to what you were doing. This is equivalent to pressing Escape. (The Escape key always closes a dialog box.) Select Help to view information on the condition reported by the dialog box.

With the mouse you select a choice by double-clicking on it with the left button. If you double-click on line 2, the box disappears. If you double-click on line 1 but the drive doesn't have a diskette in it, the box reappears.

☐ **MOUSE**

Alternatively, click once on your choice, then move the mouse pointer to the OK button and click once.

As a rule, you select the action indicated on a button by clicking on it once. If you click on OK before making a selection, the dialog box disappears. If you click on Cancel, the dialog box always disappears, returning you to what you were doing. If you click on Help, you'll see information explaining the condition reported in the dialog box or directions for completing an operation you've started.

Figure 4.3 shows a dummy dialog box with an example of every element you might encounter. At the top, of course, is the title of the dialog box, which will be the name of a command or program. The box may contain a message.

This box contains several types of items:

- An *entry line,* on which you can type additional information
- *Check boxes,* of which you can choose one or more

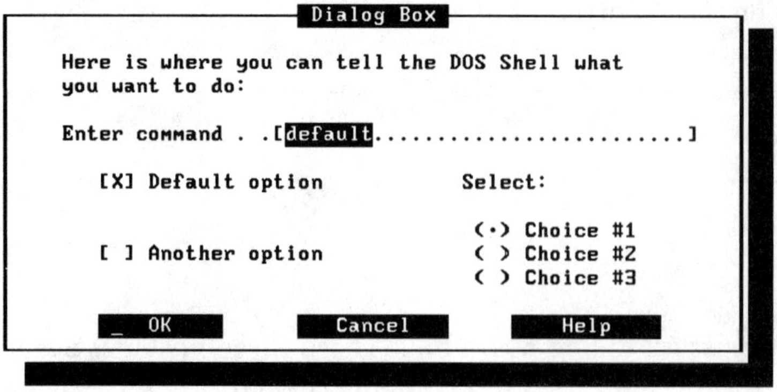

```
┌────────────────────────┤ Dialog Box ├────────────────────────┐
│                                                               │█
│  Here is where you can tell the DOS Shell what               │█
│  you want to do:                                             │█
│                                                               │█
│  Enter command . .[default........................]          │█
│                                                               │█
│    [X] Default option              Select:                   │█
│                                                               │█
│                                    (·) Choice #1             │█
│    [ ] Another option              ( ) Choice #2             │█
│                                    ( ) Choice #3             │█
│                                                               │█
│    ▁   OK              Cancel              Help              │█
└───────────────────────────────────────────────────────────────┘█
 ███████████████████████████████████████████████████████████████
```

Figure 4.3   A sample dialog box showing typical elements

- *Option buttons,* of which you can select only one
- *Action buttons,* of which you can select only one

As you do in the Shell screen itself, you move among areas in the dialog box with the Tab and Shift-Tab keys. When the dialog box appears, the cursor is on the entry line. Each press of Tab moves the cursor in turn to the bracketed space before each check box, to the space in parentheses before each option in the list, and to each action button, from left to right.

Editing the Entry Line.   A *default value* appears on our sample entry line. If you select OK, this value will be acted on. If you prefer to enter a different value, type it in and the default will disappear. Pressing Enter when you finish typing is the same as selecting OK at this point.

A Shell entry line gives you many more ways to correct mistakes than a DOS command line does. The ← key moves the cursor back across the text you typed without erasing it. Home moves the cursor to the beginning of the line. To insert additional characters, you just type them in, and the characters on the line will move to the right as you type.

To replace characters that are already present, you must first press the Ins key. This toggles between *insert* mode and *overtype* mode. In overtype mode, characters you type replace those at the current position of the cursor, instead of moving them to the right. The Del key deletes the character at the cursor, and the Backspace key deletes the character to the left of the cursor.

You don't have to move the cursor back to the end of the line to execute the command. Just press Enter or select OK.

Toggling Options On and Off.   In our dummy dialog box, you'll see two *check boxes* below the entry line, on the left. You select an option by moving the cursor to it and pressing the space bar. Or place the mouse pointer between the brackets and click. An X appears next to the option selected.

Selecting an Option from a List.   To the right of the check boxes is a list containing *option buttons*. You can select only one item from an option list. To do this, move the cursor to the desired button and press the space bar. Or click the mouse button between the parentheses.

At the bottom of the box are the action buttons. Of course you can select only one. Doing so closes the box, completes or cancels the action, or brings up another dialog box.

Selecting Screen Areas

To move between screen areas, use Tab or Shift-Tab (refer to Figure 4.1). Pressing Tab once selects the Directory Tree window. You'll know it's selected because a little arrow appears to the left of the highlighted directory. Pressing Tab a second time selects the file window. The arrow appears next to the selected program. Pressing Tab a third time selects the program group window. As you'd expect, the arrow appears next to the first item in the group. Pressing Tab a fourth time returns you to the drive icons. Pressing Shift-Tab selects in the opposite direction. Thus if you've selected the file window, pressing Shift-Tab selects the Directory Tree window.

Once you've selected an area, you use the arrow keys to move among items inside it (as you did when selecting a disk drive). To move to the file window, use the Tab key. Press ↓ twice. You'll see the highlight move down to the third file name in the window. If there are more items in a

■ **KEYBOARD**

▶ **HINT**
You can move quickly through lists in the DOS Shell by using the other keys on the cursor keypad. Home automatically selects the first item in the list, and End the last. Each press of PgDn or PgUp displays a full window's worth of items below or above those previously displayed.

list than can fit in the window, you can see them by continuing to press ↓, which *scrolls* the list. That is, the selection bar moves to the next item on the list, bringing it into the window, while the first item disappears from the top. Pressing ↑ moves the selection bar upward. When it reaches the top of the list, pressing it again reveals the items that have scrolled beyond the top of the box.

☐ **MOUSE**

To select an item with the mouse, just click. When you click in an area, you select not only the area but the item on the line where the mouse pointer falls. Thus you can select the third file in the file window in a single step just by clicking the mouse once.

To view items that don't fit in the windows, use the *scroll bar* at the right edge of each window. The scroll bar has four parts: two arrows (one at each end), a shaded area, and a slider (a solid rectangle). Placing the mouse pointer at one arrow and holding down the button causes the contents of the window to scroll in the direction the arrow points. Clicking once on an arrow scrolls the contents one line at a time in the direction of the arrow. Clicking in the shaded area of the scroll bar moves the slider to the point at which you clicked. What appears in the window then depends on the length of the list. For example, if you click three-quarters of the way down, you'll see the part of the list that's three-quarters of the way to the bottom.

Using Menus

We'll be exploring the Shell menus thoroughly in later chapters. For now let's just get an overview of how they work, using the File menu as an example. Figure 4.4 shows how the menu appears when the file window is selected. The Create Directory... command appears in inverse video, because it's available only when the Directory Tree window or a disk drive icon is selected. (On some monitors such a command may not appear until you select the item with which it can be used.)

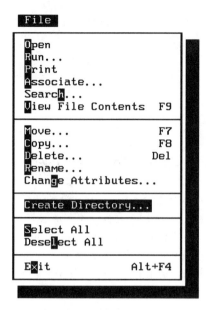

Figure 4.4   The File menu

Notice that each command has one letter highlighted. When the menu is on view, you can select the command by pressing the corresponding key. Some commands also have "shortcut" keys listed to their right. You can use them to carry out the command even when the menu is not visible, so long as the appropriate type of object is selected. Thus, for example, you can use F9 to execute the View File Contents command if the small pointer arrow is in the file window. But if you press this key when another screen area is active, the computer will beep but nothing else will happen.

Some command names are followed by three dots. When you select these, you will be asked for further information before you can proceed.

In some cases you'll see an additional menu. A few commands—not including any on the File menu—are *toggles*. That is, they let you determine whether a setting is turned on or off. These selections have a small diamond to the left of the command name when they are turned on.

■ **KEYBOARD**

You'll notice that the status line shows two possible actions you can take with the keyboard:

```
F10=Actions   Shift+F9=Command Prompt
```

Pressing F10 activates the menu bar. You'll see a series of highlights, as shown in Figure 4.5. The word *File* is highlighted, indicating that if you press Enter or ↓, the File menu will "drop down" and become visible. Each of the other menus has one letter highlighted. To pull one of them down, press the highlighted letter. Alternatively, press ← or → until the menu's name is highlighted completely. Then display the menu by pressing Enter or ↓. Once the menu is visible, you execute a command by moving the highlight to it with ↑ or ↓ and pressing Enter. Or press the key corresponding to the highlighted letter.

▶ **HINT**

Once you have pulled down a menu, pressing ← or → automatically closes the menu on display and pulls down the next menu in the direction you're moving.

You can access the menus in yet another way. Pressing the Alt key by itself has the same effect as pressing F10. However, holding down Alt and pressing the first letter of a command on the menu bar automatically displays the menu.

The arrow keys "wrap" when moving through menus. That is, when you reach one end, pressing the same key again moves you to the other end.

To back out of a menu and return to the main Shell screen, press Escape.

□ **MOUSE**

To display a menu using the mouse, just click the mouse on the menu's name on the menu bar. To execute a command, click on the command. You can move to another menu just by clicking on its title on the menu bar.

To back out of a menu, press the right mouse button. Or click anywhere on the screen outside the menu.

```
  File  Options  View  Tree  Help
```

Figure 4.5   The menu bar when it's active

Getting Help

The Shell will be happy to teach you how to use itself. Any time you've selected a command or are viewing a dialog box, you can get assistance on how to proceed by pressing F1. Most dialog boxes also have a Help button, which will give you information about how to use the box.

For more comprehensive help, use the Help menu, shown in Figure 4.6. Much of the material in the Help menu parallels what you've read in this chapter. For a comprehensive introduction, choose Shell Basics. The Commands submenu gives you essentially the same information you'll see if you select a command and press F1. The Keyboard submenu lists all keys that have special effects in the Shell. This command may be confusing to you at first, because the Shell has many advanced features requiring special keystroke combinations. The Procedures menu gives you step-by-step instructions. Using Help gives you instructions on using the Help menu itself. Finally, the Index command displays an alphabetical index of topics on which you can request further information. Don't be afraid to ask for help when you need it. It's free.

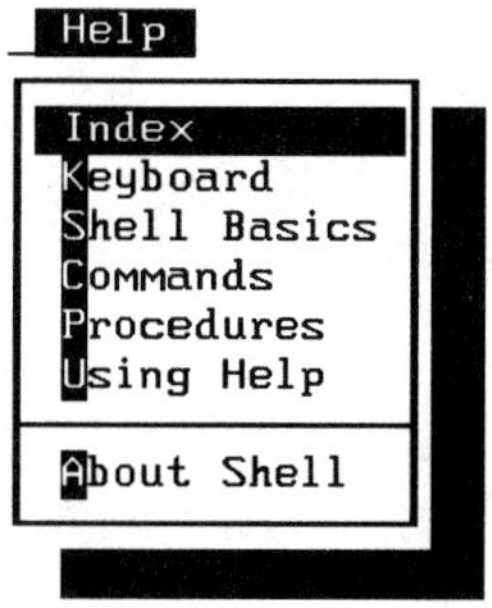

Figure 4.6
The Help menu

The Shell in Graphics Mode

On most monitors you can display the Shell in *graphics mode* as well as in text. Pull down the Options menu and select Display. You'll see the list box shown in Figure 4.7, with a variety of text and graphics modes. You can preview any mode by selecting the Preview button, or simply select a mode and see how it suits you. You can also just go ahead and choose OK. You can always change back later if you don't like the result.

After you've chosen a different mode, you'll notice a subtle change in the appearance of almost everything on your screen. Figure 4.8 shows the Shell screen transformed into graphics mode. Let's start at the top. The disk drive icons now show small pictures of different types of disks.

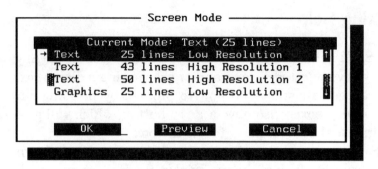

Figure 4.7   The Display dialog box

You'll know right away whether a letter refers to a hard disk or a diskette drive.

In the Directory Tree window, the brackets have been replaced by file folders, an apt metaphor for directories. In the file window, two different kinds of icons appear next to the file names. Programs are marked by a rectangle with a horizontal line through it. You'll see this same icon in the

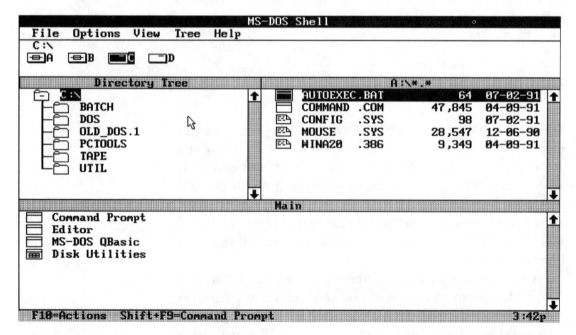

Figure 4.8   The Shell in graphics mode

program group window as well as icons with a double row of rectangles inside them. The latter signifies that there are more items inside the one you see. Data files are marked by an icon representing a page of text with the corner folded over.

Menus are also subtly changed. Instead of the highlight that marks the action letter, you'll find an underscore. If your monitor shows more than two colors, unavailable commands appear in a paler shade of the text color.

Dialog boxes are changed only slightly. The action buttons have curved ends, so they look more like buttons. The option buttons are now circles. The default option has its circle filled in.

The mouse pointer is now an arrow instead of a rectangle. The scroll bars, too, are subtly changed.

You may prefer the graphic display because it presents more information through the use of graphic symbols. It's much easier to recognize a program by its icon, for example, than by the last three letters of its name. Nonetheless, the actions you take in graphics mode are exactly the same as those in text mode.

Changing the Display Colors

Even if you have a monochrome monitor, you can change the colors in which the Shell appears. Pull down the Options menu and select Colors. You'll see a list box similar to the one you used to select a screen mode. For monochrome monitors you can choose among two or four shades of black and white, or inverse colors. If you have a color monitor, you can choose any of the fancifully named color schemes you'll find in this list box.

The procedure for selecting color schemes is the same as that for selecting graphics modes. As with graphics modes, you can try them out before you settle on one, and you can change them any time you like.

Trying Out Some Shell Commands

One advantage of the Shell is that it lets you do some things you can't do at a DOS prompt. Let's look at a few.

Viewing a File

In Chapter 3 you used the TYPE command to view a file you created. Using the Shell, you can view all parts of your file at will. If you don't yet have any long text files, you won't be able to use all the tools the Shell gives you. However, the screen will give you hints as to their power.

To view a file, follow these steps:

1. Select the file window and the name of the file to view. You can select with either the Tab and arrow keys or the mouse.
2. Pull down the File menu either by clicking on File or by pressing Alt-F.
3. Select the View File Contents command. You can do this in any of four ways:

   - Press V
   - Press F9
   - Use the arrow keys to move the selection bar to the command and press Enter
   - Click on the command with the mouse

   Use whichever method you like best.

You'll see the screen shown in Figure 4.9.

As you can see, the Shell displays your file in a window, where you can control your view. As the messages indicate, you can move back and forth within the file by using various keys. Pressing PgUp or PgDn displays the previous or next screenful of text, respectively. The ↑ and ↓ keys scroll the text one line at a time. The Enter key, as the status line notes, is equivalent to the PgDn key. Unfortunately you can't try any of these keys because the file is too short to take more than one screen.

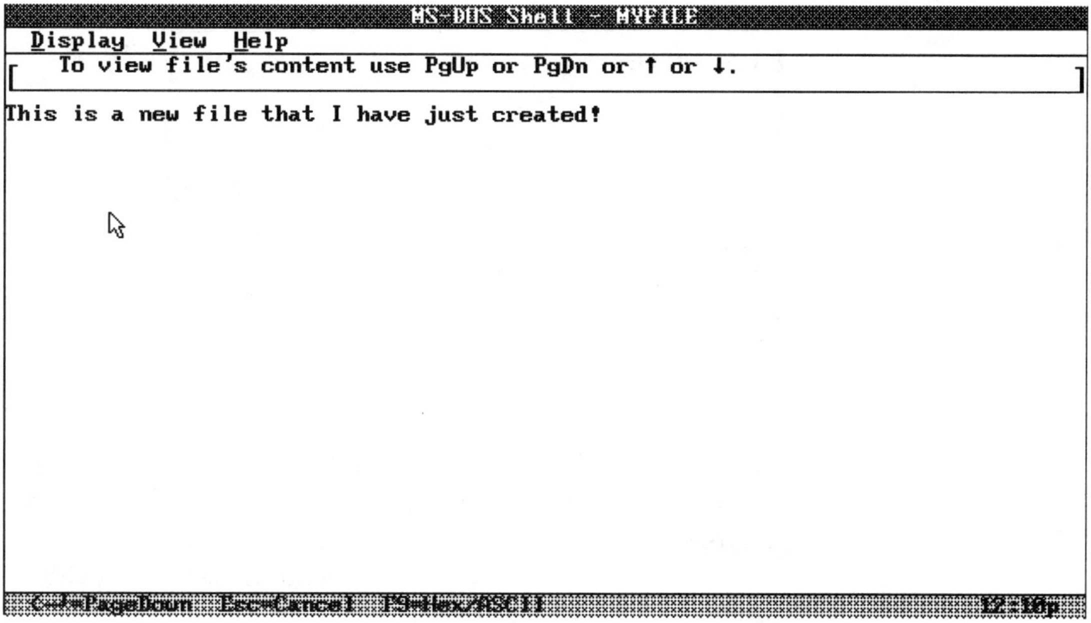

```
                        MS-DOS Shell - MYFILE
 Display  View  Help
┌──────────────────────────────────────────────────────────────────────┐
│    To view file's content use PgUp or PgDn or ↑ or ↓.                  │
└──────────────────────────────────────────────────────────────────────┘
This is a new file that I have just created!



        ⍾



 C=PageDown   Esc=Cancel   F9=Hex/ASCII                         F2=Help
```

Figure 4.9   Viewing a file in the Shell

You have several additional options. Notice that there is
a new menu, with three commands. The Help menu is the
same as that at the main Shell screen. The Display menu
lets you switch to *hexadecimal* mode, to view program files.
We won't go into this at present. However, as you can see
from the status line, you can accomplish the same thing just
by pressing F9. You might try it just for fun. Press Escape
when you're finished to return to the main Shell screen.

Searching for a File

Let's use another facility of the Shell that is unavailable on
the command line—locating all copies of a file. Again, make
sure the file window is selected. Now pull down the File
menu. Select Search. ... You'll see the dialog box in Figure
4.10. Notice that the default given to you on the entry line is
., the wild-card pattern that means "all files." Also, the
check box for Search entire disk is selected. If you just

Figure 4.10   The Search dialog box

press the space bar or select OK, you'll see a list of every file
on your disk. It will whiz by too fast to read, but as with
View, you'll be able to move the list around in your window
and read any part you like.

The power of the Search command becomes evident
when you restrict the search. Type

```
command.com
```

on the entry line and press Enter. After a few moments, you
should see something like Figure 4.11. This indicates that
there are two copies of COMMAND.COM (the DOS command processor) on your disk. One is in the root directory
(indicated by C:\) and the other is in another directory,
called C:\DOS. Setup installs this program in both places,
so don't be surprised to find it twice.

As you can see, the menu is the same as at the main
Shell screen. For instance, you can search for a group of
files. Then you can use some commands on the File menu
to work with them—compare them, delete duplicates, and
so on.

Running Programs from the Shell

The Shell gives you several ways to run programs, which are
summarized below. We'll try a few shortly.

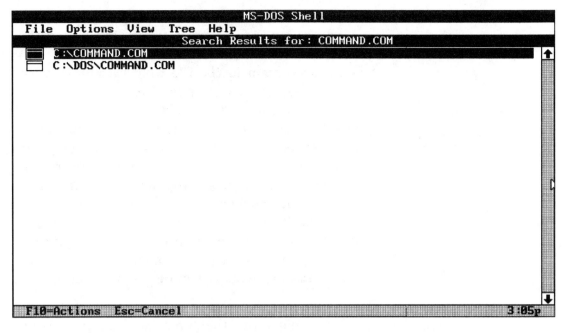

Figure 4.11   The result of searching for a file

- Move the selection bar in the file window to a program's name and press Enter.
- Double-click on a program's name with the mouse.
- If a program is present in the program group window,
  select it in that window. You will probably be asked to
  supply command-line parameters.
- Press Shift-F9, as the status line suggests. You can
  then enter a command line at a DOS prompt. Enter

      exit

  to return to the Shell.
- Select Command Prompt in the program group window, either with the mouse or the keyboard. This too
  gives you a DOS prompt. Enter

      exit

  to return to the Shell.

- Pull down the File menu. Select the Run command. You can then enter a command line from within the Shell.
- Select a program in the file window, pull down the File menu, and select Open. The program will run automatically, with no parameters.
- As you'll learn in Chapter 14, you can set up associations between specific file types and the programs that created them. You can then run a program by selecting one of its files in the file window and pressing Enter or double-clicking. The program will then automatically open the file if it's capable of doing so.
- As you'll also learn in Chapter 14, you can add programs to the program group window. Once you do, you can have them prompt you for the requisite parameters.

The easiest way to run a program is to select it in the file window. You'll recall that program files have names ending in COM, EXE, or BAT. If your screen resembles the ones we've been looking at, you have only two programs in the file window: COMMAND.COM and AUTOEXEC.BAT. DOS runs both for you when you start up, so there's no point to your doing so.

Using the Run Command

One of the ways to run a program is to select the Run command from the File menu. You'll be given an entry line on which you can type a DOS command. Enter

```
edit
```

just as you did in Chapter 3. The Editor will appear again. When you're finished looking at it, press Escape Alt-F X to close the Editor. You'll also see the message

```
Press any key to return to MS-DOS Shell...
```

at the bottom of the display. This message appears any time you run a program from the Shell, unless you use one of the methods in which you ask for a command prompt. When you use these, nothing will tell you that the Shell is still in memory. The only way you'll know is to enter the EXIT command, as described earlier.

Using the Program Group Window

Let's try out the program group window at the bottom of the screen. You'll recall that the item [Disk Utilities] is a program group. Select this. The contents of the window change to match Figure 4.12. Note that [Main] now appears as a group, along with several new commands. You can return to the Main group by selecting [Main].

Select the Disk Copy command. This activates the DOS command DISKCOPY, which, naturally enough, copies disks. Specifically, it copies the contents of one diskette to another diskette of the same type. When you select DISKCOPY, you'll see a dialog box like the one in Figure 4.13. The entry line contains two pieces of information: the name of the disk drive containing the diskette to be copied (the *source*) and that of the drive containing the diskette onto which the copy should be made (the *target*).

If you have only one drive, the entry line will contain the default value

```
a:  a:
```

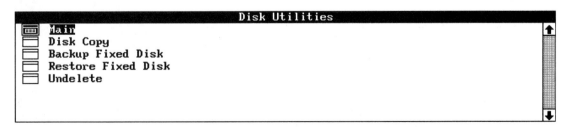

Figure 4.12   *The Disk Utilities program group*

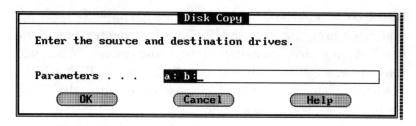

Figure 4.13   The Disk Copy dialog box

instead of

```
a: b:
```

This implies that you must place *both* the source and the target in the same drive—but not at the same time. Note, however, that if you have two drives, you can't copy from one to the other unless both are of the same type.

We're not going to complete this command now. We'll wait until Chapter 5, when you'll gain a more thorough understanding of disks. The important point to remember is that you're selecting the DISKCOPY command from a menu and entering its parameters in a dialog box. Once you select OK, you're executing a DOS command as surely as if you had typed

```
diskcopy a: a:
```

on the DOS command line.

Dealing with Disks

Chapter 5

What You Will Learn

- How to prepare a diskette for use
- How to copy and compare diskettes
- How to care for diskettes
- How to prepare a diskette to start your computer
- When and how to format hard disks

As you learned in Chapter 1, disks and disk drives come in a variety of sizes and capacities. They are essential to your computer system because they give you a place to store work when it's not actively in your computer's memory. In this chapter you'll learn the special commands for dealing with disks as such. In the following two chapters, you'll learn the commands for dealing with what you put on the disks.

What Is Formatting?

When you take a new diskette out of the box, the magnetic medium contains only random magnetic patterns. Your computer can't store information on it until those patterns have been organized so that DOS can later locate the information. This is called *formatting* the diskette. Not surprisingly, it's done by the FORMAT command.

The Parts of a Disk

DOS creates fundamentally the same structure on all the disks it formats. First, it divides the disk into *tracks,* or *cylinders.* These are invisible concentric rings in the magnetic medium. Each track is divided into *sectors.* All sectors are the same size, but different types of disks have different numbers of tracks and sectors. The more tracks and sectors a disk contains, the greater its capacity for storing data. Your computer locates data in part by its *address* expressed as a track number and a sector number.

At the beginning of each disk, DOS places three very important structures that together make up the DOS *reserved area. First comes the boot record,* containing the bootstrap program that starts your computer, a description of the disk's physical structure and capacity, and a few other necessities. Following that are two copies of the *file allocation table,* often abbreviated FAT. This is a map of addresses that tells DOS exactly where to find any data contained in a file and, not incidentally, where to write new data so that it won't destroy existing data. (Problems in the FAT result in many dire error messages.) Following the FAT is the root, or main, directory. This is where file names are written. Figure 5.1 shows the location of these items on a 360K diskette. Note that the tracks are not drawn to scale; nor does the diagram show 40 tracks.

The rest of the disk is used to store your data. The sectors are grouped into units called *allocation units,* or *clusters.* Clusters are simply groups of a fixed number of sectors, the number depending on the type of disk. When DOS writes a file, it allocates space for it in whole clusters, hence the alternative name.

Why do you have to know all this? Well, you need to know the capacity of a diskette in order to format it. Also you'll see messages at various times referring to sectors, tracks, and allocation units. It's a lot easier to respond to messages if you know what they mean. For reference, Table 5.1 shows the capacity of the most common types of diskettes.

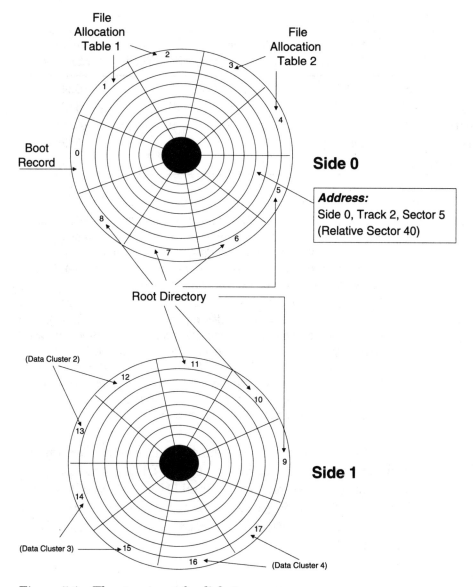

Figure 5.1   The structure of a diskette

Formatting a Diskette

✳ NOTE

Disk capacity is measured in kilobytes, *symbolized by a* K, *or in* megabytes, *symbolized by* Mb. *These measurements are multiples of* bytes. *A byte is computer lingo for a specific measurement*

Table 5.1 Common diskette formats

Diskette Type	Nominal Capacity	Number of Tracks	Sectors Per Track	Cluster Size (bytes)
5¼" double density	360K	40	9	1024
5¼" high density	1.2Mb	80	15	512
3½" double density	720K	80	9	1024
3½" high density	1.44Mb	80	18	512
3½" extra high density	2.88Mb	80	36	1024

of storage space. If the data to be stored is in the form of characters, as it might be in a document, a single byte holds a single character. If it's another type of data, such as program code or the formulas necessary to recreate a drawing or a spreadsheet, bytes represent something other than characters.

The reason that the prefixes kilo- *and* mega- *refer to something other than a thousand and a million (1024 and 1,024,000, specifically) has to do with the way computers "think." No matter what you appear to be putting into your computer, it must be broken into a series of 0s and 1s before the CPU understands it and can do anything with it. Computers use the* binary *number system. Not coincidentally, 1,024 is equivalent to 2^{10}—a nice round number in computer terms, if not in human terms.*

Let's format a diskette now. We'll use the command prompt first. The steps you take, and DOS's responses, are essentially the same in the Shell. However, you'll understand the formatting process better if you enter the commands yourself, rather than letting the Shell enter them for you.

Formatting at the Command Prompt

Because FORMAT is an external command, you must have the FORMAT program available. If you're using diskettes, you'll find FORMAT on your Startup diskette. If you're using a hard disk, FORMAT was already placed there by Setup.

We'll begin by formatting a diskette that's never been used. Take a new diskette that will fit in drive A. If you have a high-density drive, use a high-density diskette. (A bit later you'll learn how to format a double-density diskette in a high-density drive.) At the command prompt, enter

```
format a:
```

This command tells DOS to execute FORMAT on the diskette in drive A (you must always specify the drive). DOS will respond with the prompt

```
Insert new diskette for drive A:
and press ENTER when ready...
```

When the diskette is safely in the drive and the latch is closed, press Enter. You'll see the message

```
Checking existing disk format.
```

DOS is attempting to read the boot record to find out whether the diskette has ever been formatted. This will take a while. When it discovers that the diskette has no boot record, DOS assumes you want to format the diskette to the drive's maximum capacity. DOS will tell you:

```
Formatting 1.2M
  0 percent completed.
```

(If you're not using a 1.2Mb drive, the number will be different.) The percentage noted on the screen gradually increases until the second line of this message is replaced by

```
Format complete.
```

✔ NEW FEATURE
Automatic prompt-
ing for a volume
label

You will then be prompted to enter a volume label:

```
Volume label (11 characters, ENTER for none)?
```

A volume label is a name given to a disk for your convenience. If you don't want one, just press Enter. However, it's
useful to have a quick guide to what's on a diskette, so you
might as well get into the habit of entering volume labels.
You can enter up to 11 characters, excluding ones that are
used as parts of DOS commands (which are * ? / \ , : ; | " +
< > = & ^[ ] ( )—you can't use most of these in file names,
either). If you enter lowercase letters, DOS will convert
them to uppercase.

When the formatting process is finished, DOS reports
on the results:

```
1213952 bytes total disk space
1213952 bytes available on disk
    512 bytes in each allocation unit.
   2371 allocation units available on disk.


Volume Serial Number is 0945-17F8

Format another (Y/N)?_
```

This report on a 1.2Mb diskette tells you the number of
bytes (1,213,952 ÷ 1,024,000 = 1.2), the size of the clusters
(512 bytes), and the number of clusters on the disk. If DOS

encounters any unusable (bad) sectors while formatting, it will mark them so they won't be used and will tell you how much of the disk they take up. It also tells you the volume serial number (which you don't need to know).

✴ NOTE

A bad sector is a part of a disk that won't reliably hold data. Data written to a bad sector cannot be read. A program written to a part of a disk containing a bad sector won't run. If the FORMAT command tells you a diskette contains bad sectors, don't use it. If it has a lifetime guarantee, save it until you have enough disks with bad sectors to send them back to the manufacturer, otherwise throw it away. Hard disks, in contrast to diskettes, almost always have some bad sectors. This need not be a cause for alarm.

The prompt at the last line of the FORMAT message tells you to press N (and Enter) if you don't want to format another diskette or Y (and Enter) if you do want to format another. Unless you want to format another diskette of the same capacity in the same drive, press N. FORMAT assumes you want to use the same settings for other diskettes you format at the same time.

Your diskette is now ready to store data. When you place files on it, attach a label to the outside of the diskette explaining the contents. This is especially important if you work in an environment where several people use computers, because it's easy to get unlabeled diskettes mixed up. If the label is already attached to the diskette, write on it with a soft, felt-tip pen. Alternatively, write the label before you place it on the diskette.

The label should include:

- Your name
- The date you created the diskette
- The file name or names of the documents on the diskette
- The name of the program with which the file(s) were created (often, you can deduce that from the file name extensions)

Formatting a Used Diskette

As a rule, when you format a diskette, you erase everything on it. This can be a lot quicker than erasing all the files and removing a volume label. And it's the only simple way to empty a diskette that has DOS on it.

✔ **NEW FEATURE**
Quick formatting

DOS 5 has a special quick-format feature for reformatting used diskettes. It's not only fast, it enables you to undo the format if you've accidentally erased a vital file. Add the /Q switch to the FORMAT command:

```
format a: /q
```

This is where checking the existing format matters. DOS reads the description of the disk in the boot record. It then quickly displays the messages

```
Checking existing disk format.
Saving UNFORMAT information.
QuickFormatting 360K
Format complete.
```

! **WARNING**
Your chances of unformatting a diskette successfully depend on your doing it before you write any new information to it.

When DOS saves the unformat information, it copies the map that tells where the files are—the FAT and root directory—to a known location on the disk. In Chapter 10 you'll learn how to use this information to bring back the files you erase when you quick-format a disk.

As you can see, the diskette used was a double-density 5¼-inch diskette. Even though it was placed in a high-density drive, DOS was able to read the old disk's description and format it correctly. As you might guess, you can quick-format disks of different capacities in the same drive when asked

```
QuickFormat another (Y/N)?
```

because DOS always checks the boot record to find out the current format.

✳ NOTE

When should you not use quick-format to format a diskette? First, you must do a full format if the diskette has never been used. Second, you should do one if you suspect something is wrong with the diskette. The quick-format process just copies the unformat information and erases the original file allocation tables and root directories. It doesn't check for bad sectors and lock them out.

Formatting a Double-Density Diskette in a High-Density Drive

As you've learned, DOS always attempts to format a new diskette to the drive's full capacity. And if you don't use the /Q switch, DOS will do the same with a used diskette. If you attempt to format, say, a used 360K diskette in a 1.2Mb drive without the /Q switch, DOS provides the helpful messages

```
Existing format differs from that specified.
This disk cannot be unformatted.
Proceed with format (Y/N)?
```

Thus to format a new double-density diskette in a high-density drive, you must specify the diskette capacity with the /F switch. For 360K diskettes this takes the form

```
format a: /f:360
```

For 720K diskettes it takes the form

```
format b: /f:720
```

(Of course, if your drives A and B aren't the same size as these, you'll use different drive letters.) Otherwise the procedure is exactly the same, as are the messages.

Formatting in the Shell

If you're not in the Shell, type

```
dosshell
```

at the DOS prompt.

☐ MOUSE

To format a diskette, double-click on the Disk Utilities program group in the lower window. When the group appears, double-click on Format. You'll see the dialog box shown in Figure 5.2.

■ KEYBOARD

To format a diskette, press Tab until the title bar of the program group window is highlighted. Press the ↓ key until the Disk Utilities group is highlighted. Then press Enter. Press ↓ until Format is highlighted and press Enter. You'll see the dialog box in Figure 5.2.

The only parameter supplied on the entry line is the drive name, A:. If you want to format a diskette in drive B, format a double-density diskette in a high-density drive, or do a quick format, you must type in the parameters and press Enter or select OK. Your screen clears and you take exactly the same steps as though you had entered FORMAT at the DOS prompt. All the Shell does is enter the FORMAT command and supply the name of the drive it thinks you want to use. In Chapter 14 we'll change this to make it easier to format diskettes from the Shell. When you've responded to the Format another prompt, you'll see the message

```
Press any key to return to the Shell...
```

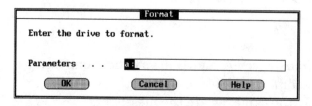

Figure 5.2   The Format dialog box

at the bottom of the screen. Press a key.

You can also quick-format a diskette from the Shell.

Click on `Quick Format` from the Disk Utilities program group, just as you selected `Format` in the previous exercise.

 **MOUSE**

■ **KEYBOARD**

Press Tab until the title bar of the program group window is highlighted. Press the ↓ key until the `Disk Utilities` group is highlighted and press Enter. Press ↓ until `Quick Format` is highlighted and press Enter.

You'll see the dialog box shown in Figure 5.3. The Shell puts together the FORMAT /Q command, leaving space for the drive name. Again, `a:` appears on the entry line. Proceed as you would with the FORMAT command.

Making a DOS Diskette

If you run your system from diskettes, you will want to have several diskettes that can start your system. First, you can't start your system without one. Second, you'll probably want to set up your main program diskettes so that you can start the system with them and have the program load automatically. Even if you have a hard disk, you should always have a few diskettes that can start the system without accessing the hard disk. If something goes wrong with your hard disk or if you make a mistake that locks up the computer while customizing your system, you won't be able to correct the damage unless you boot from a diskette.

There are two ways to make a diskette capable of starting your computer (a *boot diskette*). One is to add the /S (system) switch when formatting the diskette. This switch

```
┌──────────────────────────────────────────┐
│            Quick Format                    │
├──────────────────────────────────────────┤
│ Enter the drive to quick format.           │
│                                            │
│ Parameters . . .   a:                      │
│   ( OK )      ( Cancel )     ( Help )       │
└──────────────────────────────────────────┘
```

Figure 5.3   The Quick Format dialog box

tells DOS to copy the system files and COMMAND.COM to the diskette. After you enter a volume label (or press Enter to leave one out), you see a report similar to the following (which is for a 720K diskette):

```
730112 bytes total disk space
118784 bytes used by system
611328 bytes available on disk
  1024 bytes in each allocation unit
   597 allocation units available on disk
```

This report adds some information to the normal FORMAT report. You may have noticed that when you formatted a diskette without the /S switch, the number of bytes available was equal to the total disk space. This time you can see that the system files take up about 116K. This leaves you less space for storing other files.

If your diskette is already formatted, you can make it a startup, or *bootable,* diskette with the SYS command. Take the data diskette you made at the beginning of this chapter, place a label on it saying "Emergency Recovery Disk," and use it in this exercise. In later chapters we'll complete this diskette.

! WARNING

You cannot use the SYS command to copy the operating system files to a diskette in the same drive as the one containing the files themselves. If you have only one drive, or if your drives are of different types and you want to make a system diskette of the same type as your Startup diskette, you must use the FORMAT command with the /S switch.

A disk with the system files on it must be in your computer. Since SYS is an external command, you must also have the SYS program in your computer. If you use diskettes, you can accomplish both by placing the Startup diskette in one drive. Make it current (by entering the drive name at the prompt) before you issue the command.

DOS 5 is the first release in which you can copy the system files to any formatted diskette, even if files are present. The only restriction is that the target diskette must have 116K of free space.

✔ **NEW FEATURE**

To copy the system files to a diskette, just enter SYS followed by the name of the drive containing the target diskette. If the system files are not on the current drive, tell DOS where to find them. For example, if drive B is current and the system files are on drive C, enter

```
sys c: a:
```

You'll soon see the message

```
System transferred
```

as long as there is enough room on the target diskette. If there isn't, you'll see the message

```
No room for system on destination disk
```

or

```
Could not copy COMMAND.COM
```

Just try another diskette that has more free space, or delete some files.

Volume Labels

As you already learned, DOS asks you to give a volume label to a disk when you format it. You can use the LABEL command to change an existing volume label, delete one, or add one to a disk that doesn't have any. To add or change a label, enter the LABEL command at the command prompt or on the Run entry line in the Shell, then follow it with the drive name and the desired label. For example, you could type

```
label c:my system
```

If the label doesn't contain any illegal characters, DOS simply writes it to disk. (As you can see, you can use this command on hard disks as well as diskettes.)

To delete a volume label, just include the drive name. For example:

```
label a:
```

When you see the prompt

```
Volume label (11 characters, ENTER for none)?
```

press Enter. The label will be removed.

To check a volume label without viewing an entire directory, use the VOL command. Enter it followed by the name of the drive you want to look at. For example:

```
vol a:
```

You'll see something like the following:

```
Volume in drive A is STARTUP
Volume Serial Number is 164C-6CD0
```

The serial number is something you needn't pay attention to. It's created by DOS for its own purposes.

Copying a Diskette

DOS has a special command just for copying diskettes—DISKCOPY. If you're still in the Shell, go back to the command prompt and we'll try this command now. (You can either press Alt-F4 or F3 to remove the Shell from memory, or press Shift-F9 to get a command prompt with the Shell still in memory.)

DISKCOPY can only copy one diskette to another of the same type. If you want to copy to a different type, you must copy the files individually (you'll learn how to do that with the COPY command in Chapters 6 and 7). A disk copy differs from a file copy in that everything on the source disk—including the actual arrangement of the files—is copied exactly to the target. The COPY command, which simply copies files, copies all the useful information but not necessarily in the same arrangement as the original. And there is one other vital difference. The command for copying files won't copy hidden files, such as the DOS system files. To copy these, you must either use DISKCOPY or one of the techniques described earlier for making a DOS diskette.

To copy a diskette (the source), you must tell DOS which drive contains it and which one contains the diskette to be copied onto (the target). The basic form of the command is

diskcopy *source target*

 NOTE

You can copy hidden files using the Copy command on the File menu in the Shell. But copying the system files with this command won't make the target disk bootable.

where *source* and *target* are drive names (remember to include the colon). Which drives you can use for the source and the target depends on the types you have:

- If you have one diskette drive, both the source and the target must be in the same drive.
- If you have two diskette drives of different sizes, both the source and the target must be in the same drive.
- If you have two drives of the same size but different capacities (such as a 1.2Mb 5¼-inch drive and a 360K 5¼-inch drive), you can copy from one drive to the other only if you're copying double-density diskettes. If so, use the high-density drive as the source.
- If you have two diskette drives of the same size and capacity, either drive can be the source or the target.

How do you manage to put two diskettes in the same drive? Well, DOS is smart enough to tell you to switch the diskettes in the drive at the appropriate times.

A Single-Drive Diskette Copy at the Command Prompt

It's always a good idea to have an extra copy of an important diskette, in case something goes wrong with it. Let's copy your DOS Startup diskette. Place it in drive A and enter

```
diskcopy a: a:
```

You'll see the message

```
Insert SOURCE diskette in drive A:

Press any key to continue...
```

In a little while, DOS will tell you it's reading the diskette:

```
Copying 40 tracks
9 sectors per track, 2 side(s)
```

As you know from Table 5.1, this tells you you're copying a
360K diskette, the only kind that has 40 tracks of 9 sectors.
If you're copying another type, the numbers will be different. When DOS has read as much of the diskette as it can fit
into the computer's memory, it will tell you to

```
Insert TARGET diskette in drive A:

Press any key to continue...
```

Take out the Startup diskette, put in a blank diskette (or
one you don't need any more), and press a key. If the diskette
is blank, you'll see the message

```
Formatting while copying
```

Depending on the diskette capacity and the amount of memory in your computer, you may have to swap the diskettes
one or several more times. However, after you've made the
first swap, the only way you'll know the copy is proceeding
is that the light on the diskette drive is on. When the entire
diskette is copied, you'll be asked

```
Copy another (Y/N)?
```

As with FORMAT, if you press Y, your next copy will have to
be of the same type as the last.

A Two-Drive Diskette Copy
at the Command Prompt

If you have two diskette drives of the same type, copying is a bit simpler. Enter the command

```
diskcopy a: b:
```

You'll be prompted to

```
Insert SOURCE diskette in drive A:

Insert TARGET diskette in drive B:
Press any key to continue...
```

HINT

If you see a message beginning with the words Error writing, *it means the target diskette is damaged and the copy won't be accurate. Press Ctrl-Break or Ctrl-C to interrupt the command. Start over with a different diskette.*

Once you press a key, DOS reads the diskette in drive A and writes to the one in drive B. You don't have to swap disks at all.

Copying Diskettes in the Shell

As you saw in Chapter 4, you can copy diskettes in the Shell by selecting Disk Copy from the Disk Utilities program group. The Shell assumes you will copy from drive A to drive B if you have two drives (you'll learn how to change that in Chapter 14 if your drives don't match). You can change the source and target drives by editing the entry line. Once you enter the command, the prompts, messages, and procedures are exactly the same as at the command prompt.

Comparing Diskettes

When you copy a diskette, how do you know the copy is accurate? Most of the time it is. If you want to be doubly sure, you can use the DISKCOMP command. (If you're using diskettes, it's on the Utility diskette.) The procedure is exactly the same as for copying diskettes. Try comparing your copy of the Startup diskette with the original. At the command prompt, or on the Run entry line in the Shell, enter the command

```
diskcomp a: a:
```

or if you have two drives of the same size,

```
diskcomp a: b:
```

If you use one drive, you'll be prompted to

```
Insert FIRST diskette in drive A:

Press any key to continue...
```

If you use two, you'll be prompted to

```
Insert FIRST diskette in drive A:

Insert SECOND diskette in drive B:

Press any key to continue...
```

DOS will tell you the dimensions of the first diskette with a message such as

```
Comparing 80 tracks
9 sectors per track, 2 side(s)
```

If you're using one drive, you'll be prompted at some point to

```
Insert SECOND diskette in drive A:

Press any key to continue...
```

You may have to swap diskettes several times. If they are identical, DOS tells you

```
Compare OK
```

If they aren't, it displays the message

```
Compare error
```

and tells you the track and side at which the discrepancy occurs. It beeps at each discrepancy. If you hear a series of beeps, assume the diskettes are not even nearly identical. Press Ctrl-Break to stop the noise. When the comparison is finished, you'll be asked

```
Compare another diskette (Y/N)?
```

 HINT

Even if you copy all the files from one diskette to another, the diskettes will probably not be identical, even though the information on them is. In Chapter 9 you'll learn how to compare files. If you try to compare diskettes of different types, you'll be told they aren't compatible. DISKCOMP works only with identical diskettes.

Formatting a Hard Disk

As a rule, you do not want to format a hard disk. When your hard disk is set up properly and used regularly, it contains most of your software and data. Although it is possible to undo the effects of formatting (you'll learn how in Chapter 10), you'll still want to format a hard disk only in a few very restricted circumstances. Because of the rarity with which you are likely to perform this operation, DOS allows you to format a hard disk only at the command prompt.

Hard disks are set up in much the same manner as diskettes, with a few important differences. First, instead of two sides, hard disks have several *platters,* each of which has two sides. You might think of these as resembling a stack of phonograph records. Second, each track on one side of a platter can hold a minimum of 17 sectors. Depending on the type, your hard disk may have many more sectors per track.

One other significant difference is that hard disks almost inevitably have some bad sectors. This is no cause for alarm.

Why Format a Hard Disk?

As on a diskette, a hard disk has a magnetic coating that must be organized before it can hold data. Again, this organization is imposed by the FORMAT command. You'll want to format a hard disk if:

- It's never been formatted.
- You have changed its apparent size (see Appendix A for details).
- You want to lock out bad sectors.
- Your files have become fragmented.
- Your data has become scrambled beyond hope of recovery.

If your hard disk is brand new and has never been formatted, you must format it. You'll probably know if this is the case. One clue is that when you try to read the drive or make it current you'll see the message

! WARNING

If your hard disk is not brand new, you should always make a backup copy of its contents before you format it. You'll learn how to do that in Chapter 10.

```
General failure reading drive C:
```

✔ **NEW FEATURE
Large hard disk
partitions**

This may also be a sign of serious trouble, however.

Another reason to format a hard disk is to take advantage of the new features in DOS 5 for handling large hard disks. With DOS 3.3 if your hard disk was larger than 32 megabytes, you had to divide it into *partitions* of not more than 32 megabytes. With DOS 4 you could use larger partitions but you had to take steps to ensure that they didn't cause problems. If you're interested in pursuing this matter, see Appendix A.

Hard disks are subject to much more intensive use than diskettes. Eventually the patterns that tell DOS where to find information become weaker. Also the physical surface may begin to deteriorate. Bits of the magnetic medium may flake off or dust may get on the platter. If these things happen, parts of the disk will no longer hold data. This results in a bad sector.

Although you can't get rid of bad sectors, the FORMAT command will mark them in the file allocation table so that DOS doesn't try to write data to them.

For reasons that will become clear in Chapter 10, after you use a disk for awhile, the files on it get broken into fragments and scattered all over the disk. It takes DOS longer to read such files than it does to read those that appear in consecutive sectors. Your system may appear to have slowed down. To remedy this situation, first make a backup copy of the information on the hard disk. Then format the hard disk and restore the backup. When the files in the backup copy are written to the now-empty disk, they will again be written to consecutive clusters.

Finally, sometimes for a variety of reasons—including thunderstorms or the passing of a stray cosmic ray—the data on a hard disk becomes hopelessly scrambled. You try to read a directory and see gibberish instead. Or your file allocation table becomes scrambled, so that DOS doesn't know where to find your files. In these circumstances the only way out *may* be to reformat your hard disk. You'd better pray that you made a backup copy of its contents recently, because you won't be able to if DOS can't read the disk.

Steps to Formatting a Hard Disk

Formatting a hard disk is essentially the same as formatting a diskette. But DOS presents a few obstacles to remind you that you shouldn't take this step lightly.

If the hard disk to be formatted is drive C (the boot drive), there are additional complications. Drive C has to have the operating system on it. If DOS is already on drive C (which it may not be, if the hard disk is new), it will be wiped out by formatting, so you'll need to run FORMAT from the Startup diskette. You'll also need to copy the DOS system files from diskette to the newly formatted drive C.

To format drive C, first place your Startup diskette in drive A. Make that drive current by entering

```
a:
```

Next enter the FORMAT command. Specify drive C as the drive to be formatted and tell DOS to copy the system files:

```
format c: /s
```

DOS is smart enough to know you're asking it to format a hard disk. It displays the message

```
WARNING, ALL DATA ON NON-REMOVABLE DISK
DRIVE C: WILL BE LOST!
Proceed with Format (Y/N)?
```

HINT

If your hard disk appears to be unreadable, try reading it after booting your system from a diskette. If it's still unreadable, the problem is something other than scrambled data.

If you press any key other than Y, you'll return immediately to the DOS prompt. If you press Y, DOS first makes sure you can recover from the format, displaying the message

```
Saving UNFORMAT information.
```

It then completes the format in much the same manner as for a diskette, prompting you for a volume label and reporting on the results.

If you have more than one hard disk and you want to format a drive other than C, you needn't start from a diskette. You can use the copy of FORMAT on drive C. Also you shouldn't use the /S switch. The only hard disk that can start your system is drive C, and there's no point to copying the system files to any other hard disk. For example, to format a hard disk designated D, just enter

```
format d:
```

Again, you'll be cautioned that you will lose data and must confirm your intention.

Diskette Do's and Don'ts

Diskettes can become damaged in a number of ways. The 5¼-inch flexible diskettes are subject to more kinds of damage than the 3½-inch ones, which have a hard shell. However, you should use care when dealing with either. You'll find a partial list of potential problems on the back of many diskette sleeves. Although diskettes can wear out under the best of circumstances, you'll prolong their life by following these guidelines:

Do:
- Keep diskettes at temperatures between 50 and 125 degrees Fahrenheit

- Insert diskettes carefully into their drives
- Keep them dry

Don't:

- Touch the magnetic medium through the oval-shaped hole on a 5¼-inch diskette or through the rectangular hole protected by the metal slide on a 3½-inch diskette
- Place diskettes near objects that generate a magnetic field, such as telephones and video display screens
- Stick diskettes to a refrigerator door with a magnet
- Take a diskette out of a drive while the drive is spinning (except with certain commercially available backup programs)
- Get food, coffee, or other liquids on them
- Take diskettes through airport security checks—instead pass them by hand to the guard

With 5¼-inch diskettes, which are flexible, observe the following additional cautions:

- Keep them in their sleeves when you're not using them
- Don't bend, crease, or use paper clips on them
- Write on the label only with a soft, felt-tip pen

Managing Files and Directories in the Shell

Chapter 6

What You Will Learn

- The nature of directories and files
- How to view and select directories
- How to create, name, and delete directories
- How to name files
- Options for sorting and selecting files
- How to copy, delete, and move files

Most of the things you can do with directories and files can be done either in the Shell or at the command prompt. In this chapter you'll be using Shell commands from the File menu, which appears in Figure 6.1.

Working with Directories

Every file must have a home. Its home is a directory. On a hard disk, the root directory can hold 512 entries. A hard disk, however, can hold considerably more than 512 files. Therefore you need some means of storing larger numbers of them.

In a sense your hard disk is your file cabinet, and a directory is a smaller unit of storage—a drawer in the cabinet, a hanging folder holding a group of files, or a manila

 NOTE

From here on, examples are for a hard disk, unless otherwise noted. You can make adjustments by finding the appropriate DOS files among your diskettes and using a blank diskette in drive B for the exercise files.

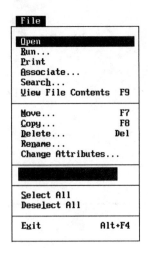

Figure 6.1   The File menu

 MOUSE

■ **KEYBOARD**

folder inside a hanging folder. This is why the Shell indicates directories with icons of file folders. You use this structure to keep track of your data and store your programs efficiently.

This organizational structure—large storage areas containing smaller ones—suggests another common metaphor for disk directories: the tree. If the "root" directory is the base of the system, you can have other directories arranged as branches off the trunk. These branches can have still other branches off them.

You've already looked at the root directories of several disks. Now let's examine the relationship between the root directory and other directories, which are called *subdirectories*. If you're not in the Shell, load it now. You'll see the familiar Directory Tree window on the left (now you know why it's called a tree) and the file window on the right. We're going to change the screen arrangement so we can concentrate on these items.

✳ NOTE

Subdirectory *is a relative term. It expresses the relationship between an included directory and the containing directory. But every subdirectory is a directory that has all the characteristics of a root directory. In this book the term* directory *is used to refer to all directories, unless the relationship between specific directories is being discussed.*

If you're using a mouse, click on the View menu, then on the option Single File List.

If you're using the keyboard, press Alt-V S to choose the Single File List command from the View menu.

The program group window will disappear, leaving you with tree and directory windows the length of the screen. It will look something like Figure 6.2, but the details won't be the same because your files and directories are different than mine. The files listed in the file window are contained in the directory that's highlighted in the Directory Tree window (c:\). If you move down through the tree with the cursor keys or click on a different directory, the list in the

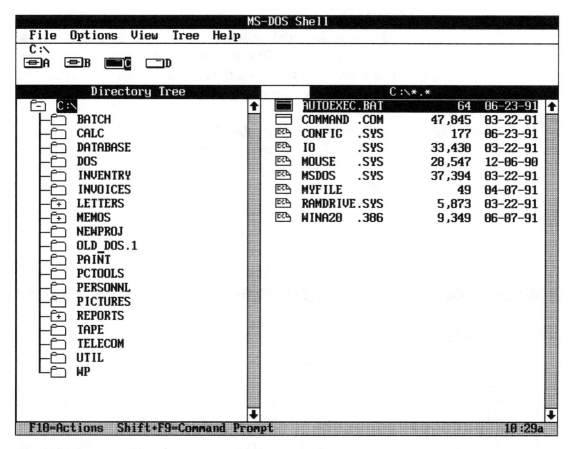

Figure 6.2   The Single File List display

file window will change. At the same time, the file window's
title bar tells you the name of the directory whose files are
displayed. If a directory contains no files or only other directories, in the directory window you'll see the message

```
No files in selected directory.
```

Click on the DOS directory, and you'll see a list similar   □ **MOUSE**
to the one in Figure 6.3. Note that you have two copies of

COMMAND.COM on the disk, one in the root directory and one in the DOS directory. This is quite significant. As we've noted, no two files in a single directory can have the same name, but files in different directories can. Thus you can keep a backup copy of a file in another directory on the same disk.

■ **KEYBOARD**

To select the DOS directory with the keyboard, press Tab until the title bar of the Directory Tree window is highlighted. Then use ↓ to move the highlight to the DOS directory.

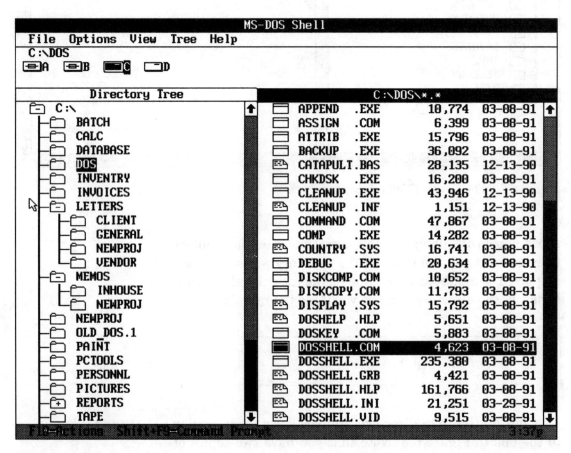

Figure 6.3   The DOS directory

Viewing a Directory

Figures 6.2 and 6.3 point out some other important features of the DOS directory structure and the Shell's management of it. Notice that the root directory's folder has a minus sign in it. Notice also that several other folders—LETTERS, MEMOS, and REPORTS—have a plus sign in them in Figure 6.2 and a minus sign in Figure 6.3. The minus sign means that a directory has subdirectories and that these are displayed in the windows. The plus sign indicates the presence of subdirectories that are not currently displayed.

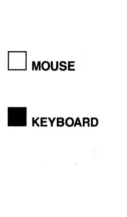

MOUSE

To display hidden directories using a mouse, click your mouse on a folder with a plus sign. To hide directories, click on a folder with a minus sign.

KEYBOARD

To display hidden directories using the keyboard, move the cursor to a folder containing a plus sign and press the Plus key on the numeric keypad. To hide them, press the Minus key on the numeric keypad when a folder with a minus sign is selected. Figure 6.3 shows the Directory Tree window with the hidden directories displayed.

You can also change what's displayed in the Directory Tree window by using the Tree menu, shown in Figure 6.4. As you can see, you can show or hide (*expand* or *collapse*) one branch or the entire tree, with a single keystroke combination.

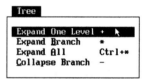

Figure 6.4   The Tree menu

Making a Directory Current

Just as only one disk drive can be the current or default drive, only one directory can be the current directory on a disk. When you're using the Shell, selecting a directory in the Directory Tree window makes it the current directory of the current drive. That is the directory you'll see in the file window at the right.

Every drive in your system always has a current directory. If the drive has only a root directory—as is likely on a diskette—it will be current. If you haven't done anything to change it, the root directory will be current on other drives as well. To make a directory on another drive current, select its icon (as explained in Chapter 4). Then select the directory in the Directory Tree window. The directory that was current on your previous drive will remain current. This doesn't seem important now, but it will when you begin working with files.

Creating a New Directory

You'll need many directories to keep your files in order, just as you need many folders for your paper files.

 MOUSE

To create a directory in the Shell, first click in the Directory Tree window. Click on the directory *below* which you want the new directory to appear. Then click on File and on the Create Directory command. You'll see the dialog box in Figure 6.5.

 **KEYBOARD**

To create a directory in the Shell, press Tab until the Directory Tree window is selected. Use ↑ and ↓ to move the highlight to the directory *below* which you want the new directory to appear. Press Alt-F E to select the Create Directory command from the File menu. You'll see the dialog box in Figure 6.5.

For this exercise select the root directory of drive C. On the entry line, enter

```
shell
```

In a little while the tree diagram will change to show the new directory in alphabetical order.

Figure 6.5   Creating a directory

Make another directory below the root. Call it DUMMY. We'll use this directory in the following exercises. Make a third called TEMP. The Shell will use this directory, as will many other programs, once you've told them how to find it. (You'll learn how to do that in Chapter 12.)

Naming a Directory

Every directory must have a name. Directory names follow the same rules as file names, which are discussed in detail later in this chapter. For now, if you remember that directory names can be up to eight alphanumeric characters, you'll be safe. Like file names, directory names can have extensions of up to three characters, separated from the main part of the name by a period. However, as a matter of convenience, most people don't give their directory names extensions. When you have to type a series of names, you'll find the extra characters burdensome.

Some software packages may create a number of nested subdirectories with complex names. As a rule, you don't have to worry about those—the software package will deal with them itself.

However, when you have the opportunity to choose a name for a software directory, a short name is better than a long one, even if the long one seems to make more sense. More on this point in Chapter 8.

Renaming a Directory

To rename a directory, first make sure the Directory Tree window is selected. Select the directory to be renamed, either with the keyboard or the mouse. Use the Rename command on the File menu. You'll see the dialog box in Figure 6.6. Select the DUMMY directory and enter

on the entry line. When you click OK or press Enter, the dialog box disappears, the DUMMY directory disappears,

 NOTE

Although you can create and delete directories at the command prompt, you can rename them only in the Shell.

Figure 6.6   Renaming a directory

and the TRIAL directory appears in its proper alphabetical order. (Actually, this isn't what happens. What really happens is that the directory name appears in the root directory in its old position with its new name. The Shell sorts the tree display so that it seems to be in order.)

Deleting a Directory

! WARNING

If your keyboard has both Del and Delete keys, only the Del key will delete files and directories in the Shell. Use this key even if Num Lock is on, which usually makes it issue a decimal point.

To delete a directory from within the Shell, select the Directory Tree window and the directory to delete (for now, the TRIAL directory). You can then either use the Delete... command on the File menu or press the Del key. You'll see the dialog box in Figure 6.7, asking you to confirm your intention.

It was easy to delete this directory because there were no files in it. If there had been, you'd see the dialog box in Figure 6.8. As the message indicates, a directory must be completely empty before you can delete it.

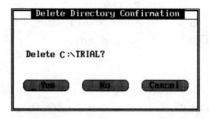

Figure 6.7   Confirming your decision to delete a directory

Figure 6.8   When you can't delete a directory

Working with Files

In computer terms a file is any set of data that is treated by the system as a unit. A note you write in your word processor is saved as a file. So is the data you create in a spreadsheet or database program.

A file may be something other than data. Every program you execute is a file as well—often more than one. DOS itself includes multifarious files of several types.

A file has several important characteristics:

- It consists of a series of consecutive bytes.
- It has a specific location on disk.
- It has a name.
- If it is executable—i.e, if it is a program—it has a name of a particular form.

Naming Files

On a computer that runs DOS, a file name follows a strict set of rules:

- It may be up to eight characters long.
- It may include any alphanumeric characters, plus the characters ~ @ # $ % ^ & ' { } - ! $ ( ) _.
- It may not include the characters * . ? / \ | % , ; : " [ ] + = or the space. These characters are used as operators in DOS commands.
- It may have an optional extension of up to three characters. Some types of files *must* have a particular

extension. In general, an extension identifies the type of file.

- If the name has an extension, you must type a period between the name proper and its extension.

The most important rule regarding file names is that no two files in a directory can have the same name. If you want two copies of a file in the same directory, they must have different names. There is no problem with having two files with the same name if they are on different disks or in different directories.

Extensions, as noted, are used to identify file types, and some are reserved for specific types. EXE and COM are used for executable programs. BAT is used for batch files, which are files, or programs, consisting of a series of DOS commands. (You'll learn how to create and use batch files in Chapter 13.) Many software packages assign specific extensions to the files they create. (As you'll learn in Chapter 14, you can use this fact in the Shell to streamline access to your files.) You shouldn't change these extensions unless you want to make an identical copy of a file in the same directory as the original.

Naming files is not a trivial matter. The eight-character limitation doesn't leave much room for describing a file's contents. If you don't establish a system, you can quickly find yourself drowning in a sea of cryptic eight-character codes. Some companies use a standardized system in which each position in the file name represents a particular category of information. For example, the first two characters might be a department code, the second two a personal code, and the last four a project code. This can be hard to decode without a map. At the other extreme, simply calling a letter LETTER can land you in trouble. Eventually you'll write another letter, and you won't be able to name it LETTER as well (without losing the first LETTER).

As a rule, it's best to stick with alphanumeric characters. Although programmers like to insert underscores to separate parts of a file name, such nonalphanumeric characters make the name harder to type. The following list shows some valid—though not necessarily useful—file names:

COMMAND.COM
garbage
TIN.TYP
$DIR@.(&)
19910620.LST
A
myfile.new
New_Book.txt
NEW-BOOK.TXT
3.14
#$@-'-!._^_

The file names in the following list are all invalid for one reason or another. Do you know what's wrong with them? If you don't, reread this section.

NEW BOOK.CH1
OLD.BOOK.TXT
yes[but]
mynew.file
THIS?.ONE
too.good
BADFILE:TMP

Develop the habit of using the extension as a type identifier rather than an extra three characters. If your software permits it, you might separate letters, memos, and reports by giving them the extensions LTR, MMO, and RPT, for example. Remember, these things aren't exactly English. I once saw a file in someone's directory called

```
UNCLE ST.EVE
```

Somehow this fellow's software allowed him to save a file with a space in its name. However, since DOS regards the space as a separator, it thereafter regarded the file name as UNCLE and the remainder as `Too many parameters`. Needless to say he could never open that file again.

It's good to develop a system for naming files. As noted, if your software permits, you can use extensions to classify files. However, if, say, your word processor imposes an extension such as DOC (document) or TXT (text), you can use part of the file name to distinguish among types of documents. For example, you might reserve the first character for something that indicates the type of document, such as L, M, or R (for letters, memos, and reports, respectively) and use the subject or recipient as the main part of a file name:

LSAMUEL.DOC
MCARMICL.DOC
ROZONLYR.DOC

These file names might represent a letter to Ms. Samuel, a memo to Mr. Carmichael, and a report on the ozone layer.

Remember that the directory shows the date you created the file, so you needn't try to include that information in the name. If you want to name your files by date, however, it's best to use the form *yyyymmdd*. For a file created on November 20, 1991, for example, use

`911120.LOG`

This will ensure that your files are sorted by date when they are also sorted by name. If you want to use this format for several file names in a directory, you can use the last two characters to distinguish them.

Ways to Display and Delete Files

Turn your attention now to the file window. You're going to perform some operations using commands on the File menu. The first thing to understand about managing files in the Shell is that the commands you execute always work on *selected* files. There are two aspects to selecting files. First, you can narrow down the list of files displayed by using a *wild-card pattern*. Then you can select one or more files.

Rearranging the Directory Display

The File Display Options dialog box (shown in Figure 6.9) allows you to sort file names in the directory window using various criteria. You can sort by

- Name
- Extension
- Date
- Size

or leave the list unsorted, so that it reflects the actual order in which the file names appear on the disk. Sorting by extension groups the files by type, so you can see quickly what files of a given type you have in a directory. Sorting by date, especially if you also choose Descending Order, makes it easy to find the files you've worked on most recently. (As you'll see in Chapter 12, you can select a default sorting order for directories even if you don't use the Shell.) To see how helpful changing the sorting order can be, reenter *.* in the File Display Options dialog box and select Extension as the order to sort by. The directory window will now group the files by extension. You may find this especially useful when trying to locate the files created by a particular software package. Many database-management programs, for example, use the extension DB

Figure 6.9   The File Display Options dialog box

or DBF, and many spreadsheet programs use an extension beginning with W, for "worksheet."

Selecting a Single File and Groups of Files. Whether or not you sort the list of files shown in the directory window, you can select more than one to be acted on by a command.

☐ **MOUSE**

To select a single file, just click on it. To select a group of files that are listed consecutively, take these steps:

1. Select the first file of the group by clicking on it.
2. Hold down the Shift key.
3. Select the last file of the group by clicking on it.

To select files that are not listed consecutively, hold down the Ctrl key and click on each file you want to select.

■ **KEYBOARD**

To select a single file, move the highlight to it with ↑ or ↓. To select a group of files that are listed consecutively, move the highlight to the file name at one end of the list, hold down the Shift key, and extend the selection upward or

Table 6.1 File selection keys in the Shell

Key	Effect
Shift-F8	Turns Add mode on or off. In Add mode you can select nonconsecutive items from the file list. When Add mode is on, the word ADD appears on the status line.
Shift-↑	Extends the selection to the file above the selected file.
Shift-↓	Extends the selection to the file below the selected file.
Shift-PgUp	Extends the selection upward to include a full window of files before the selected file.
Shift-PgDn	Extends the selection downward to include a full window of files below the selected file.
Alt-F S (File, Select All), Ctrl-/	Selects all files in the window.
Alt-F L (File, Deselect All), Ctrl-\	Turns off the current selection, leaving only the file name under the highlight selected.
Shift-space bar	In Add mode selects all files between the previously selected file and the highlight.
Space bar	In Add mode adds the highlighted file to the group of selected files.

downward with ↑ or ↓. To extend the list further, use PgUp or PgDn.

Alternatively, press Shift-F8 to put the Shell in Add mode. This allows you to select multiple files by several means. Table 6.1 shows the keys you can use to select files. Figure 6.10 shows a group of consecutive selected files, and Figure 6.11 shows several files selected individually.

How Wild-Card Characters Work. Wild-card characters are vital to all aspects of your work in DOS, both in the Shell and on the command line. You use them to refer to, or select, groups of files. There are two wild-card characters, * and ?. The asterisk stands for any (or no) charac-

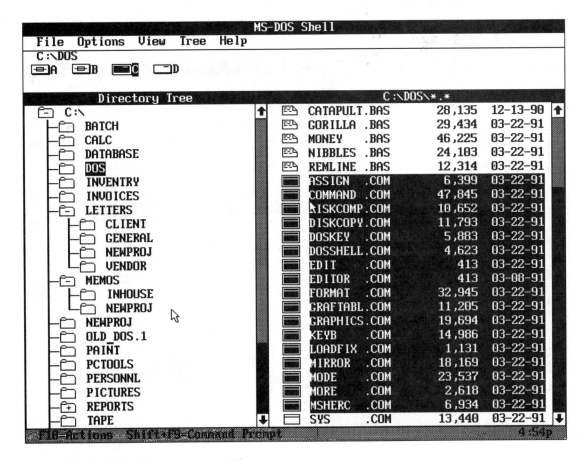

Figure 6.10   Selecting contiguous files

ters appearing after it in the position in the part of the name in which it appears. If it's the first character, it stands for any file name or any extension. The question mark stands for any character in a particular position. Let's examine how this works.

As you've already learned, the pattern

```
*.*
```

stands for all files in a directory. You don't need to type

```
dir *.*
```

```
                        MS-DOS Shell
 File   Options   View   Tree   Help
 C:\DOS
 ▭A    ▭B    ▬C    ▭D

    ══════Directory Tree══════              ══════C:\DOS\*.*══════
 ▭ C:\                            ↑    ▣ MYSHELL .INI      18,163   03-29-91 ↑
    ├─▭ BATCH                          ▣ NIBBLES .BAS      24,103   03-22-91
    ├─▭ CALC                           ▭ NLSFUNC .EXE       7,052   03-22-91
    ├─▭ DATABASE                       ▣ PACKING .LST       2,637   03-22-91
    ├─▭ DOS                            ▭ PRINT   .EXE      15,656   03-22-91
    ├─▭ INVENTRY                       ▣ PRINTER .SYS      18,804   03-22-91
    ├─▭ INVOICES                       ▭ QBASIC  .EXE     254,799   03-22-91
    ├─▭ LETTERS                        ▣ QBASIC  .HLP     130,810   03-22-91
    │  ├─▭ CLIENT                      ▣ README  .TXT      31,349   03-22-91
    │  ├─▭ GENERAL                     ▬ RECOVER .EXE       9,146   03-22-91
    │  ├─▭ NEWPROJ                     ▣ REMLINE .BAS      12,314   03-22-91
    │  └─▭ VENDOR                      ▭ REPLACE .EXE      20,226   03-22-91
    ├─▭ MEMOS                          ▬ RESTORE .EXE      38,294   03-22-91
    │  ├─▭ INHOUSE                     ▭ SETVER  .EXE      12,007   03-22-91
    │  └─▭ NEWPROJ        ▭            ▭ SHARE   .EXE      10,912   03-22-91
    ├─▭ NEWPROJ                        ▭ SORT    .EXE       6,938   03-22-91
    ├─▭ OLD_DOS.1                      ▭ SUBST   .EXE      18,478   03-22-91
    ├─▭ PAINT                          ▭ SYS     .COM      13,440   03-22-91
    ├─▭ PCTOOLS                        ▭ TREE    .COM       6,901   03-22-91
    ├─▭ PERSONNL                       ▣ UMB     .TXT      27,574   12-13-90
    ├─▭ PICTURES                       ▬ UNDELETE.EXE      13,924   03-22-91
    ├─▭ REPORTS                        ▬ UNFORMAT.COM      18,576   03-22-91
    └─▭ TAPE                      ↓    ▭ XCOPY   .EXE      15,804   03-22-91 ↓
 F10=Actions   Shift+F9=Command Prompt                          10:34a
```

Figure 6.11   Selecting noncontiguous files

because the DIR command acts on all files in a directory by default. Other commands, as you'll learn, require you to enter a file name as a parameter.

In the * . * pattern (often called "star-dot-star"), the first asterisk stands for any characters in the main part of the file name, the period is the separator between the main part and the extension, and the second asterisk represents any characters in the extension. Using question marks, the pattern

```
????????.???
```

is exactly equivalent to * .*. In fact, there are many commands in which, if you enter the pattern * .* and make a mistake on the command line, DOS will respond with an error message including the pattern ????????.???.

Let's look at question-mark characters more closely. Say you had a directory containing the following files:

```
FREDDIE.BAS
FRANCES.LTR
FRANCIS.TXT
FRANKLIN.BAT
CHANCES.BA
```

You could select only FRANCES.LTR and FRANCIS.TXT by using the pattern

```
FRANC?S.*
```

You could select all the files beginning with FR by using

```
FR*.???
```

or

```
FR*.*
```

You could select FRANCES.LTR and CHANCES.DB with the pattern

```
??ANCES.*
```

There's one tricky part. The question mark also substitutes for a nonexistent character at the position it occupies. Thus,

```
*.BA?
```

would include FREDDIE.BAS, FRANKLIN.BAT, and CHANCES.BA. There is no wild-card pattern that can select the first two files but not the third.

Entering a Wild-Card Pattern for the Directory Window. Now let's see some things you can do with wild-card characters. Let's begin by looking at the question-mark pattern.

MOUSE

Click on the title bar of the directory window, so the Shell knows you want to work there. Click on the Options menu, then on File Display Options. You'll see the dialog box in Figure 6.9. Type

```
????????.???
```

on the entry line and click on OK.

KEYBOARD

Press Alt-O F to display the Options menu and select the File Display Options command. You'll see the dialog box in Figure 6.9. Type

```
????????.???
```

on the entry line. Press Tab until the cursor appears in the OK button. Press Enter. As you'll see, although the wild-card pattern in the title bar of the directory window changes, the list of file names does not.

Next we'll enter a new wild-card pattern for the directory window. First make the DOS directory current. Repeat the procedure for bringing up the File Display Options dialog box and enter

```
*.com
```

When you complete the command by selecting OK, your screen should change to resemble Figure 6.12. Now only those files with the COM extension are listed.

As you remember, COM signifies a type of executable file, or program. This is one way to get a picture of the programs you can run from a given directory. (You'd have to repeat the procedure entering *.exe to see the rest.) If you use extensions consistently, you can list all files of a given

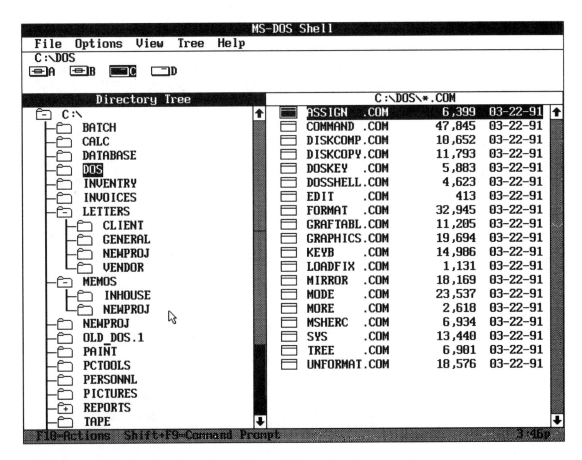

Figure 6.12   Narrowing your view with a wild-card pattern

type by using the asterisk wild-card character for the file name plus the file type extension.

You needn't restrict yourself in quite this way. Type

```
dos*.*
```

on the entry line. This should display all files in the directory whose names begin with the characters DOS. As you can see, these include the DOSSHELL files plus a few others. If you wanted to copy the Shell to another disk or directory, a wild-card pattern would certainly make it easier for you to find the relevant files!

Copying Files

Now that you know how to select directories and files, let's apply that knowledge to something useful.

Copying a file is the easiest way to make sure you have a backup if the original becomes damaged. It's also useful for grouping files on particular diskettes or in particular directories.

Copying a Single File. To copy a single file, select it using one of the methods just described, then select the Copy... command from the File menu. Select the root directory in the Directory Tree window and then select MYFILE (which you created) in the file window. Next select the Copy... command from the File menu (or just press F8). You'll see the dialog box in Figure 6.13. Put a diskette in drive A. Type

```
a:
```

in the entry line and select OK. You'll soon see the message shown in Figure 6.14.

Now repeat the procedure. You'll see the message in Figure 6.15, warning you that you're about to copy over, or *overwrite*, another file by the same name. The dialog box kindly shows you the dates and sizes of both files, so you can decide whether to proceed. At present there is no harm in

```
                    Copy File
  From :   MYFILE
  To :     C:\
            OK         Cancel        Help
```

Figure 6.13   The Copy File dialog box

doing so, but there are times when you'll be glad you were
warned.

There's an even easier way to copy files. If your target is
another directory on the same drive, first select the file to
copy. Then hold down the Ctrl key, click the left mouse
button on one of the selected files, and drag the mouse
pointer to the target directory in the Directory Tree window.
If the target directory isn't visible in the window, stop at
that window's scroll bar, still holding the key and the button.
Move the mouse pointer up or down the scroll bar until the
target directory appears. When it does, drag the pointer to it
and release the button. You'll be asked to confirm that you
want to copy the files.

You can also copy to another drive. Dragging to the drive
icon will copy the selected file to the current directory on
that drive. If you want to copy to a different directory, use
the Dual File List display and make the target directory of
the target drive current in the second window. Then you can
copy by dragging the file from the file window of one pair of
windows to the Directory Tree window of the other pair. You
don't need to hold down the Ctrl key.

☐ **MOUSE**

```
  Copying file:  MYFILE          1 of    1
```

Figure 6.14   The copy-file message

Figure 6.15   The Replace File Confirmation dialog box

Copying a File with a New Name.   You can copy a file to the same disk if you give it a different name; to a different disk using the same name; or to a different disk using a different name. You are not permitted to copy a file into its current directory with the same name as the original because DOS wouldn't know which copy you wanted when you asked for it. In fact if you try, you'll see the message

```
File cannot be copied onto itself
```

To make a second copy of the file in a given directory, the new name must differ from the old by at least one character, either in the file name or its extension. If you are making a backup copy of a file in the same directory, a common way of changing the name is to use the extension BAK.

To do this, you simply enter the new name on the entry line. Try this now. Select drive A. You should see MYFILE in the file window. Select it and press F8. When you see the Copy dialog box, type

```
myfile.bak
```

on the entry line and select OK. You'll soon see MYFILE.BAK below MYFILE in the file window.

You can rename a file while you copy it to a different destination. To try this, select MYFILE on drive A and select the Copy... command, or press F8. Type

```
c:yourfile
```

on the entry line and select OK. When you select drive C and the root directory, you'll see YOURFILE in the file window.

Copying a Group of Files.   You've already been given a hint as to how to copy a group of files. You select the files to be copied, then fill in the destination in the Copy dialog box. Get out the Emergency Recovery Disk you made in Chapter 5. Make the DOS directory on drive C current. Next select the Options menu and the File Display Options command. Change the sorting order to Name, which will make it easier to complete the following steps.

Select a group of files. Hold down the Ctrl key as you click on each with the mouse. Or press Shift-F8 to go into Add mode and press Shift-space bar as the highlight reaches each one. The files are:

CHKDSK.EXE
FDISK.EXE
FORMAT.COM
RECOVER.EXE
RESTORE.EXE
SYS.COM
UNDELETE.EXE
UNFORMAT.COM

 HINT
You can move to the list of files in the From *line in the dialog box either by clicking on it or pressing Shift-Tab. You can then edit or delete file names, if you wish. This works with the Move Files dialog box and the* Delete: *line in the Delete Files dialog box as well.*

Now choose the Copy... command, and again enter a: as the destination. When the process is complete, you'll have backups of all the files necessary for rebuilding your system on a single diskette. If you have a mouse, the dragging technique described earlier can be used here too.

Renaming Files

Now that you know how to copy files, both in the Shell and at the command prompt, you should have little trouble with renaming or deleting them. We'll deal with renaming files first.

To rename a file in the Shell, you follow essentially the same procedure as for renaming a directory. If the file is not in the current directory, use the Directory Tree window to make the directory containing it current. (If you're not sure where you left the file, use the Locate command in the File menu.) Make the file window current. Select the file to rename (MYFILE in the root directory of drive C). With either the mouse or the keyboard, select the Rename command from the File menu. You'll see the dialog box in Figure 6.16. Enter

```
myfile.old
```

on the entry line. The Shell will display a message box similar to the Copy-File message box, telling you that it's renaming the file.

Deleting Files

Deleting files is a bit more fraught than copying or renaming them. Fortunately, there are safeguards to help keep you from deleting the wrong file. The safeguards are different in

> **! WARNING**
>
> *You can't really rename several files at once in the Shell. You can select more than one, then select the* Rename *command. But you will be presented with each name in turn and asked for the new one. You can, however, rename groups of files at the DOS prompt by using wild-card patterns.*

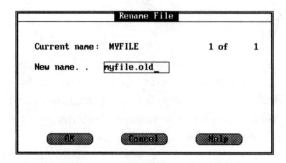

Figure 6.16   The Rename File dialog box

Figure 6.17   Deleting a group of files

the Shell and at the command prompt. You can also recover files you've deleted, but the procedure doesn't always work. (You'll learn it in Chapter 10.) Therefore be careful when deleting files and keep backups of all your work.

To delete one or more files in the Shell, simply select them and select the Delete... command from the File menu. You'll see a list of the selected files in a dialog box like the one in Figure 6.17. When you press Enter or select OK, you'll be presented with each file name in turn and asked to confirm your intention as shown in Figure 6.18. Therefore if you accidentally selected some files, you can skip those by choosing No and still delete the rest.

Moving Files

In the Shell you can move files from one directory to another. There's no equivalent command at the prompt, except to copy the files to the target directory and then delete them from the source directory. (In short, that's the essence of moving a file—copying it and then deleting it.) Let's move YOURFILE (by now the sole remaining copy of MYFILE on your hard

Figure 6.18   Confirming your intention to delete

disk) to the C:\TEMP directory. Make the root directory current by selecting it. Select YOURFILE in the file window. Now press F7 or select Move from the File menu. You'll see the dialog box in Figure 6.19. On the entry line, type the name of the directory to which you want to move the file:

```
\temp
```

Click OK or press Enter. The Shell will move the file for you, displaying the typical message telling you what it's doing.

The Shell's Move command is very powerful. Not only can it move a file from one directory to another, it can move files to other drives simultaneously and rename them. To move a file to a different drive, begin the entry line with the drive name. (The rules of currency apply. That is, to move the file to the current directory of the target drive, just type the drive name.) To change the file's name, add the new name after the path name.

You can move files to another directory on the same drive (but not to another drive) by dragging with the mouse. Just select the files, hold down the left mouse button, and drag the pointer to the target directory in the Directory Tree window. As with copying, you can use the scroll bar to bring the target directory into view.

✔ **NEW FEATURE**
Moving files across drives

☐ **MOUSE**

❗ **WARNING**
If you specify a nonexistent directory as the place to which the directory should be moved, the Shell will simply rename the file with the name you gave as the target directory, rather than moving it.

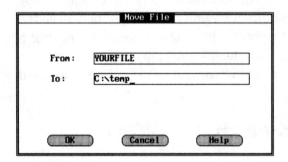

Figure 6.19   Moving a file

Managing Files and Directories at the Command Prompt

Chapter 7

What You Will Learn

- How to use path names
- How to create and delete directories
- How to create, rename, and delete files
- How to copy files
- How to tailor the directory display using switches

If you're not using the Shell, you may have skipped Chapter 6. If so, go back and read the sections "Naming a Directory," "Naming Files," and "How Wild-Card Characters Work." You'll need to be familiar with this information before you proceed. If you're using the Shell, press Shift-F9 to get to a command prompt.

Specifying a File's Location

So far, everything you've done has been simplified by the fact that in the Shell you could make current the directory from which you were copying and that the target was the root directory of another disk. What happens if you want to copy to some other destination? One way is to select the target disk and make the target directory current. But what if you want to copy from one directory to another on the same drive? Now you've got a problem. Fortunately DOS provides a solution: *path names.*

A path name is simply a description of a file's location in terms of drive and directories. A complete path name consists of

- The drive name
- A backslash, to signify the root directory
- The names of all the directories between the root and the directory containing the file, separated by backslashes
- The name of the file, if it's appropriate to the command

To take an example, look at Figure 7.1. The file called FRANKLIN.LTR is in the directory GENERAL, which is a subdirectory of LETTERS, which is itself a subdirectory of the root. The full path name of this file would therefore be

```
C:\LETTERS\GENERAL\FRANKLIN.LTR
```

Relative Path Names

When using path names, the general rule is that you must specify any part that's not current. You can give DOS directions either from the root directory of the drive, as in the above example (the *absolute* path name), or from the current location. Thus if drive C is current, you could refer to this file by the path name

```
\LETTERS\GENERAL\FRANKLIN.LTR
```

If the LETTERS directory is current, you can simply use

```
GENERAL\FRANKLIN.LTR
```

This is the *relative* path name.

HINT

Notice that you don't put a backslash before GENERAL. A backslash at the beginning of a path name always refers to the root directory. In fact you could think of \ as the root directory's name.

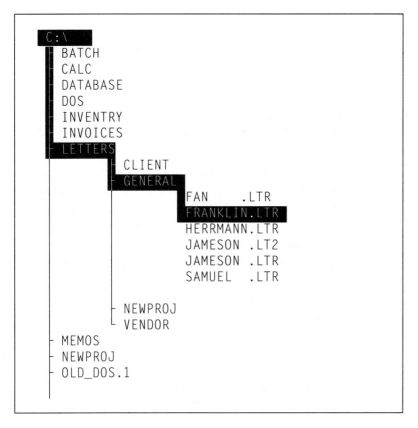

Figure 7.1   The path from the root directory to a file

If the LETTERS directory is current on drive C but the current *drive* is drive A, you could refer to the file as

```
C:LETTERS\FRANKLIN.LTR
```

Relative Directories

When you view a directory other than a root directory at a command prompt, you will see the following two names at the beginning of your file list:

```
    .                <DIR>      01-23-91    3:04p
    ..               <DIR>      01-23-91    3:04p
```

The single period refers to the current directory, and the double period refers to the directory directly above it (often called the *parent* directory).

You can use these directory names as parts of path names. Most commands allow you to use the single period to refer to the current directory. This will become useful shortly.

It's a bit easier to envision the uses for the double period. For example, suppose you had a directory tree like the one in Figure 7.1. If you wanted to copy FRANK-LIN.LTR to the \LETTERS\CLIENT directory, you could select \LETTERS\GENERAL in the Directory Tree window, select the file in the file window, and enter

```
    ..\client
```

on the Copy entry line. This means, "Go up to the directory above this one (in this case LETTERS), and go down from there to CLIENT."

❊ NOTE

Path names reflect the underlying structure of the directories on disk. Although the Shell represents your directories as a tree diagram, in fact the tree is only implicit on disk. When a directory is a subdirectory of another directory, its name appears as an entry in the directory it's subordinate to. You don't actually see the current directory's place in the structure. However, the command prompt shows you its name, along with the complete path from the root, so you'll always know your absolute location.

Working with Directories

Now that you understand path names and currency, you can use the DOS commands for dealing with directories. All the directory commands come in two forms, a short form that's easy to type, and a longer form that's somewhat more mnemonic. After both are introduced, we'll use the short forms.

Making a Directory Current

The two forms of the command to make a directory current are CHDIR and CD, both of which stand for "change directory." Enter the command followed by the directory path name. You may use either an absolute or relative path name. Thus when you're at the root directory of drive C, to make the DOS directory current, just enter

```
cd dos
```

because DOS is a subdirectory of the root. Do this now. You'll see the prompt change to

```
C:\DOS>
```

to let you know where you are.

Next suppose you want to make the TEMP directory current. Type

```
cd temp
```

You see the message

```
Invalid directory
```

and the prompt remains

```
C:\DOS>
```

But you know you created the TEMP directory! What's going on here? Remember the rules of currency. Because you didn't specify a path name, DOS looks for the directory you named only in the current directory. TEMP is not a subdirectory of DOS. To get there from where you are, you must enter

```
cd \temp
```

 HINT

The double-period abbreviation for the directory above the current one is quite useful in all the directory commands. You could change from DOS to TEMP by typing cd ..\temp *because DOS and TEMP are parallel directories—both subordinate to the root. However, this abbreviation is most useful for changing from one directory to another when both are subordinate to another subdirectory. You'll use the double period to move up one level even more often. To move from TEMP to the root, for example, you could just type* cd ...

Creating Directories

Sensible management of your hard disk requires a well-organized set of directories, with different ones for various software packages, for different types of files, and for other specialized purposes. You should already have at least two directories: DOS and TEMP. In this section you'll create a few more that you'll use in Chapter 8, when you organize your directory tree.

The two forms of the command to create a directory are MKDIR and MD, both of which stand for "make directory." Simply type the command followed by the name of the new directory. But there's more to it than that. (You knew that, didn't you?) The important points to consider are which directory you want as the parent for your new directory and which directory is current when you're creating it. The path name you specify in the command must reflect these considerations. Thus if you're at the root directory and you want to create a subdirectory of it (say, C:\BATCH), just enter

```
md batch
```

If another directory is current, you would have to specify the
path:

```
md \batch
```

You'll be using the BATCH directory later, when you begin
to customize your system.

To create a directory on another drive, specify the drive
as well as the path. Make sure you have a diskette in drive
A and the door is closed. Enter

```
a:
```

Now enter

```
md c:\util
```

Now enter

```
dir c:\
```

to see what you've done. Among the items in the directory
display should be the directories TEMP, BATCH, and UTIL.

If your current directory is not the root, you can make a
subdirectory of the current directory by entering MD followed by the simple directory name. For example, to make a
subdirectory of TEMP when TEMP is the current directory,
you could just enter

```
md temp2
```

If you wanted to make this directory when, say, C:\DOS is
the current directory, you'd have to enter

```
md \temp\temp2
```

See if you can create this directory from your current
location.

 HINT

*To be on the safe side,
make a habit of always
specifying the complete
path name when you
use MD, until you're con-
fident about the shape of
your tree.*

Deleting Directories

The two forms of the command to delete a directory are RMDIR and RD, both of which stand for "remove directory." The steps for deleting a directory are the same as those for creating one. Enter the command, followed by enough information about the path for DOS to find the directory to delete.

As noted earlier, a directory must be empty before you can delete it. To find out what happens if it isn't, enter

```
rd c:\temp
```

You'll see the message

```
Invalid path, not directory,
or directory not empty
```

Obviously this means that one of three conditions is present:

- You entered the name of a path that doesn't exist (if you typed a single character incorrectly in a path that's otherwise valid, you've specified a path that doesn't exist; a computer can do only what you tell it to do, not what you meant to tell it to do).
- The path name you entered leads to a file, not a directory. You'd get the above message, for example, if you entered

```
rd \temp\yourfile
```

- There are files in the directory (true in this case) or there are subdirectories subordinate to it (also true).

You will also see this message if you attempt to delete the current directory. To delete a directory, you must first make some other directory current. Make the TEMP2 directory current. Now enter

```
rd c:\temp\temp2
```

You'll see the invalid path message. Enter

```
rd temp2
```

You'll see the message again. Now enter

```
cd ..
```

to make the TEMP directory current. Enter

```
rd temp2
```

again. You won't see any message. That means that the directory has been deleted.

Viewing Directories in Sorted Order

DOS 5 permits you to view your directories in sorted order at the command prompt. To do so, you use the /O *(order)* switch, followed by a letter denoting the proper order. N sorts by name, E by extension, S by size, and D by date. To see how this works, look at Figures 7.2 and 7.3. Figure 7.2 shows a directory with the file names in random order, as they appear on disk. Figure 7.3 shows the same directory displayed with the /ON switch. As you can see, the files now appear to be sorted by name, even though you have done nothing to change what's on the disk.

✔ **NEW FEATURE**
Sorting the directory display

To reverse the effect of these switches, place a minus sign before the letter signifiying the sorting criterion. You can also use more than one criterion, to create a secondary sort. For example, to sort the directory by date in reverse order and sort the files for each date by name, enter

```
dir /o-dn
```

You can also use switches to display either the list of files in a directory without any subdirectories (as they appear in the Shell's file window) or the list of directories without any files. To restrict your view in this manner, use

✔ **NEW FEATURE**

```
D:\DICT>dir
 Volume in drive D is SOFTWARE
 Volume Serial Number is 012C-1020
 Directory of D:\DICT

DICTUTIL EXE      21405 10-20-89  12:00p
.                <DIR>       01-23-91   1:50p
..               <DIR>       01-23-91   1:50p
WSSPL001 OVR      24707 07-03-90   6:00p
G4CVTWP  EXE      23173 10-20-89  12:00p
G4       DIC     158745 11-17-89   2:00p
USER     DIC       1585 04-12-91   5:21p
MASTER   DIC     136743 10-20-89  12:00p
COMPUTER DCT       4418 04-11-91  11:26a
INTERNAL DCT      25600 12-30-86   1:04p
THESR001 DCT     100674 07-03-90   6:00p
SPLMN001 DCT     140672 07-03-90   6:00p
WSTHS001 OVR      17190 07-03-90   6:00p
DEFIN001 DCT     250219 01-18-90   6:00p
README   G4        1013 11-15-89   2:07p
G4       EXE     201039 10-20-89  12:00p
G4       HLP     118871 10-20-89  12:00p
G4       WPS      13376 10-20-89  12:00p
G4       PRF        947 11-07-90   1:34p
G4       G4B     158745 10-20-89  12:00p
G4PROF   EXE      65207 10-20-89  12:00p
G4RHED   EXE      91517 10-20-89  12:00p
G4RUNWP  EXE      13245 10-20-89  12:00p
        23 file(s)     1569091 bytes
                       2091008 bytes free

D:\DICT>_
```

Figure 7.2   An unsorted directory

the switches /A-D and /AD, respectively. (These make use of the *attribute byte,* which you'll learn about in Chapter 9.) Figures 7.4 and 7.5 show their effects. As you can see, both figures are displays of the same disk directory—the root directory of drive D.

```
D:\DICT>dir /on

 Volume in drive D is SOFTWARE
 Volume Serial Number is 012C-1020
 Directory of D:\DICT

 .               <DIR>        01-23-91    1:50p
 ..              <DIR>        01-23-91    1:50p
 COMPUTER DCT       4418      04-11-91   11:26a
 DEFIN001 DCT     250219      01-18-90    6:00p
 DICTUTIL EXE      21405      10-20-89   12:00p
 G4       DIC     158745      11-17-89    2:00p
 G4       EXE     201039      10-20-89   12:00p
 G4       HLP     118871      10-20-89   12:00p
 G4       WPS      13376      10-20-89   12:00p
 G4       PRF        947      11-07-90    1:34p
 G4       G4B     158745      10-20-89   12:00p
 G4CVTWP  EXE      23173      10-20-89   12:00p
 G4PROF   EXE      65207      10-20-89   12:00p
 G4RHED   EXE      91517      10-20-89   12:00p
 G4RUNWP  EXE      13245      10-20-89   12:00p
 INTERNAL DCT      25600      12-30-86    1:04p
 MASTER   DIC     136743      10-20-89   12:00p
 README   G4        1013      11-15-89    2:07p
 SPLMN001 DCT     140672      07-03-90    6:00p
 THESR001 DCT     100674      07-03-90    6:00p
 USER     DIC       1585      04-12-91    5:21p
 WSSPL001 OVR      24707      07-03-90    6:00p
 WSTHS001 OVR      17190      07-03-90    6:00p
        23 file(s)      1569091 bytes
                        2091008 bytes free

D:\DICT>_
```

Figure 7.3   A directory with files sorted by name

Copying Files

Now that you understand path names, you are ready to try
out the file commands at the command prompt. There are a
few complications to copying files (or indeed, to any com-

```
D:\>dir /a-d
 Volume in drive D is SOFTWARE
 Volume Serial Number is 012C-1020
 Directory of D:\

CHANGES   CRC      1839 08-23-90    5:29p
FNTTBL    WRK        22 10-12-90    9:53a
HELP      CRC      8578 08-23-90    5:29p
MIRORSAV  FIL        41 04-15-91    3:19p
MIRROR    FIL     50688 04-15-91    3:19p
MIRROR    BAK     50688 04-15-91   11:55a
PCTRACKR  DEL     36768 04-15-91    3:41p
TREEINFO  NCD       555 04-12-91   12:35p
PBRUSH    OV1     14468 06-15-89    3:04p
FIG                 909 04-15-91    3:57p
        10 file(s)      164556 bytes
                       2088960 bytes free

D:\>_
```

Figure 7.4   A directory listing with the subdirectories removed

mand you can execute from the File menu). First, you can't select groups of files except by using wild-card patterns. Thus it doesn't matter in what order they appear in the directory. And you can't copy files in one operation that don't match a wild-card pattern. You either have to repeat the procedure for each file or repeat it with a series of wild-card patterns. This is one reason why you'll probably want to use the Shell to do any serious file reorganization.

Second, as you might have guessed, you *must* specify both the source and the target of a copy, except in a few circumstances. Third, there's no warning when you might be copying over another file of the same name.

To copy one or more files at the DOS prompt, use the COPY command. Its basic form is

COPY *source target*

```
D:\>dir /ad
 Volume in drive D is SOFTWARE
 Volume Serial Number is 012C-1020
 Directory of D:\

BASIC        <DIR>      01-23-91    1:00p
COLLAGE      <DIR>      01-23-91    1:00p
DICT         <DIR>      01-23-91    1:00p
EFAX         <DIR>      01-23-91    1:00p
FW           <DIR>      01-23-91    1:00p
GV           <DIR>      01-23-91    1:00p
HIJAAK       <DIR>      01-23-91    1:00p
HSG          <DIR>      01-23-91    1:00p
IMCAP        <DIR>      01-23-91    1:00p
INSET        <DIR>      01-23-91    1:00p
PARADOX      <DIR>      01-23-91    1:00p
PBRUSH       <DIR>      01-23-91    1:00p
PCINDEX      <DIR>      01-23-91    1:00p
QPRO         <DIR>      01-23-91    1:00p
TELECOM      <DIR>      01-23-91    1:00p
WS           <DIR>      01-23-91    1:00p
WS4          <DIR>      01-23-91    1:00p
QUOTES       <DIR>      04-12-91   12:21p
          18 file(s)             0 bytes
                 2088960 bytes free

D:\>_
```

Figure 7.5   A directory of subdirectories

The rule for specifying the source and the target is, essentially, that you must give DOS enough information to locate what it is you want to copy (using drive and path names, if necessary), and you must make it equally clear where you want the files copied to. The command prompt gives you more flexibility than the Shell in that neither the source nor the destination must be current. But there's an advanced Shell command that gets around this limitation, which you'll learn about in Chapter 9.

To see how this works, make your DOS directory current. Let's copy YOURFILE to drive A once more. You must specify its location in the command:

```
copy c:\temp\yourfile a:
```

DOS indicates a successful copy with the message

```
1 file(s) copied
```

Conversely, if drive A were current, you wouldn't have to specify the target at all:

```
copy c:\temp\yourfile
```

DOS always assumes that the target is the current drive and directory unless you tell it otherwise. (That's why the current drive and directory appear on the entry line in the Shell.)

To simultaneously rename the copy, use a command of the form

**copy [*sourcepath*\]*oldname.ext* [*targetpath*\]
    *newname.ext***

where *sourcepath* and *targetpath* are needed only when one (or both) is not current, and *oldname.ext* and *newname.ext* represent the old and new file names.

To copy groups of files, specify them with a wild-card pattern. For practice, copy the Shell files to the C:\SHELL directory while the root directory is current. Enter the command

```
copy c:\dos\dosshell.* c:\shell
```

DOS displays the name of each file as it's copied and tells you how many files were copied altogether, as Figure 7.6 shows.

If you were to attempt to copy these files to a 360K diskette, you would run out of room, because their combined size is over 450K. You would see all the file names, but at the end you'd see the message

```
Insufficient disk space
 5 File(s) copied
```

! WARNING

If you copy a group of files to a disk with insufficient room, and a copy of the last file was already on the disk, the disk will contain neither version of the file when the process is complete.

When you see this message, the last file name on the screen has *not* been copied to the target. If the same thing happens in the Shell, you'll see a similar message in a dialog box.

Renaming Files

To rename files, you use either of two commands: REN or RENAME. As with the COPY command, you must specify both the old and the new name. Also as with COPY, you must specify the path to the file to be renamed if it's not in the current directory. The basic form of the command is

REN[AME] [*path*\\]*oldname.ext newname.ext*

If you want to rename a single file, just enter the complete

```
C:\>copy c:\dos\dosshell.* c:\shell

C:\DOS\DOSSHELL.INI
C:\DOS\DOSSHELL.VID
C:\DOS\DOSSHELL.COM
C:\DOS\DOSSHELL.EXE
C:\DOS\DOSSHELL.GRB
C:\DOS\DOSSHELL.HLP
        6 file(s) copied
C:>_
```

Figure 7.6 Copying files with a wild-card pattern

file name as the old name. If part of the name will remain unchanged, you can use a wild-card character for that part. For example, if you wanted to rename FRANKLIN.LTR to FRANCES.LTR, you could type

```
ren franklin.ltr frances.*
```

Let's take advantage of the ability to rename multiple files. First make the root directory current. Now enter

```
ren \myfile.* 1stfile.*
```

The backslash tells DOS to look for the file in the root directory. The asterisk tells it to rename all files with the basic name you entered, no matter what extension they have. (You don't need to include the drive name because the drive is current.) Now enter

```
dir \
```

You'll see the root directory, with files 1STFILE.OLD and 1STFILE.BAK appearing where the files MYFILE.OLD and MYFILE.BAK used to be.

✳ NOTE
Be careful to enter the file name correctly. If you use a space instead of a period, DOS will tell you Too many parameters *and refuse to proceed. If you use a space instead of a period in the old name, DOS will tell you* File not found *unless of course there's another file with the same basic name but no extension. Then it will display the* Too many parameters *message.*

Deleting Files

As with renaming files, you can use either of two commands to delete files at the command prompt: DEL or ERASE. The basic form of the command is

DEL [*path*]*filename.ext*

or

ERASE [*path*]*filename.ext*

If no switch is used, you get no warning whatsoever of the command's consequences unless you are deleting all the files in a directory. You can erase multiple files by using a wild-card pattern; when you press Enter all matching files will quietly disappear. It's therefore a good idea to preview the directory from which you're planning to delete files.

If you mistype the command so that DOS can't find any matching file, it displays the message

```
File not found
```

You can protect yourself from accidentally deleting files by adding the /P *(permission)* switch to the command. DOS presents you with the complete path name of each matching file and prompts you with

✔ **NEW FEATURE**
Selectively deleting files

```
Delete (Y/N)?
```

If you don't want to delete the file, just press N. Figure 7.7 shows the effect of using the /P switch.

To completely erase a directory, use a command of the form

```
del *.*
```

or

```
del .
```

```
C:\TEMP>del *.* /p

C:\TEMP\SWAPDT.SW3,      Delete (Y/N)?n
C:\TEMP\VME22199.TMP,      Delete (Y/N)?y
C:\TEMP\TEST.BAT,      Delete (Y/N)?n
C:\TEMP\ARCHIVE.ZIP,      Delete (Y/N)?n
C:\TEMP\VME44707.TMP,      Delete (Y/N)?y
C:\TEMP\7D8CDOSC.BAT,      Delete (Y/N)?n
C:\TEMP\TESTFILE.TMP,      Delete (Y/N)?y
C:\TEMP\6630DOSC.BAT,      Delete (Y/N)?y
C:\TEMP\FIG0701.TXT,      Delete (Y/N)?n
C:\TEMP\FIG0701.BAK,      Delete (Y/N)?y
C:\TEMP\TEMP.BAK,      Delete (Y/N)?y
C:\TEMP\TEST.BAK,      Delete (Y/N)?y
C:\TEMP\7D8CDOSC.BAK,      Delete (Y/N)?y
C:\TEMP\6630DOSC.BAK,      Delete (Y/N)?y

C:\TEMP>_
```

Figure 7.7   Deleting files selectively with the /P switch

Note that you can use the single period that stands for the current directory. If the directory isn't current, just give DOS its name. For example:

```
del c:\shell
```

This command deletes all the files in C:\SHELL but not the directory itself.

When you enter a command that will delete all the files in a directory, DOS warns you with

```
All files in directory will be deleted!
Are you sure (Y/N)?
```

If you press N and Enter, the command is canceled.

In this chapter you've learned to perform the most common and fundamental DOS operations at the prompt. You've also learned the very important principles of currency and path names. You can now feel confident that you've come a long way toward mastering your operating system.

Organizing Your Directory Tree

Chapter 8

What You Will Learn

- Factors to consider when setting up your directories
- How to use a drive name to represent a directory
- How to delete earlier versions of DOS
- How to go back to earlier versions of DOS

 NOTE

Skip this chapter if you don't have a hard disk.

As you've already learned, the purpose of your directory structure is to help you keep track of your files. When you first start out with computers, you may think you won't ever accumulate enough files to need to worry about where you put them. Trust me—it ain't so. If you just chuck everything into the root directory, you'll certainly know where everything is. But you still won't be able to find anything. Even if you use the Shell, the files will be so numerous that you'll have a hard time locating a specific one. And besides, as you've already learned, the root directory can't hold more than 512 files, a limitation not imposed on subdirectories.

A Question of Strategy

There are other reasons for ramifying your directory structure. First, many software packages consist of large numbers of files. If you allow several to share a single directory, you'll have a dreadful time if you delete or upgrade one of them. How would you know, for example, which program uses the printer file EPSLQ.PRD and which uses EPS25.PDV? And what happens if both include a program called INSTALL.EXE, which you must run before you use the software package?

Indeed, to some degree your software limits control over your tree. Some software packages create subdirectories subordinate to their main directory and expect to find specific files in them. That needn't be a problem except esthetically, because the software will manage these directories itself.

You'll also want some systematic organization that helps you find data files. What that should be depends on several factors:

- How much you use the Shell
- What software packages you use
- Your work habits
- Whether you share your computer with anyone else
- Whether you have more than one hard disk
- If you have a large hard disk, whether you want to treat it as though it were several smaller disks or one large one (see Appendix A to combine hard disks into a single drive)

Beyond that, the tree structure is only one consideration in setting up your system. You'll learn ways to tweak your system to support your directory organization in Chapter 14.

Plan Ahead

Remember that the more advance planning you do, the less frustration you'll encounter later. Careful planning helps you create a tree that makes sense to you and directory names that you can remember, all of which helps you understand your system. Of course, if you want to reorganize a hard disk that's already set up, the process is a bit more difficult. It is not impossible, however. First, you must make a complete backup (see Chapter 10). Then create the directories. And finally, restore the files from your backup and, if necessary, move them to different locations. (Many commercially available utility programs can simplify this process.)

Obviously if you have more than one hard disk, you should plan all disk structures at the same time. Let's now examine these issues in greater depth.

How Will You Run Your Programs?

The way you get to your software affects the way you set up your tree. If you use the Shell as your system gateway, you can set it up to include program groups for each major application. When you do this, you give DOS complete instructions on how to find your software. At the same time, you remind yourself what help you must give DOS to complete the task.

If you don't plan to use the Shell, other factors come into play. When you type a command at the prompt, as you know, DOS tries to run an internal command, a DOS external command, or a program in the current directory of the current drive. What you probably don't know is that Setup arranged your system so that DOS can find the external programs, which are in the DOS directory. It does this by executing a command called PATH. In Chapter 12 you'll learn how to use this command to help DOS find software on other directories as well. But there are limits to how many directories you can access this way. The shorter your directory names, the more you can access automatically—but it's harder to remember what's in them.

How Many Hard Disks?

As noted, with DOS 5 you may be able to combine several "logical" hard drives into one. That is, if you actually have only one hard disk but several hard drive names, you can reorganize your disk so that it has only one drive name. This can be an advantage or a disadvantage. With a single hard drive, you may want to have fewer branches from the root, with many more at one level below that. This is no problem if you use the Shell's Directory Tree window. The plus signs in the folders will remind you which directories have subdirectories.

But if you work at the prompt, executing DIR on the root directory will show only the first level of subdirectories. You may forget what subdirectories they contain. However, some switches to DIR, and some other DOS commands, can remind you.

✔ **NEW FEATURE**
Large disks with standard-size clusters

It's easier to work with large hard drives in DOS 5 than in DOS 4. Large drives created using DOS 4 tended to have extra-large clusters, which tended to waste disk space. In contrast, large drives created using DOS 5 have the standard 2K clusters. Therefore, if you created a large drive using DOS 4, you may want to restructure it using DOS 5. See Appendix A for details.

Who Uses Your Computer?

If you share your computer with other people who do separate work, it's best to give each person a single subdirectory at the root directory. Let them create their own directories beneath their individual directories. If your hard disk is large enough and the number of users is small enough, you could give each person a single logical hard drive.

Of course you still have to work out some agreement as to how you'll access the software. Given the fact that DOS can be taught to find only some directories automatically, you'll have to agree on which ones. (However, DOS is flexible enough to allow you some other options, as you'll learn in Chapter 13.)

Some General Principles

The first rule to follow is Occam's razor, one of the basic principles of science: *Entities should not be multiplied needlessly.* In other words, don't create more directories than you need. The second rule is to *keep your root directory simple.* The third is, to the degree that your software permits, *keep your data files out of your software directories.* Let's expand on these principles.

How Much Nesting?

Many experts suggest that you place subdirectories beneath the software directories, one for each person who uses the computer, and beneath that, one for each type of file. An example of this type of organization appears in Figure 8.1. You may not need this much complexity. Indeed, hardly anybody does. Besides, you'll have a hard time using some software if you have to go through long path names to get to your files.

In addition, DOS limits a complete path name, including the drive name and file name, to 63 characters. If you must open a file with a long path name once you're inside a software package, you may be out of luck. You'll also have a terrible time remembering the names of intervening directories, and if you mistype a character, you're back to square one. Granted, software is becoming smarter, and it may enable you to work your way back up and down through the tree—but it's easier if you don't have to.

For these reasons, try to minimize the levels of subdirectories. The less ramification your tree has, the easier it is to swing through its branches. Many people can get along just fine with only one or two levels (except of course for those created by the software).

How Do You Work?

The way you work and the type of work you do will affect the directories you create for your data files. If you create most of them using one software package, you won't want to place them all in a single directory, any more than you'd cram all your business records into a single file drawer. However, if you occasionally use other packages and have just a few files for each, you may be able to maintain a single data directory for these files.

Suppose you characteristically work on one project at a time but refer to work from previous projects. The obvious organizational principle is to separate current files from noncurrent ones. But if you work on many projects, you may

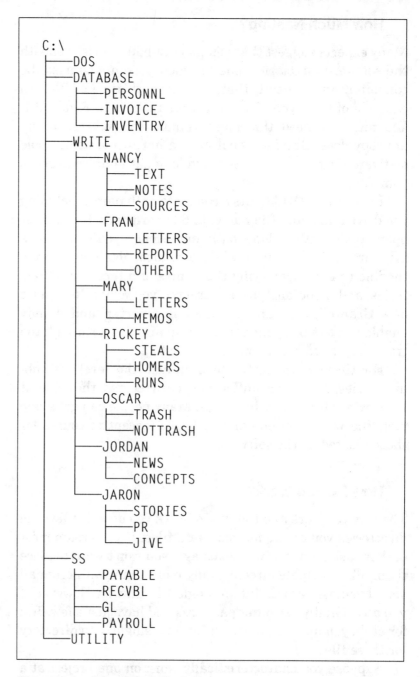

Figure 8.1   A heavily nested directory tree

prefer to keep all files for a given project in a single directory, rather than separate them according to the software you used to create them. Or you may prefer to combine these two principles.

In any case you should have one miscellaneous directory for odds and ends that don't exactly fit into any of your other categories.

You can follow any basic organizing scheme with only two levels of nesting. But the number of files in a directory is also a factor. When a directory gets so full you can't find files, work out some basis for separating them and create another directory. You can use the Shell's File Move command to move some of the files into your new directory.

 HINT

When in doubt, remember the KISS principle, learned by every novice programmer: "Keep it simple, stupid!"

Pruning the Roots

The root directory of your hard disk—the core of your organization—should function primarily as a jumping-off point for your actual work. Think of it as a "you-are-here" spot on the map, to which you can return easily to get your bearings. Your root directory *should* contain:

- COMMAND.COM
- Your AUTOEXEC.BAT file
- Your CONFIG.SYS file
- Any programs used by CONFIG.SYS but by no other programs (you won't know what these are for a few chapters yet)
- All your principal subdirectories

Your root directory is thus your startup directory. It contains everything necessary to get your system up and running, and virtually nothing else except subdirectories. (Your CONFIG.SYS and AUTOEXEC.BAT files *must* be in the root directory, or they won't be executed.)

You don't *have* to place the files used by CONFIG.SYS in the root directory. (Many people place them in a subdirectory of DOS called BIN, for "binary files." But all program files are binary files, so it's not too clear why you should do this.) You just have to tell CONFIG.SYS where to find the necessary files by using a path name. But it's easier to modify your configuration if all your startup files are in the root directory. You'll learn about these startup files in Chapter 12.

Separating Software and Data

A few software packages fit nicely onto a single 360K diskette and involve only a few files. However, over the last several years, software has tended toward suburban sprawl. Programs that once came on a single disk, or at most on 2, now include a suite of 11 diskettes and take megabytes of hard disk space.

It's no problem to keep in the software's directory the two or three data files used exclusively by, say, a calendar program. But with a larger program, you can easily lose your data files among the dozens of files that make up your software. Some programs put data into the software directory regardless. You don't have to stand for this. DOS gives you the tools to put your data files almost anywhere you want and still enables your software to find them.

You don't know enough DOS yet to use these tools—the PATH command, the APPEND command, and batch files. These are among the subjects of Chapters 12 and 13. For now, just rest assured that you *can* separate data from software and that your life will be easier if you do.

Essential Subdirectories

It is almost essential that your hard disk include the following four subdirectories:

- DOS
- BATCH
- UTIL
- TEMP

These are your keys to a well-designed, smoothly functioning hard disk system. The DOS directory contains your DOS files. The BATCH directory is where you place files that help run your system (as will be described in Chapter 13). Use the UTIL directory for *utility software*—programs to help keep your system running smoothly. The TEMP directory is a separate directory for temporary files. As you'll learn later, many programs use such a directory if they can find it. This keeps your other directories from becoming cluttered with files you didn't create and don't know what to do with. You should also have some kind of directory for miscellaneous stuff—call it MISC or UNFILED or something equally suitable.

Some Sample Directory Organizations

In this section you'll look at a few styles for directory trees and learn their advantages and disadvantages. Each will illustrate some principles and approaches just discussed.

Viewing Your Tree at a Command Prompt

The diagrams in the following pages were generated by the TREE command. This command displays a diagram of the subdirectories of the current directory or of whatever drive and directory you enter as a parameter. To see a diagram of your hard disk's directory at the command prompt, enter

```
tree c:\
```

To print it on paper, enter

```
tree c:\ >prn
```

(You'll learn what this command means in Chapter 15.)

A Heavily Nested Tree

Let's begin by examining the tree in Figure 8.1. You'll see that there are only five directories one step below the root. Each is a software directory: DATABASE is for a file management program, SS is for a spreadsheet, and WRITE is for a word-processing program. Nested beneath each software directory is a series of data directories. Thus each software directory contains the files for a single software package plus a group of subdirectories.

If you examine the WRITE directory, you'll see that beneath it are main directories, identified by name, for the people who use the word processor. These people have created their own subdirectories. It's not clear whether the main directories have anything in them. But it doesn't matter. Some prefer to keep their main directories empty, whereas others store data files in them.

This tree has certain drawbacks. It's easy to navigate in the Shell's Directory Tree window but hard to do so at the command prompt. Also, it's hard to remember which files are nested under which set of directories. And to view a file on-screen, you may have to type something ungainly, such as

```
type c:\write\oscar\nottrash\inventry.txt
```

Reducing the Nesting

This system can be simplified considerably by moving the principal data directories up one level, to become sub-directories of the root (see Figure 8.2). The subdirectories below them still exist.

This arrangement has one other advantage. Now that every worker has a personal directory off the root, it can be used to store any type of file, not just word-processing files.

A Sensible System for a Single User

Figure 8.3 shows the tree diagram you have seen in the Shell in previous chapters. As you can see, it has the DOS, BATCH, UTIL, and TEMP directories. OLD_DOS.1 is the directory created by Setup. DATABASE, WP, CALC, PAINT, and TELECOM are application software directories. PCTOOLS and TAPE are directories for a large package of utility software and a program to back up the hard disk to tape, respectively.

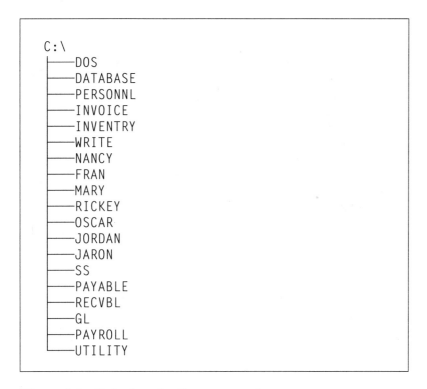

```
C:\
    ├──DOS
    ├──DATABASE
    ├──PERSONNL
    ├──INVOICE
    ├──INVENTRY
    ├──WRITE
    ├──NANCY
    ├──FRAN
    ├──MARY
    ├──RICKEY
    ├──OSCAR
    ├──JORDAN
    ├──JARON
    ├──SS
    ├──PAYABLE
    ├──RECVBL
    ├──GL
    ├──PAYROLL
    └──UTILITY
```

Figure 8.2   Reducing the directory nesting

The remaining directories all contain data files. PIC-TURES contains files created by PAINT. Most others are self-explanatory. As you can see, this directory reflects the fact that the worker separates projects (represented by NEWPROJ) from ongoing, everyday business.

There are several different ways you might organize this directory tree. It might make sense to have separate REPORTS, MEMOS, and LETTERS directories subordinate to NEWPROJ, for example, rather than the other way around. (Presumably there are enough files to warrant separate directories.) At some point, organization becomes a matter of preference.

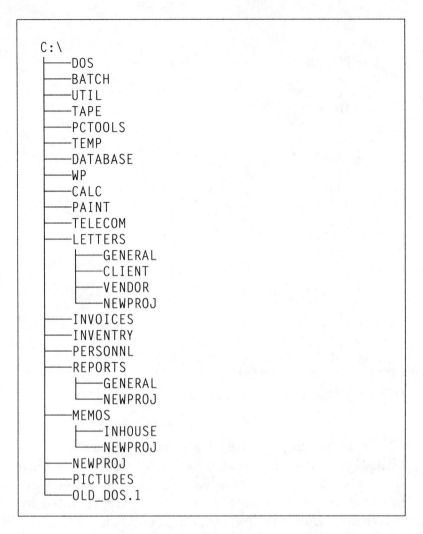

Figure 8.3   Yet another sample directory tree

Separating Software and Data on Two Drives

Figure 8.4 shows a system with two hard disk drives. Drive C contains the software directories, and drive D the data directories. This arrangement has two advantages. First, you have a head start when you look for a file, because you know software is on one drive and data on the other. Second, if the drives are separate physical units rather than logical subdivisions of a single physical drive, the system will run faster because each drive has a separate read-write head to process data. The head reading drive C stays relatively near the open program file, and the head reading drive D near the data file. With logical subdivisions, however, there is only one head, which must jump back and forth between the software and the data.

Incidentally, if you examine the tree for drive C, you'll see how many contemporary software packages develop their own directories. The spreadsheet has special directories for fonts and clip art. The database has directories for

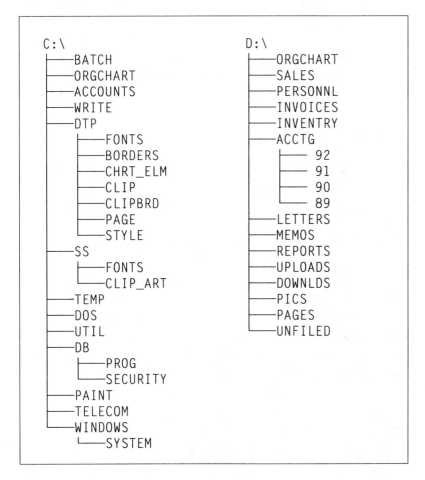

Figure 8.4   A system with two drives

programming tools and tools to maintain security and integrity. The desktop-publishing package has numerous directories—for fonts, borders, chart elements, clip art, page layouts, style sheets, and a clipboard for cutting and pasting.

Note also the relationship between the directories on drive C and drive D. The ORGCHART directory on drive C contains a program for setting up and printing organization charts. The ORGCHART directory on drive D contains the data files created by the program on drive C. There are also special directories for UPLOADS and DOWNLDS (downloads). *Uploading* is the term for sending a file to another computer using telecommunications software, and *downloading* is the term for receiving such files. Because all files to be transmitted are kept in one directory (on drive D), the telecommunications program can easily find them. The DOWNLDS directory contains received files, which the user will either delete or move elsewhere after examining them.

A Single Large Drive

Given DOS 5's ability to handle very large drives, you may prefer to turn all your hard disk real estate into a single drive. If you do, it's almost essential to use several levels of nesting. This need not be a problem if you use the Shell or some other utility software to help you get around and remember where you have put things.

Figure 8.5 shows a sample directory tree for a large hard drive. WINDOWS is a directory for Microsoft Windows, the graphical operating environment you'll meet in Chapter 16. The application programs specific to Windows are nested beneath a directory called WINAPPS, except for the graphics applications, which are nested beneath GRAPHICS. The standard DOS applications are nested beneath a directory called APPS. The data directories are divided by project. A separate INHOUSE directory contains subdirectories for files pertaining to internal company affairs.

There are several ways to approach navigation here. First, as you can see in Figure 8.6, the root directory gives

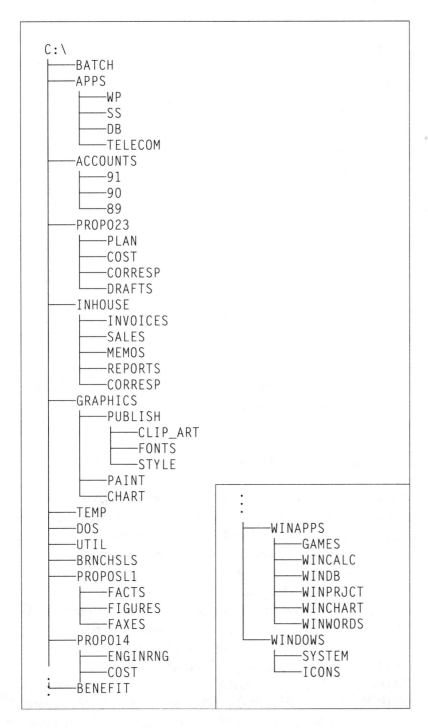

Figure 8.5   A tree for a large hard drive

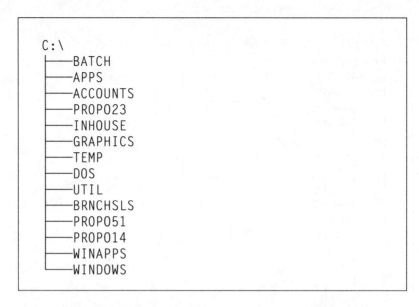

```
C:\
   ├──BATCH
   ├──APPS
   ├──ACCOUNTS
   ├──PROPO23
   ├──INHOUSE
   ├──GRAPHICS
   ├──TEMP
   ├──DOS
   ├──UTIL
   ├──BRNCHSLS
   ├──PROPO51
   ├──PROPO14
   ├──WINAPPS
   └──WINDOWS
```

Figure 8.6   The first-level directories of the large drive

you a concise system overview. Using DIR on a subdirectory of the root displays a manageably short list of subdirectories. From there it's easy to see how to proceed.

Treating a Directory as a Drive

DOS includes a command—SUBST (substitute) that lets you treat a directory as though it were a separate drive. If you assign a drive name to a directory, you can thereafter refer to the directory either by the new drive name or its original path name. (The new drive name is another instance of a logical drive.) If you use a drive name in place of a directory name, you have a lot less typing to do when you want to refer to files in that directory or when you want to make it current.

You might find SUBST useful with a tree structured like that in Figure 8.5. You could assign drive letters to the PROPO23, INHOUSE, GRAPHICS, WINAPPS, APPS, PROPOSL1, and PROPO14 directories. To do this, you may need a special command called LASTDRIVE in your

CONFIG.SYS file. You'll need this command if any of the drive names you want to use comes after the letter E. You'll learn how to use the LASTDRIVE command in Chapter 12.

To give a directory a drive name, enter a command of the form

SUBST *d1*: *d2*:*path*

where *d1*: is the drive name to give the directory, and *d2*:*path* is the actual name of the drive and directory. For example, you might make the INHOUSE directory drive D by entering

```
subst d: c:\inhouse
```

If you did, entering `dir d:` or `dir c:\inhouse` would display substantially the same information.

You need not restrict yourself to subdirectories of the root. You could, for example, enter

```
subst e: c:\proposl1\facts
```

Then you could load a file (called, say, INFO.DOC) in that directory into your word processor just by entering

```
wp e:info.doc
```

To undo a substitution, add the /D (delete) switch:

```
subst e: /d
```

Entering the SUBST command with no parameters shows you a list of the substitutions in effect:

```
D:  => C:\INHOUSE
E:  => C:\PROPOSL1\FACTS
```

A Bit of Housekeeping

If you upgraded to DOS 5, you may want to remove the previous release from your hard disk—but don't do it until you've used DOS 5 for several weeks. If you encounter problems, you may want to look at the text files APPNOTES.TXT, UMB.TXT, and README.TXT. You can read them using the View File Contents command in the Shell. After following any instructions you find, you may safely delete these text files. To remove your earlier version of DOS, just enter the command

```
deloldos
```

Before going further you may want to browse through your DOS directory to see if you want to eliminate any files. Some are necessary only for very specialized functions. Remember, you can always get deleted DOS files back if necessary, providing you've made the diskette copies as suggested in Chapter 2. To replace deleted files, simply copy them from the diskette to your hard disk.

DOS can remap the keyboard so that various keys display foreign-language characters. (The commands that accomplish this are beyond the scope of this book.) If you don't plan to use these, you can safely delete the following files:

4201.CPI
4208.CPI
5202.CPI
EGA.CPI
LCD.CPI
COUNTRY.SYS
DISPLAY.SYS
KEYBOARD.SYS
KEYB.COM
NLSFUNC.EXE
PRINTER.SYS

NOTE

If you want to revert to your old version, place your Uninstall diskette in drive A and reboot the computer by pressing Ctrl-Alt-Del. The screen will tell you how to proceed.

If you don't have a color graphics adapter (a low-resolution color display) you also don't need to have the file GRAFTABL.COM.

If you won't do any programming, you don't need EXE2BIN.EXE. QBASIC.EXE is the QuickBASIC programming language, which you may not need. However, it must be present if you use the DOS Editor, which is discussed in Chapter 11. If you prefer another word processor that can create ASCII (unformatted text) files, you can delete the following:

EDIT.COM
EDIT.HLP
QBASIC.EXE
QBASIC.HLP
MSHERC.COM

You can also delete files with the extension BAS. These are program files in the QuickBASIC language.

If you find you don't want to use the DOS Shell, you can delete all files whose names begin with DOSSHELL as well as the DOSSWAP.EXE file.

You can safely delete EDLIN.COM. It was included in DOS 5 only for consistency with earlier releases. It's a rather clumsy line editor, which to all intents and purposes has been replaced by EDIT.COM, the new DOS Editor.

Advanced File Management

Chapter **9**

What You Will Learn

- How to rearrange the Shell for advanced file management
- How to copy files from multiple sources
- How to make a drive behave as a subdirectory on another drive
- How to compare directories
- How to compare files
- What file attributes are and how to use them

Extending the Range of Shell Commands

You've learned the basics of using the Shell to manage files. In this section you'll learn to use all the Shell's advanced file-management features. This is less a matter of using the commands on the File menu than it is of changing the behavior of the Shell itself. To do this, you'll be using commands on the Options menu, shown in Figure 9.1, and on the View menu, shown in Figure 9.2.

Figure 9.1 *The Options menu*

Figure 9.2 *The View menu*

179

Viewing Information About Selected Files

Select any file and choose the Show Information command from the Options menu. Your screen will look something like Figure 9.3.

The Show Information box tells you a great deal about what you've been up to and the state of your system, as well as about the selected file. Let's examine it line by line. At the top you see the file name. Immediately below that is the text Attr:, which stands for "attributes." You'll learn about file attributes later in this chapter. At the moment note that there are four periods after the attribute indicator, signifying that the file has none of the four possible attributes.

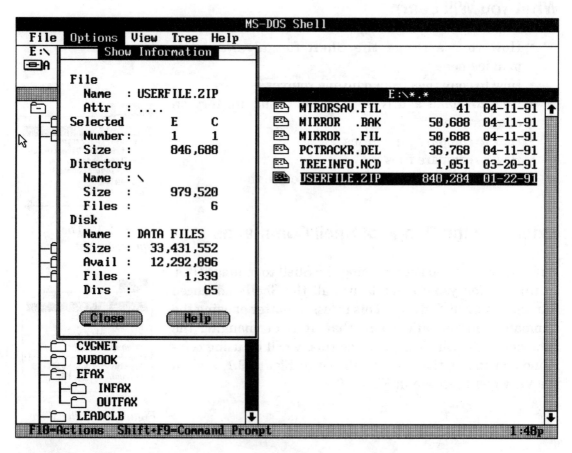

Figure 9.3   Viewing information about your Shell activities

Below the information about the selected file are the sections `Selected`, `Directory`, and `Disk`. The section `Directory` is more or less self-explanatory. It tells you the directory name, the number of bytes in the files it contains (`Size`), and the number of files, just like the top and bottom of the display produced by the DIR command.

The `Disk` section is also fairly clear. It shows you the disk's volume label, its size in bytes, the number of bytes free, and the number of files and directories. (You can get similar information from the CHKDSK command, which you'll learn about in Chapter 10.)

More interesting, and more difficult, is the `Selected` section. The first line shows the last two drives you've worked with. The second shows how many files are selected on each drive. You can see that drives E and C have been selected and that one file is selected on each drive.

What exactly does this mean? As you may have noticed, the first time you select a drive, a message box similar to Figure 9.4 tells you the Shell is scanning it. When you select a second drive and then switch back to the first, the Shell doesn't rescan the drive. Rather, it uses the information it has already gathered. One file is selected on each drive because you cannot have less than one file selected. Thus the value displayed next to `Size:` in this section is the combined size of all the *selected* files. You can verify this by comparing the value to the size of USERFILE.ZIP, the selected file on drive E, as shown in the file window. The difference between the size shown in the file window and that in the Show Information window is the size of the selected file on drive C. As you become more sophisticated in selecting files, the information in this window will become more valuable.

> **! WARNING**
> *If you run a program that adds, deletes, or edits files on a disk, the information in the Shell will not be current because it doesn't automatically rescan your drive. To force it to do so, use the* Refresh *command on the View menu or press the shortcut key F5.*

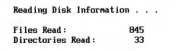

```
Reading Disk Information . . .

Files Read:          845
Directories Read:     33
```

Figure 9.4   Scanning a drive

Selecting Files from Multiple Directories

Suppose your directory tree is organized by project, and you want to copy all the files created by one software package to a backup diskette. Alternatively, suppose your files are grouped in directories by type, and you want to copy all files pertaining to a given project to a particular directory. The Shell gives you several ways to accomplish this without selecting files one at a time.

As you've already learned in Chapter 4, you can use the Search command on the File menu to list all files on your disk matching a wild-card specification. You can then select individual files or groups of files from the resulting window as you would in the file window. Let's look at a few other ways of accomplishing the same thing.

Selecting Across Directories. From the Options menu, choose Select Across Directories. You won't notice any change immediately. But the next time you view the Options menu, you'll notice a dot next to the command, indicating that it has been turned on. You now can go through directories one at a time, in the Directory Tree window, selecting files to copy or move. When you change directories, files stay selected. When you've finished, select the appropriate command from the File menu and it will act on all selected files. (The dialog box for the command will list the files without their path names, so you'll have to remember what you've done.) To turn off the Select Across Directories command, choose it again. The dot will disappear from any selected files.

A Global View of Your Files. The methods described above do the job, but they're a bit tedious. Let's take advantage of another Shell option to streamline the process further. From the View menu, select All Files. Your screen will rearrange itself radically. The Directory Tree window will be replaced by the Show Information window. The file window will show all the files on the selected drive, in the order you've chosen with the File Display Options command. The result should resemble Figure 9.5. You need the information displayed on the left because you no longer have the tree diagram to tell you which directory a file resides in.

By itself this list isn't terribly useful, but you can make it more so by changing your File Display Options. Figure 9.6 shows a list of files matching the wild-card pattern *.DB?. The resulting file list shows files created by several database-management programs. Some have the extension DB, others the extension DBF. As you move the highlight through the file window, the information on the left changes to reflect the selected file and the directory in which it's located. (This will slow the highlight

```
                              MS-DOS Shell
   File  Options  View  Tree  Help
   E:\BUSINESS\OLDFILES
   ⌸A   ⌸B   ▭C   ▭D   ▰E

                                                  *.*
                              11E      .REV     3,712   03-15-91   12:12p ⬆
   File                       12-1     .SCR     8,128   03-27-91    2:17p ▨
     Name  : 1988.LOG         12-2     .SCR     8,128   03-27-91    2:09p
     Attr  : ....             1987     .LOG     1,820   12-31-88    2:27p
   Selected           E       1988     .LOG    29,988   01-03-89    1:44p
     Number:          1       1988ALL  .TL     15,503   03-11-89   12:49p
     Size  :     29,988       1988PER  .TL      3,320   03-11-89   12:46p
   Directory                  1STSHELT .SCR     8,128   02-28-91    5:09p
     Name  : OLDFILES         250GTO   .PCX    26,689   05-02-89    5:55p
     Size  :    370,525       303REV   .GEM     6,582   11-24-89   11:36p
     Files :         11       305REV   .GEM     2,752   11-21-89    4:14p
   Disk                       411_0601 .GEM     2,330   03-31-88   11:02a
     Name  : DATA FILES       411_0602 .GEM     1,180   03-08-88   11:15p
     Size  : 33,431,552       411_0603 .GEM    13,482   03-08-88   10:36p
     Avail : 12,005,376       411_1001 .GEM     1,204   03-27-88    5:35p
     Files :      1,337       411_1002 .GEM     2,382   03-27-88    5:50p
     Dirs  :         65       411_1003 .GEM     3,158   03-27-88    5:44p
                              411_1004 .GEM     2,892   03-27-88    5:54p
                              411_1005 .GEM     2,970   03-27-88    6:01p
                              411_1010 .GEM     5,954   03-27-88    5:58p
                              411_1101 .GEM     6,930   03-25-88    7:54p
                              411_1102 .GEM     9,802   03-25-88    8:04p
                              411_1103 .GEM     5,278   03-25-88    7:51p ⬇
   F10=Actions  Shift+F9=Command Prompt                          3:18p
```

Figure 9.5   A global file list

down noticeably.) It's a good way to get an overview of a subset of your files.

The All Files display has other uses. Suppose you want to view the work you've done in the last few days but don't remember exactly which files you've worked on. From the Options menu, choose File Display Options. Use the wild-card pattern *.* in the Name: entry line. Sort the files by date and select Ascending order. This will give you a list similar to Figure 9.7, with the most recent files at the top of the window.

Selecting Files from Multiple Drives. The options you've just tried give you a lot of scope. But suppose you

```
                            MS-DOS Shell
   File   Options   View   Tree   Help
   E:\BUSINESS\INVOICES
   [=]A   [=]B   [=]C   [=]D   [=]E

                              *.DB?
                    INVCES1 .DB      4,096    04-02-91    9:55a  ↑
   File             INVCES2 .DB      4,096    03-14-91    5:47p
     Name  : INVCES1.DB  INVCES3 .DB      4,096    03-14-91    5:55p
     Attr  : ....       INVENTRY.DB      8,192    03-28-91   12:17p
   Selected        E    INVOICE .DB      4,096    04-03-91   12:44p
     Number:       1    JAZZALBM.DB     37,175    09-27-89    6:25p
     Size  :   4,096    JAZZAN1 .DB      5,369    09-14-89   10:06p
   Directory            JAZZMAP .DB      4,324    06-06-89    5:48p
     Name  : INVOICES   MASTORDR.DB      1,531    09-21-89    1:07p
     Size  :  160,040   MEMBERS .DB     10,240    04-02-91    3:08p
     Files :      57    OLDALBUM.DB     10,472    06-06-89    4:20p
   Disk                 OLDANTH .DB      1,244    06-06-89    3:52p
     Name  : DATA FILES OLDENTRY.DB      1,462    01-28-90    9:30a
     Size  : 33,431,552 OLDIEMAP.DB      3,300    06-06-89    2:24p
     Avail : 12,005,376 OLDIES  .DB     33,059    06-06-89    4:20p
     Files :    1,337   ORDERS  .DB      4,096    03-28-91   11:50a
     Dirs  :      65    ORDRHIST.DB      4,096    03-28-91   11:50a
                        PERFORMR.DB    158,967    09-27-89    6:31p
                        REISSUE .DB     19,738    09-26-90    2:39p
                        ROLODEX .DB      5,446    02-08-91    1:50p
                        ROLODEX .DBF    66,722    04-11-91   12:27p
                        SALESPER.DB      2,338    10-24-89    9:34a
                        SOFTWARE.DB      8,192    03-29-91    2:54p  ↓
   F10=Actions   Shift+F9=Command Prompt                    3:21p
```

Figure 9.6   Displaying selected files from all directories

want to view items on several hard drives at once. Can you? The fact that the Show Information window displays information about two drives might suggest that you can. But you can't. However. . . .

A rather obscure DOS command lets you treat several drives as though they were a single, large disk. Suppose you have two hard disks, C and D. The procedure is to create a directory beneath the root of one drive and join the second drive to that directory. The directories on the second drive will then be treated as subdirectories of the new directory.

Create a directory on drive C called DDRIVE. To do this in the Shell, select drive C. Use the File Display Options command to display a Directory Tree window.

```
┌──────────────────────────── MS-DOS Shell ────────────────────────────┐
│  File   Options   View   Tree   Help                                  │
├───────────────────────────────────────────────────────────────────────┤
│  E:\PRIMA                                                             │
│  ▣A   ▣B   ▭C   ▭D   ▭E                                               │
│                                                                       │
│                                              ┌──────── *.* ─────────┐  │
│                              ▷          ▣ DOS5     .GV   36,704  04-11-91  3:43p ▲│
│  File                                  ▣ MEDMIL   .WQ1  23,991  04-11-91  3:42p  │
│    Name  : DOS5.GV                     ▣ FIG0806  .PCX  67,027  04-11-91  3:22p  │
│    Attr  : ...a                        ▣ FIG0805  .PCX  68,554  04-11-91  3:19p  │
│  Selected          E                   ▣ FIG0807  .PCX  66,124  04-11-91  3:17p  │
│    Number:         1                   ▣ PCTRACKR.DEL  36,768  04-11-91  2:50p  │
│    Size  :    36,704                   ▣ FIG0804  .PCX  24,098  04-11-91  1:59p  │
│  Directory                             ▣ FIG0803  .PCX  46,340  04-11-91  1:49p  │
│    Name  : PRIMA                       ▣ LABEL    .FOR     320  04-11-91  1:39p  │
│    Size  :   367,092                   ▣ MENUS    .TXT     426  04-11-91  1:39p  │
│    Files :        37                   ▣ FIG0801  .PCX  73,408  04-11-91  1:26p  │
│  Disk                                  ▣ FIG0802  .PCX  73,624  04-11-91  1:25p  │
│    Name  : DATA FILES                  ▣ APPOINT  .TM    6,388  04-11-91  1:24p  │
│    Size  : 33,431,552                  ▣ ROLODEX  .DBF  66,722  04-11-91 12:27p  │
│    Avail : 11,866,112                  ▣ ROLODEX  .FOR     443  04-11-91 11:54a  │
│    Files :     1,339                   ▣ MIRROR   .FIL  50,688  04-11-91 11:47a  │
│    Dirs  :        65                   ▣ MIRORSAV.FIL      41  04-11-91 11:47a  │
│                                        ▣ MIRROR   .BAK  50,688  04-11-91 11:39a  │
│                                        ▣ ADDRESS  .ENV     256  04-11-91 11:31a  │
│                                        ▣ STEINER  .LTR   2,560  04-11-91 11:27a  │
│                                        ▣ FIG0501  .GEM   5,316  04-11-91 10:45a  │
│                                        ▣ FIG0502  .PCX  11,395  04-10-91  5:36p  │
│                                        ▣ HS       .CFG     512  04-10-91  5:27p ▼│
├───────────────────────────────────────────────────────────────────────┤
│  F10=Actions  Shift+F9=Command Prompt                          3:43p │
└───────────────────────────────────────────────────────────────────────┘
```

Figure 9.7   Finding the most recently changed files

Choose the `Create Directory` command from the File menu. Enter the name

```
\DDRIVE
```

in the entry line.

Alternatively, press Shift-F9 to get to the command prompt and enter

```
MD C:\DDRIVE
```

If you're at the command prompt, next enter

```
join d: c:\ddrive
```

and then

```
exit
```

If you're in the Shell, select R̲un from the File menu and enter

```
join d: c:\ddrive
```

When you return to the Shell, press F5 to rescan the drive. Figure 9.8 shows what happens when you use JOIN. Both DOS and the Shell treat the joined drive as part of the "host" drive. You lose all access to it as an independent drive. However, you can still select its directories in the Directory Tree window or refer to its files with a path name beginning with C:\DDRIVE.

✳ NOTE

In the Shell you no longer have access to a joined drive. You can select it, but no files will appear. Instead you'll see the message `No files in selected directory.` *To view the files on drive D, select the directories subordinate to DDRIVE.*

Any attempt to access the joined drive at a command prompt will result in the message `Invalid drive specification.`

Now that you've joined the drives, select Search from the File menu. Enter a wild-card pattern that selects files on both drives. As you can see from Figure 9.9, matching files from both drives are displayed. If Select Across Directories is turned on, you can select files from either drive. If you use the All Files display option, files from both drives appear in the file window.

Other Aspects of the JOIN Command. If you have still other hard drives, there's no reason you can't join them all into a single drive. The only restriction is that each drive must be joined to an empty subdirectory of the root.

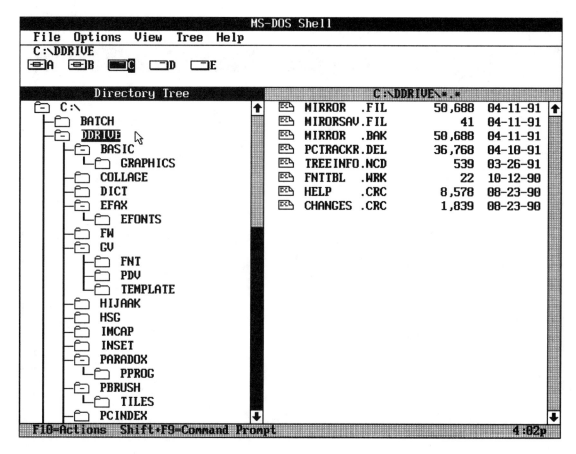

Figure 9.8   Joining one drive to another

Entering

```
join
```

displays a list of joined drives, such as

```
D:  => C:\DDRIVE
```

When you're through using your joined drives, be sure to undo the join. Enter a command of the form

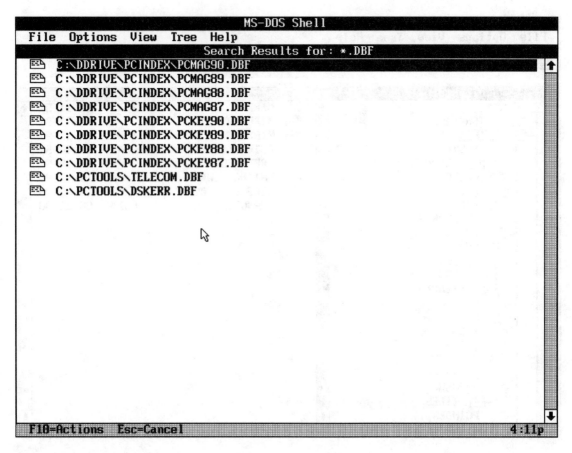

Figure 9.9   Selecting files from joined drives

```
join d: /d
```

where *d*: is the name of the joined drive. (The /D switch
stands for "delete.")

Comparing Directories Using the Shell

At times you need to compare two directories. Suppose, for
example, you have copies of files on various diskettes and
others on your hard disk. You want to be sure the hard disk
contains the most recent copies. Alternatively, you may want
to back up your most current files on a diskette.

Begin by selecting the Dual File Lists command
from the View menu. Your screen will show two Directory
Tree and file windows. At the moment the lower windows
will display information about the root directory of the current drive.

To select any window, move the mouse pointer into it and
click. To select the drive to be displayed in either pair of
windows, click on the drive icon above them.

□ **MOUSE**

To move among the four windows and the two drive
selection bars, use the Tab and Shift-Tab keys, just as you
would with a single pair of windows. The highlighted drive
icon above a pair of windows determines the drive about
which those windows will display information.

■ **KEYBOARD**

Let's use the dual display to compare the contents of two
directories. From the upper drive list, select the hard drive
containing one set of files you want to compare. Next insert
a diskette containing the other files and select the drive
from the lower drive list. You will see a screen like the one in
Figure 9.10. You may have to scroll through each file window several times to match up the file names you're interested in. However, this is by far the easiest way to compare
two directories.

The Shell doesn't give you any further assistance at this
point. It doesn't assume, for example, that when you select
the Copy command you want to copy to the other displayed

directory. You still have to specify the target. But you can see the results quite clearly.

Other Shell Options

You've already encountered most of the commands on the Options and View menus. Enable Task Swapper on the Options menu is an advanced command that you'll learn about in Chapter 14. At that point we'll also go into the Program List and Program/File list views in detail.

Two other options are worth noting. The Repaint Screen command (and the Shift-F5 shortcut) on the View

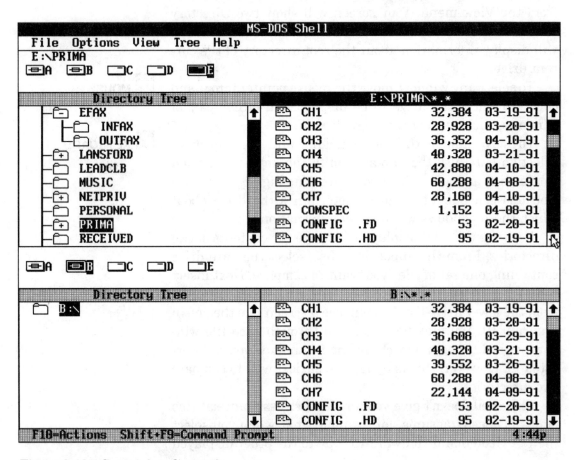

Figure 9.10 Comparing directories

menu simply fixes the display's appearance. Occasionally something may look wrong when you return to the Shell from another program. This is most likely to happen when the computer must switch between video modes. This command does not cause the Shell to rescan the drive, just to update the screen.

Finally, as you become more confident, you may wish to reduce the number of times you must confirm deletions, copying over files with the same name, and certain mouse operations. These are controlled in the Shell by the Confirmation dialog box (see Figure 9.11), which you access by choosing the Confirmation... command on the Options menu. Initially each operation in this box is marked with an X, which means the Shell asks you to confirm that operation for each selected file. To turn off confirmation, press the space bar and select OK. (More about this in Chapter 14.)

There is no rule about whether you should have the Shell prompt you regarding each selected file. Choose whatever you're comfortable with. If you're not sure of yourself, leave the options as they are.

The Confirm on Replace option is actually quite useful, however. When you select a group of files to be moved or copied, it's possible to replace a later version of a file without realizing it. With Confirm on Replace selected, you'll be warned by a dialog box such as the one in Figure 6.15. It gives you the size and date of both files, so you can be sure you're copying in the right direction.

Figure 9.11   The Confirmation dialog box

File Attributes

At a few points, you've seen some mention of *file attributes.* These are values that affect the way DOS treats a file in some contexts. A file can have one of four attributes: *read-only, hidden, system,* and *archive.* There are also two other attributes: one that distinguishes a volume label and one that distinguishes a directory name. A file that has none of these is a normal, or *read-write,* file. The vast majority of your files, including most commercial software, is of this type. An attribute is placed in a hidden byte in the directory entry. This is called the *attribute byte.* When a file has one of the attributes, it is said to be *set;* when it doesn't, the attribute is *cleared.*

All this may sound arcane, and in fact you can ignore attributes most of the time. But it's helpful to know about their effects and occasionally to control them. Let's look at the effects first.

Read-Only Files

If the read-only attribute is set, the file may be neither modified nor erased, even though it appears in the directory listing. If you try to erase a read-only file, DOS displays the message

```
Access denied
```

You can, however, copy a read-only file and modify or erase the copy.

If you work with other computer users, you may want to protect your files with the read-only attribute.

Hidden Files

Hidden files do not appear in directory listings at the command prompt. This means they aren't affected by commands that use the listings, including COPY *.* and DEL *.*. However, they *are* affected by DISKCOPY and FORMAT. To manipulate a hidden file, you can either change the attribute or use the Shell.

By default the Shell displays hidden files in the file window, and you can copy or delete them there. If you don't want them displayed, turn off the `Display hidden/ system files` option in the File Display Options box.

✳ NOTE

When you erase all the files from a bootable diskette using the DEL command, the hidden system files will still be present. All you need do to make the diskette bootable again is copy COMMAND.COM onto it. Adding the hidden attribute to a file will protect it from other users who use the DIR command but not from those who use the shell.

Many copy-protected software packages create hidden files on the root directory of a hard disk. You should not change their hidden status if you want the software to run. However, if for some reason you have deleted the software from your hard disk without following its "uninstall" procedure, you may want to delete these files.

System Files

A system file is, by definition, any file that has the system attribute set. Otherwise it is just like any other read-only file. The DOS files IO.SYS and MSDOS.SYS have both the hidden and system attributes set, which is why they are called hidden system files.

System files, like hidden files, are listed in the Shell's file window and can be copied or deleted there but not at the prompt.

Archive Files

The attribute to which you need to pay the most attention is the archive attribute. When a file is first created, copied to a new destination, or edited, this attribute is set. This indicates that it is a new copy of the file, one which has never been backed up (archived, in a sense). Two DOS commands, BACKUP and XCOPY, can selectively copy only those files whose archive attribute is set, thereby copying only files that have never been backed up in their present form. BACKUP automatically clears the archive attribute, so it won't copy the same file again. You can optionally have XCOPY do the same thing. You'll learn about XCOPY later in this chapter, and BACKUP in Chapter 10.

✳ NOTE

When you move a file using the Shell, its archive attribute is not changed in the new location.

Changing File Attributes in the Shell

❗ WARNING

Don't change a file's attributes without good reason. Doing so can cause unexpected and unpleasant things to happen. If you make all your program files read-only, for example, software installation may fail when you upgrade. If you remove an archive attribute, you may find that some vital files are missing when you need to restore a hard disk.

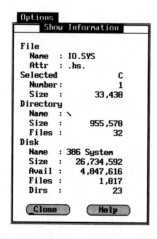

Figure 9.12   The Show Information box when attributes are set

Let's look at how the Shell handles file attributes. As you saw in Figure 9.3, the Shell indicates the four important bits of the attribute byte by dots in the Show Information box. If any attributes are set, the dots are replaced by lowercase letters corresponding to the first letter of the attribute name. Make the root directory of drive C current, select the file IO.SYS, and display the Show Information box. As Figure 9.12 shows, the hidden and system attributes are indicated by the letters *h* and *s* in place of the two middle dots. (On your system, an *a* will appear in place of the last dot unless you've already backed up your hard disk.)

Now close the Show Information box and select Change Attributes from the File menu. As you can see in the resulting dialog box (Figure 9.13), attributes that are set are indicated by a pointer next to their name.

For practice, you can safely turn on the read-only attribute of IO.SYS, because system files are already protected from editing by the system attribute. Here's how you use the `Change Attributes` command.

To change an attribute using a mouse, just click on it. If it's on, it will be turned off and vice versa. Click on `OK` to record the changes or on `Cancel` to ignore them.

☐ **MOUSE**

To change an attribute using the keyboard, press Shift-Tab to select the `Hidden` attribute. Use ↑ and ↓ to move among the attributes. Press the space bar to toggle them on and off. When you are finished, press Tab to move the cursor until you select `OK` to record the changes or `Cancel` to cancel them. Then press Enter.

■ **KEYBOARD**

Viewing Attributes at the Command Prompt

Two DOS commands give you information about file attributes: DIR and ATTRIB. As you learned in Chapter 7, you can use the /A switch to view a directory listing showing file

✔ **NEW FEATURE**
Viewing directories by attribute

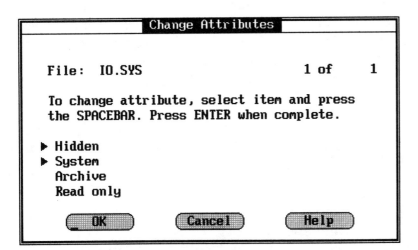

Figure 9.13   The Change Attributes dialog box

names without subdirectories or subdirectories without file names. You can also use /A, followed by the letter of an attribute, to view lists of files having specified attributes. To list the hidden files on your root directory, for example, you could enter

```
dir c:\ /ah
```

This will produce a display something like the following:

```
Volume in drive C is MY SYSTEM
Volume Serial Number is 012C-1030
Directory of C:\

IO        SYS      33430 03-22-91    5:10a
MSDOS     SYS      37394 03-22-91    5:10a
 2 file(s)       70824 bytes
                4853760 bytes free
```

Be aware that when you add attributes to the /A switch the effect is cumulative. The switch /ASHRA will produce a list of *only* those files that have all four attributes set. To see all the files that do *not* have a given attribute, precede the letter denoting the attribute by a minus sign. For example, to view a directory of files that don't have the archive attribute set, enter

```
dir /a-a
```

You can also view file attributes using the ATTRIB command. ATTRIB with no parameters produces a display similar to Figure 9.14.

Changing File Attributes at the Command Prompt

The ATTRIB command also allows you to modify a file's attributes. Unlike virtually all other commands, its switches

```
C:\>attrib
     SH        C:\IO.SYS
     SH        C:\MSDOS.SYS
               C:\COMMAND.COM
               C:\ANSI.SYS
               C:\DRIVER.SYS
               C:\EMM386.EXE
               C:\RAMDRIVE.SYS
               C:\MOUSE.SYS
  A    R        C:\MIRROR.FIL
  A    R        C:\MIRROR.BAK
  A    S        C:\PCTRACKR.DEL
               C:\SMARTDRV.SYS
       R        C:\WINA20.386
  A            C:\AUTOEXEC.BAT
  A            C:\CONFIG.SYS
  A   SHR       C:\MIRORSAV.FIL
               C:\HIMEM.SYS
C:\>_
```

Figure 9.14   Displaying file attributes with ATTRIB

appear *before* any file or path parameters. To set an attribute, you enter a plus sign followed by its letter. To clear it, you enter a minus sign followed by its letter. The general form of the ATTRIB command is

ATTRIB [+A] [*path \][filename.ext] [/S]*

As you've seen, if you don't specify a file name, the command applies to all files in the directory. You can restrict its scope by giving it a file name, optionally prefaced by a path name and optionally including wild cards. You can also extend its scope by adding the /S (subdirectories) switch after the file name. This switch tells the command to carry out your instructions on every subdirectory of the specified path, or if none is specified, of the current directory.

You can affect several attributes at once by including them in a single command. For example, to make all program files in a directory read-only while clearing the archive attribute, you would enter the following two commands:

```
attrib +r -a *.com
attrib +r -a *.exe
```

To do the same thing to all the program files on a disk, regardless of their location, enter the command in the form

```
attrib +r -a \*.ext /s
```

Advanced File Copying at the Command Prompt

DOS includes two commands that give you extended control over the way files are copied. Both commands—XCOPY (extended copy) and REPLACE—are powerful and useful.

Extended Copying

The XCOPY command allows you to copy an entire directory or all files matching a wild-card pattern. (If you're using diskettes, this command is on the Support diskette.) It can also copy all matching files in the subdirectories of the source. It is considerably faster than the COPY command because it reads the files in groups, rather than one at a time, filling all your memory before writing them. In addition, if the destination disk does not have subdirectories matching those on the source disk, XCOPY will create them and place the files appropriately. The basic syntax for the command is

XCOPY *source* *[target]* *[/switch]*

You must specify the source. If you specify only a path name, all files on the source meeting the characteristics specified by the switches will be copied. If the target is the current drive and directory, you can leave it out. If you place a backslash after the target, XCOPY will automatically assume it is a directory. If you don't and if the target directory doesn't exist—for example, if you issue the command

```
XCOPY *.* \WORDS\TEMP
```

you will be prompted with

```
Does TEMP specify a file name
or directory name on the target
(F = file, D = directory)?
```

If you press D or if you type the initial command as

```
XCOPY *.* \WORDS\TEMP\
```

the TEMP directory will have copies of all files found in the current directory.

Let's look at some examples that illustrate the power of this command. Figure 9.15 shows XCOPY simultaneously reading all files matching the wild-card pattern CH*, then copying them to the directory CHAPTERS, which it creates if it doesn't already exist.

```
C:\BOOK>xcopy ch* \chapters\
Reading source file(s)...
CH1
CH2
CH4
CH6
CH5
CH3
        6 File(s) copied

C:\BOOK>_
```

Figure 9.15   Copying files with XCOPY

The only differences between XCOPY in this form and COPY are that XCOPY is faster and creates the target directory if necessary. In addition, XCOPY has some useful and powerful switches. Let's examine some of them.

Perhaps most powerful, and useful, is the /S (subdirectories) switch. This tells XCOPY to copy all files matching the source specification in any subdirectories of the source, as well as the source. It recreates all the relevant subdirectories on the target if they don't already exist, as Figure 9.16 shows. Here all the files are copied from a diskette in drive A that contains subdirectories to a new directory on drive C. The subdirectories are reproduced on drive C.

The effect of the /S switch is even greater if you specify a wild-card pattern. As Figure 9.17 shows, XCOPY can search

```
C:\>xcopy a: c:\book\ /s
Reading source file(s)...
A:CONTENTS
A:INDEX
A:NOTES
A:CHAPTERS\CH1
A:CHAPTERS\CH2
A:CHAPTERS\CH4
A:CHAPTERS\CH6
A:CHAPTERS\CH7
A:CHAPTERS\CH5
A:CHAPTERS\CH3
A:CHAPTERS\CH9
A:CHAPTERS\CH8
A:TABLES\TBL0701.TXT
A:TABLES\TBL0702.TXT
A:TABLES\TBL0703.TXT
A:TABLES\TBL0704.TXT
A:TABLES\TBL0705.TXT
A:TABLES\TBL0901.TXT
        18 File(s) copied

C:\>_
```

Figure 9.16   Copying from subdirectories and creating new subdirectories

an entire drive for matching files and copy them all to a different location.

If you're not sure what files are on your source disk, add the /P (prompt) switch. XCOPY will ask you to confirm each one. This gives you the chance to exclude files you don't want, as Figure 9.18 shows.

Following is an overview of the remaining switches.

/W (wait)	Prompts you to press any key to begin copying files. This is useful mainly when you have to read the XCOPY program from the Support diskette and must remove it from the drive to insert the source diskette.
/M (modified)	Copies only files with the archive attribute set (that is, those that have been modified) and clears the archive attribute of the source copy.
/A (archive)	Copies only files with the archive attribute set but does not clear the archive attribute.
/D:*mm-dd-yy* (date)	Copies only files created on or after the specified date.
/V (verify)	Reads the file after writing it, to make sure it can be read; it does not ensure the accuracy of the copy.
/E (empty)	When used with the /S switch, creates subdirectories on the target to match those on the source, even if the criteria you use result in there being no files to copy to those directories. This gives you a model of your source directory structure on the target, which you may find useful.

Selective Copying

The REPLACE command is a selective copying command. (If you're using diskettes, it's on the Shell diskette.) Its general form, like that of XCOPY, is

REPLACE [*path*]*filename.ext* [*target*] [*/switch*]

You must specify a source file name, which may include wild-card characters. If the target is not current, you must

```
D:\>xcopy *.gem a: /s
Reading source file(s)..
ART\IMAGES\SHORTCUT.GEM
ART\IMAGES\TIGER.GEM
ART\IMAGES\SUNRISE.GEM
ART\PICTURES\ENTPRS.GEM
ART\PICTURES\KCSSIGN.GEM
ART\PICTURES\KCSLOGO.GEM
DVBOOK\305REV.GEM
DVBOOK\303REV.GEM
PRIMA\ILLOS\FIG0101.GEM
PRIMA\ILLOS\FIG0104.GEM
PRIMA\ILLOS\FIG0501.GEM
        12 File(s) copied
D:\>_
```

Figure 9.17   Copying selected files from many directories

```
E:\>xcopy *.gem b: /s /p
EADOS\FIG33.GEM (Y/N)?n
EADOS\FIG56.GEM (Y/N)?n
EADOS\FIG64.GEM (Y/N)?n
EADOS\FIG69.GEM (Y/N)?n
EADOS\FIG69-2.GEM (Y/N)?n
EADOS\FIG83.GEM (Y/N)?n
ART\IMAGES\DANCER.GEM (Y/N)?y
ART\IMAGES\HOUSE.GEM (Y/N)?y
ART\IMAGES\SHIP.GEM (Y/N)?y
ART\IMAGES\SHORTCUT.GEM (Y/N)?n
ART\IMAGES\SHORTHI.GEM (Y/N)?y
ART\IMAGES\TIGER.GEM (Y/N)?n
        4 File(s) copied
E:>_
```

Figure 9.18   Selecting individual files to copy

also specify that. With no switches, REPLACE copies only files that already exist on the target. It's not immediately apparent why this is useful, but it will become so.

The most powerful switch is /S, which works just like the /S switch to XCOPY. Perhaps the most useful switch is /U (update), which copies files only if the source is newer than the target. You can use it to make sure several users have the latest copies of specific files.

You can also reverse the effect of the REPLACE command with the /A (add) switch. This copies only files that *don't* exist on the target. By combining these two switches, you can ensure that two directories have identical files without deleting any files from the target that may not exist on the source. Using these two forms of the REPLACE command is a very handy way of making sure you have a complete current backup of the files in a given directory. For example, you might enter these two commands:

```
replace \newproj\*.* a: /u /s
replace \newproj\*.* a: /a
```

This will copy any files from the NEWPROJ directory and its subdirectories that are already on the diskette in drive A but are older than those in the NEWPROJ directory. Then it will copy any files that exist in NEWPROJ but not on the diskette. (Unfortunately you can't use the /S switch with the /A switch.)

Here is a brief overview of the remaining switches:

/R (read-only)	Replaces read-only files (useful for updating your operating system).
/P (prompt)	Prompts you for permission before writing each file, so that you can selectively exclude files.
/W (wait)	Prompts you to press any key to begin copying files. This is useful mainly when you have to read the REPLACE program from the Shell diskette and must remove it from the drive to insert the source diskette.

Comparing Files

There are times when you need to compare files. You may want to find the differences between two versions. Or you may find that a program is behaving strangely. One way to make sure a file has not become damaged is to compare the version on your hard disk or on your working diskette with the version on the original software diskette. (This assumes of course that an installation procedure hasn't changed the program file.)

DOS provides two file-comparison commands, COMP and FC. The former is relatively simple and easy to use but doesn't tell you much. The latter is powerful enough that most of it is beyond the scope of this book. But we'll take a peek at it anyway.

Simple Comparisons with COMP

To compare two files with COMP, enter the command followed by the file names. You can include path names if necessary. If the files are identical, you'll see the message

```
Files compare OK
```

If they differ in length, you'll see the message

```
Files are different sizes
```

If COMP encounters more than ten differences, it gives up.

✔ **NEW FEATURE**
Specifying the form of COMP output

COMP can now display the compared data as characters if you use the /A switch or as decimal numbers if you use the /D switch.

If the files are the same length but have differences, COMP displays the distance from the beginning of the file at which the difference is found in *hexadecimal* numbers— something you can safely avoid. It also displays the values of the bytes at that point in hexadecimal numbers. If the file is basically a text file, you can tell it to display characters instead of hexadecimal numbers by using the /A switch. You can also have it display line numbers instead of the number of bytes from the beginning by using the /L switch. When comparing program files, don't use these switches. All you want to know is whether the files are identical. Figure 9.19 shows the results of a comparison using COMP, when the text "arrange" has been replaced by "mark up."

```
C:\LETTERS>comp notation notation.bak /a /l
Comparing NOTATION and NOTATION.BAK...
Compare error at LINE 12
file1 = a
file2 = m
Compare error at LINE 12
file1 = r
file2 = a
Compare error at LINE 12
file1 = a
file2 = k
Compare error at LINE 12
file1 = n
file2 =
Compare error at LINE 12
file1 = g
file2 = u
Compare error at LINE 12
file1 = e
file2 = p

Compare more files (Y/N)?n
C:\LETTERS>_
```

Figure 9.19   Comparing files with COMP

Advanced Comparisons with FC

The FC (file compare) command is more flexible than the COMP command. If files differ in size by even one byte, COMP simply reports that they are different. To compare two text files line by line, use the FC command with the /L switch. If two lines are different lengths, the comparison continues by displaying them. Figure 9.20 shows how FC displays the differences it finds.

You can make the result even more useful by adding the /N switch to display line numbers for the mismatched lines, as shown in Figure 9.21. This makes it easy to find the differences and correct them if necessary.

```
C:\LETTERS>fc notation notation.bak /l
Comparing files NOTATION and NOTATION.BAK
***** NOTATION
as soon as possible. It goes without saying that you
can arrange the final copy to suit your needs.

***** NOTATION.BAK
as soon as possible. It goes without saying that you
can mark up the final copy to suit your needs.

*****

***** NOTATION

The result will look like figure 1.

***** NOTATION.BAK

The result will look something like figure 1.

*****

C:\LETTERS>_
```

Figure 9.20   Comparing two text files line by line

If the files are formatted differently but contain essentially the same text, use the /W switch. This forces FC to compress "white space"—tabs and spaces—so that only the actual text characters are compared. You can also force either command to compare files without regard to capitalization by adding the /C switch.

FC can also compare program files. However, if the files differ, its display will probably just confuse you. As a rule, all you need to know is whether the files are the same, which either FC or COMP can tell you.

 HINT

To record the result, press Ctrl-P or Ctrl-PrtSc before you issue the FC command. The output will go to the printer as well as the screen. Remember to press Ctrl-P again when FC is finished, or everything else will also go to the printer.

```
C:\LETTERS>fc notation notation.bak /1 /n
Comparing files NOTATION and NOTATION.BAK
***** NOTATION
11:     as soon as possible. It goes without saying that you
12:     can arrange the final copy to suit your needs.
13:
***** NOTATION.BAK
11:     as soon as possible. It goes without saying that you
12:     can mark up the final copy to suit your needs.
13:
*****


***** NOTATION
34:
35:     The result will look like figure 1.
36:
***** NOTATION.BAK
34:
35:     The result will look something like figure 1.
36:
*****
C:\LETTERS>_
```

Figure 9.21   Comparing files using line numbers

Safeguarding Your Data

Chapter 10

What You Will Learn

- How to find and correct some types of disk errors
- How to back up your hard disk
- When to back up your hard disk
- Why you should back up your hard disk <u>frequently</u>
- How to restore files from a backup
- How to recover a deleted file
- How to recover from an unintended format
- How to recover part of a mangled file

Verifying Disk Integrity

As you know, things can go wrong with disks. The first line of defense is a complete, current backup of all your files. In this chapter you'll learn to use all the DOS tools for making such a backup. You'll also learn about the other DOS tools for diagnosing and recovering from disk problems.

One important early warning system is the CHKDSK (check disk) external program. This program reports on the status of your disk(s) and memory and gives you a chance to correct any damage. The basic form of the command is

chkdsk [*drive*]

If you don't specify a drive, it reports on the current disk. If all is well, you'll see a report similar to Figure 10.1.

The first part of this report reiterates the volume label and serial number (which you've already encountered in other messages). The second part provides information about the disk's directories and files. The third part reports on the number of allocation units, or clusters, on the disk and the number in use. The final part of the report tells you how much memory your computer has and how much is in use.

Not all this information appears in every report. If you used CHKDSK on a newly formatted diskette with no bad sectors, the second through fifth lines would be absent and the number of available bytes and allocation units would equal their respective totals.

```
D:\INVOICES>chkdsk e:

Volume DATA FILES  created 01-23-1991 2:00p
Volume Serial Number is 012C-1020

 33431552 bytes total disk space
     2048 bytes in 1 hidden files
   145408 bytes in 64 directories
 21841920 bytes in 1353 user files
     4096 bytes in bad sectors
 11438080 bytes available on disk

     2048 bytes in each allocation unit
    16324 total allocation units on disk
     5585 available allocation units on disk

   655360 total bytes memory
   569632 bytes free

D:\INVOICES>_
```

Figure 10.1   The CHKDSK report

Various practices can damage your files, however. These include:

- Switching disks in a drive while a program is running. Some programs keep an image in memory of the file allocation table and root directory of the current disk. If you change disks without informing the program, files will be written as if the old disk were still in place.
- Exiting a program improperly; for example, by rebooting the computer while a file is open. The file will not be closed properly and its length will not be recorded.

If these conditions occur, CHKDSK may report various anomalous conditions. Let's look at its messages and what they mean. The most common message is

```
nnn lost clusters found in nn chains.
Write corrections to disk (Y/N)?
```

This means the file allocation table shows storage space in use that doesn't belong to any file in any directory.

What do you do in this case? It depends. First, nothing will happen whether you press N or Y. However, you've been notified that you have to make corrections. To do so, reenter the CHKDSK command, adding the /F (fix) switch. CHKDSK will make no changes without it.

Once you have entered

```
chkdsk /f
```

if you answer N, CHKDSK simply rewrites the file allocation table to deallocate the lost clusters. If you answer Y, it writes each *chain*—group of contiguous clusters—to a file in the root directory whose name takes the form FILE*NNNN*.CHK. The numbers begin with 0000 and continue until all the chains have been written or until the root directory becomes full.

Should you ask CHKDSK to write these files? First, check whether the data files you've used most recently are intact. If so, the lost clusters probably belong to deleted files and can safely be done away with. If not, press Y. Use the Shell's View File Contents command to see if you can figure out which file each chain belongs to. Delete the ones you no longer need. Try to piece the others together using the software you used to create them. If this fails, pray that you have a recent backup.

Either of the following messages means you've lost a file:

```
C:\FILENAME.EXT
    Allocation error, size adjusted.

C:\FILENAME.EXT
    Invalid cluster, file truncated.
```

The first message means the file size reported in the directory is larger than that in the file allocation table. The second message means the file allocation table shows more clusters assigned to the file than the directory indicates. When you enter

```
chkdsk /f
```

CHKDSK actually rewrites the file allocation table so that it marks as part of the file only enough clusters to match the directory entry. If possible, replace the files with copies from another disk.

If you see the following pair of messages, you've certainly lost one file and maybe two:

```
B:\FILE1.EXT
    Is cross linked on cluster nnn

B:\FILE2.EXT
    Is cross linked on cluster nnn
```

This means that, according to the file allocation table, two different files occupy the same cluster. When you enter CHKDSK with the /F parameter, DOS makes its best guess as to which file should have the common cluster and rewrites the other file so that the cluster is skipped. If either is a program file, copy it from the original diskette. If either is a data file, examine the file to make sure it's intact. If not, copy it from another disk if possible.

Checking for File Fragmentation

When DOS writes files to disk, it may need to *fragment* them, or break them up into several chains. This happens a great deal on a hard disk, where many files are updated frequently. Because it takes DOS longer to read fragmented files, your system may slow down considerably.

To find out how many files are not laid out contiguously and how many fragments they contain, use a command of the form

```
chkdsk [drive][\path\]filename.ext
```

Wild-card patterns are acceptable. Use the file name *.* to examine all files in a directory.

If the file is not laid out consecutively, CHKDSK displays a report of the form

```
C:\PATH\FILENAME.EXT
    Contains n non-contiguous blocks.
```

in addition to the standard report. If it is contiguous, you'll see the message

```
C:\PATH\FILENAME.EXT
    All specified files are contiguous.
```

This form of CHKDSK reports on only one subdirectory. To get a full report on your disk, you must repeat the command for each directory or use one of the disk-optimizing programs mentioned below.

What to do about fragmentation? If the disk is a diskette, copy all the files to a blank, formatted diskette. If it's a hard disk, the problem is more complicated. You can buy *disk-optimizing software* (such as PC-Kwik Power Disk, OpTUNE, the Norton Utilities, or PC Tools) and follow the directions carefully. If you don't want to spend the money, the only alternative is to back up the entire hard disk, format it, and restore it.

Backing Up Your Hard Disk

In Chapter 9 you learned some commands that you can use to back up a data directory: XCOPY and REPLACE. You have your original software diskettes and the backup copies the manual told you to make (don't you?). You might therefore assume that you'll be in good shape once you back up your data directories.

But what happens if something damages your hard disk's file allocation table? You won't be able to find many of your files. Of course, you can reformat your hard disk, reinstall all your software, reconfigure the software for your hardware, and then copy the data files from your backup diskettes. But wouldn't it be easier if you could complete the whole operation in one swell foop? (Yes, it would.)

Hard disks do fail. And diskettes sometimes become unreadable. It's easy to ignore this possibility until you have a crash. Then it's too late. Blessed are the pessimists, for they have made backups.

DOS includes two commands, BACKUP and RESTORE, for backing up hard disks and restoring the backed-up files. In this section you'll learn how to use these commands to make your backups relatively painless.

The BACKUP Command

The BACKUP and RESTORE commands are DOS's principal means for backing up hard disks. Both are external programs. BACKUP can back up all or part of the disk, depending on the switches you use, to diskettes or to another hard disk. (It can also back up one diskette to another.) However, you cannot use the files directly from the backup disk(s) because BACKUP condenses them into two files per backup disk. These files are called BACKUP.*NNN* and CONTROL.*NNN*, where *NNN* is the number of the backup medium (the number of a backup diskette in a series, for example).

This arrangement allows BACKUP to use all the available space on each backup diskette. It simply writes one diskette until it's full, then asks for another. If a file isn't completely backed up when a diskette becomes full, it is continued on the next diskette. BACKUP can thus copy files that won't fit on your most capacious diskette.

The basic form of the BACKUP command is

BACKUP *source target* [*/switches*]

As usual, the source can be any valid path name. (This means that you can back up anything from a single file to an entire hard disk.) You can specify the source using wild-card patterns and back up all matching files on the target. In this, BACKUP is as sophisticated as XCOPY. You can also back up only files whose archive attribute is set and have BACKUP clear the archive attribute.

✳ NOTE

In the following examples, it's assumed that you'll back up a hard disk designated C to diskettes in drive A. If you're backing up a different hard disk, or backing up to drive B, change the commands accordingly.

HINT

If you have two hard disks but only enough data to fill one, you can use the XCOPY command to make a complete working backup of one drive on the other. To make your first backup of, say, drive C to drive D, enter xcopy c:\ d:\ /s. *To keep the backup up-to-date, each day enter* xcopy c:\ d:\ /s /m. *This will copy only files whose archive attribute is set and clear the attribute so that they won't be copied again until they are modified.*

Examine the switches available for the BACKUP command in Table 10.1. Then I'll walk you through the procedure for a complete backup and a daily supplementary backup.

Note that the /T switch ignores the date. If you want to back up files created or modified after a certain date *and* time, you must specify both.

Quirks of the BACKUP Command

The BACKUP command has a few peculiarities of which you should be aware. First, unless you use the /A switch, it erases all files in the root directory. However, if there are sub-

Table 10.1 Switches for the BACKUP Command

Switch	*Effect*
/M (modified)	Backs up only files whose archive attribute is set, clearing the attribute afterwards.
/A (append)	Adds the files to the diskette. Normally BACKUP erases all files on the diskette before writing to it.
/D:*mm-dd-yy* (date)	Backs up files created or changed only on or after the specified date.
/T:*hh:mm*a/p (time)	Backs up files created or changed only at or after the specified time. Use the form displayed in directories: hours and minutes, followed by *a* for a.m. or *p* for p.m.
/L[:*path\filename.ext*] (log)	Creates a disk file containing a log of the backup. If you don't specify a file name, it will be called BACKUP.LOG and appear in the root directory of the source drive.
/F:*nnnn* (format)	Tells BACKUP to what capacity to format the target diskette if it isn't already formatted. Use as you would the /F switch for the FORMAT command.

directories on the target diskette, it leaves them alone. You can have a backup diskette whose root directory looks like Figure 10.2. Note the two files made by the program, BACKUP.001 and CONTROL.001, among the subdirectories. Also note how BACKUP changes the diskette's volume label.

Second, be aware of how BACKUP treats unformatted diskettes. If it finds one in the target drive, it calls the FORMAT command. If you don't specify the disk capacity, it will try to format the disk to the capacity of the drive. Therefore if you're not sure whether all your disks are already formatted, be sure to use the /F switch unless they match the drive's maximum capacity.

Third, if you back up to another hard disk, BACKUP will create a subdirectory of the root called BACKUP and place the backup files there.

! WARNING

Don't mix diskette capacities when backing up to diskettes. It will only cause trouble.

```
Volume in drive A is BACKUP   001
        Volume Serial Number is 095B-15F6
        Directory of A:\

NOTES        <DIR>      03-19-91    2:28p
STRUCTUR     <DIR>      03-19-91    3:01p
DOCUMENT     <DIR>      04-09-91    3:36p
BACKUP    001    164786 04-15-91    4:20p
SALES        <DIR>      05-23-91    2:29p
SOURCES      <DIR>      04-09-91    2:29p
MEMOS        <DIR>      04-09-91    2:30p
MISC         <DIR>      04-09-91    2:30p
DOWNLDS      <DIR>      05-23-91    2:42p
CONTROL   001      1031 04-15-91    4:20p
ICE          <DIR>      07-08-91    1:48p
REPORTS      <DIR>      09-12-91   12:31p
TABLES       <DIR>      09-12-91   12:30p
UPLOADS      <DIR>      04-09-91    2:31p
INDEX        <DIR>      03-19-91    2:31p
        15 file(s)     165817 bytes
                       178176 bytes free
```

Figure 10.2   Directory of a backup diskette containing subdirectories

✱ NOTE

You could, of course, use the JOIN command to back up everything to a single series. But if you do, you'll have to be sure that the same join is in effect when you restore files. Otherwise they won't end up in the right place. Better to work with the BACKUP command than try to overcome its limitations.

Finally, you can back up only one hard disk at a time. If you have several, you'll have to keep a separate backup series for each drive.

Making a Complete Backup

At best, backing up a hard disk is tedious. Before you begin you ought to do some housekeeping. First, run the Shell and scan your directories for old files you no longer need. Delete any with the extension BAK (except MIRROR.BAK, which you'll learn about later in this chapter). You may want to use XCOPY to copy directories of inactive data files to diskettes and delete them from your hard disk. You may also want to delete directories (and files in them) for programs you no longer use.

Next, run CHKDSK to make sure no lost clusters or cross-linked files are present (see earlier section, "Verifying Disk Integrity"). BACKUP will not operate properly if they are present.

Third, enter the command

```
dir c:\ /s
```

This will give you a complete directory of all files on your hard disk. Although you can ignore most of the on-screen information, take note of the last lines, which will read something like

```
Total files listed:
    1543 file(s)    20263890 bytes
                     11479040 bytes free
```

The number of bytes listed after the number of files is the amount of data you have to back up. Alternatively, use the Shell's Show Information box and subtract the number after Avail: from the number after SIZE:. Divide that number by 1024 to get the number of kilobytes. Divide the result by the capacity of the diskettes you plan to use, remembering that the diskette's data capacity is somewhat less than its total capacity. (A 360K diskette holds 354K of data; the remainder is occupied by the DOS reserved area.) The result is the number of diskettes you'll need. Gather them and label them with the drive name, consecutive numbers, and today's date; for example:

```
Backup C1 7/13/91
```

You are now ready to begin.

To begin your backup, enter

```
backup c:\ a: /s /l
```

The /S switch tells BACKUP to back up subdirectories as well as the current directory. The /L switch tells it to create the BACKUP.LOG file in the root directory. You'll find this very useful when you restore your disk. You'll see a message such as the one in Figure 10.3.

Insert your diskette labeled C1 in drive A and press a key. If it's formatted, you'll quickly see the message

```
*** Backing up files to drive A: ***
Diskette Number: 01
```

HINT

To find out the true storage capacity of a diskette in kilobytes, format it (with the /Q option if you like), read the total disk space, and divide by 1024.

```
C:\>backup c:\ a: /s /l

Insert backup diskette 01 in drive A:

WARNING! Files in the target drive
A:\ root directory will be erased
Press any key to continue...
```

Figure 10.3 Beginning a full backup

If it's not, you'll see all the messages associated with the FORMAT command, and you'll have to wait while the disk is formatted. As soon as the format is complete, the screen displays the names of the files being backed up, as shown in Figure 10.4. You will be prompted for the next diskette as each one becomes full. As you might have guessed from Figure 10.2, the volume label and file extensions all reflect the position of the diskette in the backup series.

When a file has been backed up, its archive attribute is cleared. You can then arrange for BACKUP to skip it the next time you back up the disk.

If this is the first time you've ever backed up your hard disk, repeat the procedure on a second series of diskettes. There may be a bad sector on one diskette, or one may mysteriously appear after the backup. If this happens to

```
Logging to file C:\BACKUP.LOG

\ART\ROLEX.SCR
\ART\CONFETTI.SCR
\ART\EYE.EXE
\ART\ROLEX.COM
\ART\CONFETTI.COM
\ART\SQUARES.EXE
\ART\SATURN.EXE
\ART\PCX\BOX.PCX
\ART\PCX\CAMERA.PCX
\ART\PCX\DISH.PCX
\ART\PCX\DIVER.PCX
\ART\PCX\FISH.PCX
\ART\PCX\BYTE.PCX
\ART\PCX\CIRCLES.PCX
\ART\PCX\DISKETTE.PCX
\ART\PCX\EAGLE.PCX
\ART\PCX\INSTR.PCX
\ART\PCX\INTRO.PCX
```

Figure 10.4   A backup in progress

your only backup of a vital file and your hard disk crashes, you'll have lost the file forever.

You should do a complete backup once a month—more often if you use your computer intensively. The next time you do one, reuse *one* of your two backup series. Alternate between the series for successive backups. Thus you will always have two generations of complete backups. You may find this useful if an error is introduced to a file at some time between the two backups.

The Daily Backup

Backing up a hard disk with the BACKUP command can be tedious. At best, it takes about 2½ minutes to back up each megabyte of data on a fast 80306 computer. It can take longer with a slower computer or with unformatted diskettes. However, once it is done, you can use the switches to set up a system whereby you back up only the previous day's files.

First you must decide whether to add your daily backups to your full backup or keep them in a separate series. Barring compelling reasons to the contrary, it's better to start a new series. You will probably change the same files regularly over a period of days. And you probably don't need twelve or more iterations of each file. That being so, you can alternate between two sets of diskettes for your daily backups, just as you do for your monthly complete backups. Just start a new series each Monday, using the diskettes from two weeks earlier. You will still have from one to two weeks' worth of file copies on hand at all times.

Again, begin by numbering a series of diskettes. To find out how many you'll need, enter

```
dir c:\ /aa /s
```

and read the next-to-last line. This command will produce a directory of all files on the disk whose archive attribute is set. Multiply the number on that line by 5 to get a

HINT

There are commercially available software packages that can back up your hard disk more quickly, using fewer diskettes. They also give you a great deal more control over exactly what gets backed up and when. Examples include Central Point Backup, Fastback Plus, and Norton Backup.

guesstimate for a week's supply. Label them Daily Backup Series #1 or #2 and number them sequentially.

To begin a new series of daily backups, enter

```
backup c:\ a: /s /m
```

This command scans the entire disk but copies only modified files (those whose archive attribute is set). In the process it clears the archive attribute.

The next day alter the command to

```
backup c:\ a: /s /m /a
```

The /A switch tells BACKUP to *add* the new files to the previous diskette. (This is also the command for appending the daily backup to the complete backup.) You'll be prompted to

```
Insert last backup diskette in drive A:
Press any key to continue...
```

HINT

As noted, you can enter a single directory, or a file name with wild-card characters, as the backup source. This is especially useful for backing up all files of a given type. To back up pictorial files with the extension .PCX, for example, you could enter backup c:*.pcx a: /s.

Use the last diskette you used the previous day. Note that you aren't warned about losing all the files in the root directory because it is adding to that directory. When a diskette fills, BACKUP will prompt you for the appropriately numbered diskette.

The Log File

As noted, BACKUP can create a log file that tells you what's backed up on which diskette. This is extremely handy when you restore files. However, if you're using several backup series, as suggested here, you should add a file name to the /L switch so you know what's in each. You may want to create a special directory called BACKUP and have all your log files placed there. Thus you might enter

```
backup c:\ a: /s /l:c:\backup\c-all1.log
```

when you do your first full backup. If you have a drive D, replace the C in the file name with D. For your second full backup, replace the 1 with a 2.

If you use the default file name and location, when you continue a backup series on existing diskettes, BACKUP appends information on additional files to the existing log. It does the same if you give it a specific file name. Each day's backup will be preceded by the time and date.

Figure 10.5 shows a sample portion of a daily backup log. As you can see, each day's entry begins with the date and time. Each line begins with the diskette number and contains a file's complete path name (minus the drive name). The ellipses show how a large file can be divided across diskettes. At the end you can see the beginning of the next day's backup. (Unfortunately the log doesn't show exactly what command you issued to select the files. That's why you may want to make separate backup series, each with its own log file, for different purposes.)

 HINT

Include the source drive name as part of the file name if you have more than one hard disk, because the log file itself doesn't.

 HINT

Copy your log files to a diskette or print them out as described in Chapter 15. If something goes wrong with your hard disk, you'll lose your backup log along with everything else.

Backing Up Data Files Only

Backing up software and backing up data may involve different strategies. Generally your software does not change often, but data files do. One way to back up just your data is to issue a series of backup commands, each of which selects a specific directory or extension used for data files. You can continue these backups on a single series of diskettes. You might, for example, issue the commands

```
backup c:\*.ltr a: /s /m /a /l:c:\backup\datafile.log
backup c:\newproj\*.* a: /s /m /a /l:c:\backup\datafile.log
backup c:\*.db? a: /s /m /a /l:c:\backup\datafile.log
```

```
4-15-1991   16:30:59
001   \ART\ROLEX.SCR
001   \ART\CONFETTI.SCR
001   \ART\EYE.EXE
001   \ART\ROLEX.COM
001   \ART\CONFETTI.COM
001   \ART\SQUARES.EXE
  ■
  ■
  ■
002   \ART\PCX\TEST.PCX
002   \ART\PCX\SCAN3.PCX
003   \ART\PCX\SCAN3.PCX
003   \ART\PCX\SCANPLUS.PCX
004   \ART\PCX\SCANPLUS.PCX
004   \ART\PCX\SIGNATUR.PCX
  ■
  ■
  ■
005   \ART\PICTURES\LIBRARY\UTILITY\PHONE.GEM
005   \ART\PICTURES\LIBRARY\UTILITY\POWRPLNT.GEM
005   \ART\PICTURES\LIBRARY\UTILITY\TOOLS.GEM
4-16-1991   15:40:27
005   \BOOK\CH12
  ■
  ■
  ■
```

Figure 10.5   A sample portion of a backup log file

In Chapter 13 you'll learn how to construct a batch file to do all this for you.

Backing Up Using the Shell

As you may remember, one program in the Disk Utilities group in the Shell's program group window was Backup Fixed Disk. (*Fixed disk* is another name for hard disk.) If you select this, you'll see the dialog box in Figure 10.6. The default parameters in the entry line back up all of drive C to

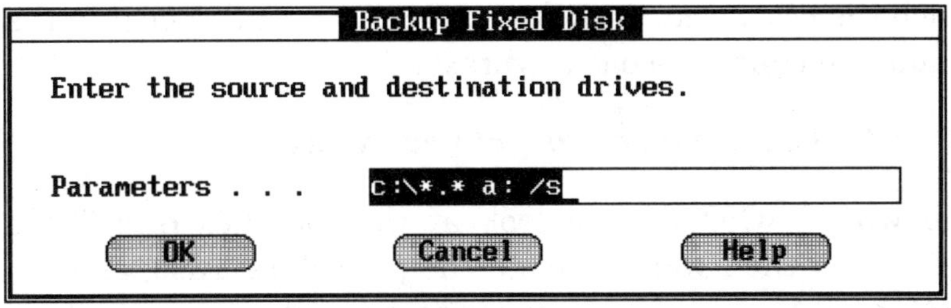

```
┌──────────────■ Backup Fixed Disk ■────────────────┐
│                                                    │
│  Enter the source and destination drives.          │
│                                                    │
│                                                    │
│  Parameters . . .    c:\*.* a: /s                   │
│    ( OK )          ( Cancel )         ( Help )      │
│                                                    │
└────────────────────────────────────────────────────┘
```

Figure 10.6   The Backup Fixed Disk dialog box

drive A without a log file. You can enter other parameters in addition to, or in place of, those in the entry line. You can also modify the Shell so that other parameters appear by default, or indeed, so that you can choose from several options. You'll learn how to make those changes in Chapter 14.

Once you enter the parameters and select OK, the BACKUP command is invoked and runs exactly as it does at the prompt.

Restoring Your Hard Disk

As with backing up, there are two choices for restoring your hard disk. You can restore the entire disk or you can restore one or several files. You'll want to restore the entire disk when:

- You've formatted it to get rid of file fragmentation
- You've formatted it to correct some damage to the boot sector, file allocation table, or root directory that CHKDSK can't fix
- You're replacing an old hard disk with a new one

You'll most likely want to restore only selected files either when CHKDSK reports damage or when you've done some editing that has left your work hopelessly mangled.

You restore all or selected files from your backup diskettes using the RESTORE command. The CONTROL file created by BACKUP shows the subdirectory from which each file was backed up. Thus RESTORE can place it in the same directory. The basic syntax is

RESTORE *source target* **[/*switches*]**

As with BACKUP, we'll look at the switches (see Table 10.2) and then walk through the procedure. Also, as with BACKUP, the date and time switches are independent, so you'll probably want to combine them.

Restoring a Complete Hard Disk

To restore a complete hard disk, start by getting out your Emergency Recovery Disk, which you made in Chapter 5. You'll need it to complete the operation.

One peculiarity of the RESTORE command is that it won't restore the three DOS files IO.SYS, MSDOS.SYS, and COMMAND.COM. There's a good reason for this. You may have backed up and reformatted your hard disk to upgrade to a new DOS version. If so, you won't want to restore the system files from the earlier version. Therefore if you're restoring the hard disk from which you started your com-

Table 10.2 Switches for the RESTORE Command

Switch	Effect
/S (subdirectories)	Restores files to subdirectories of the specified target. Use when you want to restore an entire hard disk.
/A:*mm-dd-yy* (after)	Restores files created or modified on or after the specified date.
/B:*mm-dd-yy* (before)	Restores files created or modified on or before the specified date.
/E:*hh:mm*a/p (earlier)	Restores files created or modified at or earlier than the specified time.
/L:*hh:mm*a/p (later)	Restores files created or modified at or later than the specified time.
/M (modified)	Restores only those files that have been modified since the last backup, replacing later versions with earlier ones.
/N (not)	Restores files that no longer exist on the destination disk.
/P (prompt)	Prompts you for permission to restore when the target file is read-only.

puter, you should first use the SYS command to transfer the DOS 5 operating system files to it, as explained in Chapter 5. You'll find the SYS command on your Emergency Recovery Disk.

If your disk is newly formatted, you won't have the RESTORE program file on it, so you'll have to run it from a diskette. This too is on the Emergency Recovery Disk.

To restore your complete hard disk, make drive A current and enter

```
restore a: c: /s
```

You'll see the message

```
Insert backup diskette 01 in drive A:
Press any key to continue...
```

! WARNING

The root directory of the target drive must be its current directory or the RESTORE command won't work.

This gives you the chance to replace the Emergency Recovery Disk in the drive with the first diskette of your most recent backup series. (If something has gone wrong recently, you may prefer a previous backup series.)

DOS will show you the path name of each file being restored and prompt you to insert the next diskette as each diskette is completed. If the paths no longer exist on the target, RESTORE will create them.

When you've finished, repeat the procedure using your daily backup series. If you have two current ones, use both. Then you'll have restored the current versions of your recent data files, as well as all those in your complete backup.

Restoring Selected Files

Suppose you have deleted a large chunk of a file while editing it and you can't get it back. Or suppose you have saved a file with the same name as another important file, thereby destroying the file that originally had the name.

In these circumstances you'll probably want to restore the missing or damaged file from an earlier copy.

Here's where your backup logs will come in handy. Search them to find out which diskette contains the file. Place that diskette in drive A and enter the RESTORE command, giving the file's complete path name as its target. You'll be asked for diskette 01 and told that what you've entered is out of sequence, but don't worry about it. Figure 10.7 shows the message given when a single file was restored from diskette 04.

 HINT

You may want to search all your logs to make sure you have the most recent iteration of the file. If you haven't modified it since the complete backup, it will appear only there. If you have, it may appear several times. Since RESTORE updates the log each time you use it (if you give it a log file name) and marks each new backup with the date and time, you can easily find the most recent copy.

```
C:\>restore a: c:\art\pcx\signatur.pcx

   Insert backup diskette 01 in drive A:
   Press any key to continue . . .

   *** Files were backed up 04-15-1991 ***

   WARNING! Diskette is out of sequence
   Replace diskette or continue if OK
   Press any key to continue . . .

   *** Restoring files from drive A: ***
   Diskette: 04
   \ART\PCX\SIGNATUR.PCX

   C:>_
```

Figure 10.7   Restoring a single file

You may also need to restore a group of files. The
RESTORE switches let you select the group, using very
precise criteria. You can select all files in a directory by
using the directory path name plus the wild-card pattern
.. Or you can select all files created within a range of dates
by using both the /B and /A switches. Suppose, for example,
you have deleted a group of files in a data directory pertaining to a completed project since your full backup. Now you
need to refer to those files again. Use a command such as

```
restore a: c:\newproj\*.* /a:2/25/91
/b:6/20/91 /n
```

Your file names won't have to match a wild-card pattern,
and the /N switch will avoid overwriting the current files.
The dates in the switches will select only files created during the specified period.

Restoring Using the Shell

One of the programs in the Disk Utilities group in the
Shell's program group window is Restore Fixed Disk. If
you select this, you'll get the dialog box in Figure 10.8. As
you can see, no parameters are given; you must enter the
source and target yourself. You can also modify the Shell so
that parameters appear by default, or indeed, so that you
can choose from several options. You'll learn how to make
those changes in Chapter 14.

Figure 10.8   The Restore Fixed Disk dialog box

Once you have entered the parameters and selected OK, the RESTORE command runs exactly as it does at the prompt.

Protecting Yourself Against Unfortunate Formats and Deletions

As you already know, when you format a hard disk you don't actually erase it. DOS merely rewrites the reserved area. The files are still on the disk, but all names (including directory names) are erased from the root directory.

Similarly DOS doesn't erase the data in a file when you issue the DEL or ERASE command. It just makes the file name invisible in the directory and deallocates its storage clusters. When you write a new file, however, it *may* use the directory space formerly occupied by the old file's name. If your disk is especially full, it may also use the deleted file's clusters.

However, if there is room to spare on your hard disk and you haven't overwritten the file name, DOS 5 makes it relatively easy to get back an erased file. Similarly, it allows you to undo a FORMAT command (as you learned in Chapter 5) by saving a copy of the DOS reserved area before completing a format.

Saving Format and Deleted-File Information

✔ **NEW FEATURE**
Saving unformat information

You can give DOS some assistance in retrieving erased files by executing a program called MIRROR. The basic syntax is

MIRROR [*drive*]

Enter this command at the command prompt or from the Shell's Run command. If you don't specify a drive, MIRROR acts on the current drive. When you execute MIRROR, it creates a copy of the DOS reserved area in a file called

MIRROR.FIL. The next time you run the program, it renames this file MIRROR.BAK and creates a new MIRROR.FIL. It also creates a hidden, system, read-only file called MIRORSAV.FIL. This file gets written to the very last disk cluster and contains the location of MIRROR.FIL, so DOS can find it on a disk that's been formatted.

You can *undelete* files easily if you haven't written anything else to the disk—and again, you can extend this ability by giving DOS some help. For this you must *install* the MIRROR program. Enter

```
mirror /td
```

where *d* is the letter of drive you want to protect. You can protect several at once by entering them all on the command line:

```
mirror /tc /td /te
```

This places the MIRROR program in your computer's memory, where it stays until you reboot. Every time you run MIRROR, it writes to a system file called PCTRACKR.DEL. This file records all the files you've deleted and their locations. The more often you run MIRROR, the better your chances of recovering a deleted file. In Chapters 12 and 14, you'll learn ways to install MIRROR automatically and run it automatically when you return from your application programs to the prompt or the Shell.

Recovering from a Format

To recover from a format, use the UNFORMAT command, which you've placed on your Emergency Recovery Disk. This command works on diskettes that you have quick-formatted as well as on hard disks. Tell it which drive to unformat and wait while it searches for current or old copies of MIRROR.FIL and MIRROR.BAK. When it finds them, it asks which copy you want to use. As a rule, you should use the most recent. You may prefer to use an earlier one if you

✔**NEW FEATURE**
Undoing a format

```
A:\>unformat d:

Restores the system area of your disk by using the image file created
by the MIRROR command.

    WARNING !!        WARNING !!

This command should be used only to recover from the inadvertent use of
the FORMAT command or the RECOVER command.  Any other use of the UNFORMAT
command may cause you to lose data!  Files modified since the MIRROR image
file was created may be lost.

Searching disk for MIRROR image.

The last time the MIRROR or FORMAT command was used was at 12:24 on 04-17-91.
The prior time the MIRROR or FORMAT command was used was at 11:42 on 04-17-91

If you wish to use the last file as indicated
above, press L.  If you wish to use the prior
file as indicated above, press P.  Press ESC
to cancel UNFORMAT.
l

The MIRROR image file has been validated.

Are you sure you want to update the system area of your drive A (Y/N)? y

The system area of drive D has been rebuilt.

You may need to restart the system.

A:\>_
```

Figure 10.9   Unformatting a disk

suspect something has gone wrong with your file allocation table before the last time you ran MIRROR. Select a copy of the file and follow the prompts, as shown in Figure 10.9.

Undeleting Files

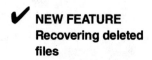
NEW FEATURE
Recovering deleted files

As noted, you have the best chance of undeleting a file if you have not written anything else to the disk since the deletion. And your chances of success are increased if MIRROR is installed and you use it frequently. But it's not impossible to undelete files under other circumstances.

Just enter the UNDELETE command, optionally followed by a file name or wild-card pattern. You can enter this command at a prompt or using the Shell's Run command. (You may also include a drive and path name to recover files not in the current directory.) If you don't enter a file name, UNDELETE assumes you've entered *.*. The program searches through both PCTRACKR.DEL and the directory you named.

UNDELETE presents you with each matching file name that has at least some available clusters and asks whether you want to undelete it. If you answer Y, it proceeds automatically unless another copy of the undeleted file with the same name exists in the directory. As you can see from Figure 10.10, this is quite possible. Choosing which version to recover is pretty much a matter of trial and error. After you choose, you'll be asked for a new name.

Once you've recovered the file, press Ctrl-Break to end the UNDELETE process.

Recovering Part of a Damaged File

Sometimes a bad sector develops after you've formatted a disk. DOS won't know about the sector and may write a file to it. Or a sector may go bad after you've written a file to it. When you attempt to access the file, DOS gives you the message

```
Data error reading drive d:
Abort, Retry, Fail?
```

Press R for Retry several times. You may get lucky. If you do, rewrite the file to another drive.

 HINT

If you see the "Data error" message when you have entered a command line specifying both a program and a file name parameter, either could be the file containing the bad sector. To find out, reenter the program name with a different parameter. If you still see the message, it's the program. If not, it's the data file.

```
D:\BOOK>undelete

Directory: D:\BOOK
File Specifications: *.*

    Deletion-tracking file contains  187 deleted files.
    Of those,  130 files have all clusters available,
               22 files have some clusters available,
               35 files have no clusters available.

    MS-DOS directory contains    7 deleted files.
    Of those,   3 files may be recovered.

Using the deletion-tracking file.

     CH10      $G$      512  4-17-91   1:15p
...A  Deleted:  4-17-91   1:15p
All of the clusters for this file are available. Undelete (Y/N)?n
     CH10      BAK    50944  4-17-91   1:13p
...A  Deleted:  4-17-91   1:15p
All of the clusters for this file are available. Undelete (Y/N)?n
     CH10      BAK    46464  4-17-91  12:51p
...A  Deleted:  4-17-91   1:06p
All of the clusters for this file are available. Undelete (Y/N)?n
     CH10      BAK    45312  4-17-91  12:44p
...A  Deleted:  4-17-91  12:51p
All of the clusters for this file are available. Undelete (Y/N)?y

The filename already exists. Type a different filename.
Press F5 to bypass this file.
temp.bak

     TEMP      BAK    45312  4-17-91  12:44p
...A  Deleted:  4-17-91  12:51p

File successfully undeleted.
     CH10      BAK    50944  4-17-91  12:23p
...A  Deleted:  4-17-91   1:15p
All of the clusters for this file are available. Undelete (Y/N)?^C

D:\BOOK>_
```

Figure 10.10   Undeleting files

Whether or not you get lucky, the next step is to use the RECOVER command. Enter

```
recover filename.ext
```

where *filename.ext* is the name of the unreadable file. You can enter this command at a prompt or using the Shell's Run command. This command will read the file from the beginning, skip over the bad sector(s), and continue reading until it reaches the end. It then writes all the readable parts to a file called FILE0000.CHK, which it places in the root directory. When it's finished, it erases the original file and marks the bad sectors in the file allocation table, so they won't be used again.

❗ WARNING

Always *use a file name with the RECOVER command. If you don't, it will rewrite all the files on the disk, giving each a different number. You'll have the Devil's own time unscrambling that mess!*

If the damaged file is a program file, copy it from its original source or a backup diskette. If it's a data file and you don't have another copy, try to load it into the program you created it with and piece it together. If it's a text file, it's possible you'll have lost only a few pages.

A Word to the Wise

Back up all your files frequently.

Using the DOS Editor

Chapter 11

What You Will Learn

- How to start the DOS Editor
- How to use the Editor menus and command keys
- How to enter and edit text
- How to load and save files

What Is the DOS Editor?

✔ NEW FEATURE
DOS Editor

The DOS Editor is new in DOS 5. It is essentially a programmer's editor, not a word processor. (In fact it's included as part of the QuickBASIC program language, also a new feature in DOS 5.)

Although you don't get the sophisticated text- and page-formatting features you expect in a word processor, the Editor is in fact quite powerful. It gives you everything you need for editing configuration and batch files. You can also use it to edit any other file that uses unformatted text: text files for displaying on the screen, files to be sent via a fax board, and the like.

✱ NOTE

Previous versions of DOS included a line editor called EDLIN. It's still included in DOS 5 for those who prefer it. But it's hard to learn and hard to use compared to the DOS Editor.

✳ NOTE

In the next two chapters, you'll need an editor to customize the configuration files and to create batch files. If you have an editor or word processor you like that can create files in ASCII or nondocument mode, you can safely skip this chapter.

What the Editor Can Do

The DOS Editor is a full-ASCII editor. This means you can enter virtually any character in your computer's set of 256, not just those you can type at the keyboard. You can enter all the control characters (except Ctrl-@, Ctrl-J, Ctrl-M, and Ctrl-N) and see their graphic symbols in the Editor window. You enter most control characters by pressing Ctrl-P, then the control-key combination. If this doesn't work, you can enter any control character except the four mentioned by holding down the Alt and Shift keys and typing the character's ASCII code on the numeric keypad. This is also how you enter the extended ASCII characters.

✳ NOTE

ASCII is an acronym for American Standard Code for Information Interchange, an agreed-upon set of computer symbols (a character set). There are three parts to the character set. The first two, 95 keyboard characters and 32 control characters, make up the standard ASCII character set. Control characters are special characters that usually have some effect on your hardware, but are also represented by graphic symbols. In addition, your computer has 128 extended ASCII characters. These include foreign-language characters, mathematical symbols, and characters for creating boxes and borders around text on the screen.

The most important difference between a programmer's editor and a word processor is that lines don't "wrap" at the right-hand edge of the screen. You can type up to 255 characters on a line before you must press Enter. Text will continue on the line until you do. Thus if you type a long line, you won't be able to see all of it on the screen. In contrast, word-processing programs arrange text to fit established screen page margins, and you press Enter only to start a new paragraph.

The fact that lines *don't* wrap is a very important feature. Many programming languages—including the one built into DOS—regard the text on a single line as a command to be executed. If text wrapped automatically, your files would become unintelligible to the command interpreter.

The Editor has an *auto-indent* feature. This means that if you indent a line by pressing Tab, the following line will have the same indentation. This feature is useful for indenting code segments to indicate their structure. (But in this book you won't use indentation at all.)

The Editor has several small menus, which appear in Figure 11.1. As with the Shell menus, you can select a command by pressing Alt plus the first letter of its name on the menu bar, followed by the highlighted key within the menu. You can click on the menu bar then on a command in the menu that appears. However, you can perform many operations directly with the keyboard or mouse. A status line at the bottom of the screen displays a list of keys you can use to get help, display menus, or proceed with whatever you're doing. If a key name appears in angle brackets—for example, <Esc>—you can activate the command associated with the key by clicking on the key name with the left mouse button.

If you are familiar with WordStar or any editor or word processor that uses WordStar commands, you'll have little trouble learning the keyboard commands. Many WordStar commands, especially those for moving the cursor, work in the Editor.

※ NOTE

Programs that use WordStar commands include SideKick, Side-Kick Plus, early versions of PC Tools, the 1Word editor in the XTree programs, VDE, ThinkTank, GrandView, PC-Outline, and the editors in virtually all programming languages published by Microsoft and Borland. However, the DOS Editor doesn't use WordStar commands for marking blocks of text. You'll need to learn the DOS Editor commands for doing this or use the mouse

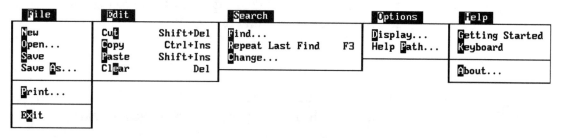

Figure 11.1   The Editor menus

and menus, which you may well find more efficient. But even if you don't know WordStar, the DOS Editor is easy to learn and use.

If you're familiar with almost any other Microsoft program or any program for the Macintosh computer, you'll find the mouse operations familiar.

In this chapter we'll use the Editor to create and edit a list. Since you can easily learn everything you need to know about the Editor by studying Table 11.1 (see the next section) or the Survival Guide (which appears automatically when you load the Editor), this chapter just gives you a brief overview.

Entering and Editing Text

In this exercise we'll create a brief outline of a plan to upgrade your company's computers to DOS 5. To begin, bring up the Editor. If you're at a command prompt, enter

```
edit
```

If you're in the Shell, select Editor from the program group window. If you've used the Editor before, the name of the last file you edited appears in the entry line. If not, the file selected in the file window appears there. Clear the entry line by pressing the space bar. When the Editor appears on your screen, press Escape to get rid of the opening message and reach the editing screen.

To enter text, just start typing at the *text cursor,* a flashing underscore. Enter the text in Figure 11.2. It's OK if you make some mistakes—it's easy to correct them. Be sure to press Enter at the end of each line.

Getting Around

Once you've entered the text, you'll need to get around in the window to edit it, using the mouse or the keyboard.

☐ **MOUSE**

The mouse cursor appears as a rectangle. To move around the window, just click the mouse where you want

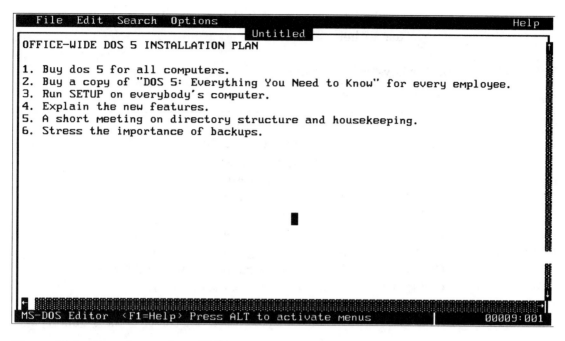

File   Edit   Search   Options   Help
                                    Untitled
OFFICE-WIDE DOS 5 INSTALLATION PLAN

1. Buy dos 5 for all computers.
2. Buy a copy of "DOS 5: Everything You Need to Know" for every employee.
3. Run SETUP on everybody's computer.
4. Explain the new features.
5. A short meeting on directory structure and housekeeping.
6. Stress the importance of backups.

MS-DOS Editor   <F1=Help> Press ALT to activate menus   00009:001

Figure 11.2   Sample text for a file

to enter or change text. If the text isn't visible, use the scroll bars at the right and bottom edges of the window to move through the file. Hold down the left mouse button on the arrows at the ends to move a line at a time up or down, or a character at a time left or right.

Clicking the left button at a point on the horizontal scroll bar moves the cursor to the corresponding position on the text line. Click on the square next to the ← or → to move to the beginning or end of the line, respectively. Clicking the left button on the vertical scroll bar moves to the corresponding position in the file. To move to the end of the file, click on the square just above the ↓. To move to the beginning, click on the square just below the ↑.

The first part of Table 11.1 lists the cursor keys. ■ **KEYBOARD** Although you can move through the file using the four arrow keys alone, practice with the ones that move a word or a page at a time. You'll find them much more efficient. When the table shows both a cursor key (or cursor-key combination) and a WordStar Ctrl-key sequence, you can use either.

Table 11.1 DOS Editor keystroke commands

Cursor Key	WordStar Key	Effect
		Moving the Cursor
←	Ctrl-S	Moves left one character
→	Ctrl-D	Moves right one character
Ctrl-←	Ctrl-A	Moves left one word
Ctrl-→	Ctrl-F	Moves right one word
↑	Ctrl-E	Moves up one line
↓	Ctrl-X	Moves down one line
Ctrl-Enter		Moves to the beginning of the next line
	Ctrl-Q S	Moves to the beginning of the current line
End	Ctrl-Q D	Moves to the end of the current line
Home		Moves to the beginning of text on the current line; if the line is blank, moves the cursor to the beginning of the line
	Ctrl-Q E	Moves to the top of the window
	Ctrl-Q X	Moves to the bottom of the window
Ctrl-Home	Ctrl-Q R	Moves to the beginning of the file
Ctrl-End	Ctrl-Q C	Moves to the end of the file
		Scrolling Text in the Window
Ctrl-↑	Ctrl-W	Scrolls up one line
Ctrl-↓	Ctrl-Z	Scrolls down one line
PgUp	Ctrl-R	Scrolls to the previous screen
PgDn	Ctrl-C	Scrolls to the next screen
Ctrl-PgUp		Scrolls left one screen
Ctrl-PgDn		Scrolls right one screen
		Selecting Text
Shift-←		Selects the character to the left of the cursor, up to the beginning of the line
Shift-→		Selects the character to the right of the cursor, up to the end of the line
Shift-↑		If at the beginning of a line, selects the line above the current line; otherwise selects the current line and the line above it
Shift-↓		If at the beginning of a line, selects the line below the current line; otherwise selects the current line and the line below it

Shift-Ctrl-←		Selects the word to the left of the cursor; if at the beginning of a line, selects the line above the current line
Shift-Ctrl-→		Selects the word to the right of the cursor; at the end of a line, selects the line below the current line
Shift-Home		Selects to the beginning of the line
Shift-End		Selects to the end of the line
Shift-PgUp		Selects the current line and one screen above it
Shift-PgDn		Selects the current line and one screen below it; scrolls the selection beyond top of the screen, so you can't see what's selected
Shift-Ctrl-Home		Selects from the current line to the beginning of the file
Shift-Ctrl-End		Selects from the current line to the end of the file
Escape		Cancels selection

Copying Text

Ctrl-Ins		Copies selected text to the clipboard
Shift-Del		Copies selected text to the clipboard and deletes it from the file
	Ctrl-Y	Copies the current line to the clipboard and deletes it from the file
	Ctrl-Q Y	Deletes text from the cursor to the end of the line; copies it to the clipboard
Shift-Ins		Pastes the contents of the clipboard into the file at the cursor position

Deleting Text

Del	Ctrl-G	Deletes the character at the cursor; deletes selected text
Backspace	Ctrl-H	Deletes the character to the left of the cursor
	Ctrl-Y	Deletes the current line; saves the deleted text on the clipboard
	Ctrl-Q Y	Deletes from the cursor to the end of the line; saves the deleted text on the clipboard
	Ctrl-T	Deletes the portion of a word to the right of the cursor
Shift-Tab		Deletes leading spaces from all lines in a selected block
Ctrl-Del		Deletes selected text and saves it on the clipboard

Searching and Replacing

	Ctrl-Q F	Finds specified text
	Ctrl-Q A	Finds specified text and replaces it with new specified text

continued

F3	Ctrl-L	Finds the next instance of the last text specified for a find or replace operation
	Other Keys	
Ins	Ctrl-V	Toggles between insert and overtype mode
End Enter		Inserts a line below the current line
	Ctrl-N	Inserts a carriage-return character (inserts a line at the left edge of the screen; otherwise breaks the line)
	Ctrl-K *n*	Inserts a place marker, where *n* is a number from 0 to 3
	Ctrl-Q *n*	Goes to place marker *n*, where *n* is a number from 0 to 3
	Ctrl-P	Allows entry of a control character in the file; press the Ctrl-key combination after pressing Ctrl-P
F6		Switches between the help and editing windows

Changing Text

By default the Editor is in *insert mode*. This means that if you enter a character in an existing line, the characters to the right of the cursor will move to the right. To change a single character, you can proceed in two ways. You can enter the new character and then delete the old one. Or you can switch to *overtype mode* by pressing Ins or Ctrl-V and typing the new character to replace the old one.

Let's change the word SETUP so that it has only an initial capital. Move to the beginning of the word and press Ins. You'll see the cursor change from an underscore to a flashing rectangle. Type

```
Setup
```

and press Ins again when you're done.

Now let's change the word *every* in line 2 to *each*. This time we'll do it by deleting the word.

☐ **MOUSE**

Click at the beginning of the word. Hold down the left button and drag the mouse to the right. You'll see a highlight extend across the word, showing that it's *selected*. Many operations require you to select text. When the highlight covers the entire word and nothing else, release the mouse

button. Press Del. Type

```
each
```

Move the cursor to the beginning of the word. Press
Ctrl-T to delete it. Type ■ **KEYBOARD**

```
each
```

Saving Your Work

Before you go any further, you should save your file. Select
the Save command from the File menu. You'll see the dialog
box in Figure 11.3. This box (as well as others in the Editor)
has a method of choosing options not found in the Shell. If
you press and release Alt, one letter in the name of each
option becomes highlighted. You can then choose an option
by pressing Alt again plus the highlighted letter. Or you can
just hold down the Alt key and then press the highlighted
letter of the option you want.

Note that you can save your file to any drive or directory
by going into the box listing the drives and the directories on
the current drive, scrolling until you see the one you want,
and selecting it by pressing Enter or clicking on it with the
mouse. Scroll by pressing ↑ and ↓ or by holding down the left
mouse button over an arrow on the scroll bar. If you select a
drive or directory from the window, it will appear in the entry

Figure 11.3   The Save dialog box

line, followed by * .. Backspace to erase this name, and type

```
install.txt
```

When you've entered the file name, either click on OK or press Enter.

Notice that the file name now appears at the top of the window, where Untitled formerly appeared. The next time you save your file, it will keep this name. To change it, select the Save As command from the File menu. You'll see the dialog box again, with the current name on the entry line. If you enter a different name, you'll have two copies of the file.

Working with Blocks of Text

To edit more than a few characters—to rearrange lines, for example—you use *block operations*. You select text to be copied, deleted, or moved (with the keyboard or mouse). As you already saw when you marked a word for deletion, selected text is highlighted in inverse video. You then select the appropriate command from the Edit menu (or type its keystroke equivalent). The portion of Table 11.1 called "Selecting Text" lists the keys you can use to select text, and the portions called "Copying Text" and "Deleting Text" tell which keys—in addition to those on the menu—you can use to copy, delete, or move text.

To understand block operations, you have to understand the difference between *cutting, copying,* and *deleting*. When you delete text, it is gone; you can't get it back. When you cut text, it disappears from your file but is stored temporarily in an area of memory called a *clipboard*. You can *paste* what's on the clipboard into your file. When you copy text, it remains in your file but appears on the clipboard as well. The clipboard, however, holds only the text that you cut or copied most recently.

Let's try some of these techniques now.

Click on the letter *A* after the numeral 5. Hold down the   ☐ **MOUSE**
left button and drag the mouse to the right until

```
A short meeting
```

is highlighted. Then release the button. Click on Edit to
pull down the Edit menu, then on Cut. The selected text will
disappear from the screen.

Move the cursor to the letter A̲ after the numeral 5.   ■ **KEYBOARD**
Press Shift-Ctrl-→ three times to select the words

```
A short meeting
```

Now you can either press Alt-E T to use the Cut command
on the Edit menu or press Shift-Del, the shortcut key. The
selected text will disappear from the screen.

Now move your cursor to the numeral 3. Press Ctrl-N to
create a blank line. Here you'll paste the text you've just cut.

Click on the Edit menu, then on Paste. The text   ☐ **MOUSE**
appears following the cursor.

Press Alt-E P to activate the Paste command from the   ■ **KEYBOARD**
Edit menu or press Shift-Ins. The text appears following the
cursor.

Press → once, and enter

```
genda for a
```

You've just decided that with the help of this book and the
relatively straightforward Setup program, your staff can do
their own installation.

Now let's try copying. Move the cursor to the word
Explain.

Select the word by holding down the left mouse button   ☐ **MOUSE**
and dragging across it. Now click on Edit, then on Copy.

■ **KEYBOARD**

Select the word by pressing Shift-Ctrl-→. Now press Alt-E C to select the Copy command, or use the shortcut key Ctrl-Ins. Now move to the line above, after the numeral, and press Shift-Ins, or Alt-E P, or click on the Edit and Paste commands. Do the same on the line below.

Now it's time to clean up the text. Delete the numerals, press the Tab key at the beginning of each line, and edit the remaining text to match Figure 11.4.

Searching and Replacing

Let's try another feature of the Editor—searching for and replacing text. Display the Search menu by pressing Alt-S or clicking on the Search command. Now select Find. (Alternatively, press Ctrl-Q F.) You'll see the dialog box in Figure 11.5. Type

    dos

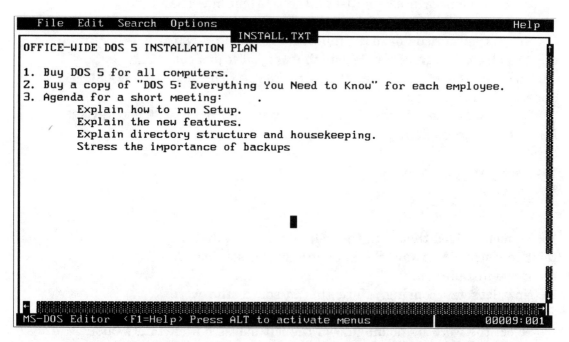

```
   File   Edit   Search   Options                                    Help
┌─────────────────────────────── INSTALL.TXT ───────────────────────────────┐
│OFFICE-WIDE DOS 5 INSTALLATION PLAN                                         ↑│
│                                                                            ║│
│1. Buy DOS 5 for all computers.                                            ║│
│2. Buy a copy of "DOS 5: Everything You Need to Know" for each employee.   ║│
│3. Agenda for a short meeting:        .                                    ║│
│        Explain how to run Setup.                                          ║│
│        Explain the new features.                                          ║│
│     ╱  Explain directory structure and housekeeping.                      ║│
│        Stress the importance of backups                                   ║│
│                                                                           ║│
│                                                                           ║│
│                                ▌                                          ║│
│                                                                           ║│
│                                                                           ║│
│                                                                           ║│
│                                                                           ║│
│←                                                                          →│
│ MS-DOS Editor  <F1=Help> Press ALT to activate menus          00009:001   │
└────────────────────────────────────────────────────────────────────────────┘
```

Figure 11.4   The edited outline

Figure 11.5   The Find dialog box

and press Enter. A highlight will appear over the word DOS in the first line of your installation plan list.

Now press Ctrl-L. The highlight moves to dos in item number 1. Press F3. It moves to DOS in item number 2. Press either of these keys, and the highlight moves back to the title. The Find function will repeat infinitely, cycling through the file each time you reach the end. Either the F3 or the Ctrl-L key repeats the operation.

Now let's try replacing text. We'll replace the lowercase dos in item number 1 with uppercase characters. Select the Change command. (Alternatively, press Ctrl-Q A.) You'll see the dialog box in Figure 11.6. Notice the Editor assumes that the word the cursor is on is the text to find.

Enter

dos

as the text to find and

DOS

as the text to change to. Press Alt-M Alt-W Alt-C to select Match Upper/Lowercase, Whole Word, and Change All. Now press Enter or select OK. The dialog box will look like Figure 11.7. The Editor will replace the lowercase text with uppercase and display the message

Change complete

in a dialog box.

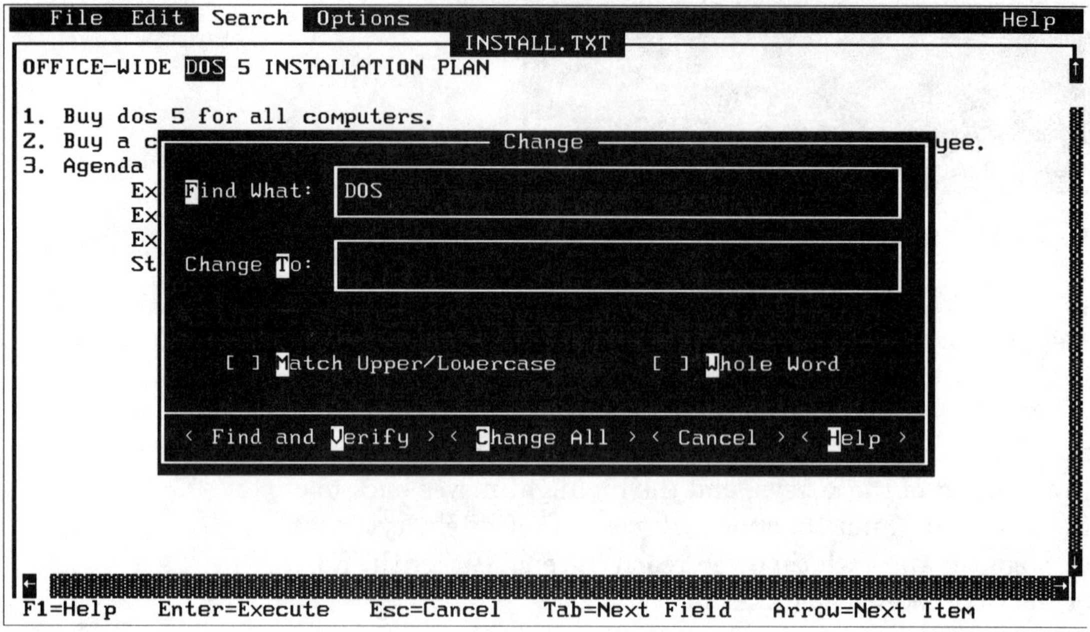

Figure 11.6   The Change dialog box

Let's note the other options. If you don't select Whole Word, the characters *dos* would be replaced with uppercase characters in words like *endosperm*. If you don't want to replace every instance of something, choose Find and Verify. Before changing the text, the Editor will display the dialog box in Figure 11.8. You can skip any given instance or cancel the procedure.

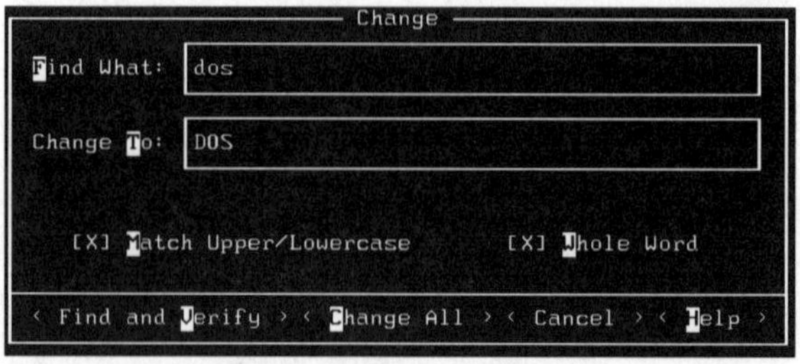

Figure 11.7   A filled-out Change dialog box

Figure 11.8   Selectively changing text

Other File Operations

If you want to edit another file once you're in the Editor, select New from the File menu. If you haven't saved your current file since the last change, you'll be asked whether to do so before proceeding. Once you save or choose not to, the window clears and the word Untitled appears again as the title. (You can clear the window without saving your text by choosing Clear from the Edit menu.)

You can also edit files that already exist so long as they are ASCII (unformatted text) files. If you're in the Editor, choosing Open from the File menu gives you the dialog box in Figure 11.9. As you can see, you can choose the drive and directory from the Dirs/Drives box and choose a file from the Files box. To select a file name, click on it or move the highlight to it with the arrow keys and press Enter.

Note that the entry line displays *.TXT. Correspondingly, only files with the extension TXT appear in the Files box. If you want to choose from among files with other extensions, enter a different wild-card pattern. Or enter

Figure 11.9   The Open dialog box

. to see all files in the chosen directory. Alternatively, you can type a file name, optionally including a path, in the entry line.

If you're starting the Editor from the Shell, as you've seen, you can enter the name of the file to open in the entry line of the Shell's dialog box or first choose it in the files window.

If you're starting the Editor from the command prompt, you can enter a file to open as a parameter. For example, to edit the file you just created, you would enter

```
edit install.txt
```

To print your file, choose Print from the File menu. You'll see the dialog box in Figure 11.10. If your printer is properly hooked up and turned on, the text will be printed when you select OK.

You can also print part of a file. Select the text to be printed with either the keyboard or the mouse. Select the Print command then the Print selected text option, and finally, OK.

Editor Options

You can customize several aspects of the way the Editor appears on the screen. If you have a monochrome monitor and you can't see the screen clearly, add the /B (black-and-white) switch to the command line. If you have a low-resolution color monitor, you can use the /G (graphics) switch. This

Figure 11.10   The Print dialog box

will update the screen more quickly, but you may also see "snow," especially when you scroll through a file.

To change other aspects of the display, choose the Dis-play command from the Options menu. This produces the dialog box in Figure 11.11. As you can see, you can choose from 16 foreground and 8 background colors. If you don't use a mouse, you may want to turn off the scroll bars to allow more room for text. Finally, you can change the number of spaces between tab stops. The default of 8 matches what the Tab key does at the command prompt and is commonly used by programmers. If you prefer, you can change the tab interval to 5 spaces, or 4, or anything else.

There's one other option on the Options menu: Help Path. You won't need this unless you're using diskettes exclusively. Because DOS needs QBASIC.EXE to run the Editor, both are on the BASIC/Edit diskette. The help files for both programs are on the Help diskette. If you're using the Editor with diskettes, set the help path to B:\ and insert your Help diskette in drive B. After you've loaded the Editor from drive A, you can replace the BASIC/Edit diskette with the data diskette containing the file to edit.

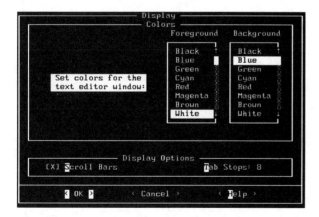

Figure 11.11   The Display dialog box

Using the Survival Guide

You can use the help system at any time, not just when you first open the Editor without a file. As you may have noticed, every dialog box includes a Help button. You can also display the opening Survival Guide screen by pressing Shift-F1 or selecting Getting Started from the Help menu. In addition, pressing F1 displays help on whatever the Editor thinks you're doing. Figure 11.12 displays the screen that explains the keys you use to move around in the help system.

You may have noticed references to the "Editor window" in this chapter, even though the Editor appears to take up the full screen. You get a window when you bring up the help system while a file is open. The help screen occupies one window while your file occupies the other. To move between the two, press F6 or click on <F6=Window> on the status line. To close the Help window, press Escape.

```
  File   Edit   Search   Options                                    Help
                            HELP: Help Keys
     ◄Getting Started►  ◄Keyboard►  ◄Back►                                ▲

  View Help on the MS-DOS Editor environment    F1 (or click the
                                                right mouse button)
  Exit Help                                     Esc

  View Getting Started                          Shift+F1
  Display the Help menu              ■          Alt+H

  Move cursor to next Help topic                Tab
  Move cursor to previous Help topic            Shift+Tab
  Move cursor to next Help topic with starting  character
  character
  Move cursor to previous Help topic with starting  Shift+character
  character
  View previous Help topic (repeat up to 20 times)  Alt+F1 (or double-click
                                                the <Back> button)

  View the next topic in the Help file          Ctrl+F1
  View the previous topic in the Help file      Shift+Ctrl+F1
                        ─── INSTALL.TXT ───
  OFFICE-WIDE DOS 5 INSTALLATION PLAN
  <F1=Help> <F6=Window> <Esc=Cancel> <Ctrl+F1=Next> <Alt+F1=Back>
```

Figure 11.12   Help keys

Now that you know how the Editor works, let's use it to tailor your system to your needs. In the next chapter, you'll edit the CONFIG.SYS and AUTOEXEC.BAT files to take advantage of many DOS facilities. In the following chapter, you'll create batch files to take further control of your system.

Fine-Tuning Your Configuration

Chapter 12

What You Will Learn

- The nature of the DOS configuration files
- How to help DOS find your programs
- How to install DOS resident programs
- Dealing with the DOS environment space
- How to set configuration defaults
- What device drivers are and how to install them

Throughout this book the CONFIG.SYS and AUTOEXEC.BAT files have been mentioned. These two files determine much of the way your computer behaves and the face it presents to you. When DOS 5 installs itself, it creates very simple versions of these files. If you already have them, Setup modifies them slightly. (It saves the original versions on the Uninstall diskette, under the names CONFIG.DAT and AUTOEXEC.DAT.) In this chapter you'll tailor these files to your system and your preferences. We'll begin with AUTOEXEC.BAT because it's easier to understand and you'll modify it more often.

Before you make any modifications, scan this whole chapter. The changes you make in one file may depend on settings in the other. It's best to understand what you're doing before you proceed.

What Is the AUTOEXEC.BAT File?

AUTOEXEC.BAT is simply a file of DOS commands to be executed sequentially, that is, a *batch file*. When you start your computer, DOS looks for this file in the root directory of your boot disk. If it finds it, DOS executes all the commands in it during the startup process. Therefore AUTOEXEC.BAT should include any command you want executed every time you start up—and no others.

You'll learn a great deal more about batch files and the commands specific to them in Chapter 13. Here we'll just look at the ones you'll use to set up your system.

Examining the AUTOEXEC.BAT File

Let's examine the contents of your AUTOEXEC.BAT file. Exactly what you'll find depends on your system and whether you installed DOS on diskettes or a hard disk. Begin by making the root directory of your boot disk current. This will make it easier to modify the file. If you have a hard disk and prefer to use the command prompt, enter

```
type autoexec.bat
```

You can examine AUTOEXEC.BAT in the Shell by making the root directory of drive C current, selecting the file in the file window, and selecting View File Contents from the File menu.

If you told Setup to run the Shell whenever you start your system, your AUTOEXEC.BAT file will probably look like Figure 12.1. If you use diskettes, your AUTOEXEC.BAT file will look like Figure 12.2. To see it, just enter

```
type autoexec.bat
```

at the command prompt.

The first line of both files tells DOS not to display the command prompt nor each command before executing it. Thus AUTOEXEC.BAT executes almost invisibly. (Although

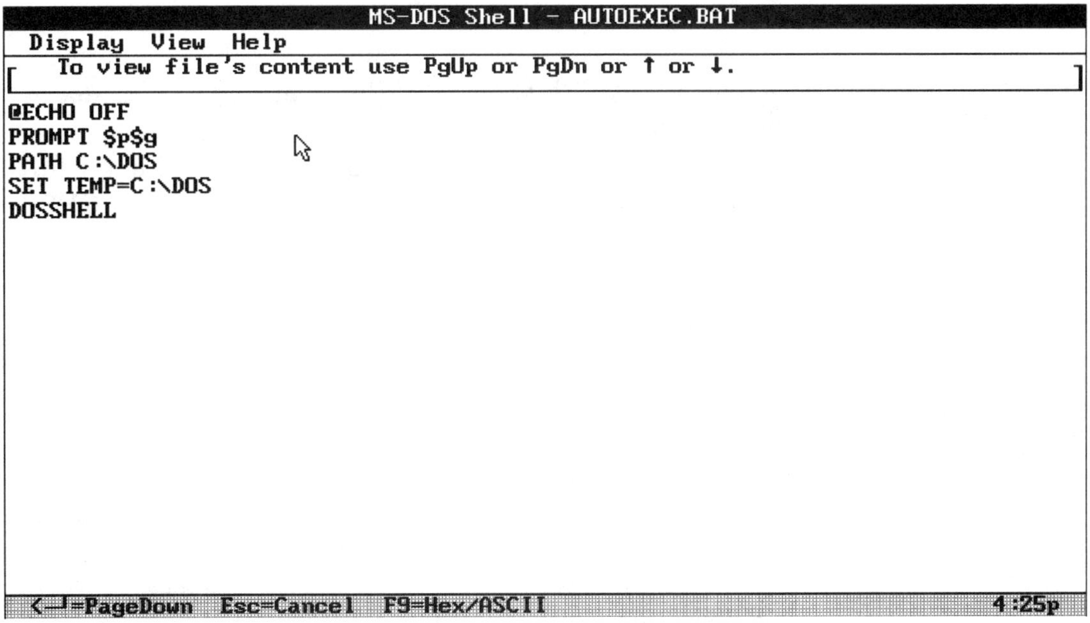

```
                    MS-DOS Shell - AUTOEXEC.BAT
  Display  View  Help
      To view file's content use PgUp or PgDn or ↑ or ↓.
 @ECHO OFF
 PROMPT $p$g            ↳
 PATH C:\DOS
 SET TEMP=C:\DOS
 DOSSHELL




 <─┘=PageDown  Esc=Cancel  F9=Hex/ASCII                        4:25p
```

Figure 12.1   The default AUTOEXEC.BAT file for a hard disk system

the commands don't appear, any messages they display will.) The second line, the PROMPT command, determines what your prompt looks like. As you've noticed, it displays the name of the current drive and directory, followed by the symbol >. If you didn't have this command, your prompt would just be A> or C>, though you can further customize it to your liking. The PATH command tells DOS to look in any directories specified in it when you type a command that runs a program. The SET command places information in an area of memory where programs can find it. The final line in Figure 12.1 issues the command to run the Shell.

Edit your AUTOEXEC.BAT file in the DOS Editor or in a word processor that can save files as ASCII (unformatted text) files. If you're not sure how to create ASCII files in your word processor, consult its documentation. Every line in the file must begin at the left margin, and all but the last must end with a carriage return.

```
@ECHO OFF
PROMPT $p$g
```

*Figure 12.2
The default
AUTOEXEC.BAT file
for a startup diskette*

259

HINT

Don't put any extraneous information in the file, because DOS will try to interpret it as a command or something that modifies a command. However, if you like, you can add comment lines to explain the other lines in the file. Begin the line with the command REM (remark) so that DOS does not attempt to execute it.

Setting the Date and Time

When an AUTOEXEC.BAT file is present, DOS doesn't prompt you for the date and time. That's fine if your system has an internal clock. But if your files are all dated 01-01-80, add the following commands right after @ECHO OFF:

```
DATE
TIME
```

DOS will execute these commands when it comes to them, just as if you had typed them at the prompt.

✳ NOTE

If you have a PC-XT or clone that has an expansion board with a clock, you may have to use a command such as SETCLOCK to read the time from the board's clock and tell it to your computer's system clock. Check the board's documentation for the exact command and substitute it for DATE and TIME. (You will probably have to copy from a diskette that came with the board a file whose basic name is the same as the command.)

Customizing Your Prompt

As you've seen, the default command prompt displays the current drive and path. This is very useful. However, you may want yours to do more. You can insert any text you like into a prompt. In addition, certain combinations of characters act as command symbols. These combinations always begin with a dollar sign. They allow you to include things such as the date and time, plus characters that would otherwise be interpreted as commands. Table 12.1 lists the special command characters to be used in a prompt.

A PROMPT command can be up to 127 characters long, including the word *PROMPT* itself. Let's look at some examples. You've already seen the effect of pg. We'll try a few more complex prompts. You can enter them at the current prompt and see it change. When you find one you like, use it to replace the one in your AUTOEXEC.BAT file.

Table 12.1 Prompt command characters

Symbol	Effect
b	Inserts a bar character, |
d	Inserts the current date
e	Inserts an escape character (use in conjunction with the ANSI.SYS device driver to set screen colors)
g	Inserts a greater-than symbol, >
h	Backspaces one character
l	Inserts a less-than symbol, <
n	Inserts the name of the current drive
p	Inserts the current drive and path name
t	Inserts the current time
v	Inserts the DOS version (equivalent to VER)
_	Places what follows on the next line of the screen

Try entering

```
prompt [Date=$d]$_[Time=$t]$_$p$g
```

Your prompt will then look like Figure 12.3.

As you can see, the characters [Date=, [Time=, and] were translated literally. The $t turned into the current time, to the nearest hundredth of a second, and the $d turned into the date. The $_ symbol broke the date, time, and path name into separate lines.

Let's make the time display a bit more readable. We'll add five backspace characters to delete the seconds and hundredths:

```
prompt [Time=$t$h$h$h$h$h]$_$p$g
```

```
[Date=Thu 04-25-1991]
[Time=16:39:21.06]
C:\>_
```

Figure 12.3 A prompt showing the date and time

```
[Time=16:55]
C:\>_
```

Figure 12.4 A prompt showing the hour and minute

The prompt should now appear as in Figure 12.4.

Additional text could include a cheery greeting:

```
prompt Hi! I'm at your service!$_What can I do
for you?$_Current directory: [$p]
```

This would produce the prompt in Figure 12.5.

! WARNING

If your PROMPT command is too long to fit on the screen, your word processor may wrap it to the next line. Make sure that there isn't a carriage return where the line breaks. If there is, DOS won't know how to interpret the second line and part of your prompt will be lost. However, the DOS Editor automatically keeps all text on a single line.

Later, after you've learned about the CONFIG.SYS file, you'll be able to use the PROMPT command to change your screen colors.

Helping DOS Find Your Programs

Take a close look at the third line of Figure 12.1:

```
path c:\dos
```

This is the command that Setup used to arrange for DOS to find the DOS external programs. Remember, when you type a command, DOS looks for it only in COMMAND.COM

```
Hi! I'm at your service!
What can I do for you?
Current directory: [C:\]_
```

Figure 12.5 A prompt with a greeting

and then in the current directory unless you include a full path name. But if you have a PATH command, DOS also looks in any directory named in it. PATH thus sets up a *search path* for your programs. If you type the name of a COM, EXE, or BAT file that is in any directory named in the PATH command, DOS executes it.

The PATH command consists of the word *PATH*, followed by a space and one or more path names, separated by semi-colons. Don't put any spaces between the path names.

What Should Go on the Search Path?

As a general rule, you should place on the path any directories containing programs you might want to execute when any of several directories is current. These include the directory containing your DOS external programs (which Setup placed on the path for you), the UTIL directory you created to hold programs to help manage your system, and your BATCH directory, which will contain batch files to help DOS run programs whose directories *aren't* on the search path. (You'll learn how to create these files in Chapter 13.)

You'll also probably want to add the directories containing your most commonly used application programs, especially if there are only a few. But if you use many and you add them all, you may run out of characters. Just because you *can* use 127 characters for the command doesn't mean you *should*. It takes DOS longer to search a long path. You may become pretty discouraged when you mistype a command, and after a longish wait, DOS returns the message

```
Bad command or file name
```

Finally, some programs look only in the current directory for auxiliary files and can't run unless they find them. These programs should be run from their home directory and shouldn't be on the path.

HINT

The extended search time can be alleviated by commands in your CONFIG.SYS file, as described later in this chapter. And if a program needs its directory to be current, you can run it from a batch file, as described in Chapter 13. Or you can use the APPEND command to help find the auxiliary files, as described below. For now, be conservative.

Many software packages want to add themselves to your path during installation. Some even insist on being first. If you're a computer novice, you may as well let them have their way, until you find your system slowing down because DOS is always looking first in a directory containing a program you rarely use. When you become more familiar with DOS and your system, you'll want to use PATH to access programs you use on a daily basis and run the rest by using a batch file (see Chapter 13 for instructions).

In sum, your search path should include the following:

! WARNING

The PATH command affects only executable files. If you want to use the COPY, RENAME, ERASE, or TYPE commands, you must still specify the entire path to the file if it is not in your current directory.

- The DOS directory
- The BATCH directory
- The UTIL directory
- Directories containing your most frequently used programs
- Directories containing often-used utility packages complex enough to warrant their own directories

Begin with the DOS, BATCH, and UTIL directories, in that order. Since DOS always searches the directories on the path in the order in which they appear, order the rest to match the frequency with which you use their contents.

 HINT

To see what directories are on your path at any time, enter path *at the command prompt.*

The Path and the Shell

If you run your programs from the Shell, your path may not need to be as comprehensive as otherwise. When you set up a program, you include information about the directory from which it should be started. You can even have the Shell start your program from one directory and then change to another containing your data files.

This may not work for all programs, however. Some are constructed to find their auxiliary files in the same directory as the program file. Others require another means of finding their auxiliary files—an *environment variable*—which you'll learn about shortly. (Environment variables are usually placed in your AUTOEXEC.BAT file during installation by the programs that need them.) Some programs can run from any directory only if they're on the path. Check the documentation. If it suggests that you first type a CD command and then the command to run the program, the program does *not* have to be on the path.

Searching for Data Files

To assist PATH, DOS includes the APPEND command, which can locate data files as well as program files. In its most basic form, it looks just like PATH:

APPEND *d:\path;d:\path;d:\path. . .*

When you add an APPEND command to your AUTO-EXEC.BAT file, DOS looks in all the listed directories for nonprogram files.

What directories should be appended? That depends on your software. As a rule, you should use APPEND to help your software find auxiliary files it needs in order to run, not data files you plan to edit. How do you know if a program's directory needs to be appended? Again, by trial and error. If it won't run from a directory other than its home directory when it's on the path, try appending it. You may also find that programs that *aren't* on the path may run from anywhere when they are appended, if you invoke them with the full path name.

Other programs, however, may write little configuration files and such in whatever directory is current. If one does, you may prefer to cooperate with it and run it from its home directory. Or you may find it useful to have different configurations appropriate to different directories.

! WARNING

If your computer is on a network, you must run APPEND after the network is loaded. In fact it may be run for you by the network startup procedure. Consult your network administrator before you attempt to alter the APPEND list.

APPEND has two switches: /E (environment) and /X (extended). You may find the /E switch useful. It places the list of appended directories in a special area of memory where you can see it along with other useful information. You can, however, view the APPEND list just by entering `append` at a prompt.

! WARNING

The /X switch is dangerous. It extends DOS's searching abilities so that it can find any file named as a parameter to a command in any appended directory. In effect it treats all appended directories as if they were part of the current directory. Why is this dangerous? Consider the following scenario.

You have a file GOLDBERG.LTR in your LETTERS\GENERAL directory and another file by the same name in your NEWPROJ directory. The LETTERS\GENERAL directory is appended. Thinking NEWPROJ is current, you type `del goldberg.ltr`. *But the current directory is actually BATCH. DOS dutifully searches through the appended directories and deletes the file in LETTERS\GENERAL. That's not what you had in mind at all.*

Worse yet, when you use the /X switch, you can open a data file in an appended directory just by giving its name. However, when you write the file, it will appear in the current directory unless you include the complete path. Some programs don't let you do that.

If you use either switch, you must enter two APPEND commands, the first with the switch and the second with the list of directories. For example, you might enter

```
append /e
append c:\video;c:\dict
```

This example also indicates some types of directories that should be appended. The VIDEO directory contains screen configuration files for various programs. The program that loads them is on the path but can't find the configuration files without assistance. Similarly the DICT directory contains dictionary files for a spelling-check and thesaurus program. The program can be invoked by typing a complete path name, but it won't find the dictionaries without help, not even if DICT is on the path.

✳ **NOTE**

APPEND is our first example of a terminate-and-stay-resident program, or TSR. We'll call it a resident program for short. Resident programs run once, then leave some active code in memory. DOS includes several resident programs, some of which you'll encounter in this chapter. They generally sit in memory and don't bother you. Many commercially available resident programs, however, are considerably more complex. You can call them to the foreground, over the top of the application you're working in, by pressing a "hot key." When you're done, you return them to the background with a hot key. Resident programs all occupy memory you may need for applications. (See Appendix B for help.) They may also conflict with one another.

Installing Deletion Tracking

In Chapter 10, you learned how to keep a record of deleted files by installing MIRROR. It's a good idea to put the MIRROR command in your AUTOEXEC.BAT file, with the appropriate switches. Even if you don't install deletion tracking, placing MIRROR in AUTOEXEC.BAT will copy the DOS reserved area at least once a day to protect you from an unintended format.

To copy the DOS reserved area, just add the command

```
mirror c: [d:]
```

where *d* is any hard drive letter, including the names of all your hard disks. To install deletion tracking, add the /T switches:

```
mirror /tc /td d:
```

This makes MIRROR a resident program.

When you install MIRROR, it automatically copies the reserved area of drive C. You must add other drives to be scanned as parameters on the command line. This example installs deletion tracking for drives C and D and copies the reserved area of both drives.

Setting Environment Variables

You've been hearing a bit about the environment. We're not talking about ecology at the moment but about an area of memory set aside by COMMAND.COM for information it needs. The full name for this area is the *DOS environment space*. To see what's in it, enter

```
set
```

at a prompt or on the Run entry line. If you haven't yet changed your AUTOEXEC.BAT file and you have a hard disk, you'll see something like Figure 12.6.

These four lines represent *environment variables*—values placed in the environment to assist DOS. The command to set an environment variable takes the form

SET *variable=value*

You probably recognize the last three lines in Figure 12.6 from the AUTOEXEC.BAT file in Figure 12.1. The PROMPT and PATH variables are established by the PROMPT and PATH commands, respectively.

✔ **NEW FEATURE**
Temp variable required

Selecting the Directory for Temporary Files

The Shell looks in the environment for a directory name assigned to the variable TEMP. It places temporary files in

```
C:\>set
COMSPEC=C:\DOS\COMMAND.COM
PROMPT=$p$g
TEMP=C:\DOS
PATH=C:\DOS
C:\>_
```

Figure 12.6   The contents of the DOS environment space

that directory. Because Setup doesn't know what directories you have, it assigns your DOS directory to the TEMP variable by adding the line

```
SET TEMP=C:\DOS
```

to your AUTOEXEC.BAT file.

Normally, temporary files are erased when you exit the Shell. But if you have to reboot the computer unexpectedly, your DOS directory may acquire useless files with names like 1824DOSC.BAT, D597DOSC.BAT, and DOSSHELL.SWP.

To keep the contents of your directories predictable, create a TEMP directory and make the TEMP environment variable point to it. If you examine the command above, you'll see how to establish an environment variable: Enter the SET command, followed by the variable name, an equal sign, and a value. Don't place spaces around the equal sign unless you want DOS to regard them as part of either the variable or the value. Now change the line to read

```
set temp=c:\temp
```

Of course if you placed the TEMP directory on another drive, use the correct drive name.

As you become a more sophisticated user, you'll find that many programs (among them Microsoft Windows) use the directory designated by a TEMP variable. DOS itself does so whenever you use a command involving redirection (See Chapter 15). As a rule, you can ignore anything a program places in this directory. If you find unknown files in the TEMP directory after restarting your computer, you can safely delete them.

You may find that some application programs and utilities create environment variables. They will usually tell you so during installation and offer to place them in your

AUTOEXEC.BAT file. Since such programs require their environment variables in order to function, you should let them do so. You may, however, want to group them in your AUTOEXEC.BAT file, perhaps after the PATH command. Here are some sample environment variables created by various software packages:

```
TEMP=E:\TEMP
NU=C:\NORTON
EFAX3=D:\EFAX
PCPLUS=D:\TELECOM\PCPLUS\
PCTOOLS=C:\PCTOOLS\DATA
LIB=D:\QBASIC\LIB
```

Changing Some Other Environment Variables

You can change the PATH and PROMPT variables with commands of the form

```
set path=d:\path
```

and

```
set prompt=$p$g
```

HINT

If you see the message Insert disk with COMMAND.COM in drive A: Press any key when ready..., *DOS is trying to load COMMAND.COM from drive A. If you use diskettes, you may want to copy COMMAND.COM to all your program diskettes.*

as well as with the PATH and PROMPT commands. If you use the /E switch for the APPEND command, the APPEND list appears in the environment like any other variable, and you can change it the same way.

Now what about that COMSPEC variable in Figure 12.6? That's established automatically by DOS. Some programs use the memory occupied by the portion of COMMAND.COM that normally remains in memory. When you exit from such a program, DOS loads COMMAND.COM, using the COMSPEC variable to locate it. It's usually best to leave COMSPEC alone. One circumstance where you might change it is if you have started a hard disk system from a diskette. Entering

```
set comspec=c:\command.com
```

will cause DOS to look for COMMAND.COM on the hard disk, so you can safely remove the diskette. Otherwise you may be told periodically to place a diskette with COM-MAND.COM on it in drive A.

The value assigned to the COMSPEC variable is the directory from which DOS originally loaded COM-MAND.COM. However, it may be established in the CON-FIG.SYS file, which you'll learn about later in this chapter. In this it contrasts with other environment variables, which must be established either through AUTOEXEC.BAT or at a command prompt.

✔ **NEW FEATURE**
Setting COMSPEC
location in
CONFIG.SYS

Selecting a Default Directory Display

DOS 5 lets you decide how the DIR command displays your directories by setting an environment variable called DIRCMD (directory command). You assign to this variable any combination of DIR switches that creates the desired display. For example, you might use the command

✔ **NEW FEATURE**
Selectable direc-
tory display format

```
set dircmd=/oe-d/l/p
```

to display any directory in lowercase, sorted by extension, and sorted within extensions by date and time in reverse order, pausing after each full screen. The result might look like Figure 12.7. To occasionally get a different display, enter DIR with different switches or enter minus signs before switches you want to override. To get the original default display, for example, you'd have to type

```
dir /-o/-l/-p
```

```
C:\>dir temp

 Volume in drive C is SYSTEM
 Volume Serial Number is 012C-1020
 Directory of C:\TEMP

d597dosc bat          26 04-26-91 11:49a
.              <DIR>     01-23-91  2:46p
..             <DIR>     01-23-91  2:46p
1824dosc bat          29 04-26-91 11:41a
temp     bat          61 09-27-90 10:43p
test     bat          46 09-27-90 10:40p
swapdt   sw3        4096 04-26-91 11:58a
swapsh   sw3        4096 04-26-91 11:58a
dosshell swp       26937 04-26-91 11:50a
5        zip      199809 10-18-90  9:56a
4        zip      321879 10-18-90  9:45a
3        zip      169782 10-18-90  9:39a
2        zip      165363 10-18-90  9:33a
1        zip      195356 10-18-90  9:32a
        14 file(s)   1087480 bytes
                     9775104 bytes free

C:\>_
```

Figure 12.7   Viewing a directory with customized settings

Changing and Deleting
Environment Variables

You can change a variable's value by entering a SET command with the new value. For example, even if you don't change your AUTOEXEC.BAT file, you can change TEMP so that it points to the TEMP directory instead of the DOS directory by entering

```
set temp=c:\temp
```

at a command prompt. This setting will remain until you change it or restart the computer.

To get rid of an environment variable, enter the SET command with the variable name followed by the equal sign. For example, to delete the TEMP environment variable, enter

```
set temp=
```

If You Run Out of Environment Space

By the time you've established a long path, a complex prompt, an APPEND list, and a few other environment variables, your environment space may be getting awfully full. DOS allocates 128 bytes at a minimum and more under some circumstances. However, if you use all the allotted space, you'll see the message

```
Out of environment space
```

You'll need to make your environment space larger by modifying your CONFIG.SYS file, as described below.

Speeding File Access

DOS includes a command for speeding up some types of disk access: FASTOPEN. This command sets aside a small area in memory (a *buffer*) for the complete path name of each file you open. The next time you open the file, DOS reads the information from the buffer rather than searching the disk.

To install FASTOPEN, enter the command followed by the drive(s) to be kept track of:

```
fastopen c: d:
```

FASTOPEN automatically keeps track of 48 file names for each drive. There's no compelling reason to change this. If

HINT

To get an estimate of how many files you open on each drive, install DOSKEY as described below and review its log of commands. Don't forget, however, that you may open several files within a program in one session before returning to the prompt or the Shell.

NOTE

If you have expanded memory, you can place the FASTOPEN in it by adding the /X switch.

NEW FEATURE
Command stack

you want to track more or fewer files for a given drive, you can specify the number of file names to track:

```
fastopen c:=60 d:=12
```

Place an equal sign after the drive name followed by the number of file names to be remembered.

If you had your software on drive C and your data files on drive D, you might want an arrangement such as the one illustrated. It presumes you use only a few data files on any given day but that you use a variety of tools to edit them and manage your computer. Base your estimates on the number of files you use on each drive.

The slower your hard disk (or your computer), the more of a difference FASTOPEN can make. If your disk is very fast, you probably don't need it.

Installing a Command Stack

DOS 5 includes DOSKEY, a resident program that creates a *command stack*—a list of DOS commands you have already entered. By default it remembers about 20 to 40 commands, depending on how long the commands are. You can reenter any command by scrolling through the list and selecting it. DOSKEY also gives you a great deal more flexibility in editing command lines.

To install DOSKEY, enter

```
doskey
```

As with all DOS commands, you can enter it at a command prompt. However, if you don't use the Shell, you'll want to install this program in your AUTOEXEC.BAT file so that it's always available. Table 12.2 lists the keys you can use to recall and edit commands.

You will probably come to find DOSKEY invaluable. It has many other capabilities (described in your DOS manual) that are beyond the scope of this book. However, you will immediately find it useful when you start creating

Table 12.2 DOSKEY command keys

Key	Effect
↑	Displays the previous command in the list
↓	Displays the next command in the list
F7	Displays a numbered list of commands you have entered
F8	If you type the first few letters of a command, each press of F8 displays the previous command that begins with those letters
PgUp	Displays the oldest command still stored in the list
PgDn	Displays the command most recently issued
Escape	Clears the command line
Ins	Toggles between insert mode (the default) and overtype mode
Home	Moves the cursor to the beginning of the command line
End	Moves the cursor to the end of the command line
←	Moves the cursor left one character on the command line
→	Moves the cursor right one character on the command line
Ctrl-←	Moves the cursor left one word on the command line
Ctrl-→	Moves the cursor right one word on the command line
Backspace	Deletes the character to the left of the cursor
Del	Deletes the character at the cursor
Ctrl-Home	Deletes from the cursor to the beginning of the line
Ctrl-End	Deletes from the cursor to the end of the line

batch files. You'll often find yourself editing a file, testing it, then editing it again. To switch between the command that invokes your editor and the one that runs the batch file, you'll only have to press ↑ and ↓.

Putting It All Together

Let's assume you've decided to use all the facilities thus far described. Your AUTOEXEC.BAT file might look like Figure 12.8. Note that the commands don't appear in the order in which they were discussed. Some resident programs are quite fussy about what's loaded before and after them.

If you're using commercial resident programs, their documentation will generally tell you where they should be

```
@echo off
prompt $d$_$p$g
date
time
path c:\dos;c:\batch;c:\util;c:\wp;c:\ss;c:\db
set temp=c:\temp
set doscmd=/p
mirror /tc /td c: d:
fastopen c: d:
append /e
append c:\video;c:\dict
doskey
c:\dos\dosshell
```

Figure 12.8   An expanded AUTOEXEC.BAT file

loaded, or their installation program may place the command at the appropriate point in AUTOEXEC.BAT. DOS resident programs are on the whole less fussy, but MIRROR likes to be loaded first.

Testing the Results

When you've finished modifying your AUTOEXEC.BAT file, you should test the results. If it doesn't load any resident programs, you can test the file by entering

```
autoexec
```

If it does load resident programs, most of them will simply display a message saying that they are already installed. (A few ill-behaved programs will load a second copy of themselves into memory.)

To be absolutely sure that what you're seeing is what you intended, reboot the computer by pressing Ctrl-Alt-Del. Watch the messages that appear on the screen. If you see Bad command or file name, File not found, or Syntax error, you may need to make further changes.

To find out which commands are causing problems, delete the line

```
@echo off
```

from the beginning of the file. DOS will then display each line of the file at a prompt before executing it. Then you can easily see which commands result in error messages. When the file is running correctly, test all the programs you have loaded to make sure they are behaving as you want them to. Then put the @echo off statement back.

What Is the CONFIG.SYS File?

The CONFIG.SYS file, as you remember, is a text file DOS looks for while it starts your computer. If DOS finds the file in the root directory of your startup disk, it executes the commands in it.

The CONFIG.SYS file includes two types of commands: *configuration commands,* which establish default settings and reserve memory for them; and *device driver commands,* which either tell your computer about installed hardware or change the way the hardware behaves. We'll look at both, beginning with the configuration commands.

Each command takes the form of a name, followed by an equal sign, followed by a value:

COMMAND=VALUE

If you like, you can add comment lines to explain the other lines in the file. Begin comments with the REM command, so that DOS does not attempt to execute them.

As with your AUTOEXEC.BAT file, each line in CONFIG.SYS *must* begin at the left margin. And the file must be saved as an ASCII (unformatted text} file, in either your word processor or the DOS Editor.

The commands in CONFIG.SYS are executed only while the computer is booting. You must reboot to make changes take effect.

Examining the CONFIG.SYS File

Exactly what you find in your CONFIG.SYS file depends on your system and whether you installed DOS on diskettes or a hard disk. You can examine this file at the command prompt by making the root directory of your boot disk current and entering

```
type config.sys
```

as shown in Figure 12.9. If you have a hard disk, you can alternatively examine the file in the Shell by making the root directory of drive C current, selecting the file in the file window, and selecting View File Contents from the File menu. Commands that load device drivers all begin with DEVICE. All the others are configuration commands.

If your system is controlled by an 8088 microprocessor (i.e., if it's a PC-XT or clone), you'll see something like Figure 12.9. If it has an 80286 (PC-AT), 80386, or 80486 microprocessor and more than 640K of RAM, you'll see additional lines as shown in Figure 12.10. The extra commands for the higher-powered computers are designed to manage and use the additional memory. If you're working with diskettes,

```
C:\>type config.sys

DEVICE=C:\DOS\SETVER.EXE
FILES=10
SHELL=C:\DOS\COMMAND.COM C:\DOS\ /p

C:>_
```

Figure 12.9   A CONFIG.SYS file for an 8088 computer

drive C will be replaced by drive A and the line beginning with SHELL will be missing.

You'll find a complete explanation of memory on PCs and the DOS programs that control it in Appendix B.

Configuration Commands

In this section you'll learn about the most common configuration commands. There are others, but you'll need them only in extraordinary circumstances. You can add any of these commands, and change the values they establish, by editing the CONFIG.SYS file. Table 12.3 gives a brief overview of all of them.

As you read the following sections, you may be tempted to maximize the values established by configuration commands. While increasing the values of many may make your computer more efficient, it will leave less memory for your

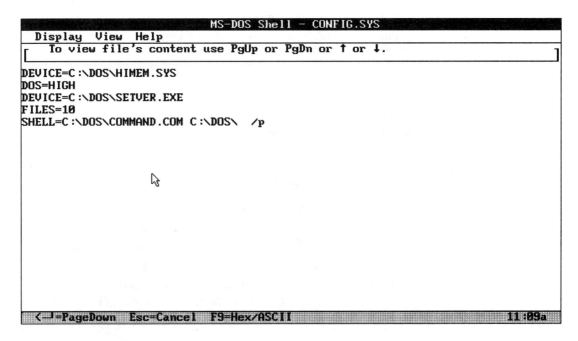

```
                    MS-DOS Shell - CONFIG.SYS
     Display   View   Help
       To view file's content use PgUp or PgDn or ↑ or ↓.

DEVICE=C:\DOS\HIMEM.SYS
DOS=HIGH
DEVICE=C:\DOS\SETVER.EXE
FILES=10
SHELL=C:\DOS\COMMAND.COM C:\DOS\ /p




                    ⌐




 ←┘=PageDown   Esc=Cancel   F9=Hex/ASCII                    11:09a
```

Figure 12.10   A CONFIG.SYS file for an 80386 computer

Table 12.3 Configuration commands

Command	Effect
BREAK	Establishes how frequently DOS checks for presses of the Ctrl-Break or Ctrl-C key combination
BUFFERS	Specifies the amount of memory reserved for storing data recently read from disk for quick access
COUNTRY	Selects a nationality for keyboard layout, character set, decimal separator, and currency symbol
DRIVEPARM	Allows you to enter a description of the structure of a drive; needed for some external drives
DOS	Determines which portion of memory the resident parts will occupy
FCBS	Establishes the maximum number of files that are accessed by file control blocks that can be open (file control blocks are used mainly by older programs)
FILES	Establishes the maximum number of files that are accessed by file handles that can be open
INSTALL	Loads resident programs in the lowest part of memory, such that they cannot be unloaded
LASTDRIVE	Establishes the maximum number of virtual drives that can be created
SHELL	Tells the name and location of the command processor to be used; optionally sets the location referred to by the COMSPEC variable and sets the size of the environment space
STACKS	Reserves an area for storing information needed by the microprocessor about recent hardware activities

programs. Also, you can set some values so high that your system actually becomes *less* efficient.

How Many Files Can Be Open?

The FILES command establishes the maximum number of files that can be open at one time. If you remove this command from your CONFIG.SYS file, DOS allows a maximum of 8 open files. Since you'll nearly always have the two hidden system files, COMMAND.COM, an application program, and a data file, this doesn't leave much flexibility. Setup conservatively increases the number to 10.

If you work with a database program, you'll probably need a minimum of 20 files. Some software requires more. If you run resident programs, you'll need still more.

Your software documentation should tell you if you need a minimum number of files. Some packages' installation programs automatically edit your CONFIG.SYS file. If you're not sure what setting to use, 20 or 25 should give you flexibility without costing you too much memory. Edit the FILES command so that it reads

```
FILES=20
```

or

```
FILES=25
```


Speeding Up Disk Access

DOS sets aside a small portion of memory as a *disk buffer*, in which it stores the information most recently read from disk. If the information you need is already in the buffer, DOS reads it from there. This is much faster than reading from the disk itself.

The buffer size depends on the size of your disk drives and the amount of memory in your computer, but it's very small. You can add blocks of memory (which for convenience we'll also call "buffers") by putting a BUFFERS command in your CONFIG.SYS file:

```
BUFFERS=20
```

While each increase in the FILES command uses only a few additional bytes of memory, buffers take about ½K each—more if you have a hard disk on which a single letter refers to more than 32 megabytes.

Unfortunately the ideal number of buffers can be established only by trial and error. As a general rule, you'll want one buffer for each megabyte of hard disk storage. On a hard disk system, you should have at least 20 buffers. However, as hard disks become large (say, over 40 megabytes), you may not want to give up additional memory. Also, if you make the number too high, it will take DOS longer to read from the buffers than it would from disk.

Another factor in determining the number of buffers you need is the type of software you use. The performance of database programs is improved more markedly than other types of software by an increase in the number of buffers.

There are other ways to speed up your hard disk, especially if you have more than 640K of memory. One is a *disk cache*—a program that provides more sophisticated disk buffering. DOS 5 includes a disk cache called SMARTDRV.SYS, which you'll learn about later in this chapter. (Other disk-caching programs, which you may prefer, are available commercially. Some are included with PC Tools and the Norton Utilities. Other popular caching programs include Super PC-Kwik and Lighting.) If you use FASTOPEN and a disk-caching program, you can maximize disk efficiency with only a few buffers.

Increasing the Number of Drive Letters

In Chapter 8 you learned how to assign a drive letter to a directory with the SUBST command. But there's a catch. If the highest drive letter in your system for a physical drive or a drive established by a device driver is B, C, or D, DOS allows only for drive letters up to E. If you already have drives with letters of E or beyond, no other letters are available.

You may need more than one virtual drive if you're trying to simplify complex directory paths. You'll also need multiple virtual drives if your computer is on a network. If you want to use SUBST to create more than one virtual drive, you have two choices. You can reuse letters by entering a command such as

```
subst b: c:\ss\invoices\1990\west
```

but you'll lose access to drive B until you delete the substitution. Obviously the better solution is to increase the number of drive letters available.

To increase the number of drive letters, use the LASTDRIVE command. It takes the form

```
lastdrive=d
```

where *d* is a drive letter. You can set LASTDRIVE equal to Z if you wish, but remember that each additional drive requires a little more memory.

Locating the Command Processor

Setup may have established a SHELL command in CONFIG.SYS that tells DOS where to look for COMMAND.COM. One purpose of this command is to allow programmers to substitute another command processor. (You sometimes find this with games that run only from a diskette.) It's also essential if COMMAND.COM is not in the root directory of your boot disk.

Let's look at SHELL closely. The general form is

SHELL=*path*\COMMAND.COM *path* /P [/E:*nnnn*]

The first *path*—A:\ or C:\DOS\—tells DOS where COMMAND.COM is located. The /P switch tells DOS that this is a *permanent* copy of COMMAND.COM that can't be unloaded.

If you see the message

```
Out of environment space
```

while your system is booting, use the /E (environment) switch as shown in the general form for SHELL. It is followed by a colon and the number of bytes to reserve for the environment. By default DOS reserves at least 128.

 NOTE

When you go to a DOS prompt from within a program (such as the Shell), you're loading a second copy of COMMAND.COM into memory, above the memory occupied by your program. The EXIT command unloads that copy and returns you to your previous program.

You might start by using /E:256. Save the file and reboot the computer. If you still see the message, repeat the procedure, increasing the amount by 16. Keep increasing by 16 until the message disappears.

If COMMAND.COM is in the root directory of your boot disk and you have enough environment space—or if you don't have a SHELL command but your system works fine— leave well enough alone.

✔ **NEW FEATURE**
Loading DOS in
high memory

Where Do the DOS Files Go?

If your computer has memory beyond 640K, you'll probably see this pair of commands in your CONFIG.SYS file:

```
DEVICE=C:\DOS\HIMEM.SYS
DOS=HIGH
```

The first command tells DOS how to talk to the extra memory in your system, and the second tells DOS to load the buffers and other storage areas established by CON-FIG.SYS into the extra memory. This gives you an additional 20 to 50K for your programs. (On one system I was able to leave 620K free for executing programs by using these commands.)

If you find these commands in your CONFIG.SYS file, leave them there unless you have reason to do otherwise. For further information about managing memory, see Appendix B.

Installing Device Drivers

A *device driver* is a small file that either tells DOS how to address hardware that it may not know is present or alters the way it does so. Many types of peripheral equipment are packaged with a disk that includes a device driver to be installed. For example, a mouse almost invariably needs either a device driver or an executable resident program to handle communications between itself and the computer.

DOS includes quite a few device drivers you can install. You've already briefly encountered two: SETVER.EXE and HIMEM.SYS. (Most device drivers use the extension SYS.) In this section we'll look at SETVER.EXE and several others. ANSI.SYS allows you to customize your screen colors. SMARTDRV.SYS establishes a disk cache. And RAM-DRIVE.SYS allows you to treat a portion of memory as a disk.

You install device drivers with the DEVICE command. Its general form is

DEVICE=d:\path\filename.ext [/switches]

Notice that the path and extension are *not* optional. Since DOS executes the command in CONFIG.SYS before anything else, no path has been established. The only time you can leave out the drive and path name is when the device driver is in the root directory of the boot disk. (This is why this book suggests placing them there.)

The ANSI.SYS Device Driver

If you have a color monitor, you may want to install the ANSI.SYS device driver, which provides what are called *extended screen and keyboard functions*. We'll look at one extended function: screen color. (For information about other functions, see your DOS manual or the extensive discussion in Jonathan Kamin's *Expert Advisor: DOS,* Addison-Wesley, 1989.) When ANSI.SYS is installed, you can embed codes called *escape sequences* in your prompt and in batch files to control the colors you see when you're working in DOS. An escape sequence is so called because it begins with the character assigned to the Escape key. As you may remember, you represent this character in a prompt by the characters $e. (You can't enter it by pressing Escape because that has other effects.)

To install the device driver, add the line

```
device=c:\dos\ansi.sys
```

to your CONFIG.SYS file if ANSI.SYS is in the DOS directory, or

```
device=ansi.sys
```

if it's in the root directory.

Now you can modify your prompt so that it automatically sets your screen to the colors of your choice. Add the following to the PROMPT command in your AUTOEXEC.BAT file:

```
$e[f;b;im
```

where f is the code number for the foreground color, b is the code for the background color, and i is a 0 for normal text or 1 for high-intensity (bright) text. Choose the numbers from Table 12.4.

Let's look at an example. Say you want your screen to display bright white characters against a blue background. If your prompt command reads prompt pg, you'd change it to

```
prompt $e[37;44;1m$p$g
```

Table 12.4 Color codes for ANSI escape sequences

Color	Foreground Code	Background Code
Black	30	40
Blue	34	44
Green	32	42
Cyan (blue-green)	36	46
Red	31	41
Magenta	35	45
Yellow	33	43
White	37	47

What Does SETVER.EXE Do?

Setup installs a device driver called SETVER.EXE (set version) in your CONFIG.SYS file because some programs don't run properly in the DOS 5 environment but do if they think they are running in an earlier version. You use SETVER as a command (at the prompt or on the Run entry line) to tell DOS to notify the program that it's running under another version. SETVER includes a table of such programs that the device driver reads while booting the program. To see the table, enter

```
setver
```

at a prompt.

The table includes many programs that have been certified to run correctly with the false version information supplied by SETVER. But you can add others. If you have a program that runs well under your old version of DOS but doesn't run in DOS 5, use the command

```
setver c:\dos filename.ext n.nn
```

The drive and path tell SETVER where SETVER is located, so it knows where to write the information. *Filename.ext* is the name of the program that didn't run, and *n.nn* is the number of the DOS version that worked. For example, to run GeoWorks Ensemble, you would type

```
setver c:\dos geos.exe 4.01
```

When you reboot the computer, SETVER will be installed with the new version table, and the program should run.

If the program doesn't run any better after you've added it to the version table, delete it from the table with the command

```
setver c:\dos filename.ext n.nn /d
```

✔ **NEW FEATURE**
Reporting version information to a program

▶ **HINT**
If you try to run a program that runs under an earlier version of DOS and instead of locking up the system it displays the message Packed file corrupt, *try running the program with a command of the form* loadfix d:\path\ filename.ext.

NEW FEATURE
Disk cache

Installing a Disk Cache

If you have more than 640K of memory, you may want to set some of it aside as a disk cache. Enter the line

```
device=c:\dos\smartdrv.sys [size] [min]
```

in your CONFIG.SYS file *after* the line that installs HIMEM.SYS. The *size* and *min* parameters are measured in kilobytes. *Size* is the total size of the cache, and *min* is the minimum size to which it can be reduced by other programs (specifically, Microsoft Windows) that use some cache memory for other purposes.

If you don't specify a size, SMARTDRV.SYS will establish a cache of 256K, outside the memory used by programs. The driver itself, however, occupies some of your regular memory.

Generally speaking, the larger the cache, the better your hard disk performs. You can probably also reduce the number of buffers in your BUFFERS statement with no loss of performance. If you have lots of memory, allocate at least a megabyte for the cache:

```
device=c\dos\smartdrv.sys 1024
```

NOTE

If you have expanded memory, use the /A switch to place the cache buffer in it.

Installing a RAM Disk

A RAM disk is a portion of your computer's memory that DOS treats as though it were a disk. It has a directory. You can read from it and write to it as though it were a physical disk. But it is very fast. Because it's so fast, it's a good place to put files that have to be read from disk often. You may want to copy the following types of files to a RAM disk:

HINT

A RAM disk is also a good location for temporary files, because RAM disks aren't permanent. To place temporary files on a RAM disk, assign its root directory to the TEMP variable.

- Files you use many times a day
- Large batch files
- Overlay files (distinguished by the extension OVR or OVL) used by your favorite programs

You'll find a RAM disk especially useful if your system doesn't have a hard disk. It's a good way to keep programs such as FORMAT on hand.

The disadvantage of a RAM disk is that whatever is on it disappears when the power goes off, even for a moment. Therefore it's not a good place to put a file you're editing.

To install a RAM disk, enter a line of the form

```
device=c:\dos\ramdrive.sys [size /e]
```

in your CONFIG.SYS file *after* the line that installs HIMEM.SYS (*size* is measured in kilobytes). The default (and the minimum) is 64K. Match the size to that of the files you want to place on the RAM disk.

The RAM disk will automatically receive the drive letter that comes after your last hard disk. If you have two hard disks, C and D, your RAM disk will be drive E.

You can install a RAM disk in your computer's regular memory (though you may find it cramps your programs). To do so, leave out the /E switch. To install one in expanded memory, use the /A switch instead of /E. For more about expanded memory, see Appendix B.

You can install more than one RAM disk by placing a separate command in the CONFIG.SYS file for each one. For example, to create two RAM disks, one of 64K and the second of 256K, you would use the lines

```
device=c:\dos\ramdrive.sys 64 /e
device=c:\dos\ramdrive.sys 256 /e
```

 HINT

For a noticeable speed-up, install a RAM disk and set the TEMP variable in AUTOEXEC.BAT to point to its root directory. If you use the Shell, include the RAM disk on the AUTOEXEC.BAT search path, before the DOS directory, and add the command copy c:\dos\dosshell.exe e: *(assuming your RAM disk is drive E).*

Installing a Mouse

As noted, your mouse needs a device driver because many programs (including the Shell) won't be able to use it otherwise. If you've upgraded from an earlier version of DOS, the driver is probably already installed. If you're setting up a new system, you'll have to install one.

The place to start is your mouse manual. Follow its instructions for installing the software. Note that many brands of mice include a group of special mouse menus for software that doesn't normally use a mouse—including software you may not have. If you don't want to use this software, you can safely delete it, along with its special directory. Just make sure that you keep the mouse driver file and the mouse test program (if there is one).

Many mice come with two programs that can act as device drivers. MOUSE.SYS is installed in your CONFIG.SYS file, and MOUSE.COM can be run from your AUTOEXEC.BAT file. You need only one of these. You may need the Shell's Search command to find these files. If you're not using the mouse menus, I suggest moving MOUSE.SYS to the root directory and MOUSE.COM to the UTIL directory.

Once you have found them and/or moved them, you can install one. Begin by adding the line

```
device=mouse.sys
```

NOTE

If you have a serial mouse, you'll probably have to tell the driver the name of the serial port to which the mouse is attached. See Chapter 15 for information about serial ports.

to your CONFIG.SYS file. Add any parameters recommended by your mouse manual. If all is well, stop there. If you experience problems, try deleting this line from CONFIG.SYS and add

```
mouse
```

followed by any recommended parameters, to your AUTOEXEC.BAT file at some point after the PATH command.

So What Have You Got Now?

If you've tried everything suggested here, your CONFIG.SYS file might resemble the one in Figure 12.11. This assumes that you have an 80286, 80386, or 80486 microprocessor, several megabytes of memory, a color monitor, a mouse, a long path, and a complex prompt. To go with it, you might use an AUTOEXEC.BAT file such as the one in Figure 12.12.

```
device=c:\dos\setver.exe
files=30
buffers=10
shell=c:\dos\command.com c:\dos\ /e:256 /p
lastdrive=h
device=himem.sys
dos=high
device=smartdrv.sys 1024
device=ramdrive.sys 512
device=mouse.sys /1
device=ansi.sys
```

Figure 12.11   A complex CONFIG.SYS file

Notice that the path now begins with drive E, the RAM disk created in the CONFIG.SYS file. The Shell files are also copied to the RAM disk, so that the Shell will load quickly. Together these two configuration files take advantage of most of the facilities DOS offers you for speeding up your system and protecting your data.

```
@echo off
prompt $e[0;30;42m$t$h$h$h$h$_$e[37;44;1m$p$g
path e:\;c:\dos;c:\batch;c:\util;c:\wp;c:\ss;c:\db;c:\video
set temp=e:\
set dircmd=/p /on
mirror /tc /td c: d:
fastopen c:=60 d:=10
copy c:\dos\dosshell.* e:\
append /e
append c:\video;c:\dict
doskey
dosshell
```

Figure 12.12   A complex AUTOEXEC.BAT file

Batch Files

Chapter 13

What You Will Learn

- How to construct a batch file
- When to use batch files
- How to process command-line options in a batch file
- Special batch file commands

In this chapter you'll learn to create and use batch files. If you work primarily from the prompt, you will find them indispensable. If you work from the Shell, you should read this chapter anyway, because the principles governing batch files also apply to installing programs to run from the Shell.

You'll see many examples of batch files here. You probably won't be able to use them yourself unless you modify them. You may have to change a command or directory path to match your system. But if you learn the principles, you'll be able to create your own batch files to meet your needs.

Why Use Batch Files?

As you learned in Chapter 12, a batch file is a list of DOS commands to be executed sequentially. It can contain any commands you execute at a prompt, plus some special commands. Any time you find yourself repeating the same series of commands more than twice, you can save time with a batch file. You can use batch files to:

- Run programs not on the search path using a single command
- Record a set of parameters for a command you use often
- Use a single command to execute a series of commands
- Create alternative names for commands

Batch files can thus greatly streamline your work.

Creating Batch Files

As you'll remember from editing your AUTOEXEC.BAT file, you can create a batch file with either the DOS Editor (see Chapter 11) or a word processor. If you use a word processor, however, you must save the file as ASCII (unformatted) text. If a batch file is short—one or two lines—you may want to create it with the COPY CON command described in Chapter 3.

Because each line in a batch file is interpreted as a command, it must begin at the left margin and end in a carriage return. Like a command typed at the prompt, a batch file command can be uppercase or lowercase. If it is a program name, the program file must be in the current directory or on the search path, unless you include sufficient path information.

A batch file name follows the same rules as other DOS file names, except it has the extension BAT. If you create a batch file to run a single application that is not on the path, you can give it the same basic name as a DOS internal command or executable file. If you do this, however, never place it in the same directory as the executable program. The batch file will never run. When you give DOS a command, it looks for and executes COM and EXE files before it even looks for a batch file.

Chapter 8 recommended creating a BATCH directory and putting your batch files in it. If you place this directory on your search path right after the DOS directory, it will be the fourth place DOS looks for a command to execute (after COMMAND.COM, the current directory, and the DOS directory).

Running Batch Files

DOS runs a batch file one line at a time. It reads a line, executes it, then reads the next line. Therefore the batch file must be available to DOS until it is finished. This may become a problem on a diskette-based system. If you start a batch file from one diskette and change diskettes before the batch file is finished, you'll see the message

```
Insert disk with batch file
Press any key to continue...
```

DOS waits until you press a key before it looks again for the batch file in drive A. If it isn't there, you'll see the message again. There are two ways around this problem. If you can, place the batch file on the search path. If not, copy it onto every diskette that's likely to be used while running the batch file.

To interrupt a batch file, press Ctrl-C or Ctrl-Break. As soon as the current DOS operation ends, you'll see the message

```
Terminate batch job (Y/N)?
```

 HINT

If you're using diskettes and you have a batch file that you use often, you may be able to solve the problem by creating a small RAM disk with RAM-DRIVE.SYS, as explained in Chapter 12. Have your AUTOEXEC.BAT file copy the batch file to the RAM disk (which will be drive C) and include the command path c:\ *in AUTOEXEC.BAT.*

! WARNING

If your batch file is carrying out a command that can itself be interrupted by Ctrl-Break (such as XCOPY), pressing the key combination will interrupt only that command. You'll have to press it again to interrupt the file.

If you press Y, no further commands will be executed. If you press N, execution will continue. If you press any other key, the message will reappear.

Special Batch File Commands

DOS includes a handful of commands that are used exclusively, or almost exclusively, in batch files. Together they make up a rudimentary programming language. Using the full complement of batch file commands, you can create programs to control complex processes. Such programming is beyond the scope of this book. Here you'll just learn how to use batch files to simplify everyday tasks. However, for reference, a complete list of batch file commands, along with short definitions, appears in Table 13.1. For further information see your DOS manual or the command reference at the end of this book. If you're interested in pursuing the matter still further, recommended books are *Expert Advisor: DOS* (Addison-Wesley, 1989) and *MS-DOS Power User's Guide, Volume 1* (Sybex, 1987), both by Jonathan Kamin.

Running Programs
That Aren't on the Path

Chapter 12 suggested that you place the directories for your most frequently used programs on the search path and run others using batch files. Let's see how this works.

Suppose you usually use a word processor but also have a text editor for specialized work. Suppose further that you've given the editor its own directory because several auxiliary files—configuration files, printer definitions, and such—have to be placed in the same directory as the program file itself. But you prefer to keep your text files in another directory. When you're working in your text file directory, you have to type the editor's full path name:

```
c:\editor\editor filename.ext
```

Table 13.1 Batch file commands

Command	Effect
CALL	Executes another batch file from within a batch file; when the second file is finished, the first continues
ECHO	Controls whether the command prompt and the commands in a batch file appear while the batch file runs; if display of commands is suppressed, can be used to display text
FOR. . .IN. . .DO	Carries out a specified command on a set of objects (files, directories, other commands)
GOTO *label*	Causes a batch file to continue executing after the line containing the specified label
IF [NOT]	Tests for a condition, performing the command that follows only if the condition is true; with the NOT modifier, performs the command only if the condition is false
PAUSE	Temporarily halts a batch file's execution until a key is pressed
REM	Creates a *remark* (a nonexecutable line) that explains what other commands do
SHIFT	Causes the command that follows to act on the next command-line parameter

To cut down on typing you could create a one-line batch file, as in Figure 13.1, on page 298.

Call this file ED.BAT and save it in your BATCH directory. Now you can call your editor by entering

```
ed
```

Instead of seeing

```
Bad command or file name
```

you'll see something like Figure 13.2 (on page 298) until your editor arrives on the screen. (You'll learn shortly how to get the batch file to open a file in your editor.) As this illustration shows, the command in the batch file is simply entered at the prompt and run as though you had typed it there yourself.

```
c:\editor\editor
```

Figure 13.1 ED.BAT, version 1

Let's try something just a bit more complex. Suppose you have a calendar-printing program that can run only from its home directory. Suppose it also keeps its data files in that directory. To run the program, you have to type three commands: a drive name to make the drive current, a CD command to make the directory current, and the program name. Figure 13.3 shows these combined into a single batch file called CALENDAR.BAT in the batch directory.

When you enter

```
calendar
```

you'll again see each command appear at the prompt. And of course your calendar program will load and run.

! WARNING

Notice that this batch file has the same name as a program file. This is all right because CALENDAR.BAT makes the CALENDAR directory current before calling the program. If the batch file didn't include these steps, it would simply execute itself over and over. The same thing happens if you use a batch file to run a program of the same name that's on the search path but further from the beginning than the BATCH directory. DOS will always find the file in the BATCH directory first and run that.

```
D:\NOTES>ed
D:>NOTES>c:\editor\editor
```

Figure 13.2 Running a program from a batch file

```
c:
cd \calendar
calendar
```

Figure 13.3   CALENDAR.BAT, version 1

Controlling What Appears
While a Batch File Executes

You can set up batch files so that they display only the text
you want to see, giving your programs a much more professional appearance. This involves both *not* displaying text
that shouldn't appear and displaying messages that should.

Hiding Batch File Commands

As you've probably noticed, you don't see all the commands
in your default AUTOEXEC.BAT file while it's setting up
your system. This is because the first line

```
@echo off
```

contains two commands that hide text. First, the @ symbol,
when used as the first character on a line in a batch file,
prevents that line from appearing when the file runs. If you
revise ED.BAT to read

```
@c:\editor\editor
```

you won't see anything new on the screen between the time
you enter the command and the time the editor takes over.

Similarly you could rewrite CALENDAR.BAT so that
each line begins with the @ symbol. Neither the prompt nor
the commands would appear, and you'd go right into the
CALENDAR program.

However, you can use the ECHO command for the same purpose. When you place

```
echo off
```

in a batch file, subsequent commands do not appear and the prompt disappears until the file is finished. The command

```
@echo off
```

at the beginning of the AUTOEXEC.BAT file uses both of these techniques. The @ symbol makes sure the `echo off` command doesn't appear, and the `echo off` command makes sure no other commands appear. You may want to get into the habit of beginning batch files of more than a few lines with this command. CALENDAR.BAT would then look like Figure 13.4.

✳ NOTE

Although the actual commands in a batch file following an ECHO OFF command don't appear on the screen, messages generated by the programs it runs do. If your batch file includes the command `del *.bak`, *for example, you'll still see the message* `File not found` *if there are no matching files in the current directory.*

Displaying Messages

You can also use ECHO to display a text message. Just type it after the word ECHO. Such messages can provide information about what's going on in a batch file. Or they can create a batch file that does no more than display information. For example, suppose you place many phone orders

```
@echo off
c:
cd \calendar
calendar
```

Figure 13.4   CALENDAR.BAT, version 2

```
@echo 5010 010 010 010
@echo Expires 6/93
```

Figure 13.5   CC.BAT

using a credit card, and you're always asked for your card number and expiration date. You can create a batch file called CC.BAT containing something like the text in Figure 13.5. If you place this file in your BATCH directory, you can look up your credit card number just by entering

```
cc
```

The result appears in Figure 13.6. No need to fumble in your purse or pocket! (But if you share your computer, or even your office, you may not want this information to be so readily available.)

 HINT

If you want to display more than a few lines of text, put them in a separate file (make sure it's an ASCII, or unformatted, file). Then in your batch file use the commands

```
cls
type filename.ext
pause
```

▶ **HINT**

To make a batch file display a blank line, enter echo . *where you want the line to appear (see Figure 13.18 later in this chapter).*

```
C:\NOTES>cc

5010 010 010 010
Expires 6/93

C:\NOTES>_
```

Figure 13.6   Running CC.BAT

where filename.ext *is the file containing the text to be displayed. (The PAUSE command is explained below.)*

Pausing for a Response

Sometimes you need to do something before a batch file can complete its instructions. For example, you may need to change diskettes in a drive or turn the printer on. The batch command PAUSE places the message

```
Press any key to continue . . .
```

on the screen and waits for a keystroke.

You might, for example, set up a batch file for your daily backup. It could both issue the proper backup command (say, to back up only files changed since the last backup) and print the log file. You don't need to remember parameters, and you can type just one command. An example is shown in Figure 13.7. (The last command copies the file BACKUP.LOG to the printer. You'll learn how it works in Chapter 15.)

A Batch File to Back Up Data

In Chapter 10 you saw three commands to back up your data files in a single backup series. I also promised you a

```
@echo off
c:
cd\
backup c: /s /m /a
echo Is the printer turned on and ready?
pause
copy backup.log lpt1
```

Figure 13.7   DAILYBAK.BAT

batch file that would automate the process. By now you've probably guessed that all you have to do is put the commands into a batch file. Figure 13.8 shows how this batch file would look.

Testing Batch Files

Batch files are relatively simple programs. If you've never written programs before, you may be unfamiliar with two basic principles of programming:

- Include enough information in the program so that you'll understand what it's supposed to do six months after you've written it, or so that someone else can understand it
- Test the program each time you make a change in it

To explain to yourself how a program works, you include comments in it. As mentioned in Chapter 12, a comment is some explanatory text preceded by the command REM (remark). If ECHO is off, remarks don't appear on the screen. You see them only when you examine or edit the file. As you already know, if you want to explain (to yourself or someone else who might use it) what a file is doing, you use the ECHO command to display appropriate messages. In the batch files that follow in this chapter, you'll see many examples of remarks.

As your batch programs become more complex, testing them becomes even more important. As suggested with

```
@echo off
backup c:\*.ltr a: /s /m /a /l:c:\backup\datafile.log
backup c:\newproj\*.* a: /s /m /a /l:c:\backup\datafile.log
backup c:\*.db? a: /s /m /a /l:c:\backup\datafile.log
```

Figure 13.8   DATABAK.BAT

AUTOEXEC.BAT, if you see error messages and you're not sure which command is causing them, delete the `@echo off` line (or put a REM command in front of it). Then you can see each command and the messages it produces on the screen.

If your batch files may delete or rename files, first create a dummy diskette or directory to try them out on. Just copy some files to a diskette and make sure that some of them have names that will match any wild-card pattern in your batch file. That way you can run your program as many times as necessary without worrying about losing precious data.

Using Parameters with a Batch File

As you saw in Figure 13.7, you can include parameters in a batch file the same way you would on the command line. This is fine when you want to use the same parameters over and over. Remembering the switches needed for a daily backup is an excellent use for a batch file.

At times you'll want a shortcut to open a particular file in a particular directory. Suppose, for example, you have a spreadsheet file of expenses called EXPENSE in a directory called BUSINESS\PERSONAL. You also have a spreadsheet file of business miles traveled called MILEAGE in a directory called CAR. You could create a pair of shortcut batch files to open both files in your spreadsheet, without having to remember the details. (These examples assume that your spreadsheet program is on the search path and that it can open a file when given its name as a parameter.) The batch file to open the expense-record file is called EXPENSE.BAT. It contains the commands in Figure 13.9. Similarly MILES.BAT contains the commands in Figure 13.10.

```
@echo off
c:
cd \business\personal
ss expense
mirror
```

Figure 13.9   EXPENSE.BAT

 HINT

Notice that EXPENSE.BAT and MILES.BAT end by running the MIRROR program, which you learned about in Chapter 10. This ensures that the copy of the unformat information is updated every time you modify the spreadsheet files. If you've installed delete tracking, as explained in Chapter 12, MIRROR also updates the delete tracking file. In all probability your spreadsheet program deletes the previous version of the file when you write a modified one. This extra step makes it much easier to get back the previous version if you need to.

But what if you don't always want to use the same parameter? Take our example, in Figure 13.2. It's nice to be able to run your editor without typing a complete path name, but you wouldn't want it to open the same file every time. For this purpose you can use *variables*. A variable consists of the percent sign followed by a number from 1 to 9. When you enter parameters on the command line that runs a batch file, the variables take on the value of those parameters. The number of the variable determines which

```
@echo off
c:
cd \car
ss mileage
mirror
```

Figure 13.10   MILES.BAT

parameter it takes on. Thus %1 is replaced by the first parameter on the command line, %2 by the second, and so on.

Let's work some variations on ED.BAT to use this facility. We could just add the %1 parameter to the existing file:

```
@c:\editor\editor %1
```

Now you can type, say,

```
ed newnote
```

and the command that DOS executes will be

```
c:\editor\editor newnote
```

Now let's suppose your editor uses style sheets for different types of files and will open a style sheet as well as a file if you enter its name as the second parameter. Change the single line of ED.BAT to read

```
@c:\editor\editor %1 %2
```

Now you can enter the command line

```
ed newnote notes.sty
```

and have the editor open the appropriate style sheet.

Variables can take as values *parts* of a command or parameter or the entire command or parameter. Let's assume all your style sheet files have the extension STY. Let's also assume that your style sheets are in the EDITOR directory but that the program doesn't know how to find them there. You can include in your batch file everything except the style sheet's file name and replace that with a variable:

```
@c:\editor\editor %1 c:\editor\%2.sty
```

Now you can just enter

```
ed newnote notes
```

The batch file will do the rest.

 HINT

A program like this is a prime candidate for having its directory on the APPEND list. If you append the EDITOR directory, DOS will find the style sheets in there even without the complete path name. However, if you revise a style sheet you have loaded, when you save it the new version will appear in the current directory, unless you save it with complete path information.

There's a catch, though. If no value is assigned to the variable, it takes on the value of nothing. If you enter only one parameter, DOS will execute the command

```
c:\editor\editor newnote c:\editor\.sty
```

This will probably result in an error message. Don't worry— a solution is forthcoming.

Testing for Conditions

To find out whether various conditions exist, DOS includes the batch file command IF. The general form is

IF [NOT] *condition command*

The modifier NOT tells DOS to execute the *command* if the *condition* is false. If you don't include NOT, the *command* is executed if the *condition* is true. The IF command can be used to test for the existence of a parameter or file. It can also be used with variables that have been placed in the environment by the SET command.

Testing for the Presence of a Parameter

To test for the existence of something—a file, a parameter, or an environment variable—the *condition* you test for is the equivalence of two values, represented by the values and a double equal sign:

value1==value2

As noted, if a value is not passed to a variable, the variable takes on the value of nothing. Nada. Zilch. But not zero. How do you represent nothing in this instance? By a pair of quotation marks with nothing between them. DOS looks for text on the command line. A zero is text. If you want to find out whether a parameter is not there, you might include the code

```
if %1==""
```

But there are circumstances where this won't work. If in fact there is no parameter, DOS will interpret this statement as

```
if ==""
```

This doesn't make any sense, and you'll get a

```
Syntax error
```

message.

To solve this problem, you have to create some kind of equivalence. One way is to enclose the variable itself in quotation marks:

```
if "%1"==""
```

The other is to add an extra character to both sides of the equation:

```
if %1!==!
```

```
if not %1=="" echo %1
if not "%1"=="" echo %1
if not %1!==! echo %1
```

Figure 13.11   NOTHING.BAT

DOS will read the first formulation as

```
if ""==""
```

and the second as

```
if !==!
```

Both statements are of course true. If you don't believe it, create the batch file NOTHING.BAT, shown in Figure 13.11. Figure 13.12 shows the results when you run it with and without a parameter.

Let's look at the logic of this test. The first time we ran NOTHING.BAT, we gave it a parameter. If you look at how DOS translated each line, it's clear that the items on the two sides of the double equal sign are not the same. We asked DOS to ECHO something if the statement was *not* true. So DOS echoed the parameter "something." The second time, we got a syntax error as expected on the first line and nothing on the following two. These two times, the values were equivalent. However, when DOS evaluated the statement

```
if not ""==""
```

```
C:\TEMP>nothing something

C:\TEMP>if not nothing=="" echo something
something

C:\TEMP>if not "nothing"=="" echo something
something

C:\TEMP>if not nothing!==! echo something
something

C:\TEMP>

C:\TEMP>nothing

C:\TEMP>if not =="" echo
Syntax error

C:\TEMP>if not ""=="" echo

C:\TEMP>if not !==! echo

C:\TEMP>

C:\TEMP>_
```

Figure 13.12   Running NOTHING.BAT, version 1

it knew that it was to do something only if the values were *not* equivalent. Therefore it stopped after evaluating the equation and didn't attempt to execute

```
echo %1
```

or more precisely,

```
echo
```

```
C:\TEMP>nothing something

C:\TEMP>if nothing=="" echo something

C:\TEMP>if "nothing"=="" echo something


C:\TEMP>if nothing!==! echo something

C:\TEMP>


C:\TEMP>nothing

C:\TEMP>if =="" echo
Syntax error

C:\TEMP>if ""=="" echo
ECHO is on

C:\TEMP>if !==! echo
ECHO is on


C:\TEMP>


C:\TEMP>_
```

Figure 13.13   Running NOTHING.BAT, version 2

To clarify the point, edit NOTHING.BAT to delete the word not from all three lines and run it again. The result appears in Figure 13.13.

This time you'll notice that DOS did nothing when it found the parameter because it was told to do something only when it found nothing. When we didn't give NOTHING a parameter, DOS attempted to execute the command

```
echo %1
```

However, since %1 was in fact equal to nothing, it executed

```
echo
```

The ECHO command, when executed with no parameters
(OFF, ON, or a message), simply reports whether ECHO is
off or on.

 HINT

*You'll notice in these examples that the prompt appeared twice
after each time the batch file ended. This happens when the last
line of a batch file ends in a carriage return. If you don't want to
see the prompt twice, don't press Enter after the last line. If you're
using COPY CON, press Ctrl-Z before you press Enter.*

Knowing what you know now, you can revise ED.BAT so
that it can behave appropriately depending on whether it has
to open a style sheet. Figure 13.14 shows the new version.

This time, different lines are executed depending on
whether a second parameter exists on the command line. The
last line runs MIRROR once again, to record any changes you
may have made.

In all the examples, we've been testing merely for the
presence or absence of a parameter. When you test for a

```
@echo off
if %2!==! c:\editor\editor %1
if not %2!==! c:\editor\editor %1 c:\editor\%2.sty
mirror
```

Figure 13.14   ED.BAT, version 2

specific parameter, DOS pays attention to the case of the letters you type. You may therefore have to include multiple tests. Moreover, you can't match *part* of a parameter.

Say you want to create a batch file for formatting diskettes of a certain size. If you expect to use the diskette size as a command-line parameter for the batch file, you have to be sure you've covered all the likely possibilities. Figure 13.15 shows what the code might look like for testing for a parameter indicating a 360K diskette.

Testing for the Presence of a File

To test for the presence of a file, use the modifier EXIST with the IF command:

IF [NOT] EXIST [*path*]*filename.ext command*

The file name can include wild-card characters. Include a path name if you want to find out about the existence of files on a directory other than the current one.

As an example, a batch file to delete backup copies might look like NOBAK.BAT in Figure 13.16. This file would work just as well *without* the IF statement. But with it DOS won't execute the command

```
del *.bak
```

```
if %1!==360!...
if %1!==360K!...
if %1!==360k!...
if %1!==360Kb!...
if %1!==360kb!...
if %1!==360KB!...
```

Figure 13.15   How to match parameters exactly

HINT
One alternative is to accept a more limited range of parameters and display a message explaining the acceptable parameters if none is entered (see Figure 13.20 later in this chapter).

```
@echo off
if exist *.bak del *.bak
mirror
```

Figure 13.16   NOBAK.BAT, version 1

unless matching files exist. This means you won't see the

```
File not found
```

message. (This can be helpful in longer, more complex batch files, where you don't know which of several commands may be generating the message if ECHO is off.)

You can use the EXIST modifier to create your own messages. Figure 13.17 presents another version of NOBAK.BAT, which takes different courses of action depending on whether there are files to delete.

Changing the Flow

Up to now we've looked at batch files that go straight through from beginning to end. You can have a batch file skip inappropriate lines, or repeat several, creating a *loop*.

```
@echo off
rem If backup files exist, delete them
if exist *.bak del *.bak
rem if no backup files, display message
if not exist *.bak echo No backup files in this directory
mirror
```

Figure 13.17   NOBAK.BAT, version 2

The GOTO command tells DOS to skip to a specified point in the batch file, indicated by a *label*. A label is a set of eight characters preceded by a colon. You can use any characters that are legal in file names.

We've revised ED.BAT so it can respond appropriately whether or not a style sheet is named on the command line. Let's take this a step further. Suppose your program won't start properly unless you give it the name of a file to open. You can have the batch file find out whether a file name appears and respond with an appropriate message if it doesn't. Figure 13.18 shows the revised version of ED.BAT.

In this version you see two GOTO commands and two labels: message and end. Here's how this program works. The third line checks for the presence of the first parameter. (If there's no first parameter, there obviously aren't any others.) If there are no parameters, it goes to the line

```
:message
```

```
@echo off
rem If no parameters, explain proper procedure
if "%1"=="" goto message
rem If only one parameter, open the file in the editor
if %2!==! c:\editor\editor %1
rem If two parameters, load style sheet as well as file
if not %2!==! c:\editor\editor %1 c:\editor\%2.sty
mirror
goto end
:message
echo You must enter the name of a file to open!
echo.
echo You may optionally enter the name of a style sheet
echo (without an extension) after the file name.
:end
```

Figure 13.18   ED.BAT, version 3

```
C:\TEMP>ed

You must enter the name of a file to open!
You may optionally enter the name of a style sheet
(without an extension) after the file name.
C:\TEMP>_
```

Figure 13.19   ED.BAT executed with no parameters

which is a label. The lines following the label display a message. If DOS finds a parameter, the test in the third line is false, so the file proceeds to the fourth through ninth lines. Notice that the ninth line reads

```
goto end
```

The end label is at the very end of the batch file. Therefore DOS skips the messages telling what to do if you've made a mistake. Figure 13.19 shows what the screen would look like if you forgot to enter a file name on the command line.

Other Uses for Batch Files

In the following examples, you'll see a few other reasons for using batch files. You'll see another example of remarks, and you'll also see a circumstance in which you might want to use the CALL command.

Alternative Command Names

You may want to use batch files to shorten command names, to provide alternative names, or to remember particular groups of parameters. For example, if you often mistype the DIR command as DRI or FIT, you could have batch files called DRI.BAT and FIT.BAT, both of which contain the following single line:

```
@dir %1 %2 %3 %4 %5 %6 %7 %8 %9
```

This allows you to enter DIR with a file name and up to eight switches. Even if you mistype the command name, you can still get the right results.

Shortening Commands and Remembering Parameters

Let's see how you can use a batch file to remember groups of parameters and shorten the command. Suppose you have two diskette drives, a 1.2Mb drive as drive A and a 1.44Mb drive as drive B. Each drive can format diskettes of two different sizes. You could create the file FMT.BAT (see Figure 13.20) to keep track of the relationship between the drive type and the diskette capacity.

This file accepts as the first parameter only a number of kilobytes. This parameter determines which part of the program to execute. Up to three other parameters may be used. The variables %2, %3, and %4 receive them as values. Otherwise these variables will have no value and will be ignored. If your first parameter is not one of the four acceptable ones, the message is displayed and the program ends. This program also shows how remarks can be used to clarify what the program is doing.

Changing the Path as Needed

Sometimes a program you don't use very often absolutely must be on the path and be appended. But your path is too long to include its directory. You can create a temporary path in a batch file, then restore the regular path at the end. To begin, create a file called MYPATH.BAT that con-

```
@echo off
rem **** Test for an acceptable parameter ****
if %1#==360# goto 360
if %1#==720# goto 720
if %1#==1200# goto 12
if %1#==1440# goto 14
rem     **** If no acceptable parameter, display message and quit ****
echo Please enter the capacity of the diskette to be
echo formatted as a number of kilobytes; for example:
echo .
echo FMT 720
echo .
echo You may optionally enter FORMAT switches after the diskette size.
goto end
rem     **** Format a 360K diskette in drive A
:360
format a: /f:360 %2 %3 %4
goto end
rem     **** Format a 720K diskette in drive B
:720
format b: /f:720 %2 %3 %4
goto end
rem     **** Format a 1.2Mb diskette in drive A
:12
format a: /f:1200 %2 %3 %4
goto end
rem     **** Format a 1.44Mb diskette in drive B
:14
format b: /f:1440 %2 %3 %4
:end
```

Figure 13.20   FMT.BAT

tains your regular PATH and APPEND commands. Then create a batch file that creates the correct path for your program and starts it. Let's say it's called DOTHIS.EXE. DO.BAT, in Figure 13.21, shows how to change your path for a single program.

As you can see, all you have to do to call one batch file from another is enter its name just like a regular program name. However, to return to your original batch file after executing the second one, you must use a CALL command.

```
@echo off
rem Set temporary path
path c:\dothis;c:\dos;\c:batch;c:\util
append c:\dothis
rem Run DOTHIS
dothis %1 %2 %3 %4
mirror
rem Restore regular path
mypath
```

Figure 13.21   DO.BAT

One place you might use CALL is in your AUTOEXEC.BAT file, in place of the PATH and APPEND commands. Now that these commands are stored in MYPATH.BAT, your AUTOEXEC.BAT could begin something like Figure 13.22. The advantage is that if you change your PATH or APPEND command, you can do it in just one place— MYPATH.BAT. You don't have to keep two files up-to-date. Notice that, because you have not yet established a path, you must include full path names both for APPEND and MYPATH.BAT. Without these DOS would look only in the root directory.

```
@echo off
prompt $p$g
c:\dos\append /e
call c:\batch\mypath
set temp=e:\
■
■
■
```

Figure 13.22   Part of an AUTOEXEC.BAT file with a CALL command

Running Your Applications from the DOS Shell

Chapter 14

What You Will Learn

- How to open a file in a program automatically
- How to associate data files with a program
- How to customize the Shell's program menu
- How to run several programs at once
- How to load resident pop-up programs

Running Programs from the File List

In Chapter 4 you saw quite a few ways to run a program from the file list. To summarize them: You can press Enter or double-click on a COM, EXE, or BAT file in the file window, select the program and use the Open command on the File menu, use the Run command and enter a command line, or run the program from a command prompt. In this chapter you'll learn how to customize the Program List so that it runs your programs exactly as you want it to.

Opening a File in a Program

Many programs can open a file if its name appears as a parameter on the program's command line. If you use a mouse, you can simulate this kind of command line in the

☐ **MOUSE**

Shell. Select the data file to open by clicking on it with the left button but don't release the button. Instead drag the mouse to the name of the program in which you want to open the file. If you're in graphics mode, the pointer changes to a circle with a line through it as it passes through names of files that aren't programs (see Figure 14.1). When the pointer arrives at a program file, it changes to the icon for a data file—a piece of paper with writing on it and the left corner bent over. When you reach the appropriate program, release the mouse button. Unless you've turned off `Confirm on Mouse Operation` in the Options menu, you'll see the dialog box in Figure 14.2. If you select `Yes`, the data file will be opened in the selected program. If you select `No`, the dialog box closes and the program isn't run.

> **! WARNING**
>
> *If you've first selected a program file by mistake, the Shell will still offer to open it in your selected program when you release the button.*

It takes some skill to use this technique. First, it works only if the program and the data file are in the same directory or if you're using the Dual File List display. If the program name isn't visible when you select the data file, move the mouse pointer to the arrow at one end of the scroll

Figure 14.1   Selecting a program to use with a file

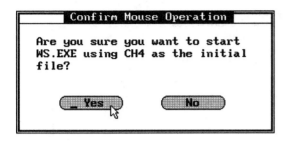

Figure 14.2   Confirming a mouse action

bar and scroll through the window until the program file appears. Be careful not to let go of the mouse button. If necessary, you can drag the pointer to the other arrow and scroll in the opposite direction.

If you're using the Dual File List, first make the directory containing the data file current in one Directory Tree window and the directory containing the program current in the other. Once you've selected the data file, you can drag to the other window and use the scroll bar to find your program.

Associating Programs and Files

There's a much simpler way to run a program from the file list and have it open a data file: *associate* a file extension with a given program. To do this, display a directory in the file window that contains a file with the appropriate extension. Select that file. Then select the Associate command from the File menu. You'll see the dialog box in Figure 14.3. Enter the program's *file* name. (That is, if the software package is called something like Whizbang Paint and the command that runs it is PAINT, you enter PAINT.COM or PAINT.EXE.) Now when you select any file with the same extension, it will be opened in the associated program.

The one prerequisite for associating file extensions is that an extension must be reserved for the data files of only one program. If you have two text editors, for example, you may have to assign the extension TXT to one and DOC to the other. And the effectiveness of both associating extensions

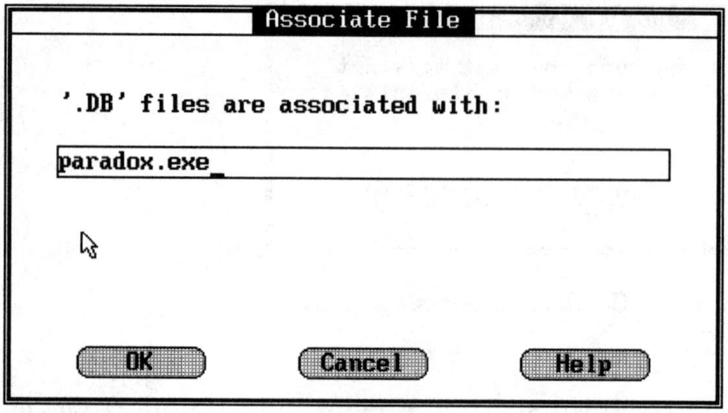

```
┌──────────────────────────────────────────────────────┐
│                  ▓ Associate File ▓                    │
├──────────────────────────────────────────────────────┤
│                                                        │
│    '.DB' files are associated with:                    │
│   ┌──────────────────────────────────────────────┐    │
│   │paradox.exe_                                    │    │
│   └──────────────────────────────────────────────┘    │
│                                                        │
│        ▷                                               │
│                                                        │
│                                                        │
│    ┌──────────┐   ┌──────────┐   ┌──────────┐          │
│    │    OK    │   │  Cancel  │   │   Help   │          │
│    └──────────┘   └──────────┘   └──────────┘          │
│                                                        │
└──────────────────────────────────────────────────────┘
```

Figure 14.3   The Associate File dialog box

and simulating command lines depends on how the program behaves at the prompt. If the program's home directory must be current, it won't run any better in the Shell with some other directory current. If you must enter a full path name on the command line, you should include the path name in the Associate File dialog box. If the program must be on the path or must have its directory appended, you still have to meet those conditions.

Installing Programs in the DOS Shell

As you no doubt remember, you can also run programs from the program group window. This window contains two types of objects: *program items,* which run a particular program, and *program groups,* which contain other program items. We're going to work with the program group window now, so choose the Program/File Lists option from the View menu, then select the program group window. (To display this window only and close the Directory Tree and file windows, select Program List, then the program group window.)

To refresh your memory, the Shell comes with several programs installed in the Main program group: the Editor,

QuickBASIC, the command prompt, and a program group called Disk Utilities. The latter includes Disk Copy, Backup Fixed Disk, Restore Fixed Disk, Format, Quick Format, and Undelete. You can edit or delete any items or add your own. You can add individual programs to the Main group or add new program groups.

In essence, what you do when you place a program in the program group window is create a batch file to run it. While the commands are essentially the same as those you learned in Chapter 13, there are a few additional options. Most important, you can set up dialog boxes that prompt you for input. You create one for every variable in the batch file, so you don't have to remember exactly which parameters a program requires.

You can also specify default parameters. You can ask the Shell to use the currently selected file in the file window as a parameter. Or you can ask that the last parameter used become the default for the next time you use the program. Finally, you can add a help window for any program or group.

In this section we'll translate some of the batch files from Chapter 13 into program items. You'll see that the technique is the same, but the way you have to think is different.

Strategic Considerations

Approach the creation of program groups the way you do your directory tree. Before you think through your style of working, you might be tempted to create a program item in the program group window for each of your principal software packages. That's akin to placing all your software in your root directory. It causes confusion and obfuscates the purpose of program items.

There are two sensible ways to go about creating program items. You can create an item for each program and have it prompt you for the parameters you must enter to get to the right data file. A program item of this type would resemble ED.BAT in Chapter 13. Alternatively, you can build in all the steps required, in the manner of MILES.BAT and EXPENSE.BAT in that chapter.

Additionally, you can group your programs, much as you group subdirectories under directories. You can have groups within groups. Your grouping system must make sense to you and/or those who share your computer.

You might place in a single group a set of program items that use the same program but open different files. Thus you might have a Spreadsheet group that includes items called Record Miles Driven and Record Expenses. Or you could create a group containing items for all the software you use in working on a given project. And of course you can create some groups of each type. This means you may have several program items for a given software package. That's perfectly acceptable; in fact you can copy an item from one group to another. If you wish, you can then edit the item in one of the groups.

You might use a program group to take the place of branching in a batch file. In FMT.BAT, as you may remember, we had four separate routines for formatting a diskette, one for each diskette type. If you were to install an equivalent in the Shell, you might have one group called Format Diskettes and four separate items within it. That's what we're going to create now.

NOTE

The illustrations show the Shell with the Program List window only, just to keep things clear. When you run programs, you will probably prefer to have both the program list and the file list available.

Adding a Program Group

The appropriate place for a group of commands to format diskettes is the Disk Utilities group, so select it. The File menu will look like Figure 14.4. The commands are appropriate only to program items and groups. Select New. You'll see the New Program Object dialog box in Figure 14.5. Select Program Group, either with the Tab key or the mouse. You'll now see the dialog box in Figure 14.6.

Editing the Add Group Dialog Box. The Add Group dialog box has three entry lines, a required one for adding a group title and two optional ones for help text and a password. The help text can be up to 255 characters long. The

```
┌─────────────────────────────┐
│ File                        │
├─────────────────────────────┤
│ New...                      │
│ Open            Enter       │
│ Copy                        │
│ Delete...       Del         │
│ Properties...               │
│ Reorder                     │
├─────────────────────────────┤
│ Run...                      │
├─────────────────────────────┤
│ Exit            Alt+F4      │
└─────────────────────────────┘
```

Figure 14.4   The File menu for the program group window

Shell automatically adjusts it to fit the help dialog box. If you want to begin a new paragraph, enter the characters

> ^m

To skip a line, enter

> ^m^m

If you enter a password, only a person who knows it can use the program group. The password can be up to 20 characters long and can contain any keyboard characters, including spaces. However, you must match the characters *exactly* when asked for the password. You can't substitute uppercase characters for lowercase or vice versa. And as you can see in Figure 14.7, you'll have to type the password with no assistance from the screen.

If you forget your password, all is not completely lost. Passwords (along with everything else you set up in the

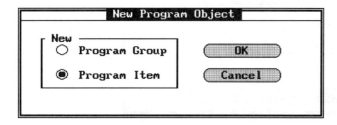

Figure 14.5   The New Program Object dialog box

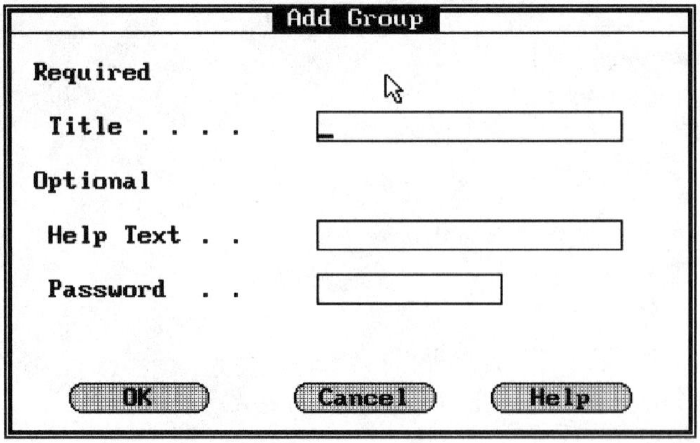

```
┌─────────────────■ Add Group ■─────────────────┐
│                                                │
│  Required                      ⊾               │
│                                                │
│    Title . . . .    ┌────────────────────────┐ │
│                     │_                       │ │
│  Optional           └────────────────────────┘ │
│                                                │
│    Help Text . .    ┌────────────────────────┐ │
│                     └────────────────────────┘ │
│    Password  . .    ┌──────────────┐           │
│                     └──────────────┘           │
│                                                │
│                                                │
│      ( OK )      ( Cancel )      ( Help )       │
│                                                │
└────────────────────────────────────────────────┘
```

Figure 14.6   The Add Group dialog box

Shell) are stored in a file called DOSSHELL.INI. This is a text file (which you can edit in the Editor), in which passwords are identified. You can, if necessary, delete the line containing the password. If you're familiar with programming structures and concepts, you should have no trouble. If you're not, get some help from a more experienced computer user.

The fact that you can delete a password by editing DOSSHELL.INI means that passwords don't really give you much security. You're protected only if everyone else who might use your computer uses the Shell and not the command prompt—and hasn't read this book!

All the dialog boxes in which you set up program group objects are in insert mode. You can use only a few text-editing keys, which are summarized in Table 14.1.

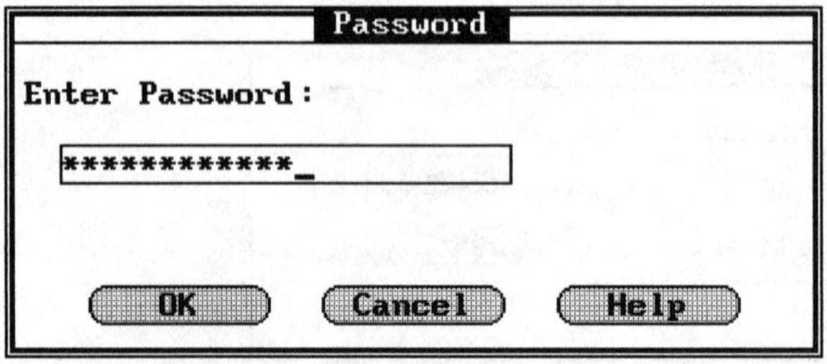

```
┌──────────────■ Password ■──────────────┐
│                                         │
│  Enter Password:                        │
│                                         │
│    ┌──────────────────────────────┐     │
│    │***********_                   │     │
│    └──────────────────────────────┘     │
│                                         │
│     ( OK )     ( Cancel )     ( Help )   │
│                                         │
└─────────────────────────────────────────┘
```

Figure 14.7   Entering a password

Table 14.1 Keys for editing entry lines

Key	Effect
Home	Moves the cursor to the beginning of the line
End	Moves the cursor to the end of the line
→	Moves the cursor to the right one character
←	If the text is not highlighted, moves the cursor to the left one character; if the text is highlighted, moves the cursor to the beginning of the line
Del	Deletes the character at the cursor
Backspace	Deletes the character to the left of the cursor

Creating a New Program Group. In the Title entry line, enter

```
Format Diskettes
```

In the Help Text entry line, you might enter something like:

```
     Use the commands in this group to format
a diskette. This process erases all the files.
Choose Quick Format to format diskettes that
contain files you might want to get back later.
```

Unless you have an overwhelming need for a password, leave the Password entry line blank.

When you've filled out the dialog box, select OK. A new icon will appear, followed by Format Diskettes, at the bottom of the program group (see Figure 14.8). If you like, press F1 to view the help text you've created, as shown in Figure 14.9.

Copying and Deleting Programs and Groups. The next step is to move the existing Format and Quick Format program objects into your new group. You can't do this in one step because you can't select more than one item in the program group window, and there's no Move command on the File menu. First select Format. Next

```
┌──────────────────────────────────────────────────────────────┐
│                        MS-DOS Shell                            │
│  File   Options   View   Help                                  │
│                        Disk Utilities                          │
│  ▦ Main                                                    ▲   │
│  ▢ Disk Copy                                                   │
│  ▢ Backup Fixed Disk                                           │
│  ▢ Restore Fixed Disk                                          │
│  ▢ Quick Format                                                │
│  ▢ Format                                                      │
│  ▢ Undelete                                                    │
│  ▦ Format Diskettes                                            │
│                                                                │
│                                                                │
│                                                                │
│                        ▷                                       │
│                                                                │
│                                                                │
│                                                            ▼   │
│  F10=Actions          Shift+F9=Command Prompt         10:10a   │
└──────────────────────────────────────────────────────────────┘
```

Figure 14.8   Adding a new program group

```
┌──────────────────────────────────────────────────────────────┐
│                     MS-DOS Shell Help                          │
│ ┌────────────────────────────────────────────────────────────┐│
│ │              Help For Format Diskettes                     ▲││
│ │    Use the commands in this group to format diskettes. This││
│ │ process erases all the files. Choose Quick Format commands to││
│ │ format diskettes that contain files you might want to get back││
│ │ later.                                                      ││
│ │                        —•—                                  ││
│ │                        ▷                                    ││
│ │                                                             ││
│ │                                                            ▼││
│ └────────────────────────────────────────────────────────────┘│
│                                                                │
│   ( Close )    ( Back )    ( Keys )    ( Index )    ( Help )   │
└──────────────────────────────────────────────────────────────┘
```

Figure 14.9   Viewing a new help screen

choose Copy from the File menu. The status line will
display the legend

```
Display the group to copy to, then press
F2. Press Esc to cancel.
```

Open Format Diskettes either by double-clicking on it or
by selecting it and pressing Enter. Press F2. Your screen
should now look like Figure 14.10. Reopen Disk Utilities (it will be selected) and repeat the procedure with
Quick Format. Now open Disk Utilities again, select
each object one more time, and press Del. The objects will be
deleted from the Disk Utilities group.

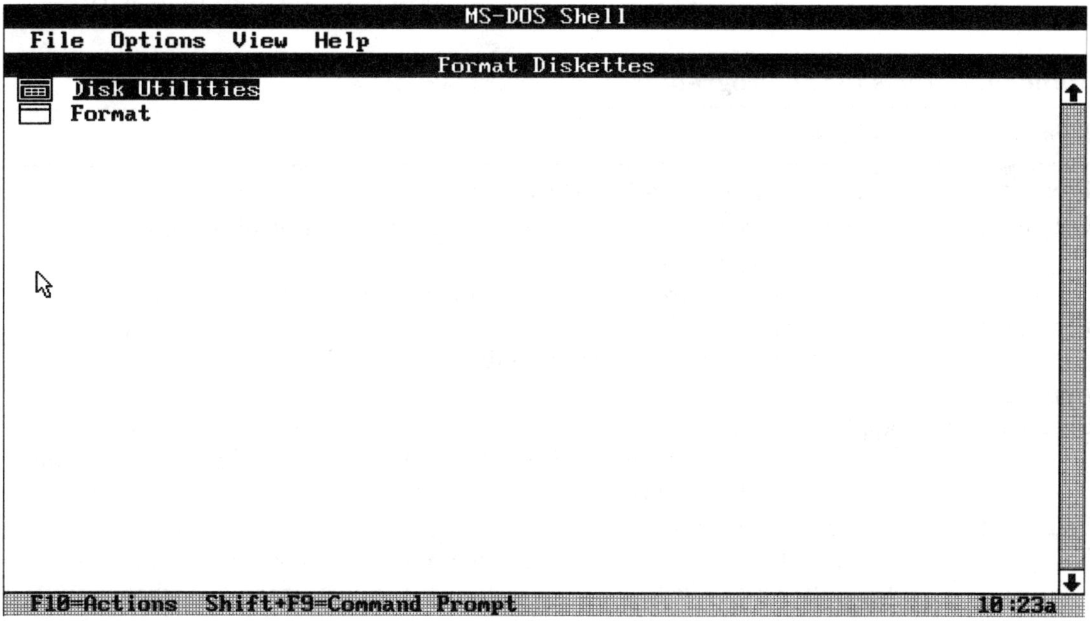

```
                            MS-DOS Shell
  File   Options   View   Help
                          Format Diskettes
  ▦  Disk Utilities                                              ↑
  ▭  Format




        ▷


                                                               ↓
  F10=Actions   Shift+F9=Command Prompt                    10:23a
```

Figure 14.10   Copying a program item

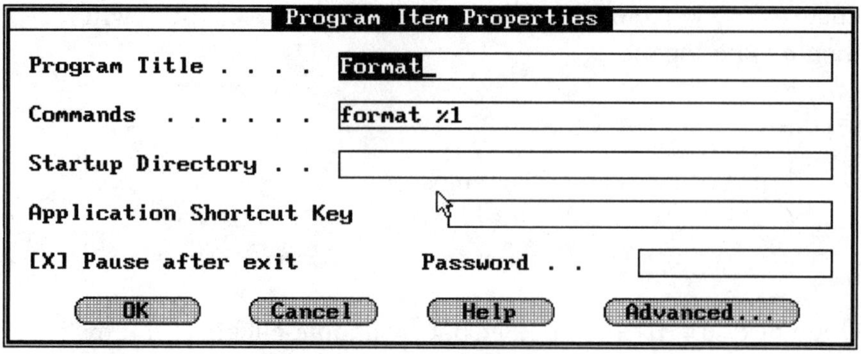

Figure 14.11   The Program Item Properties dialog box

Editing the Properties of an Object

The next step is to edit the program objects. Select For-mat, then the Properties... command. You'll see the Program Item Properties dialog box in Figure 14.11. This is where you'll create your alternative to a batch file. Table 14.2 shows the six items you have to deal with.

Table 14.2   Items in the Program Item Properties dialog box

Item	Purpose
Program Title	The name that appears at the top of the dialog box.
Commands	Here is where you write your pseudo-batch file. Multiple commands can be entered if they are separated with semicolons.
Startup Directory	If the program's directory must be current, enter it here. Alternatively, if the program is on the path and can run from anywhere but you want a specific data directory current, enter the data directory.
Application Shortcut Key	An optional key combination that switches you directly into an application when you have more than one application program running; you can use any alphanumeric key in combination with Ctrl or Alt, or Shift plus Ctrl or Alt, or any combination of these three with a function key.
Pause After Exit	If this item is checked, you'll see the message Press any key to return to MS-DOS Shell...after you leave your application program. You only need to do this if your program displays a message when it ends and you'd like to see that message.
Password	You can enter a password for each program item as well as for program groups. The same rules for passwords in program groups apply to passwords in program items.

We'll assume, as we did in Chapter 13, that you have a 1.2Mb drive as drive A and a 1.44Mb drive as drive B. For your program name, press the ← key and change the text to read

```
Format 360K Diskette
```

On the Commands entry line, press ← and change the text to read

```
format a: /f:360
```

(You pressed ← first because pressing any other key would erase everything on the entry line. This way you can just add a few characters. If you use a mouse, click where you want to insert text.) You may want to turn off Pause after exit by moving the cursor to the check box and pressing the space bar, or by clicking in the check box. Now choose OK. You're done.

Select your new item, Format 360K Diskette, choose the Copy command from the File menu, and press F2. You'll now have two copies of this item. Repeat the procedure twice. Select one of your four copies and choose Properties from the File menu. Change the title to read

```
Format 720K Diskette
```

and the command to read

```
format b: /f:720
```

Give a third copy the title

```
Format 1.2Mb Diskette
```

and the command line

```
format a: /f:1220
```

Give the fourth copy the title

```
Format 1.44Mb diskette
```

 HINT

It's a good idea to test each new item, just as you test batch files. You may have mistyped something that causes the item to fail or to respond differently than you expected.

and the command line

```
format b: /f:1440
```

Now you can choose your format by selecting a program from the Format Diskettes group.

Rearranging the Items. Your screen should now look something like Figure 14.12. This isn't the most logical arrangement. Let's change the order of the items so that Quick Format comes before Format 360K Diskette. Select Quick Format and choose Reorder from the File menu. The status line displays the message

Select location to move to, then press ENTER. Press ESC to cancel.

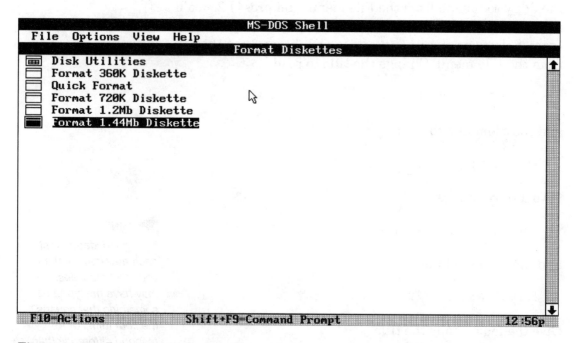

Figure 14.12   Rearranging the items in a group

Press ↑ so that the highlight moves up one position, then press Enter. The items should be grouped. You can change the position of program groups as well as program items by this method.

Prompting for Parameters

If you add variables to the commands on the `Commands` entry line, you get to set up a dialog box that asks for a value for each variable. You can make this information as explicit as you like.

As you may remember, the FORMAT commands in the FMT.BAT file in Chapter 13 included three variables. One you might certainly want to allow for is the /S (system) switch, to make a startup diskette. But if your drives can format two different diskette sizes, you may want to be able to use either as a startup diskette.

Make one more copy of the `Format 360K Diskette` item. Change the title to

```
Make a Startup Diskette
```

Change the command line to read

```
format a: /s /f:%1
```

When you choose `OK`, you'll see the dialog box in Figure 14.13. It's another `Program Item Properties` box, but it includes the explanation

```
Fill in information for %1 prompt dialog.
```

Now as a rule, the entry lines in the dialog box will be blank. However, because you've been copying a program that was configured for you, the dialog box "inherits" the original's entries. Create the dialog box that will prompt you for the diskette capacity. Change the `Window Title` to

```
┌──────────────────────────────────────────────────────────┐
│               │ Program Item Properties │                  │
│  Fill in information for % 1   prompt dialog.              │
│                                                             │
│  Window Title . . . .   ┌─────────────────────────────────┐│
│                         │Format_                           ││
│                         └─────────────────────────────────┘│
│  Program Information .   ┌─────────────────────────────────┐│
│                         │Enter the drive to format.        ││
│                         └─────────────────────────────────┘│
│  Prompt Message . . .    ┌─────────────────────────────────┐│
│                         │Parameters . . .                  ││
│                         └─────────────────────────────────┘│
│     Default Parameters . .  ┌──────────────────────────────┐│
│                             │a:                             ││
│                             └──────────────────────────────┘│
│                                                             │
│      ( ═══ OK ═══ )    ( Cancel )       ( Help )            │
└──────────────────────────────────────────────────────────┘
```

Figure 14.13   Entering text for a prompt dialog

```
Make a Startup Diskette
```

This will appear at the top of the window. `Program Infor-mation` is the text that will appear above the entry line. You can enter up to 106 characters. We'll assume that you'll usually use 360K diskettes. Enter

```
        Press ENTER to accept the default of
    360K. Enter 1200 to make a 1.2Mb diskette.
```

The text in the `Prompt Message` entry line will appear where `Prompt Message` appears in this dialog box. Enter

```
    Diskette Capacity:
```

Finally, on the `Default Parameters` entry line, enter

```
    360
```

✱ NOTE

If your command includes more than one variable, you'll be asked to fill out a dialog box for each.

Your dialog box should now look like Figure 14.14. Select `OK`. When you choose this new item, you'll see the dialog box in Figure 14.15.

Using Multiple Commands

So far we've been writing what amounts to one-line batch files with dialog boxes. That's fine—but you can do virtually

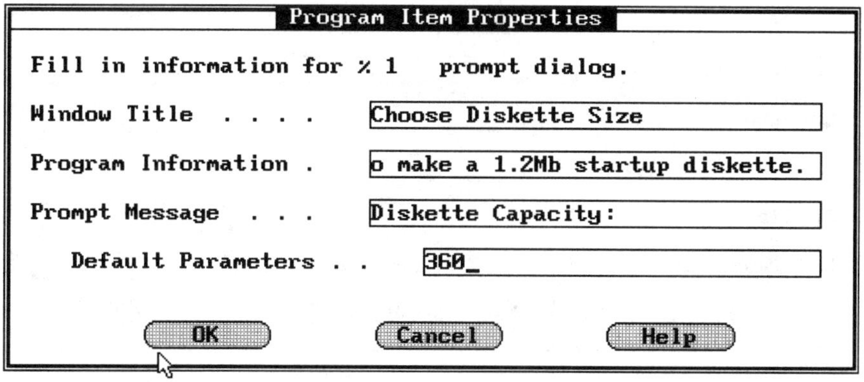

```
┌──────────────── Program Item Properties ────────────────┐
│                                                          │
│  Fill in information for % 1   prompt dialog.            │
│                                                          │
│  Window Title  . . . .    ┌Choose Diskette Size      ┐   │
│                           └──────────────────────────┘   │
│  Program Information .     ┌o make a 1.2Mb startup diskette.┐│
│                           └──────────────────────────┘   │
│  Prompt Message  . . .     ┌Diskette Capacity:        ┐   │
│                           └──────────────────────────┘   │
│     Default Parameters . .  ┌360_                     ┐   │
│                            └─────────────────────────┘   │
│                                                          │
│        ( OK )         ( Cancel )         ( Help )        │
│                                                          │
└──────────────────────────────────────────────────────────┘
```

Figure 14.14   The filled-out dialog box

anything in the Shell that you can in a batch file. Let's recreate EXPENSE.BAT from Chapter 13 as a program item. We'll put it in the Main program group for now. You can copy or delete it later if you wish. Select Disk Utilities, then select Main.

As you may recall, the EXPENSE program included the following lines:

```
@echo off
c:
cd \business\personal
ss expense
mirror
```

We won't need the @echo off command, because commands aren't echoed when you run programs from the Shell.

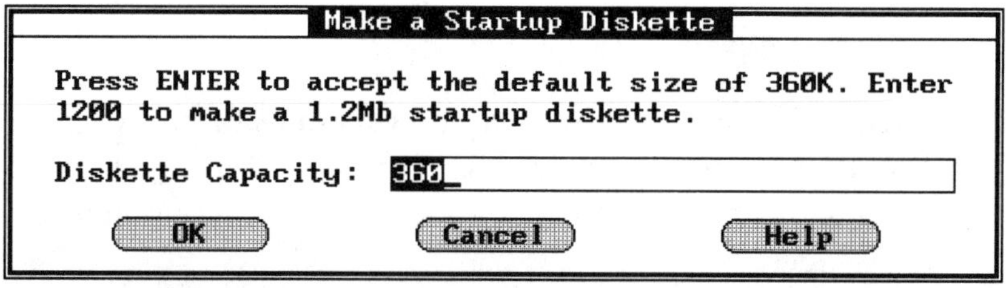

```
┌──────────────── Make a Startup Diskette ────────────────┐
│                                                          │
│  Press ENTER to accept the default size of 360K. Enter   │
│  1200 to make a 1.2Mb startup diskette.                  │
│                                                          │
│  Diskette Capacity:  ┌360_                            ┐  │
│                      └──────────────────────────────┘   │
│        ( OK )         ( Cancel )         ( Help )        │
│                                                          │
└──────────────────────────────────────────────────────────┘
```

Figure 14.15   The dialog box you created

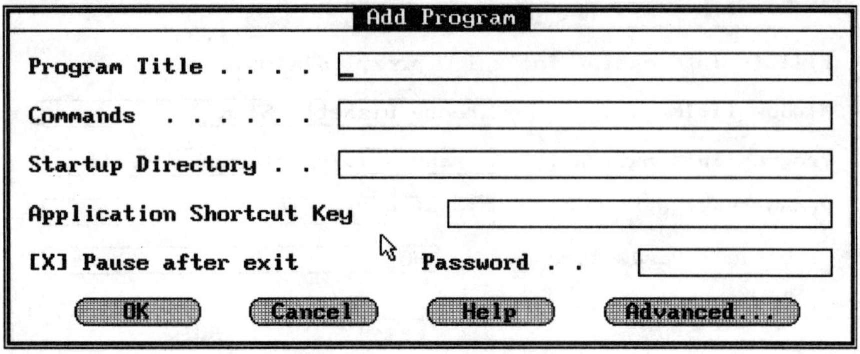

```
╔══════════════════════════════════════════════════════════╗
║                       Add Program                         ║
║                                                            ║
║  Program Title . . . . . [_                             ] ║
║                                                            ║
║  Commands  . . . . . . . [                              ] ║
║                                                            ║
║  Startup Directory . .   [                              ] ║
║                                                            ║
║  Application Shortcut Key      [                        ] ║
║                                                            ║
║  [X] Pause after exit      ⌐  Password . .  [          ] ║
║                                                            ║
║    ( OK )      ( Cancel )      ( Help )     ( Advanced...) ║
╚══════════════════════════════════════════════════════════╝
```

Figure 14.16   The Add Program dialog box

But we need to get four lines from a batch file into a single entry line. How? It's easy. You separate the lines with semicolons. Choose Ne_w from the File menu. The Program item button is selected, so press Enter or click on OK. You'll see the Add Program dialog box in Figure 14.16. Notice that it's exactly the same as the Program Item Properties dialog box in Figure 14.11. So you know how to fill it out, right?

For Program Title enter

    Record Expenses

For Commands enter

    ss expense; mirror

Wait a minute! What about making the correct drive and directory current? That's what the Startup Directory entry line is for. On that line enter

    c:\business\personal

and select OK. Because there are no variables to fill in, there will be no prompts to respond to. Run this item by double-clicking on it or by selecting it and pressing Enter. You'll see the messages

```
Bad command or file name

Press any key to return to MS-DOS Shell...
```

Did you make a mistake? Probably not. But you probably don't run your spreadsheet by entering SS or don't have a file called C:\BUSINESS\PERSONAL\EXPENSE. If you substitute actual program, directory, and data file names, you'll have something you can use.

! WARNING

You can use variables only on the Commands *entry line. If you want the program item to prompt you for a directory to make current, you can't enter a variable on the* Startup Directory *line. Instead you must include it among the commands; for example,* c: ; cd %1 ; ss %2. *You will then have to create two dialog boxes, one to prompt you for the directory and another to prompt you for the file name.*

✳ NOTE

If you wish, you can run a batch file from a program item. Place the CALL command before the batch file name. To run EXPENSE.BAT from this program item, you could have just typed call expense *on the* Commands *line. If one command in a series runs a batch file, place the CALL command before it, within the same semicolons as the command itself.*

You have now learned all the principles and techniques for creating program items and groups. With a little effort, you can create one or more program items for all your major software packages. Just plan ahead, so that your groupings make sense to you. Remember, however, that you can also run programs from the file window. If you've associated file extensions with your software packages, you can tailor the Shell environment to match your working style.

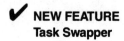

✔ **NEW FEATURE**
Task Swapper

❗ **WARNING**

You can even run several copies of a program with the same file open. This is not a good idea. Each time you save the file from one copy, you will overwrite changes you've saved with another. You can make a real mess of your files that way.

Running Multiple Programs

Now that you understand all the fundamentals of using the Shell to run your programs, let's turn our attention to a more advanced feature: loading and running several programs at once. You can even run the same program several times, each with a different file. Thus, for example, you can open a document in your word processor and a worksheet in your spreadsheet program. Say you need to look up a few figures to include in your document. You just hit a key combination to pop up your spreadsheet. Hit another combination and you're back in your word processor.

You may have heard of *multitasking,* whereby several programs simultaneously run and occupy parts of the computer's memory. The Shell does not give you true multitasking. Instead when you switch to a different program, it writes the contents of memory to a file. When you switch back to that program, it writes what's now in memory to another file and reads the previous one back. This takes a noticeable amount of time. But it is still faster than exiting one program and calling up another, and you don't lose your place in the file.

> ❗ **WARNING**
>
> *The Shell writes these files to the directory named in the TEMP variable. Therefore don't delete files with strange names from that directory while you're running multiple programs. You may be deleting the information the Shell needs to bring back another program you're using. However, if your computer has locked up while several programs are open, delete these files after you restart your computer but before starting any applications.*

The key to this wonderful feature is the command `Enable Task Swapper` on the Options menu. When you select this command, a small dot appears next to it, and your screen rearranges itself to resemble Figure 14.17. (If you choose Program List instead of Program/File Lists, only the bottom two windows will appear.) Once you activate the Task Swapper, you can move between the Shell

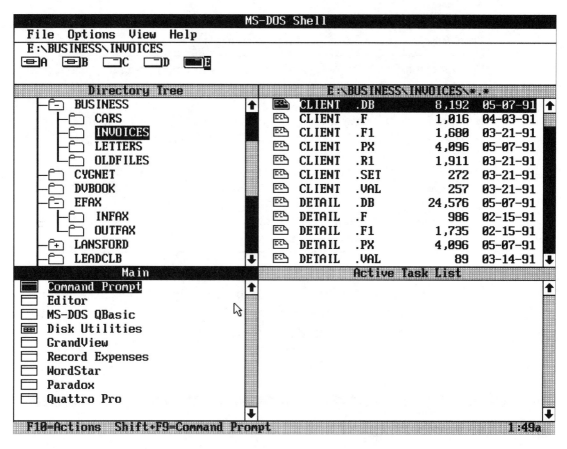

Figure 14.17   The Shell with the Task Swapper enabled

and applications you have opened by pressing one of the special key combinations shown in Table 14.3.

Figure 14.18 shows how the screen might look when you have loaded several applications. Some have Application Shortcut Keys assigned to them in the Program Item Properties dialog box. When a program has an assigned shortcut key combination, you can switch to it by pressing the keys. You need not switch back to the Shell first or cycle through all the loaded programs.

Note that some keys listed in Table 14.3 may be used by your applications. If so, you won't be able to use them for task swapping. Select the Advanced button in the Program

Table 14.3 Task-swapping keys

Key	Effect
Shift-Enter	Places a program on the Active Task List without opening it or leaving the Shell.
Ctrl-Esc	Returns from your current task to the Shell.
Alt-Tab	Switches to the next active program; hold down the Alt key and press Tab repeatedly to cycle through programs. If only two are active, toggles between them.
Shift-Alt-Tab	Switches to the previous active program; hold down the Alt and Shift keys and press Tab repeatedly to cycle backward through the programs. If only two are active, toggles between them.
Alt-Esc	Switches to the next active program.
Shift-Alt-Esc	Switches to the previous active program.

Item Properties dialog box, and you'll see the Advanced dialog box in Figure 14.19. Here you can "reserve" those keys for your application. Instead of switching to another application, the reserved key combinations will have their

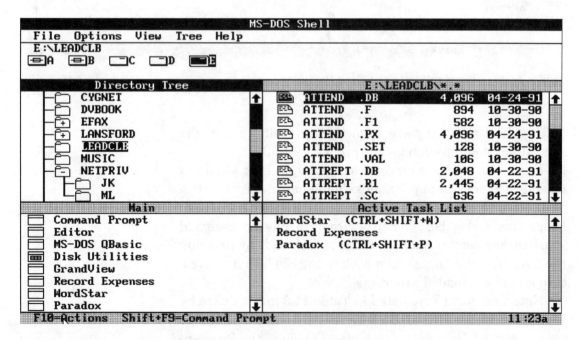

Figure 14.18   The Active Task List with several programs open

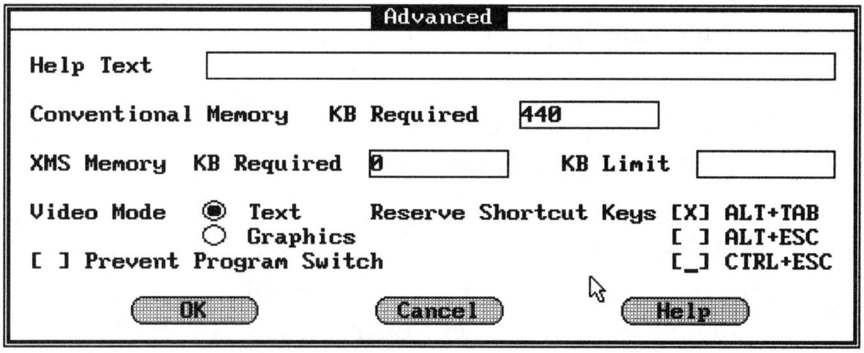

```
┌──────────────────────█ Advanced █──────────────────────┐
│                                                          │
│  Help Text    ┌──────────────────────────────────────┐ │
│               └──────────────────────────────────────┘ │
│                                                          │
│  Conventional Memory   KB Required   ┌──────────────┐   │
│                                      │440           │   │
│                                      └──────────────┘   │
│  XMS Memory  KB Required ┌──────────┐   KB Limit ┌────┐ │
│                          │0         │            │    │ │
│                          └──────────┘            └────┘ │
│  Video Mode    ◉ Text      Reserve Shortcut Keys [X] ALT+TAB │
│                ○ Graphics                        [ ] ALT+ESC │
│  [ ] Prevent Program Switch                      [_] CTRL+ESC │
│          ╭──────────╮      ╭──────────╮    ╭──────────╮  │
│          │    OK    │      │  Cancel  │    │   Help   │  │
│          ╰──────────╯      ╰──────────╯    ╰──────────╯  │
└──────────────────────────────────────────────────────────┘
```

Figure 14.19   The Advanced dialog box

normal function in that application. You will be limited to the remaining keys for swapping.

! WARNING

If all the key combinations are used by an application, try to reassign one combination within the application, rather than reserving them all. (Reserving them all is equivalent to selecting Prevent Program Switch.*) In either case once you load the application, the only way you'll be able to get back to the Shell is by quitting the application. You won't be able to swap.*

The Advanced dialog box also has some spaces to enter information about memory used by your program. If you know how much memory a program requires, enter it in the KB Required entry field. The Shell won't attempt to start the program if this much memory is not available; however, the program will get all the memory available if it can start.

The XMS Memory fields can usually be ignored. The Shell pays no attention to them in any case unless you have turned on the Task Swapper. If you have, and you specify an amount of XMS memory required, the Shell will start the program much more slowly—or not at all if the memory is not available. (See Appendix B for an explanation of XMS memory.) If your program's documentation says that XMS memory *is* required, you can limit how much it receives, so that it doesn't take all the XMS memory, by specifying a maximum amount in the KB Limit entry field.

Launching Applications with Swapping Enabled

There are two ways to start an application once you have enabled the Task Swapper. First, you can run the program from the program list, just as you would without the Task Swapper. When you select the program and press Enter, or double-click on it, it will run as usual. However, you can press Ctrl-Esc to return to the Shell. The program you started will be in the Active Task List window, and you return to it by selecting it from there. (Selecting from the Program List will launch a second copy, rather than return to the one you've already launched.) You can run another application the same way.

Alternatively, you can first move all the applications for a session to the Active Task List. To move an application to the Active Task List without actually starting it, select it and press Shift-Enter. You'll then select programs from that list.

Closing Down Active Tasks

You can't exit from the Shell if there are tasks in the Active Task List. If an application has been loaded, you should always switch to it and close it first. You *can* close an application by simply selecting it in the Active Task List and pressing Del, but as Figure 14.20 implies, you will lose data if an unsaved file is open. You must select Cancel before you close

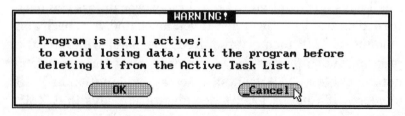

Figure 14.20   A warning about deleting active tasks

the application; otherwise it will be deleted. You might think
OK means "OK, I've understood the message and will do as
suggested," but it means "OK, close the application anyway."

The one time it's safe to delete an active task is when you
have placed it on the Active Task List by pressing Shift-
Enter but haven't yet run it. Although the Shell regards the
application as "active," no file is opened until you actually
switch to the application.

A Few Words About Resident Programs

You may like to use resident pop-up programs with some
applications. If not, skip this section. If so, give some
thought to how you want to use them.

When the Task Swapper takes a program out of memory,
it removes *everything* loaded *since* you loaded the Shell.
Therefore if you load resident programs before the Shell,
you can use them in any application you run through the
Task Swapper.

In principle you should never load a resident program
after a nonresident one (like the Shell). However, the Task
Swapper has some unusual effects on the way pop-up programs behave. On the one hand, you can load a pop-up
program as a single task. The message in Figure 14.21 will
appear over its sign-on screen. If you give the program a
Program Item in the Program List window and start it from
there, the program will appear in the Active Task List when
you run it. You can treat the program as an individual task
and switch to and from it using the Task Swapper's switch
keys. Just remember to switch back to it and press Ctrl-C
before you exit the Shell.

```
┌──────────────────────────────────────────────────────────────────┐
│              MS-DOS TASK SWITCHER'S POP-UP PROGRAM SUPPORT         │
├──────────────────────────────────────────────────────────────────┤
│ Your pop-up program has been loaded and you may activate it as you would │
│ normally.  When you have finished using this pop-up program, exit it and │
│ press Ctrl+C to return to the Shell.                              │
└──────────────────────────────────────────────────────────────────┘
```

Figure 14.21   The pop-up program message

On the other hand, you may want to load a pop-up program in conjunction with another program, as part of a task. For example, you may want to use a keystroke recorder or printer-control program with your word processor, or a pop-up calculator with your accounting program. Or you may want to use a keystroke recorder with several key-stroke files, each for a different task.

You can easily load a separate pop-up program—or a group of them—with a regular application. However, you can't just list the commands sequentially in the Commands entry line of the Program Item Properties dialog box. Suppose your Commands line contains the following, which is supposed to load your pop-up calculator, switch to a data directory, and load your accounting program:

```
popcalc /r ; cd \accounts\1991 ; accounts
```

When the Shell loads POPCALC, it will immediately display the message in Figure 14.21. You will be able to either pop up your calculator, switch to another task, or press Ctrl-C to return to the Shell. You'll never get to your accounting program.

However, you *can* load both a pop-up program and an application from a batch file. Enter

```
call shellac
```

in the Commands line for that program item. Create a batch file (in your BATCH directory) called SHELLAC.BAT, containing the text in Figure 14.22. This allows you to execute all the commands, and your pop-up calculator will pop up

```
@echo off
popcalc /r
cd \accounts\1991
accounts
```

Figure 14.22   SHELLAC.BAT

over your accounting program. When you exit the accounting program, the message in Figure 14.21 will appear. You can then safely press Ctrl-C and return to the Shell.

You can load your calculator with another program the same way. The numbers you enter in conjunction with one task won't affect the other, because one copy of the calculator will be in a swap file on disk.

Controlling the Flow of Information

Chapter **15**

What You Will Learn

- How to print files
- How to print command output
- How to send output to the serial port
- How to alter command output and files with filters
- How to set up and use serial devices
- How to use a print queue
- How to print graphic screens

As a rule, when you work at your computer, you type at the keyboard and the result appears on the screen. Thus not surprisingly, DOS regards the keyboard as the *standard input device* and the screen as the *standard output device*. Together they form the *console.*

But output doesn't have to go to the console, nor does input have to come from it. DOS includes a feature called *redirection,* with which you can direct output to a file or to another device. Under some circumstances you can also force a program to accept input from a point other than the console. Moreover you can sometimes send the output from one program to another for further processing by means of a *pipe.*

In this chapter you'll learn about the DOS logical devices—the potential destinations for data for which DOS has special names—and the commands that communicate with them. You'll also learn to use pipes and redirection to direct data to points other than the screen and to direct input to a file from points other than a program.

The DOS Logical Devices

In a practical sense, the destinations to which you can send output include files plus printers, modems, and other devices attached to the back of your computer. In a logical sense (from the computer's point of view), these destinations are actually the ports to which the peripheral equipment is attached. Each port has a *logical device name* by which DOS knows and addresses it. The ports are of two types: *serial* (or *COM*) and *parallel*. These terms refer to the way the computer handles data going to and from each type of port. Table 15.1 lists the DOS logical devices.

Although DOS provides for three logical printer ports and four logical communication ports, you may not have that

Table 15.1 DOS device names

Name	Function
CON	The console; i.e., the keyboard and screen
PRN	The default printer (parallel) port
LPT1	The first printer (parallel) port
LPT2	The second printer (parallel) port
LPT3	The third printer (parallel) port
COM1	The first communication (serial) port
AUX	An alternative name for the first communication port
COM2	The second communication (serial) port
COM3	The third communication (serial) port
COM4*	The fourth communication (serial) port
NUL	The null (i.e., "nowhere") device, also known as the "bit bucket"

*PS/2 computers can theoretically have four more ports named COM5 through COM8.

many. Ports have to be physically present for you to use them, either built in or on an expansion card. (Monochrome video cards normally include a printer port.) If you have an internal modem, it uses a logical port name but doesn't require an additional serial port. Most computers today are sold with one printer port and two communication ports, named LPT1, COM1, and COM2, respectively.

Directing Files to Devices

Logical device names can take the place of file names in commands. You used a device name when you created MYFILE in Chapter 3 with the command

```
copy con myfile
```

This told DOS to copy the information coming from a device—the console—to MYFILE. You can also use CON— or any other logical device—as the command destination. For example, you can display your CONFIG.SYS file on the screen by entering

```
copy config.sys con
```

Notice that the COPY command works the same way with a device as with a source and destination file. In the first command, you copied from a device (as though it were a file) to a file. In the second, you copied from a file to a device.

You can even copy directly from one device to another. To try this, turn on your printer and enter

```
copy con prn
```

Then type

```
This text should be printed, not displayed.
```

When you press Ctrl-Z, you'll see the message

```
1 File(s) copied
```

as usual, but the text you entered should appear on your printer. This is a good way to find out whether your printer is hooked up properly.

Printing Files Using Logical Device Names. More commonly you'll use COPY to send an existing file to the printer. You'll find it especially useful for printing text files and text generated by commands such as DIR. To print an unformatted file, such as CONFIG.SYS or a batch file, just make the printer the COPY target:

```
copy config.sys prn
```

or

```
copy autoexec.bat lpt1
```

You encountered this form of the COPY command in Chapter 10, when you printed your backup log file.

Printing a File Using Redirection. You can also use redirection to print a file. The command

```
type navigate.bat >prn
```

has the same effect as

```
copy navigate.bat prn
```

Printing Command Output Using Redirection. Sometimes you want to print command output. You can of course print your screen's entire contents by pressing Shift-PrtSc or Print Screen, or you can have the printer echo everything that appears on the screen by pressing Ctrl-PrtSc or Ctrl-P. But you can also direct your computer to print specific command output. To do so, use one of the *redirection operators:* >. This symbol placed after a command tells DOS to send its output to the destination you specify. Table 15.2 describes the four redirection operators. (Think of the angle brackets as arrows pointing in the direction the information flows.)

Using a redirection operator, you can, for example, print all the directories and subdirectories of your hard disk by entering

```
dir c:\ /s >lpt1
```

The listing will appear on your printer, but nothing will appear on your screen until printing stops.

HINT

You needn't type a space after a redirection operator, but a space before it is sometimes necessary. Get into the habit of entering one.

 **WARNING**

If you placed the command set dircmd=/p *in AUTOEXEC.BAT, you'll have to type* dir /-p *to keep DOS from stopping at the end of a page. Otherwise* Press any key to continue... *will appear on your printer, and everything will stop until you press a key. This can be quite mystifying if you direct the output to a file instead of the printer, because you won't have any warning that DOS is waiting for a keystroke. Your computer will appear to be dead. Press Ctrl-Break to get your prompt back.*

You'll probably find many uses for printing command output using redirection. For example, many commands produce reports that are too lengthy to fit on a single screen. A comparison of two files using FC, for instance, may come up

Table 15.2 Redirecting operators

Operator	Effects
>	Directs command output to the destination specified after the operator
>>	Appends command output to the file specified after the operator
<	Directs input to a command from the source specified after the operator
|	Makes the output of the command before the operator the input of the command after it

with too many differences for you to see on the screen at once.

Sending Command Output to a File. Since a logical device replaces a file name in a command, it follows that the target of redirected output can be a file. You can, for example, save a directory listing in a file by entering a command such as

```
dir a: >diskette.dir
```

Once you've saved the listing (or any file), you can append information to the end of it using the redirection operator >>. For example, to record which DOS file is on which DOS diskette in a file called DOSDIRS, place each diskette in drive A and enter

```
dir a: >>dosdirs
```

for each one.

Another command that can be used creatively with redirection is the batch command ECHO. You can use it to append a line to a file or send control characters to your printer. To send a form feed character (Ctrl-L) to your printer, enter

```
echo ^L >lpt1
```

(That's Ctrl-L, not a caret mark followed by an L.) Sure enough, if your printer is on-line, a page will roll out. You might even want to save this command in a batch file called FORMFEED.BAT (or FF.BAT). Then you'll be able to set your printer to a new page just by entering ff. You won't have to bother with printer switches.

If you need to add a line to the end of your CONFIG.SYS file, you can enter a command such as

```
echo device=c:\mouse.sys >>c:\config.sys
```

The append operator will create the file if it doesn't exist or append the text being redirected. There are only two things to watch out for. First, if you use the single > symbol by mistake and the file exists, you'll replace it with a new one by the same name. It will contain only the text you echoed. Second, if you use a text editor that places a Ctrl-Z character at the end of a file, the text will be appended. But DOS won't know it's there, because DOS stops reading a file when it encounters Ctrl-Z.

Sending Information to a Serial Port. Let's look at using redirection to send data to a device that occupies a serial port, for example, a modem. Sometimes a modem inexplicably "picks up the line," and you'll hear a dial tone; or it fails to hang up properly after a call. If your modem uses the *Hayes command set* (most modems currently available do), you can use ECHO to send commands to it. To get the modem to hang up, for example, send the Hayes hang-up command to the port. If the modem is at COM1, you would enter

```
echo +++ath0 >com1
```

To reset the modem to its starting state, enter

```
echo +++atz >com1
```

(For the rest of the Hayes command set, see your modem manual.)

Hiding Command Output. Sometimes you don't want to see the output of a command. You can hide most output by redirecting it to the NUL device. NUL is basically a black hole. Stuff you send there disappears forever. This technique is especially useful in batch files, where you may not be able to tell which command is creating messages anyway.

For example, suppose your AUTOEXEC.BAT file includes a command to copy a group of files to a RAM disk. Another command deletes all the BAK files from your

BATCH directory. The first command will display a long list of files on the screen. The second will generate the message

```
File not found
```

if there are no BAK files. You can clean up the display by adding your own text and directing the command output to NUL:

```
echo Setting up RAM disk on drive E...
xcopy c:\ramdisk e:\ >nul
echo Deleting old BAK files...
del c:\batch\*.bak >nul
```

Filters and Pipes

To send the output of one program to another for further processing, you use a *pipe*, symbolized by the pipe operator, |. When you send the output through an intermediate program, you are running it through a *filter*. DOS includes three programs that can be used as filters: FIND, SORT, and MORE. See Table 15.3 for a brief overview of these. Shortly you'll learn how to use them.

Finding Text

The FIND filter finds specified text in command output or an unformatted text file. It can search multiple files if you name them on the command line but does not accept wildcard characters. It always displays the complete line containing the text. Its general forms are

FIND *"text" file1.ext file2.ext ... filen.ext* [*/switch*]

and

COMMAND | **FIND** *"text"* [*/switch*]

Obviously in the first form, FIND is a regular DOS command; in the second, it's a filter. You may ask, What makes this a filter when the output isn't passed on to another destination? Actually it *is* passed on—to the console. You might think of the second form as

COMMAND | **FIND** *"text"* >CON

Of course you can also send the output to a file or the printer by using the redirection operator and specifying a different destination.

Let's try both versions of FIND. Chapter 12 suggested that you include MIRROR in batch files that run programs to update the deletion tracking file. To do so, you might go through a procedure like the one shown in Figure 15.1, which also illustrates FIND's limitations.

For each file you ask FIND to search, it displays the file name followed by each line containing the text. As you can see, the first command included a wild-card character and FIND rejected it. You'll also see that FIND is "case-sensitive." That is, it won't find uppercase characters if you ask for lowercase and vice versa. The command had to be

Table 15.3 DOS filters

Command	Effect
FIND	Finds specified text and displays the lines containing it. Optionally displays only lines *not* containing the text, the line numbers of the text displayed, or counts the number of lines containing the text.
SORT	When given text with no formatting codes, sorts lines in alphabetical order. Optionally sorts in reverse alphabetical order or sorts on any column of characters.
MORE	When more than a screenful of text is displayed, stops when the screen is full and displays - -More- - Press a key to see the next screen.

```
C:\BATCH>find "mirror" *.bat

File not found - *.BAT

C:\BATCH>find "mirror" busmil.bat cars.bat medmil.bat

---------- BUSMIL.BAT
mirror e:

---------- CARS.BAT

---------- MEDMIL.BAT
mirror e:

C:\BATCH>find "MIRROR" busmil.bat cars.bat medmil.bat

---------- BUSMIL.BAT

---------- CARS.BAT
MIRROR F:

---------- MEDMIL.BAT

C:\BATCH>_
```

Figure 15.1   Using FIND to search for text in files

used twice, once with mirror and once with MIRROR to find all instances in the specified files.

FIND has three switches, which alter its effects. They are listed in Table 15.4.

Table 15.4 FIND switches

Switch	Effect
/V	Finds only lines that *don't* contain the specified text
/N	Places a line number at the beginning of each line displayed
/C	Counts the number of lines containing the text

Let's use FIND as a filter. Suppose you wanted to find all files that were created or changed on a certain date. Since a full directory entry contains the date on the same line as the file name, you can search directory entries for it. You'd need to search all your directories and filter out those with the correct date. You'd use a command such as the following:

```
dir c:\ /s |find "05-09"
```

You'd see a result similar to Figure 15.2.

Notice that the output format is different when you use FIND in a pipe. Since it isn't searching files, it doesn't display the names of files in which the text is found.

Let's extend the pipe. Let's say, having seen the result in Figure 15.2, you don't want to see files whose names begin with FIG. You could use FIND a second time with the /V switch to filter those out:

```
C:\BATCH>dir c:\   /s |find "05-07"
PCT1FAX            8075 05-07-91   10:56p
STATUS    GV      46144 05-07-91    4:50p
APPOINT   622        53 05-07-91   10:03p
CAR_SUM   WQ1     3297 05-07-91    2:31p
JAGUAR    WQ1    10482 05-07-91    2:31p
MEDMIL    WQ1    25740 05-07-91    2:34p
CLIENT    DB      8192 05-07-91    2:14p
INVOICE   DB      4096 05-07-91    2:15p
DETAIL    DB     24576 05-07-91    2:15p
CLIENT    PX      4096 05-07-91    2:14p
DETAIL    PX      4096 05-07-91    2:15p
INVOICE   PX      4096 05-07-91    2:15p
FIG1402   PCX    11463 05-07-91    5:35p
FIG1401   PCX    41216 05-07-91    5:27p
FIG1104   SCR     8128 05-07-91   11:03p

C:\BATCH>_
```

Figure 15.2   Using FIND to locate files with a specific date

```
dir c:\ /s |find "05-09" |find /v "FIG"
```

You'd see the result in Figure 15.3.

Sorting Text

To sort text, DOS provides the SORT command. SORT works a little differently from FIND. It's always a filter. But you can use it to sort the text in a file by directing the file to SORT as *input* with the < operator. Alternatively you can use it in a pipe the same way as FIND. Its two general forms are

SORT < *filename.ext* **[/switch]**

and

COMMAND | SORT [/switch]

SORT can work on only one file at a time. Like FIND, it works best on unformatted text files but can also work on command output. It has only two switches. One is /+*n*, which sorts on a specific column (*n* is the number of the

```
C:\BATCH>dir c:\  /s |find "05-07" |find /v "FIG"
PCT1FAX             8075 05-07-91   10:56p
STATUS    GV       46144 05-07-91    4:50p
APPOINT   622         53 05-07-91   10:03p
CAR_SUM   WQ1       3297 05-07-91    2:31p
JAGUAR    WQ1      10482 05-07-91    2:31p
MEDMIL    WQ1      25740 05-07-91    2:34p
CLIENT    DB        8192 05-07-91    2:14p
INVOICE   DB        4096 05-07-91    2:15p
DETAIL    DB       24576 05-07-91    2:15p
CLIENT    PX        4096 05-07-91    2:14p
DETAIL    PX        4096 05-07-91    2:15p
INVOICE   PX        4096 05-07-91    2:15p

C:\BATCH>_
```

Figure 15.3   Filtering a list twice

column to sort; the left column of the screen or file is column 1). The second switch, /R, sorts in reverse order.

Commonly you'll sort a file and save the results in a new file, using double redirection. For example, to sort a phone list, you might type

```
sort <phonelst.txt >phonelst.new
```

This command is most useful in a file where the data is in regularly spaced columns. If the last names all begin in the ninth column (as they might if you used the Tab key to align columns), you'd use the command

```
sort /+9 <phonelst.txt >phonelst.new
```

Figure 15.4 shows the effects of this command, first displaying the unsorted file, then the sorted file.

```
D:\BUSINESS>type phonelst.txt

Fred      Thimsfrabble  Nationwide Thimsfrabble Co. 1(904)303-9812
George    Oscarmeyer    Best Wurst Co.              501-0987
Nancy     Sassoon       Creative Designs            555-9382
Sybil     Danning       Adventures, Unltd.          555-9013
Fiona     Chatsworth    Data Processing Temps       555-8145
Howard    Franklin      Sky High Technologies       1(209)901-6027


D:\BUSINESS>type phonelst.new

Fiona     Chatsworth    Data Processing Temps       555-8145
Sybil     Danning       Adventures, Unltd.          555-9013
Howard    Franklin      Sky High Technologies       1(209)901-6027
George    Oscarmeyer    Best Wurst Co.              501-0987
Nancy     Sassoon       Creative Designs            555-9382
Fred      Thimsfrabble  Nationwide Thimsfrabble Co. 1(904)303-9812

D:\BUSINESS>_
```

Figure 15.4   Sorting a file

✻ **NOTE**

Most text editors and word processors place a tab stop at every eighth column in the mode that creates unformatted text files. DOS always *interprets tab stops being at every eighth column.*

If you want to sort a text file, be aware of how your editor or word processor handles the Tab key. Some editors insert a single *tab character* each time you press Tab, which moves the following characters to the next tab stop. If you use TYPE to display the file on the screen or print it on most printers, it will appear correct. But since SORT regards Tab as a single character, you won't get the correct results. Instead you'd get a result like Figure 15.5. To find out if there are tab characters, backspace from the beginning of a word. If the word jumps to the previous tab stop or the end of the previous word, you've deleted a tab character.

Let's use SORT as a filter. Continuing an earlier example, suppose you want to find files with a given date and have them sorted in alphabetical order. You'd add the SORT filter to the end of the pipe. Figure 15.6 shows the result of such a command.

You might wonder why you need SORT when you can sort a directory using switches. But remember, when you use the /ON switch to sort by name, it sorts *each directory* by name. When you use the /S switch, you're viewing all the subdirectories of the specified directory. Each is sorted, but the files selected by FIND won't necessarily come from a single directory and therefore may not be in order. To sort all the file names selected by FIND into a single list, regardless of their original location, you'd have to use SORT.

```
D:\BUSINESS>sort /+9 <phonelst.txt

Howard  Franklin     Sky High Technologies       1(209)901-6027
Sybil   Danning      Adventures, Unltd.          555-9013
Nancy   Sassoon      Creative Designs            555-9382
George  Oscarmeyer   Best Wurst Co.              501-0987
Fiona   Chatsworth   Data Processing Temps       555-8145
Fred    Thimsfrabble Nationwide Thimsfrabble Co. 1(904)303-9812

D:\BUSINESS>_
```

Figure 15.5 Sorting a file with tab characters

```
C:\>dir C:\ /s |find "05-08" |sort

COMMUTE  COM     545 05-08-91   9:08p
CPSDOS   GRP   12197 05-08-91   9:53p
DATAMON  PIF     545 05-08-91   9:08p
DM       PIF     545 05-08-91   9:08p
FF       PIF     545 05-08-91   9:58p
FILEFIND PIF     545 05-08-91   5:27p
FILEFIX  PIF     545 05-08-91   9:08p
NONWINDO GRP    5906 05-08-91   2:08p
PCCONFIG PIF     545 05-08-91   9:08p
PCFORMAT PIF     545 05-08-91   9:08p
PROGMAN  INI     407 05-08-91  10:02p
PROGMAN  SAV     407 05-08-91   9:08p
SI       PIF     545 05-08-91   9:08p
SYSTEM   INI    1260 05-08-91   9:08p
SYSTEM   SAV    1260 05-08-91   9:08p
VIEW     PIF     545 05-08-91   9:08p
WIN      INI    6792 05-08-91  11:20p
WIN      SAV    6655 05-08-91   9:08p
WIN      SYD    6792 05-08-91  10:00p
WINPROJ  INI     960 05-08-91  10:01p
WIPE     PIF     545 05-08-91   9:08p

C:\>_
```

Figure 15.6   Sorting a filtered directory listing

Halting the Screen Display

The MORE filter stops text from scrolling off the top of the screen. Its effect is similar to adding the /P switch to DIR. Again you can either direct input to it or use it in a pipe. Its forms are:

> **MORE <*filename.ext*
> **MORE <*COMMAND*
> *COMMAND* **I MORE**

If the TYPE command displays text too fast, you can replace it with the first form or variation on the third:

```
more <meeting.txt
```

or

```
type meeting.txt |more
```

When the screen is full, the message

```
—More—
```

NOTE

You can get results similar to MORE by pressing Pause, Ctrl-NumLock, or Ctrl-S. The text will freeze; to unfreeze it, press another key. If you're used to one of these keys, it can be much faster than MORE; but if not, you may not stop the text quickly enough to read it.

will appear at the lower left-hand corner. Press a key and another screenful will appear.

What Is Serial Communication?

You've learned that there may be up to four communication ports in your computer (and eight on PS/2 computers). What exactly do they do?

The communication ports (also known as serial ports or COM ports) communicate with *serial devices*. These include modems, fax modems and fax boards, most mice, digitizing pads, plotters, and some printers. (Most printers are *parallel devices*.)

The difference between a parallel port and a serial port has to do with the way data is sent to them. Data arrives at the parallel port eight bits (one byte) at a time. Thus each byte can represent a single character—perfect for printing.

In contrast, data arrives at a serial port one *bit* at a time. The port has to process a series of bits and format them into a byte before it knows what it's got. If you, or one of your programs, tells the port what kind of data to expect, that's no problem—but it must be told.

What you have to do about a serial port depends on the type of device attached to it. If you're using a modem with telecommunications software, you control how the modem turns the bits into bytes through the telecommunications program. The same is true if you're using a fax board or fax modem and accompanying software. With a mouse you must install a device driver, as noted in Chapter 12. If it's a serial mouse, you'll probably have to use a command switch to tell the driver which port the mouse is attached to. About the only time you need to configure the serial port yourself is if you have a printer attached to it.

If you're lucky, your computer dealer marked the ports. Otherwise there's no easy way to tell which device occupies which port. You will have to experiment. If your mouse driver requires a switch such as /1 or /2, try each switch in your AUTOEXEC.BAT or CONFIG.SYS file. If it's the wrong one, the driver will display an error message, saying that it can't find your mouse, or that the mouse is not attached. If you're configuring a serial printer, as described below, try different port numbers, then try to print something. If it doesn't print, use a different number.

Data Format

The *data format* for serial communication consists of ten bits:

- A single *start bit,* which tells the port a byte is arriving
- Either seven or eight *data bits*
- An optional *parity bit* (error-checking bit), not used with eight data bits
- Either one or two *stop bits;* two if there are seven data bits and no parity bit (DOS also allows you to set a value of 1.5)

The *start bit* is taken care of automatically. You (or software that accesses the serial port) have to determine how many data bits will be used, whether a parity bit is used, and if so, what kind, and how many stop bits will terminate a byte. You also have to tell the port at what speed the data should be transmitted, in a number called the *baud rate* (roughly, the number of characters per second).

Parity is generally represented by a single character and takes the values shown in Table 15.5.

Table 15.5 Parity values

Character	Value
N	None
E	Even
O	Odd
M	Mark
S	Space

You don't need to know what these terms mean. Just check the device's hardware manual and see what it requires.

The baud rates you can set using DOS include 110, 150, 300, 600, 1200, 2400, 4800, 9600, and 19,200. Hardly any equipment currently made requires a baud rate of less than 1200. Modems, fax modems, and serial printers use rates between 1200 and 9600. About the only use for 19,200 is to send text directly via a cable from a serial port to another computer's serial port. Not all computers will send data this fast.

Configuring a Serial Printer

You *must* configure the serial port yourself if you use a serial printer. (Check your printer manual to find out the data format it expects.) You must also tell DOS that your printer is attached to a serial rather than a parallel port. To accomplish both things, use the MODE command twice.

To redirect the output, use the command

MODE LPT*n*=COM*n*

where the *n*'s represent the port numbers. Generally you'll direct LPT1 to a serial port. Use the port number to which your printer is attached.

Once you've done that, use MODE again to configure the port. The form of the command is

MODE COM*n baud,parity,data,stop,retry*

You can enter just the values in abbreviated form (the first two digits of the baud rate and the single letter representing the type of parity) or spell them out in a command of the form

MODE COM*n* baud=*b*,parity=*p*,data=*d*,stop=*s*, retry=*r*

The most common setup for a serial printer is 1200 baud, no parity, 8 data bits, and 1 stop bit. The MODE command determines which parameter is which by its position in the sequence. If you skip one, be sure to include the comma to reserve a space for it. Otherwise each following parameter will be mistaken for the one that should have come before it.

You should use the value P for the retry parameter; this tells the computer to keep trying to send data to the printer until it accepts it. Otherwise you're likely to be bothered by many obscure printer-error messages. The command would thus look like:

```
mode com1 12,n,8,1,p
```

or

```
mode com1 baud=1200,parity=n,data=8,stop=1,retry=p
```

Once you've determined the correct parameters and port, add these two MODE commands to your AUTOEXEC.BAT file.

Accessing Ports Beyond COM2

DOS normally has no trouble addressing serial devices at COM1 and COM2. However, because of some peculiarities in the history of the personal computer and of DOS, you may have trouble if you try to use COM3 or COM4. The reasons for this are quite technical, but to put it simply, COM1 and COM3 share a line of communication with your central processing unit. So do COM2 and COM4. Thus there's no way DOS can talk to a device attached to COM3 if it's dealing with one at COM1. It's as if COM1 and COM3 were two different houses sharing a telephone number. If you called that number, you might get responses from both but you wouldn't be sure who you were talking to.

The way to avoid the conflict is to hook up your serial devices so that no two devices share a permanently occupied line. Let's say you have a mouse, a modem, and a fax board. If you attach your mouse to COM1, your modem to COM2, and your fax board to COM3, you'll never be able to use your fax board because the mouse driver permanently monitors the line from COM1, which is shared by COM3. You could solve the problem by swapping your mouse and modem, or by moving your fax board to COM4. You probably won't try to send a fax and receive a data communication call at the same time. (If you do, one of the calls will fail.)

HINT

If you have a PS/2 computer, your serial boards and devices come with a diskette containing text files with the extension ADF. These tell you how to address the ports properly.

To change a port address, you generally have to fiddle with the hardware. There may be DIP switches or jumpers to reset; check the manual. (*Dip switches* look like a row of tiny light switches attached to a box. *Jumpers* are minuscule removable sheaths that create a short circuit between two wires.) Internal modems and internal fax boards generally have DIP switches. If you're dealing with an *I/O card* that has a series of ports, you'll probably have to mess with jumpers. If you're not sure what you're doing, please consult your dealer or a computer-knowledgeable friend.

Setting Up a Print Queue

DOS contains a program to set up a *print queue*—a disk file containing everything to be printed. When it's installed, printing can go on in the background, and you can continue your other work.

Installing the Queue

The PRINT command installs a resident program that manages the print queue. Enter it followed by the name of the port to which your printer is attached:

PRINT /D:LPT*n*

You can then enter further PRINT commands directing your computer to print specific files, to add files to the list to be printed, or to delete files from the list.

PRINT has many switches to fine-tune the timing allotted to the printer. You won't need any of them unless your computer slows down inordinately while you're printing. For details see Appendix C.

Once you have installed PRINT, you tell it what to print by typing a command of the form

> **PRINT [*path*]*file1.ext* [*path*]*file2.ext*. . .**
> **[*path*]*filen.ext***

You can enter as many file names as you can fit.

Limitations of PRINT

There's a catch to using PRINT. The files you print with it must be either unformatted (ASCII) or formatted specifically for your printer. Most applications, such as word processors and spreadsheet programs, insert one set of formatting codes in the file to make it look appropriate on-screen and substitute another set when you print. If you were to print, say, a spreadsheet file formatted for the screen, you would see formulas, formatting codes, and a host of other things that you didn't want to print out.

Your printer might also operate incorrectly. So to print an application file with PRINT, you must first use the application's "print-to-file" command (if it has one). Afterwards you can include the resulting file in the print queue. (Files of this type often have the extension PRT or PRN.)

Other drawbacks of PRINT are that you can't tell it to stop while you switch to a different type of paper or an envelope. Also, PRINT blocks any other type of output (such as screen prints) you send to a printer. You'll get a message that the printer is busy.

 NOTE

If you have a serial printer, use the name of the printer port being redirected, not the name of the COM port to which you're redirecting the printer. Also, don't use PRINT until you've issued the MODE commands that set up your printer.

HINT

You may have noticed that the Print command on the Shell's File menu is always unavailable. That's because the Shell only prints files using PRINT. If you want to print from the Shell routinely, add PRINT to your AUTOEXEC.BAT file. To print from the Shell occasionally, exit from the Shell with F3, load PRINT, then reload the Shell.

Controlling the Queue

Once you set up the queue, you control what's in it by using the switches in Table 15.6.

Using these switches is tricky. The /C and /P switches apply to the file name preceding them and to all file names following them. However, you can use both in the same command. The same basic principle applies, but it's confusing. Let's look at an example.

Say your queue contains MEMO1.TXT, MEMO1.TBL, HOUSMAN.LTR, and CHART.DOC. You want to remove HOUSMAN.LTR and CHART.DOC and add HOUS-MAN2.LTR and MEMO2.TXT. The command would have to read

▶ **HINT**

All told, you may find PRINT more trouble than it's worth. If you have spare expanded or extended memory, it's easier to use a type of software called a print spooler. *A spooler is like a disk cache—it sets aside memory to capture output intended for the printer and holds it until the printer is ready.*

```
print housman.ltr /c chart.doc housman2.ltr /p
memo2.txt
```

or

```
print /c housman.ltr chart.doc housman2.ltr /p
memo2.txt
```

The /C switch applies to the file before it (if any) and all those after it, until the one *before* /P.

Table 15.6 Control switches for PRINT

Switch	Effect
/C	Deletes a file from the queue
/P	Adds a file to the queue
/T	Deletes the entire queue

Printing Graphics

On an Epson or IBM printer, or a printer that emulates one of them when printing graphics, you can print graphic screens by pressing Shift-PrtSc or Print Screen. But you have to prepare the output with a resident program called GRAPHICS. Just enter

```
graphics
```

at a prompt, not in the Shell. If you want to print graphics and you use the Shell, exit with Alt-F4 or F3 before you enter this command. Then reload the Shell by entering

```
dosshell
```

To understand what GRAPHICS does, look at a few examples. Figure 15.7 shows a Shell screen. Figure 15.8 shows how it looks printed without GRAPHICS loaded. Figure 15.9 shows the same screen printed using GRAPHICS.

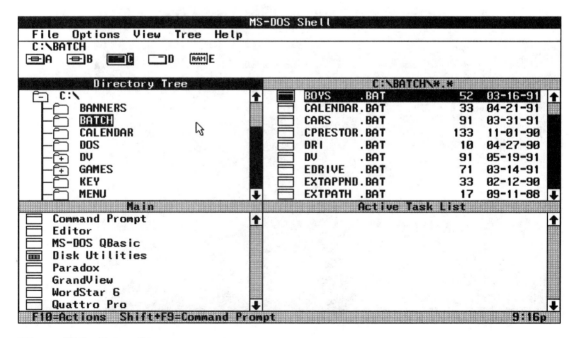

Figure 15.7   A graphic screen

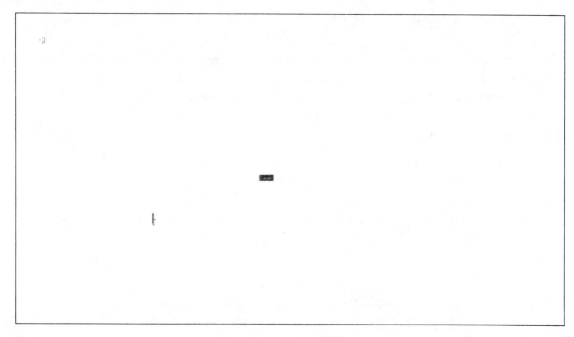

Figure 15.8   Printing a graphic screen without GRAPHICS

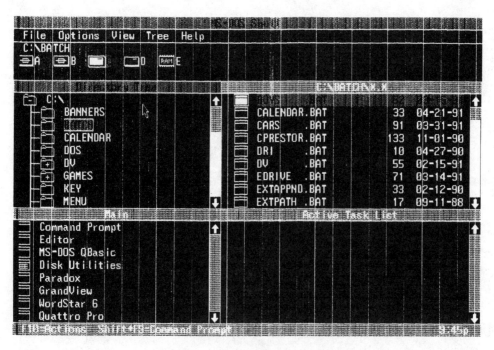

Figure 15.9   Printing a graphic screen with GRAPHICS

As you can see, GRAPHICS normally prints in reverse video from the screen—black is printed as white and vice versa. This is fine when you're in programs that use a black background. But when you're using the Shell, Microsoft Windows, or other graphics-mode programs that emulate the look of ink on paper, you'll want to reverse the printed colors. Enter the command

```
graphics /r
```

The /R (reverse) switch inverts black and white. Once you've used it, you can't switch back without rebooting. But you'll find the result much more salutary, as Figure 15.10 shows.

! WARNING

If your screen background is a color other than black or white, all colors other than black may be printed in black. If you use the /R switch, all colors other than white may be printed in black.

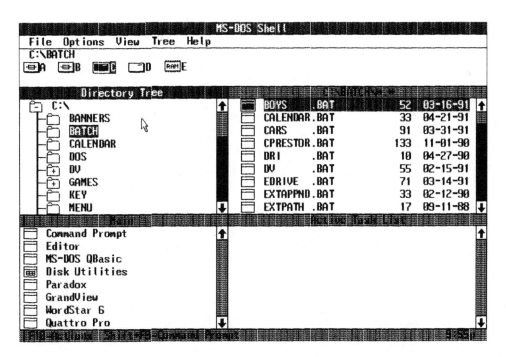

Figure 15.10 Printing a graphic screen in reverse with GRAPHICS

DOS and Windows

Chapter 16

What You Will Learn

- What Microsoft Windows can add to your computing experience
- What hardware you need to run Windows
- What alternative interfaces are available for DOS

What Is Windows?

Microsoft Windows is an *operating environment* regarded by many as the wave of the future for DOS computers. Depending on your hardware and work habits, it can open new worlds of powerful computing—or be a colossal nuisance.

An operating environment is not the same as an operating system. Rather it's an enhancement, or special interface to, an operating system. In a sense if you use the DOS Shell as the gateway to your system and use the task switcher, you're using the Shell as an operating environment.

Windows is a multitasking, windowed operating environment with a graphical user interface. This means that:

- It can run several programs at once
- It can display each running program in a separate window

- It presents information visually, so that programs and files are represented by icons, which you select and operate on with a mouse

✻ NOTE

If you've seen a Macintosh computer, you may find Windows at least moderately familiar.

Although Windows is designed to be used with a mouse, it is possible to use it entirely with the keyboard. The menus on the menu bar can be accessed by a combination of Alt plus an underlined letter, and commands on the resulting drop-down menus can be executed by pressing the underlined letter.

Additionally, when you use application programs designed specifically to run with Windows, you may have many other advantages:

- You can transfer text—even formatted text—easily from one Windows application to another.
- Since everything is displayed in a graphics mode, what you see on the screen is exactly what you'll get when you print the results. Windows includes a number of built-in fonts that will be printed as graphics, so you can create rather fancy documents.
- In many Windows programs, you can easily combine text with graphic elements—graphs, charts, logos, even photographs transferred to your computer with a scanner.

If you've learned to use all the Shell's facilities, you'll find much of Windows familiar. Its three most essential components are the Program Manager, the File Manager, and the Task Manager. These are roughly equivalent to the Shell's program group window, the Directory Tree and file windows, and Task Swapper, respectively. They even use similar commands.

The Program Manager

When you start Windows, you are presented with the Program Manager, shown in Figure 16.1. Each box, or window, is equivalent to a program group. However, there's a significant difference. In the Shell, you can view only one program group at a time. In the Program Manager, you can open several windows representing program groups. In each window you see icons representing programs. And you have a great deal of control over how the Program Manager presents itself. You can set up your own arrangement, as in Figure 16.1, or *tile* the windows, as in Figure 16.2, or *cascade* them, as in Figure 16.3, by using commands on the Program Manager's Window menu. You can have all your program group windows open or leave some closed. When closed, they appear as icons filled with document icons, as you see in all three figures. An additional advantage of Windows, as you can see, is that icons can

Figure 16.1   The Program Manager with a custom window arrangement

have descriptive names. You are not restricted to eight-character file names. You can even assign icons with meaningful names to data files.

Windows is based on the metaphor of a *desktop*. You move things around on it by dragging them with the mouse. You move open windows by holding down a button when the title bar is selected, then dragging. You can change a window's size by using special commands, or by holding down a mouse button while a margin of a window is selected and then dragging until the window is the shape and size you want. You can thus customize your "workspace" to suit the task.

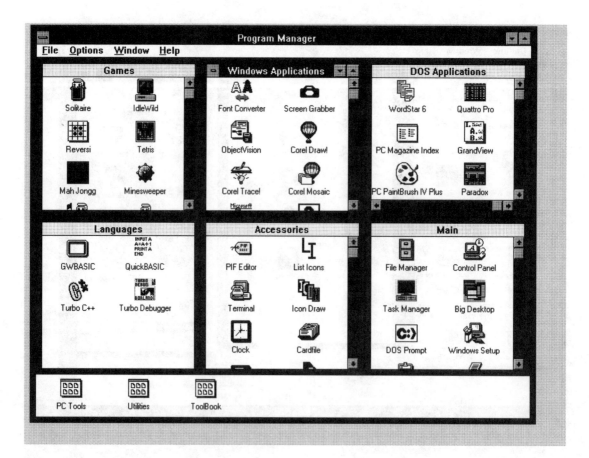

Figure 16.2   The Program Manager with tiled windows

When you install Windows, it configures itself for your hardware. Then it scans your hard disk(s) to find application programs it recognizes and builds several program groups for you automatically. The Main group contains essential programs for managing Windows. An Accessories group contains "desktop accessories" included with the software. These encompass such items as an on-screen ten-key calculator, a notepad, a datebook, a phone dialer, and a keystroke recorder for simplifying commands. If you have any programs designed specifically for Windows, they will appear in a Windows applications window. (Since Microsoft Windows includes a simple word processor and a painting

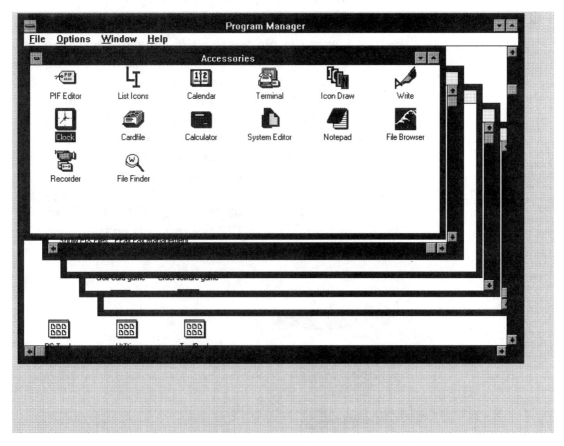

Figure 16.3   The Program Manager with cascaded windows

program, you'll have at least two applications in this window.) Another window contains those of your standard DOS applications that Windows recognizes.

You can have both programs and data files in a single group. You are encouraged to use the screen as a workspace in which you arrange all the items you need to complete a task. As with the Shell, you can place a specific program in more than one group. However, you can also create a group consisting of nothing but data files for a particular task. Since you can associate files with programs by their extensions (as in the Shell), you can start whatever program you need just by selecting a file.

Configuring Programs for Windows

One of the ways Windows recognizes programs is that they include a *program information file,* indicated by the extension PIF. This is a small file containing the information Windows needs to be able to run the program.

Figure 16.4 shows the Program Manager's File menu. As you can see, it's nearly identical to the File menu in the Shell when the program group window is selected. There's one very significant difference, however. The Properties command allows you only to specify a program name to run and an icon to associate with it. As a rule, to add programs Windows hasn't found, or to change default settings for those it has, you'll edit a PIF file rather than the Properties dialog box. You enter the information (as in the Advanced

Figure 16.4   The Program Manager File menu

dialog box in the Shell) using a special Windows program called the PIF Editor. When you use its File menu to select a PIF file, you get a list of all the PIF files in the current directory from which to select. You can change directories, if necessary, to view PIF files in other directories. With the PIF Editor, you can specify memory requirements and program parameters, reserve shortcut keys or establish new ones, and so on. Figure 16.5 shows a PIF file being edited in the PIF Editor.

There's a catch to all this of course. As with the Shell, once you've got everything set up right, Windows can simplify your work; but you need to understand even more about the behavior of your programs to get your PIF files working properly.

The Task Manager

The Task Manager is Windows' equivalent to the Task Swapper. But with enough memory and the right CPU, the Task Manager provides true multitasking. Although you can work actively in only one window, you might send files

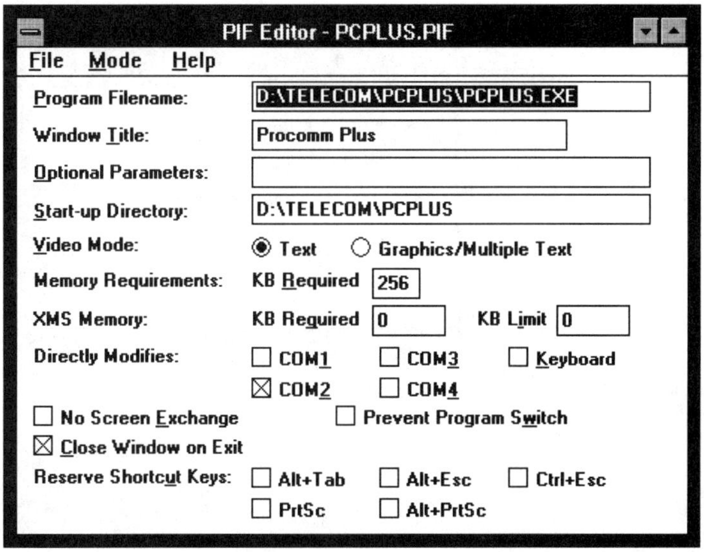

Figure 16.5   The PIF Editor

by modem, recalculate your spreadsheet, and search your database in the background, all while concentrating on preparing a presentation. If you leave the windows open for your background tasks, you'll be able to see when they're finished. You can switch to a different window by clicking the mouse on any part of it. Figure 16.6 shows the desktop with several programs open and visible.

As a rule, you're not aware of the Task Manager. When a program runs in the background, it may appear as an icon near the bottom of the screen as in Figure 16.7. These programs are said to be *running minimized*. To reopen a Windows program, double-click on it. You can also choose

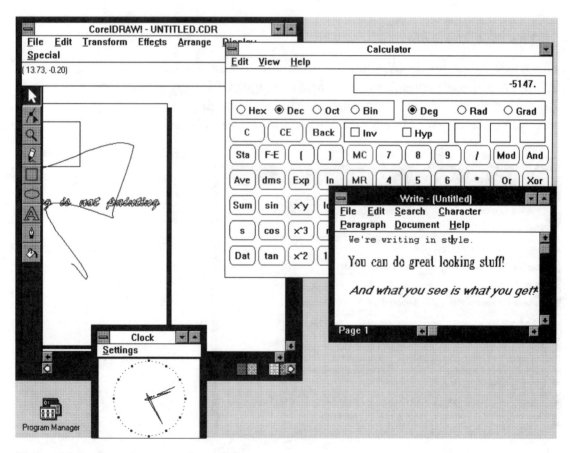

Figure 16.6   Running several programs at once

the Restore command from any program's Control menu (activated by clicking on the little box at the left-hand end of the menu bar, or by pressing Alt-space bar), and the window will return to its regular size. (If the program appears as just an icon, clicking once on it displays the Control menu. Or you can make a window fill the entire screen by clicking the mouse on the triangles in the upper right-hand corner of the window or choosing the Maximize command. Figure 16.8 shows the Control menu.

From the Control menu, you can view the Task List (see Figure 16.9) in a separate box by choosing the Switch to... command. From here you can switch directly to any

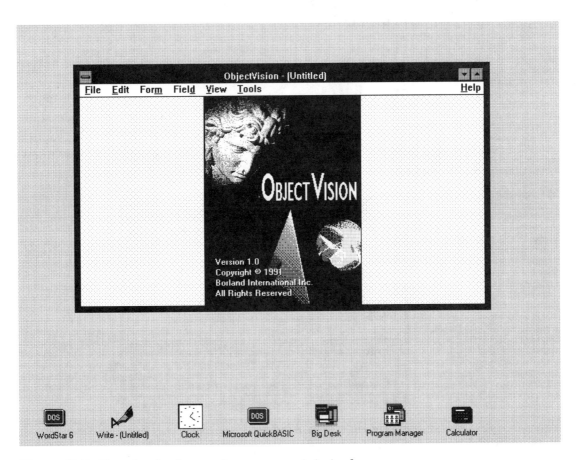

Figure 16.7   Running background programs minimized

Figure 16.8   The Control menu

active program, just as you would from the Shell's Active Task List. You can also switch to a program by clicking on its icon, if it's visible, or by using the same swap keys you'd use in the Shell.

The File Manager

The File Manager works rather like the Shell's file management system. In its windows file names rather than icons appear. Its menus are the same as the Shell's. (Figure 16.10 shows the File menu with the Directory Tree window

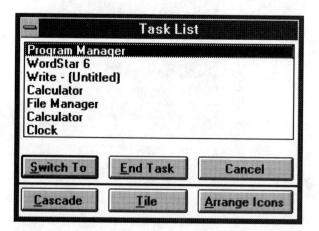

Figure 16.9   The Windows Task List

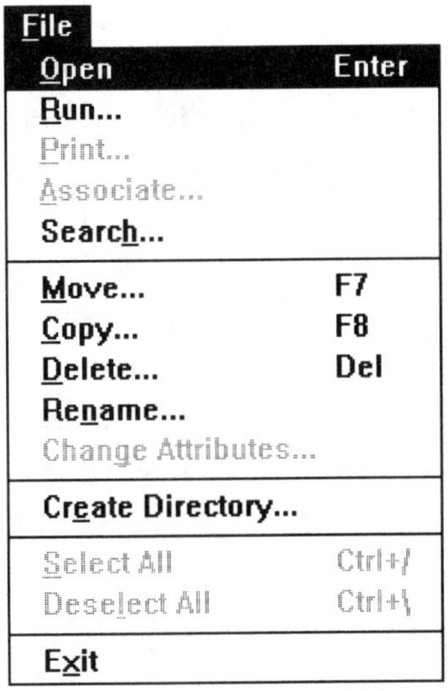

```
File
  Open              Enter
  Run...
  Print...
  Associate...
  Search...

  Move...           F7
  Copy...           F8
  Delete...         Del
  Rename...
  Change Attributes...

  Create Directory...

  Select All        Ctrl+/
  Deselect All      Ctrl+\

  Exit
```

Figure 16.10   The Directory Tree window's File menu

selected, and Figure 16.11 the same menu with a file window selected.) However, the Windows' File Manager is more powerful than the Shell and therefore somewhat harder to use.

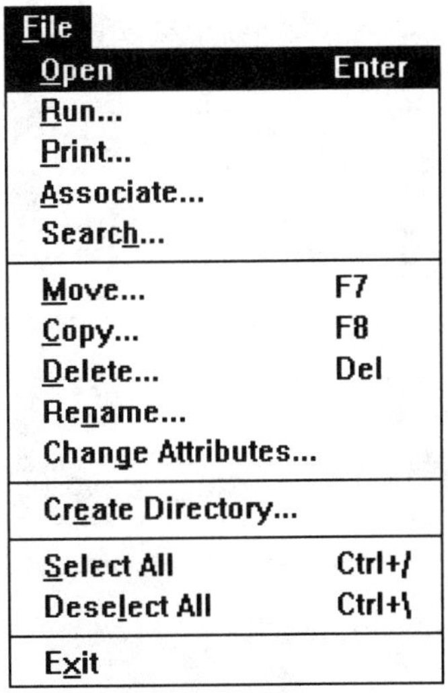

```
File
  Open              Enter
  Run...
  Print...
  Associate...
  Search...

  Move...           F7
  Copy...           F8
  Delete...         Del
  Rename...
  Change Attributes...

  Create Directory...

  Select All        Ctrl+/
  Deselect All      Ctrl+\

  Exit
```

Figure 16.11   A file window's File menu

With the File Manager, you can view more than two directories at a time. Selecting a drive opens a window displaying the drive's directory tree. You expand and collapse directory trees and navigate through them the same way as in the Shell. Once you've displayed a tree, you can open any number of directories in it by double-clicking on them. Each directory will have its own window. These windows will overlap. You may have a rather hard time finding your way through them. However, you can drag them around and change their size just as you can with other windows, so you can see only what you need to see. Figure 16.12 shows the File Manager with several windows open.

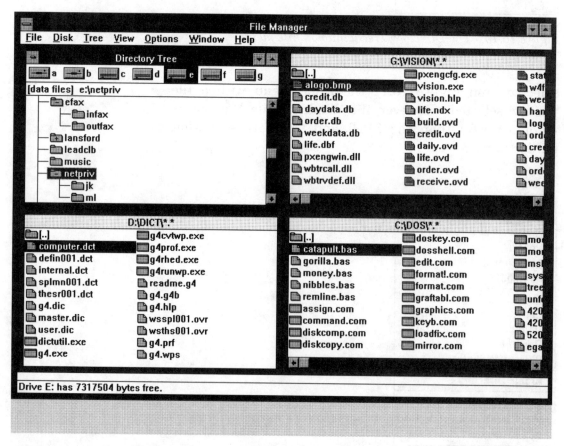

Figure 16.12   The File Manager with three directories displayed

What You Need to Run Windows

The hardware requirements for Windows are stringent—and expensive. At the minimum, Windows requires a video system that can display graphics. You can run it with a Hercules-type monographics system, but you'll probably want at least a VGA card and monitor (possibly one of the more advanced "super" or "enhanced" VGA systems, for the higher resolution). You'll also need at least an 80286 CPU and 2 megabytes of extended memory. As noted, you need a more powerful CPU to multitask DOS applications.

Those who use Windows regularly, however, say this is nowhere near enough power. On anything less than an 80386 CPU running at 25 megahertz, with a built-in memory cache, Windows can seem painfully slow. To keep Windows from bogging down when redrawing the graphics screen, you'll want a graphics card with a lot of memory—512K at a minimum. If you want Windows' multitasking capabilities, you'll need at least 4 megabytes of memory—more if you can afford it. When you've used all the memory in your system, Windows writes one or more background programs to a swap file on disk, just like the Shell. When this happens, the programs aren't running anymore, they're just waiting.

The Windows software itself requires 6½ megabytes of hard disk space. Many of the programs written for it use as much or more. You'd better have at least an 80-megabyte hard disk to store Windows itself, the programs that use it, and the graphics files you create with them.

Is Windows for You?

As with everything else in life, Windows has some significant disadvantages to go with its advantages. If you don't need the advantages it offers, obviously you won't want to use it. If you need some of its powers but are unwilling to accept the limitations it imposes, you may prefer one of the alternatives discussed below.

Some of Windows' strengths should be obvious at this point. Who wouldn't want to accomplish several tasks at once, instead of only one? If you need to combine text and graphics or require a great deal in the way of visual design elements in your documents, programs written for Windows—such as Ami Professional, CorelDraw!, Excel, or PageMaker—may be the best tools for your trade. The ease of transferring information between programs is another notable benefit. Additionally, programs written for Windows tend to have a similar menu structure. Therefore once you've learned one of them, you'll find it easier to learn others. In sum, if all of the following is true, you may find Windows an unparalleled boon:

- You're willing to spend a lot of money on hardware
- You want to use several programs written specifically for Windows.
- You need to combine text and graphics within a single file.
- You want to run several programs at once.

On the downside:

- Windows requires a lot of expensive hardware to run effectively, as you've just learned.
- It doesn't do a lot for regular DOS applications—those not specifically written for it. In most of its operating modes, it won't run these applications in a window, and it won't multitask them unless you have an 80386 or higher CPU. When you use a DOS application, it will take over the full screen. Moreover, DOS applications won't run in the background, except in Windows' most advanced operating mode, which is very slow, even on a fast computer.
- Depending on the hardware and software in your system, it can be devilishly hard to configure Windows to give you everything of which it's capable. You may find yourself spending more time tweaking your setup than working.

- Many of the Windows applications are as massive as Windows itself, requiring multimegabytes of hard disk space for all their program files, font files, clip art, and so on.

If you lack just one of the needs that Windows meets, consider the alternatives before you take the plunge.

Configuring DOS 5 for Windows

DOS 5 has many features that help Windows run faster. By carefully tuning your CONFIG.SYS file, you can ensure that Windows makes optimal use of the resources you give it.

Windows requires extended memory (see Appendix B). It also requires a lot of memory. Your CONFIG.SYS file should reflect that. Begin by installing the extended memory driver, HIMEM.SYS, to make the extended memory available to Windows.

✔ NEW FEATURE
Extended memory driver

Once you've installed HIMEM.SYS, you can tell DOS to load itself into some of the memory it makes available. The CONFIG.SYS command that does this is

✔ NEW FEATURE
Loading DOS into extended memory

```
dos=high
```

If you have an 80386 or higher CPU, you can make further memory available to Windows by loading your resident programs and device drivers into a special area of memory called the *upper memory blocks* (UMBs). You can make this area available by adding an expanded memory manager. DOS 5 includes one called EMM386.EXE. This device driver can do two things: It can make the upper memory blocks available, and it can turn some or all of your extended memory into expanded memory. Windows has no use for expanded memory, but some DOS programs you might run under Windows (such as Lotus 1-2-3 or Paradox) do. (The documentation for your programs will tell you whether they can use expanded memory.)

✔ NEW FEATURE
Expanded memory/ UMB driver

To give DOS access to the upper memory blocks, use the command

```
device=c:\dos\emm386.exe ram
```

By default it will turn *all* your extended memory into expanded memory (see Appendix B), which you don't want. To tell it to leave your extended memory alone, add the parameter noems. To restrict the amount of memory to be converted, enter the number of kilobytes to be converted. For example, if you have 6 megabytes of extended memory and you want to use 2 megabytes (2048K) as expanded memory, you'd use the command

```
device=c:\dos\emm386.exe ram 2048
```

The numeric parameter is the number of kilobytes to use for expanded memory.

Having used the RAM parameter, you can now add the UMB parameter to the DOS command, so that it reads

```
dos=high,umb
```

✔ **NEW FEATURE**
Loading drivers and resident programs into high memory

▶ **HINT**
To find out which programs have been loaded into high memory and which haven't, use the MEM /C command described in Appendix B. You may be able to load more resident programs into high memory by rearranging the order in which you load them.

Once you have made the upper memory blocks available, you can load your device drivers into them using the DEVICEHIGH command in place of DEVICE. In your AUTOEXEC.BAT file, place the command LOADHIGH (or just LH) before any command that loads a resident program. Some resident programs may not be loaded into the extra memory, but enough of them will be so that you'll notice the difference. (The more free memory you have below 640K, the larger the programs that Windows can run.)

Finally, the SMARTDRV.SYS disk-caching program is almost mandatory with Windows. Windows interacts with the cache dynamically, changing its size as needed. Therefore you should give it two parameters: a maximum and minimum cache size. Microsoft recommends that the latter figure be 256K. Figure 16.13 shows a CONFIG.SYS file for Windows on a computer with an 80386 CPU and 8 megabytes of memory. It loads DOS into high memory and allocates 1 megabyte

```
shell=c:\dos\command.com c:\dos\ /e:384 /p
buffers=10
files=35
device=himem.sys
dos=high,umb
device=c:\dos\emm386.exe 2048 ram
devicehigh=c:\dos\setver.exe
device=smartdrv.sys 1664 256
devicehigh=ansi.sys
```

Figure 16.13   A CONFIG.SYS file for Windows

for SMARTDRV.SYS and 2 megabytes for expanded memory. This leaves about 3½ megabytes of extended memory in which Windows can multitask programs.

> **! WARNING**
>
> *Windows has three operating modes—real mode, in which it doesn't use extended memory at all; standard mode, in which it uses extended memory and can swap, but not multitask, DOS programs; and 386 enhanced mode, in which it can multitask DOS applications. Even on an 80386, enhanced mode tends to be slow. However, if you want to use standard mode on an 80386, you must not use EMM386.EXE to establish any expanded memory. When you do, you can use Windows only in real or enhanced modes. To use standard mode and also use UMBs, you must use the NOEMS parameter to EMM386.EXE.*

> **! WARNING**
>
> *Occasionally you may run into problems if you load SMARTDRV.SYS with the DEVICEHIGH command. If you do, you'll see an error message telling you that SMARTDRV.SYS couldn't be loaded. If this happens, use the DEVICE command instead.*

Alternatives to Windows

You may be attracted by the enhancements Windows can bring to your computer and by how easy it is to learn and use (although it's *not* easy to set up properly). But you may not want to purchase the required hardware. If so, consider using DESQview or GeoWorks Ensemble. When you finish this chapter, you can make an informed decision as to whether you want to go beyond what DOS has to offer.

DESQview

If you use DOS applications and are happy with them; if you don't use graphics extensively; and if you want Windows' other advantages, DESQview may be your computing environment of choice. It provides multitasking with considerably less hardware than Windows (although it will take all the computing resources you give it). It can place several programs on the screen, each in its own window—even graphics programs on a monitor that displays graphics. (Some programs, however, must be given the full screen, unless you have both an 80386 CPU and a VGA monitor.) It lets you transfer text information easily between applications. And it

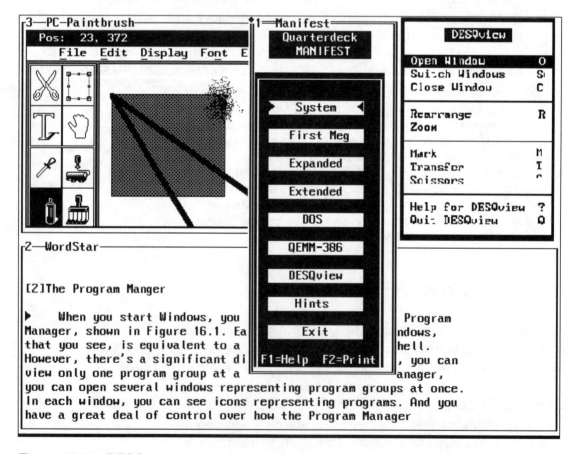

Figure 16.14   DESQview running three programs

can be much easier to use than Windows, although it may be almost as difficult to set up. Figure 16.14 shows the DESQview Main Menu with three programs running. As you can see, even a graphics program is running in a window.

You can transfer text but not graphics between applications by using a feature called "mark and transfer." Whereas Windows uses a file called a clipboard to store data in transit, DESQview hides it. But it's very smart about transferring numbers. For example, if you copied the number

```
$13,265.26
```

from a document and pasted it into a spreadsheet, the spreadsheet would treat it as a numeric value rather than text. It would appear as

```
13265.26
```

DESQview also includes a really nifty keystroke recorder. It saves keystrokes for each program in a separate file and automatically loads the appropriate file when you run the program. It has a rather desultory file manager, but you can install the DOS Shell and run it in a window if you prefer.

As you can see in Figure 16.14, each window has a number. To switch from one window to another, just press Alt followed by the number. If you can't see all your windows, the Main Menu includes a Switch Windows command, which lets you choose using a selection bar. You can also switch windows using a mouse as in Microsoft Windows.

Like Windows, DESQview scans your hard disk and automatically installs programs it recognizes. It can read Windows PIF files and recognize other programs for which it has equivalent information files of its own. Optionally you can execute a command to have DESQview scan hard disks other than the one you installed it on. If DESQview fails to find some of your software or misidentifies it, you make changes by adding the software to a list called the Open Window menu (see Figure 16.15). To install a program, you use the `Add a Program` command on that menu and fill in a screen or two of information (see Figure 16.16) about the program, rather as you would in Windows' PIF Editor. To change the information for a program, you use the `Change a Program` command, which brings you to the same screen. In addition, when you use Add a Program, you can select many popular programs from a list. You then simply tell DESQview which directory the program is in.

DESQview will run on any type of PC-compatible computer, with any CPU. However, to use it for multitasking, you must have expanded memory. On an 80386 or higher, you

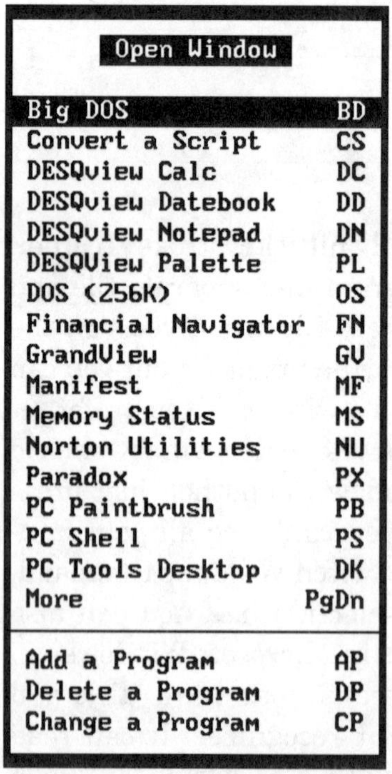

```
┌───────────────────────────────┐
│        Open Window            │
│                               │
│ Big DOS                  BD   │
│ Convert a Script         CS   │
│ DESQview Calc            DC   │
│ DESQview Datebook        DD   │
│ DESQview Notepad         DN   │
│ DESQView Palette         PL   │
│ DOS (256K)               OS   │
│ Financial Navigator      FN   │
│ GrandView                GV   │
│ Manifest                 MF   │
│ Memory Status            MS   │
│ Norton Utilities         NU   │
│ Paradox                  PX   │
│ PC Paintbrush            PB   │
│ PC Shell                 PS   │
│ PC Tools Desktop         DK   │
│ More                   PgDn   │
│                               │
│ Add a Program            AP   │
│ Delete a Program         DP   │
│ Change a Program         CP   │
└───────────────────────────────┘
```

Figure 16.15   The DESQview Open Window menu

```
┌Add=a=Program════════════════════════════════════════════════════════
│                         ▐ Specify Program Information ▌
│  Program Name..........: ▐                                        ▌
│                                        ◆
│  Keys to Use on Open Menu: ▐ ▌              Memory Size (in K): ▐200▌
├──────────────────────────────────────────────────────────────────────
│  Program...: ▐Enter pathname of program to run (C:\PROG\PROG.EXE)    ▌
│  Parameters: ▐Enter command line parameters (/SWITCH)               ▌
│  Directory.: ▐                                                      ▌
├──────────────────────────────────────────────────────────────────────
│  Options:
│              Writes text directly to screen.......: [Y]
│              Displays graphics information........: [N]
│              Virtualize text/graphics (Y,N,T).....: [Y]
│              Uses serial ports (Y,N,1,2)..........: [N]
│              Requires floppy diskette.............: [N]
├──────────────────────────────────────────────────────────────────────
│ ▐ Press F1 for advanced options ▌        Press ◄┘ when you are DONE
└──────────────────────────────────────────────────────────────────────
```

Figure 16.16   Installing a program in DESQview

can use EMM386.EXE to turn your extended memory into expanded memory, or use a third-party expanded memory manager, such as QEMM386, which is specifically designed to optimize your system for DESQview. (It also gives you access to upper memory blocks and lets you load device drivers and resident programs into them.)

If you don't have an 80386, you can add expanded memory with an *expanded memory board.* It is very important that the board conform to the Lotus-Intel-Microsoft Expanded Memory Standard, version 4.0 (LIM-EMS 4.0 for short), in hardware as well as software.

As for your computer's other resources, they needn't be extensive. DESQview itself requires less than 360K of hard disk space, although it will expand slightly as you install programs. DESQview doesn't require graphics, so it will run on any video system. And although it can use a mouse, it works quite well without one.

GeoWorks Ensemble

Yet another alternative is GeoWorks Ensemble. Like Windows, it has a graphical user interface, complete with buttons, windows, icons, and mouse control. It functions almost identically to Windows but is broken into sections that make it easy to learn. If you're a computer novice, you may find GeoWorks Ensemble ideal. It's set up on the metaphor of *rooms,* rather than a desktop. The Appliance room contains simple programs you can use with little more than the on-line help included. The Professional room contains complete applications, including a word processor, a drawing program, a simple database program, a telecommunications program, all the appliance programs, and (as of release 2.0)

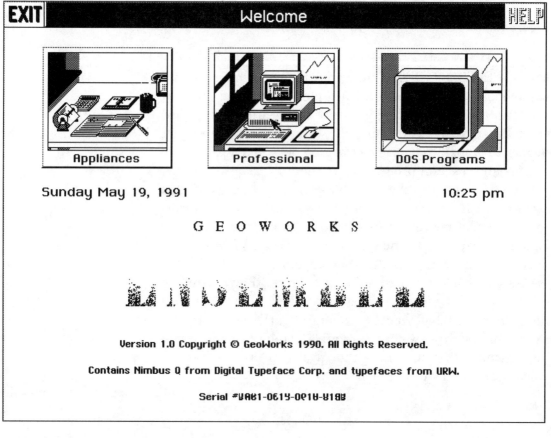

Figure 16.17   The GeoWorks welcoming screen

a spreadsheet. GeoWorks can multitask these programs, which all "talk" to each other the way Windows programs do. Finally, a DOS room lets you set up a series of buttons that launch your DOS applications. Figure 16.17 shows the welcoming screen, from which you choose a room. Figure 16.18 shows the Appliance room.

When you feel comfortable getting around in GeoWorks, you can move on to the Professional room (by way of its icon on the welcoming screen). The main window here is Geo-Works World, equivalent to Windows' Program Manager and File Manager, as you can see in Figure 16.19. Here you're in an environment very much like Microsoft Windows. You can transfer graphics and text between windows and rearrange

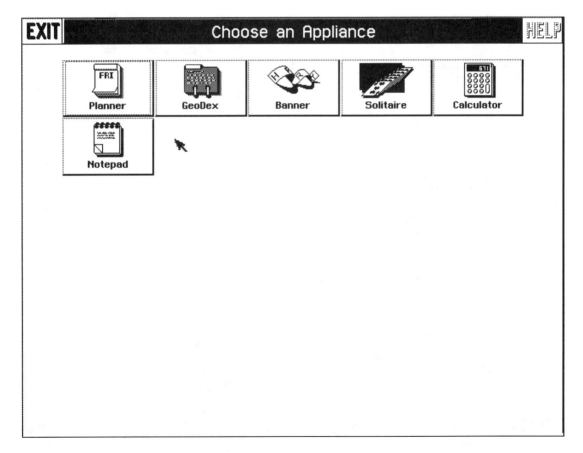

Figure 16.18   The GeoWorks Appliance room

the screen to suit your fancy.

As Figure 16.20 shows, the Control menu is quite similar to the one in Windows. However, GeoWorks has several facilities that Windows doesn't. One of them, also apparent in Figure 16.20, is the fact that you can "detach" a menu from an application and place it elsewhere on the screen. (This is what the pushpin icon on the title bar is for.) This leaves the menu open until you close it, so you can refer to it and use it as needed.

Finally, in the DOS room, you can create "buttons" for each DOS application. To start one, just click the button once with the mouse. GeoWorks won't multitask these applications, but as of version 2.0 it will allow you to switch

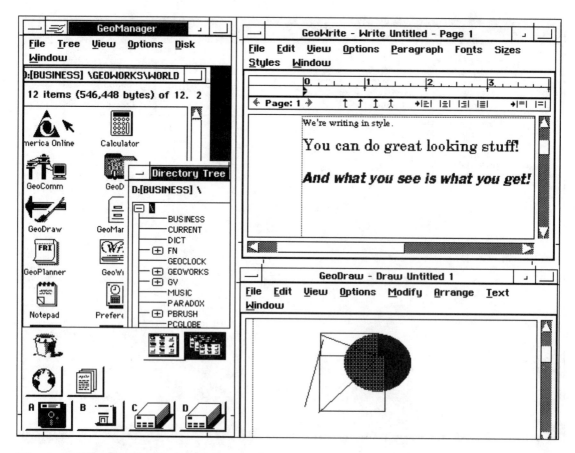

Figure 16.19   The GeoWorks Professional room

among them, as in the Shell. A future version may allow you to multitask DOS programs. Figure 16.21 shows a sample DOS room, and Figure 16.22 shows the dialog box in which you set up a button. The choice of icons is limited, but they are good-looking. Another feature of the DOS room is a batch file editor.

Although GeoWorks does require a graphics monitor and mouse, it doesn't require a fast CPU. It will run on any PC-compatible with any CPU and is even quite peppy on an 8088 (XT). It requires only about 1.5 megabytes of hard disk space. Its internal code is very efficiently written, which allows it to multitask its own applications with no memory beyond 640K.

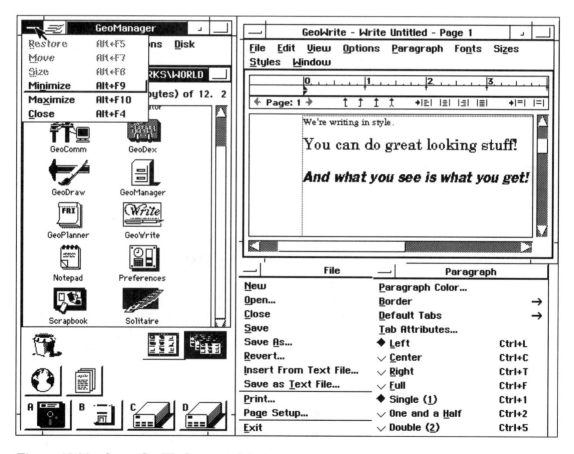

Figure 16.20   Some GeoWorks special features

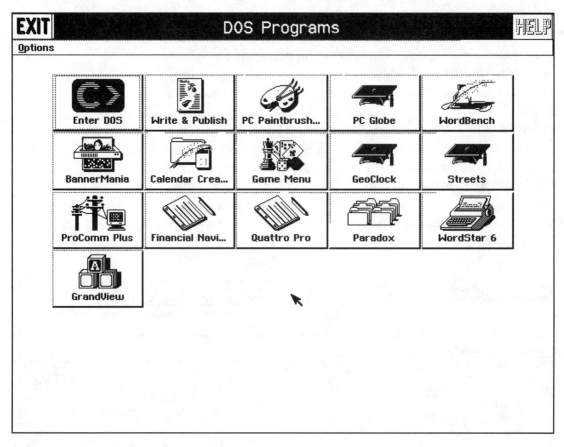

Figure 16.21   The DOS room

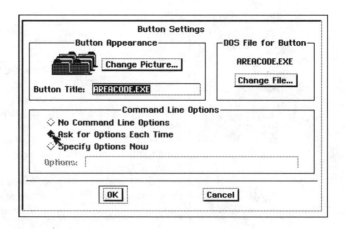

Figure 16.22   Configuring a DOS button

Restructuring a Hard Disk

A Bit of Background

Versions of DOS before release 4.0 couldn't deal with a hard disk larger than 32 megabytes as a single logical unit. If you had a larger disk, you had to break it up into *logical drives* of no more than 32 megabytes. With DOS 5 you can either partition a large drive into smaller units, each with a separate drive letter, or use it as a single logical drive with a single drive letter. DOS 5 can handle a drive of up to four gigabytes.

There are certain drawbacks to the large drives. The problem is that DOS handles them by creating larger-than-usual clusters. Many programs don't know how to handle these clusters. You'll know a program has this problem if you see a great many disk-error messages when it reads or writes files.

You can minimize the problem by creating two drives, a drive C of between 16 and 32 megabytes and a drive D comprising the remainder. Put your DOS files and your principal utility software on drive C, and your other software and data files on drive D. This may eliminate the errors.

Even so, there are pros and cons to a large drive, depending mainly on how you like to work. As noted in Chapter 8, you'll end up with a rather complex directory structure if you place most of your files on a single drive. You'll probably need utility software to keep track of your files. However, you may be more comfortable with a large drive than a multiplicity of drive names.

To partition a disk, you use the FDISK program. Partitioning wipes out all the data on the disk with no chance of recovery, so it's vital that you do a complete backup first. You can use FDISK to change the size of your partitions, and you *must* use FDISK if your drive has never been partitioned. Even if your drive is smaller than 32 megabytes, it must be partitioned into at least one logical drive before it can be formatted.

You will probably want to run FDISK from your Emergency Recovery Diskette. It's best to run it when nothing else is in memory. Also, you'll lose everything on your hard disk, so you'll need a system diskette to restart your system.

To run the program, just enter

```
fdisk
```

You'll see the menu in Figure A.1. (If you have only one physical hard disk, you won't see option 5.)

Restructuring a Partitioned Disk

If you've already been using your hard disk and you want to change its structure, you'll first have to delete your existing partitions. Choose option 3. You'll see the menu in Figure A.2.

 NOTE

A Non-DOS Partition is a portion of a physical hard disk that has been set aside for use with an operating system other than DOS. You might want to delete one if you want to use your entire hard disk with DOS, and don't plan to use another operating system. You might also want to delete one if your previous version of DOS required you to use a device driver to access your hard disk. When you repartition the drive using DOS 5, you probably won't need the device driver any more. If you're not sure, check with the dealer who sold you the system.

```
                    MS-DOS Version 5.00
                  Fixed Disk Setup Program
            (C)Copyright Microsoft Corp. 1983 - 1991

                       FDISK Options

    Current fixed disk drive: 1

    Choose one of the following:

    1. Create DOS partition or Logical DOS Drive
    2. Set active partition
    3. Delete partition or Logical DOS Drive
    4. Display partition information
    5. Choose next fixed disk

    Enter choice: [1]

    Press Esc to exit FDISK
```

Figure A.1   The FDISK main menu

```
            Delete DOS Partition or Logical DOS Drive

    Current fixed disk drive: 1

    Choose one of the following:

    1.   Delete Primary DOS Partition
    2.   Delete Extended DOS Partition
    3.   Delete Logical DOS Drive(s) in the Extended DOS Partition
    4.   Delete Non-DOS Partition

    Enter choice: [_]

    Press Esc to return to FDISK Options
```

Figure A.2   The delete partition menu

If the drive has more than one partition, the first one will be the Primary DOS Partition (containing drive C), and the second the Extended DOS Partition. Within the Extended DOS Partition will be one or more logical drives. You'll have to delete them before you can delete the Extended DOS Partition. If you're happy with the size of drive C, you can just assign the entire Extended DOS Partition to drive D after you return to the main menu. If you want a single partition, you'll have to delete the Extended DOS Partition and then the Primary DOS Partition as well. Then when you return to the main menu, you'll choose option 1 and assign the entire Primary DOS Partition to drive C.

Creating Partitions

If you can't use your hard disk with DOS or you've deleted all your partitions, you must create a DOS partition. Choose option 1, and you'll see something like Figure A.3. If you enter N, you'll be asked to enter the partition size in megabytes or as a percentage of the whole. If you already have a DOS partition, you'll see something like Figure A.4.

If you want a single logical drive occupying the entire physical disk, just press Enter when you reach the screen in Figure A.3. Otherwise specify a size for the Primary DOS Partition. Then create an Extended DOS Partition occupying the remainder of the disk. Finally create logical drives within the Extended DOS Partition, specifying their size,

```
Create DOS Partition

Current Fixed Disk Drive: 1

Do you wish to use the entire fixed disk
for DOS (Y/N).....................? [Y]
```

Figure A.3   Creating a DOS partition

```
                    Create Primary DOS Partition

  Current fixed disk drive: 1

  Partition  Status   Type   Volume Label  Mbytes  System  Usage
  C: 1         A      PRI DOS  SYS & HOME     16    FAT16    39%
     2                EXT DOS                 24             59%

  Primary DOS Partition already exists.

  Press Esc to continue
```

Figure A.4   If you already have a DOS partition

either in megabytes or as a percentage of the Extended DOS Partition. Be aware that FDISK regards a megabyte as 1,048,756 bytes (1024 x 1024 bytes), although everything else in the system regards a megabyte as 1,024,000 bytes. You may have to use a calculator to figure out what numbers to enter.

Making the Drive Bootable

Once you have established your partitions, you may be asked

```
  Do you want this partition to be the
  active partition (Y/N).........[Y]
```

The active partition is the one in which the computer will look for the DOS system files. You must have one to boot from your hard disk. If you're not sure whether you have an active partition, choose option 4. The Status column should have an A in it, on the line named PRI DOS. If it doesn't, choose option 2 and make your Primary DOS Partition your active partition. When you're finished, press Escape to leave FDISK. The computer will reboot when you press a key.

Once you're finished, you must format all the logical drives you have created, using the FORMAT command. Be sure to use the /S switch when you format drive C, so that the system files are transferred to it.

Managing Memory

DOS 5 includes many new memory management features to help Windows run faster and more efficiently. You've learned most of the procedures to accomplish this in Chapter 16. However, if you have the appropriate hardware, you can use the new features even if you don't do Windows. This appendix provides some background, so you'll know what it is you're managing.

Types of Memory

Your computer may have up to five types of random-access memory (RAM)—the memory in which the computer places data it's currently working on.

Every computer has *conventional memory,* which is the memory in which you run your programs and in which they operate on data. You can have up to 640K of conventional memory.

Many computers have no other memory. When this is the case, all the device drivers, resident programs, and DOS itself share conventional memory with the programs being run and the data they're working on. Because all these items are normally loaded into conventional memory, the amount of memory available for running programs is considerably less than the amount installed in your computer.

If your computer has 640K of RAM installed, for example, once it's up and running you may have only 560K free for programs—less if you run a lot of resident programs.

If your computer has an 80286 or higher CPU, you may also have *extended memory*. This is no different in kind from conventional memory, but because of a series of historical quirks, DOS doesn't know how to talk to it directly, even though your CPU does.

Any PC-compatible computer can have *expanded memory*, in the form of an added *expanded memory board*. This memory is accessed through a special device driver called an *expanded memory manager*, which makes the memory visible to DOS. If you have an 80386 or higher CPU and you also have extended memory, you can turn some or all of your extended memory into expanded memory by using EMM386.EXE, a device driver included with DOS 5.

Expanded memory that meets the current standard for that type of memory (EMS 4.0) can be used to run programs, including resident programs. To accomplish this, however, you need the proper hardware. If you have an 80386 or 80486 CPU, the CPU itself provides the hardware support. All you need is the device driver. With an 8088 or 80286, however, you need an *expanded memory board*. To meet the expanded memory standard, the board must have several control chips and quite a bit of additional circuitry, not just memory.

Additionally, if you have extended memory and install another DOS 5 device driver, HIMEM.SYS, you can get DOS to talk to an additional 64K of memory called the *high memory area* (HMA). This is the first 64K of extended memory.

Finally, if you have either extended or expanded memory, you may also be able to gain access to what appears to be a fifth type of memory: *upper memory blocks* (UMBs), also known as *high memory*. This memory is something of an illusion. Through a startling feat of legerdemain, these two device drivers can persuade DOS that memory exists in places where it doesn't. More on this point shortly.

The distinctions between these types of memory have to do with the way the CPU and DOS find and use memory. For various reasons DOS can address only 1 megabyte of memory. This is divided into the up-to-640K of conventional memory and a set of *memory addresses* between 640K and 1 megabyte.

There isn't actually any RAM between 640K and 1 megabyte. However, the read-only memory (ROM) on your hard disk controller, your video adapter, and some important chips on the *motherboard*—the computer's main circuit board—and on other hardware needs to be visible to the CPU as though it were RAM, so that DOS can talk to these different pieces of hardware. To make this possible, ROM takes on some of the memory addresses between 640K and 1 megabyte.

Although various hardware uses at least some of these addresses, most computers have some free. If you have extended memory, you can use EMM386.EXE and HIMEM.SYS to trick DOS into thinking that some of the extended memory is actually located at these unused addresses. DOS now regards the memory that it thinks is at these addresses as upper memory blocks. You can then load and run resident programs and device drivers there. This leaves more conventional memory free for larger programs.

✳ NOTE

Two expanded memory managers from other manufacturers, QEMM386 from Quarterdeck Office Systems and 386Max from Qualitas, both turn extended memory on an 80386 computer into expanded memory and also provide access to the high memory area and the UMBs. In addition, if you have expanded memory on an 80286 computer, you can use a program called QRAM, also from Quarterdeck, to gain access to UMBs.

Managing Memory with DOS 5

Until now there was no way DOS could deal with memory other than conventional memory. However, DOS 5 includes two device drivers for using and managing the other types of memory.

Accessing the High Memory Area

HIMEM.SYS is the driver that creates the HMA block—an area located in the first 64K of extended memory but addressable by DOS. To activate it, enter the command

```
device=c:\dos\himem.sys
```

in your CONFIG.SYS file. (Of course if your copy of HIMEM.SYS is in another directory, modify the path to reflect its correct location.) You can then have DOS load itself into the HMA block if you enter the command

```
dos=high
```

in CONFIG.SYS. This will add about 45K to your free conventional memory.

Accessing Extended Memory

Only recently have DOS programs been able to use extended memory, with the development of the eXtended Memory Standard (XMS). Programs written with a section of code called a *DOS extender* can use the properties of the 80286 and later chips to keep part of their data in extended memory. This allows you to create data files larger than your conventional memory can hold. It also allows programs to be larger than the 640K that conventional memory normally permits. Your documentation will tell you whether your software has these capabilities.

If you've installed HIMEM.SYS in your CONFIG.SYS file to access the high memory area, you have also installed the XMS driver. This makes extended memory available for use by Microsoft Windows and any other programs that know how to use it.

Accessing Expanded Memory

As mentioned, an expanded memory board can be added to *any* PC-compatible. It must conform to the Lotus-Intel-Microsoft Expanded Memory Standard (LIM-EMS.) You should use the expanded memory device driver that came with it.

Unlike extended memory, expanded memory is *mapped,* or *paged.* The device driver establishes an area in the upper memory blocks called a *page frame.* The driver uses this area as a sort of window, into which it maps chunks of expanded memory as they are needed.

However, the architecture of the 80386 (and later) CPUs is such that if you have extended memory, all you need is a device driver to turn it into expanded memory. With DOS 5 and an 80386, you can use EMM386.EXE as an expanded memory manager. To use it, add the command

```
device=c:\dos\emm386.exe
```

to CONFIG.SYS. (Change the path if necessary.) This will turn *all* your extended memory into expanded memory.

Using various parameters, you can control the behavior of EMM386.EXE. You determine the amount of memory to be used as expanded memory by adding a parameter specifying how many kilobytes of it you want. The rest will still be extended memory. For example, if you have 6 megabytes of extended memory and want to use 2 as expanded, use the command

```
device=c:\dos\emm386.exe 2048
```

in CONFIG.SYS. (Two megabytes is equal to 2048K.)

As with extended memory, some programs can use expanded memory and some can't. Check the documentation. A program that can use expanded memory will run much more efficiently when it's present. A large program may use expanded memory to enable you to create very large data files. Increasingly, resident utility programs are able to load some code into expanded memory and manage the interaction between conventional and expanded memory themselves, with the aid of the device driver. Such programs can stay resident and use only a small portion of conventional memory.

✳ NOTE

As you learned in Chapter 16, Windows uses extended, not expanded, memory. If you want to reserve some expanded memory for DOS programs that you plan to run within Windows, you have two choices: Either you must run Windows in 80386 enhanced mode, or you must use a memory manager other than EMM386.EXE. QEMM386, version 5.12 and later, make it possible to run Windows in any of its operating modes and will supply expanded memory to any program that needs it. In contrast to Windows, DESQview uses expanded memory exclusively but can make extended memory available to programs that need it.

Accessing Upper Memory Blocks

If you have an 80386 (or later) CPU, you can use the upper memory blocks between 640K and 1 megabyte—at least those that aren't being used by hardware. To do that, you must use another parameter with EMM386.EXE. To have EMM386.EXE map some extended memory so that it appears to be located between 640K and 1 megabyte, add the parameter RAM:

```
device=c:\dos\emm386.exe 2048 ram
```

You must also add the UMB parameter to the DOS command:

```
dos=high,umb
```

If you want to access the UMBs but want the rest of your memory beyond 1 megabyte to be extended, not expanded, add the NOEMS (no expanded-memory-standard memory) to EMM386.EXE and don't specify a numeric parameter:

```
device=c:\dos\emm386.exe noems ram
```

To gain the maximum amount of conventional memory, you should use HIMEM.SYS, EMM386.EXE with the RAM parameter, and a DOS command that both loads DOS into the high memory area and makes the upper memory blocks accessible:

```
device=c:\dos\himem.sys
dos=high,umb
device=emm386.exe ram
```

Once you have used these commands, you can load device drivers into the upper memory blocks using the DEVICEHIGH command instead of DEVICE for other devices in CONFIG.SYS. You can load resident programs into the UMBs by prefacing the commands that load them with LOADHIGH or LH.

DOS will load as many of these programs into the upper memory blocks as can fit. Those that can't will be loaded into conventional memory. To find out what's been loaded where, read the next section.

Examining Memory

The MEM command reports on the amount of memory of each type in your system. Figure B.1 shows a sample report.

Notice that this report shows the same amount of XMS memory and EMS memory. You won't see this with EMM386.EXE, but you may with memory managers from other manufacturers. Programs such as QEMM386 and 386Max take charge of both types of memory, allocating whichever is needed from a common pool comprising all memory above 1 megabyte. They also include enhancements for managing the upper memory blocks.

To get a report on what's present in all this memory, use the /C (classify) switch. Figure B.2 shows a sample report.

```
C:>mem

    655360 bytes total conventional memory
    655360 bytes available to MS-DOS
    597472 largest executable program size

   3571712 bytes total EMS memory
   1753088 bytes free EMS memory

   3145728 bytes total contiguous extended memory
         0 bytes available contiguous extended memory
   1753088 bytes available XMS memory
           MS-DOS resident in High Memory Area

C:>_
```

Figure B.1 *A report on memory*

In this report MEM displays information about all five types of memory. In addition, it displays a list of every program currently in memory, whether conventional or high. You can use such a report to optimize memory usage. For example, the above report indicates that approximately 12K of upper memory is free. There are also several programs in conventional memory that occupy less than 12K: VDD, APPEND, and SHARE.

Some programs actually take additional memory when they are loading and won't load into 12K even if that's the amount of code they leave in memory. (MOUSE, for example, takes only 12K but requires 15K to load.) You may be able to make more conventional memory available by loading smaller device drivers into high memory or by changing your loading order. Unfortunately the only way to be sure is to try different combinations. If you decide to experiment, copy your working AUTOEXEC.BAT and CONFIG.SYS files to a diskette, so you'll have backups in case things get hopelessly fouled up.

```
C:\>mem /c |more

Conventional Memory :

Name              Size in Decimal        Size in Hex
---------         ----------------       ------------
MSDOS             22496    ( 22.0K)         57E0
SETVER              400    (  0.4K)          190
BCDOS5              256    (  0.3K)          100
HIMEM              1184    (  1.2K)          4A0
EMM386             8400    (  8.2K)         20D0
SMARTDRV          37184    ( 36.3K)         9140
VDD                3824    (  3.7K)          EF0
COMMAND            2752    (  2.7K)          AC0
APPEND             9024    (  8.8K)         2340
MOUSE             12960    ( 12.7K)         32A0
SHARE              6192    (  6.0K)         1830
FREE                 64    (  0.1K)           40
FREE             550287    (537.2K)        8658F

Total  FREE :    550341    (537.2K)

Upper Memory :
--more--

Name              Size in Decimal        Size in Hex
---------         ----------------       ------------
SYSTEM           163840    (160.0K)        28000
MOUSE               336    (  0.3K)          150
EGA                3280    (  3.2K)          CD0
FREE                336    (  0.3K)          150
FREE              12336    ( 12.0K)         3030

Total  FREE :     12672    ( 12.4K)

Total bytes available to programs
            (Conventional+Upper) :       562688    (549.6K)
Largest executable program size :        549600    (536.8K)
Largest available upper memory block :    12336    ( 12.0K)
```

Figure B.2   A classified memory report

continues

Figure B.2 continued

```
     2490368 bytes total EMS memory
     2048000 bytes free EMS memory

     7733248 bytes total contiguous extended memory
           0 bytes available contiguous extended memory
     3751936 bytes available XMS memory

           MS-DOS resident in High Memory Area
  C:\>_
```

DOS and Shell Command Reference

Appendix *C*

This overview of DOS commands gives the most common uses for each.

Internal commands can be entered at any prompt.

 INTERNAL

External commands can be executed only when the executable file with the matching name is present in the computer.

 **EXTERNAL**

Configuration commands are used in the CONFIG.SYS file.

 CONFIGURATION

Batch commands are used in batch files.

⬡ **BATCH**

Resident commands stay in the computer's memory and continue to function after the command is issued and the prompt returns.

🏛 **RESIDENT**

The syntax diagrams use the following conventions:

d: stands for any drive name.

path stands for a complete path name from the root directory.

filename.ext stands for any legal DOS file name; wild-card characters are permitted unless otherwise specified.

filename.txt stands for the name of any text file.

Items in brackets are optional.

target may be any combination of drive, path, and/or file name (or a logical device), so long as you give enough information to tell the command where to place the results.

If a drive is optional, the command acts on the current drive if none is specified.

If a drive and path are optional, the command acts on the current drive and directory unless a drive and path are specified.

If a drive, path, and file name are optional, the command acts on all files in the current directory if no file is specified, or on all files in the specified directory if no file is specified.

DOS Commands

 EXTERNAL

 RESIDENT

APPEND

APPEND [*d:*]*path*[;[*d:*]*path2*][;. . .] [/*switch*]

Allows DOS to open data files in the specified directories as if they were in the current directory. Useful for helping programs find such files as overlays, printer drivers, and configuration files if they otherwise can't.

Switch	Effect
/X:ON	Allows DOS commands to locate files in the appended directories.
/X:OFF	Searches appended directories only when a command requests to open a file (the default).
/E	Places the appended directory list in the environment space. Must be used only the first time APPEND is issued.

APPEND ;

Clears the appended directory list.

APPEND

Displays the appended directory list.

ASSIGN

 EXTERNAL

ASSIGN *d1=d2*

Gives drive *d2* the name *d1*. Useful when a program can find files only on a drive with a specific name. Both drives must be physically or logically present in the computer.

This is a dangerous command. When you assign a drive, you lose access to the drive with the original name. If the ASSIGN command is on that drive, you won't be able to undo the assignment.

ASSIGN /STATUS

Displays a list of the assignments in effect.

ASSIGN

Undoes all assignments made with the ASSIGN command unless the external program ASSIGN.EXE is on the reassigned drive.

ATTRIB

◆ EXTERNAL

ATTRIB [+R] [+A] [+S] [+H]
[*d:*][*path*\][*filename.ext*] [/S]

Displays or changes file attributes.

Switch	Effect
+	Sets the specified attribute
—	Clears the specified attribute
R	Specifies the read-only attribute
A	Specifies the archive attribute
S	Specifies the system attribute
H	Specifies the hidden file attribute
/S	Changes the attributes of all matching files in subdirectories of the directory specified in the command

◆ EXTERNAL

BACKUP

BACKUP *source target* [*/switches*]
[*/L:[d:][\path\]logfile.ext*]

Backs up files from one disk to another. The root directory of the source disk must be current.

Switch	Effect
/S	Backs up files in subdirectories of the specified path.
/M	Backs up only files that have changed since the last backup.
/A	Appends backup files to an existing backup disk.
/F:*nnn*	Specifies the capacity to which the target disk should be formatted if necessary. See FORMAT for applicable values.
/D:*mm-dd-yy*	Backs up only files changed on or after the specified date.
/T:*hh:mmc*	Backs up only files changed at or after the specified time.
/L:[*d:*][*path*]*logfile.ext*	Records a list of files backed up and the disks on which they have been placed, in a file by the name specified. If no name is specified, the file will be called BACKUP.LOG and appear in the root directory of the source drive.

◆ INTERNAL

❖ CONFIGURATION

BREAK

BREAK ON

BREAK=ON

Increases the frequency with which the computer checks for presses of the Ctrl-Break or Ctrl-C key combination. Use the equal sign in configuration commands; omit it in commands at the prompt. BREAK commands entered at the prompt override commands issued via CONFIG.SYS.

BREAK OFF

BREAK=OFF

Establishes the normal frequency of break checking.

BREAK

Displays a message telling whether BREAK is on or off.

BUFFERS

 **CONFIGURATION**

BUFFERS=*nn*

Establishes the size of the disk buffer. A larger buffer, characterized by a higher value, generally speeds disk access; more so with database programs and programs that read frequently from overlay files.

The letters *nn* stand for a number from 1 to 99; the number is equal to the number of disk sectors the buffer can hold. On computers with 640K or more of memory, the default is 15.

CALL

⬡ BATCH

CALL [*d:*][*path*]*filename*[*parameters*]

Executes a second batch file from within a batch file, returning control to the original batch file after the second one terminates. Any parameters included in the CALL command are passed to the batch file being called.

CHKDSK

◆ EXTERNAL

CHKDSK [*d:*] [/F]

Checks the integrity of the specified disk and displays a report. Reports on the current drive if none is specified. If the /F switch is included, deletes or rewrites chains of lost clusters and fixes errors in the allocated length of files.

CHKDSK [*d:*][*path*]*filename.ext*

Checks the specified file(s) for fragmentation. Wild-card characters may be used.

CHKDSK /V

Displays the full path and name of every file on the disk.

◆ INTERNAL

CLS

CLS

Clears the screen.

◇ EXTERNAL

COMP

COMP [*d:*][*\path*]*file1.ext* [*d:*][*\path*]*file2.ext* /*switches*

Compares the specified files. Wild-card characters may be used to compare multiple files.

Switch	Effect
/A	Displays differences as characters
/C	Ignores the case of letters in the compared files
/D	Displays differences in decimal format (the default)
/L	Places a line number before each line in which a difference is found
/N=*n*	Compares only the first *n* lines of each file

◆ INTERNAL

COPY

COPY [*d:*][*\path*]*filename.ext target* [/V]

Copies the specified file(s) to the target. Use the /V switch to turn on read-after-write verification (*see* VERIFY).

DATE

DATE

Displays the current date as known by the computer and allows you to change it.

DEL (ERASE)

DEL *target* **[/P]**

Erases one or more files. To erase multiple files, use wild-card characters. To erase all the files in a directory, specify the directory's name as the target. If the /P switch is used, displays each file name before deleting, requesting permission to delete.

DELOLDOS

DELOLDOS

Deletes files from a previously installed version of DOS after DOS 5 installation. After you run this command, you cannot restore your previous DOS version with the Uninstall diskette.

DEVICE

DEVICE=[*d:*][*path*\]*filename.ext* /*switches*

Loads the specified device driver. See the documentation for the driver, or your DOS manual, for appropriate switches.

DEVICEHIGH

DEVICEHIGH=[*d:*][*path*\]*filename.ext* /*switches*

Loads the specified device driver into upper memory blocks, if they are available. See the documentation for the device driver for appropriate switches.

◆ INTERNAL

DIR

DIR [*d:*][*path*\][*filename.ext*] [*/switches*]

Displays a list of files and subdirectories in a directory. Wild-card characters may be used. In switches that change the sorting order, a minus sign sorts in descending order. In switches that specify a file attribute, a minus sign displays only files not having the attribute.

Switch	Effect
/P	Pauses the display after each screenful of information
/W	Displays a wide list, taking the full width of the screen (but with minimal information about each file)
/B	Lists only file names, but in a vertical list, with periods instead of spaces
/L	Displays the file and directory names in lowercase
/O[-]N	Sorts the display by name
/O[-]D	Sorts the display by extension
/O[-]S	Sorts the display by increasing size
/O[-]D	Sorts the display by date
/O[-]G	Places directories first
/A[-]D	Displays directory names
/A[-]A	Displays files with the archive attribute
/A[-]H	Displays hidden files
/A[-]R	Displays read-only files
/A[-]S	Displays system files

◆ EXTERNAL

DISKCOMP

DISKCOMP *d: d:*

Compares two diskettes, which must have the same format. DISKCOMP reports an accurate comparison only if the disks are identical byte-by-byte.

DISKCOPY

DISKCOPY *d: d: [/switches]*

Copies a diskette to another of the same format.

Switch	Effect
/1	Copies only the first side of the diskette
/V	Performs read-after-write verification (*see* VERIFY)

DOS

 CONFIGURATION

DOS=*location*

DOS=*activate/don't activate upper memory blocks*

If you have expanded memory, allows you to place the operating system in the high memory area, freeing more of the conventional memory for your programs. If you have an 80386, activates upper memory blocks so they can hold active device drivers and resident programs. Both functions may be combined in a single command—for example, `dos=high,umb`.

Switch	Effect
HIGH	Places DOS files in high memory area
LOW	Places DOS files in conventional memory
UMB	Activates upper memory blocks
NOUMB	Keeps upper memory blocks from being activated

DOSKEY

DOSKEY [/*switches***]**

Installs a program to recall and edit command lines.

Switch	Effect
/BUFSIZE=nnn	Establishes the size of the buffer used to store commands. The default is 512 bytes; the minimum is 256 bytes.
/HISTORY	Displays all commands stored in the buffer. Similar to pressing F7.
/INSERT	Puts the editing cursor into insert mode by default; change by pressing Ins.
/OVERSTRIKE	Puts the editing cursor into overtype mode by default; change by pressing Ins (this is the default setting).

⬡ BATCH

ECHO

ECHO OFF

Suppresses the display of commands and of the prompt while a batch file is running.

ECHO ON

Allows commands after the `echo on` command in a batch file to appear on the screen, along with the prompt. This is the default condition.

ECHO *message*

Displays the specified message on the screen while a batch file is executing.

ECHO .

Inserts a blank line in a display created by ECHO commands.

@COMMAND

Suppresses the display of the command following the @ symbol; use before the first echo off command in a batch file to suppress the display of all batch file commands.

EXIT

 INTERNAL

EXIT

If you have used a command within a program to access a command prompt without exiting the program, EXIT returns you to the running program. Use EXIT to return to the Shell if you have pressed Shift-F9 to get a command prompt.

EXPAND

 EXTERNAL

EXPAND [*d*:][*path*\\]*filename.ex_ target*

Used for making working copies of the DOS files from an upgrade version of DOS 5. Specify the name of the file to be expanded, using an underscore for the last character of the extension. The *target* should be the correct name of the file, along with a drive and/or path if the directory where you want the expanded file isn't current.

FASTOPEN

EXTERNAL

FASTOPEN *d*:[=*n*] [*d*:[=*n*]] ... [/X]

RESIDENT

Creates a memory buffer in which the names of recently opened files are stored. This command helps you access files more frequently.

Specify the name of the drive for which a buffer should be created, followed optionally by the number of file names to be stored (if you don't specify a number, the default is 50).

Switch	Effect
/X	Places the buffer in expanded memory

◆ EXTERNAL

FC

FC */switches [d:][\path\]file1.ext*
[d:][\path\]file2.ext

Compares files and displays their differences.

Switch	Effect
/A	Displays only first and last lines for each set of differences
/C	Regards upper- and lowercase instances of the same character as equivalent
/L	Compares the files as text
/LBn	Ends the comparison after *n* mismatches
/N	Displays line numbers before each line
/T	Treats tab characters as a single character, rather than replacing them with the equivalent number of spaces
/W	Regards consecutive spaces and/or tab characters as a single space
/nnnn	Specifies how many consecutive lines must be the same after a mismatch

FC /B *[d:][\path\]file1.ext [d:][\path\]file2.ext*

Compares two program (or other binary) files. Displays the results byte-by-byte in hexadecimal notation.

❖ CONFIGURATION

FCBS

FCBS=*files*

Establishes the maximum number of files that use file control blocks that can be open at one time. The default is 4, the minimum is 1, and the maximum is 255. Consult your software manuals for the correct number to use and use the largest number recommended by any of them. (Most contemporary programs don't require any file control blocks.)

FDISK

FDISK

Sets up a hard disk so DOS can use it. Establishes partitions and makes a partition bootable. See Appendix A for details.

FILES

FILES=*nn*

Establishes the maximum number of files that use file handles that can be open at one time.

FIND

FIND "text" [*d:*][*path*\\]filename.ext [/*switches*]

***command* |FIND "text" [/*switches*]**

Searches for the specified text, displaying the line containing it on the screen. FIND can search in one or more named files (wild-card characters cannot be used) or in the output of a command sent to FIND via a pipe.

Switch	Effect
/V	Displays lines that do not contain the specified text
/C	Shows how many lines contain the specified text
/N	Places a line number before each line displayed
/I	Regards upper- and lowercase instances of the same character as equivalent

FOR

FOR *%%c* IN (*list*) DO *command* [*%%c*]

Repeats the *command* for all items in the specified list. The list may contain file names, wild-card patterns, or variables.

The variable *%%c* takes the value of each item in the list in succession; *c* may be any alphabetic character. When used at the prompt, use a single percent sign in place of the double percent sign.

 EXTERNAL

FORMAT

FORMAT *d*: [*/V:label*] [*/switches*]

Formats a disk so you can use it.

Switch	Effect
/V:*label*	Lets you specify the volume label as part of the command, rather than waiting to be prompted for one.
/U	Formats the disk unconditionally, without saving unformat information.
/F:*nnn*	Specifies the diskette capacity. Valid values for *nnn* are 160, 180, 320, 360, and 1200 for 5¼-inch diskettes; 720, 1440, and 2880 for 3½-inch diskettes.
/B	Reserves space for the system files.
/S	Copies the system files to the formatted disk.

FORMAT *d*: /Q

Quick-formats a diskette that has already been formatted.

 BATCH

GOTO

GOTO *label*

Tells DOS to continue executing the batch file at the line containing the label *label*. A label is any combination of up to eight alphanumeric characters preceded by a colon. The GOTO command is often used in an IF statement.

EXTERNAL

GRAPHICS

RESIDENT

GRAPHICS [*/switches*]

If you have one of several supported printers, allows you to copy a graphic screen display by pressing Shift-PrtSc or Print Screen. By default, black parts of the screen remain white on paper and white parts are printed in black. If the command doesn't work immediately, see your DOS manual for further details on supported printers and ways to configure GRAPHICS for printers other than the defaults.

Switch	Effect
/R	Prints white on black as shown on the screen
/B	Prints the background in color on supported color printers
/LCD	Corrects the aspect ratio for LCD (laptop) screens

HELP

◆ EXTERNAL

HELP

Displays a summary of DOS commands and their uses.

HELP *command*

Displays help information for the specified command.

IF

⬡ BATCH

IF [NOT] EXIST [*d*:][*path*\\]*filename.ext*
   command

Carries out the specified command only if the specified file exists. With the NOT modifier, carries out the command only if the specified file does not exist.

IF [NOT] *%n==value command*

IF [NOT] *%variable%==%value command*

Carries out the specified command only if the specified variable has the specified value. Use the first form if the variable is a batch file variable, the second if it's an environment variable. With the NOT modifier, carries out the command only if the variable doesn't have the specified value.

◆ EXTERNAL

JOIN

JOIN *d1*: *d2*:*path*

Makes the drive specified as *d1*: appear to be the subdirectory *path* on the drive specified as *d2*:.

JOIN *d1*: /D

Undoes the effect of any previous JOIN command affecting the drive specified as *d1*:.

JOIN

Displays a list of joined drives.

◆ EXTERNAL

LABEL

LABEL [*d*:]*label*

Adds a volume label to the specified drive or changes an existing label.

LABEL [*d*:]

Prompts you for a new volume label for the specified drive. Press Enter to delete the current label.

❖ CONFIGURATION

LASTDRIVE

LASTDRIVE=*c*

Specifies the highest drive letter that can be used for a virtual disk created by the SUBST command or a network. By default, the last available drive letter is E, unless you have more than five drives comprising physical drives, hard disk partitions, or drives created by device drivers.

LOADFIX

◆ EXTERNAL

LOADFIX [*d:*][*path*\]*filename*

Use LOADFIX to run a program if you see the message Packed file corrupt when invoking it.

LH (LOADHIGH)

◆ INTERNAL

LOADHIGH [*d:*][*path*\]*filename*

Loads the specified program into upper memory blocks, if any are available, and runs it.

MD (MKDIR)

◆ INTERNAL

MD [*d:*][*path*\]. . .[*newdir*]

Creates the new subdirectory NEWDIR subordinate to the specified directory. Specify all subdirectories between the root directory and the one to contain the new subdirectory.

MD [*d:*]*newpath*

Creates a new subdirectory subordinate to the current directory.

MEM

◆ EXTERNAL

MEM

Displays a summary of the amount of conventional, extended, and expanded memory in your system. Shows how much of each is in use.

MEM /C

Displays a list of the programs currently in conventional memory and in upper memory blocks, including the amount of memory used by each, plus the amount available for programs in both conventional memory and upper memory blocks. Also includes the summary provided by MEM alone.

MEM /P

Displays the address and size in hexadecimal of programs currently in memory. Includes information about the type of each program, plus the summary provided by MEM alone.

MEM /D

Tells more than you want to know about every single thing using any of your conventional or expanded memory, including every DOS default that requires any memory.

 EXTERNAL

 RESIDENT

MIRROR

MIRROR [*d*:]. . .[*d*:]

Copies the DOS reserved area of the specified disk(s) to a file called MIRROR.FIL, to aid in undoing a FORMAT command.

MIRROR [/T*d*]. . .[/T*d*]

Installs the deletion tracking software for each specified hard disk, to aid in undeleting deleted files.

Both sets of parameters may be combined the first time MIRROR is run.

MIRROR /U

Unloads the deletion tracking program.

MIRROR /PARTN

Saves the hard disk partition table to a diskette, to aid UNFORMAT in restoring a damaged partition table.

MODE

 EXTERNAL

MODE COM*m* [BAUD=]*b*,[PARITY=]*p*,[DATA=]*d*, [STOP=]*s*, [RETRY=]p

 RESIDENT

MODE LPT*n*=COM*m*

Configures serial port *m* and redirects printer output directed to printer port *n* to it.

Parameter	Function
[BAUD=]*b*	Establishes baud rate *b* where *b* can have the value of 110, 150, 300, 600, 12 or 1200, 24 or 2400, 48 or 4800, 96 or 9600, 19 or 19,200
[PARITY=]*p*	Establishes the type of parity checking; *p* can have the value of N (none), E (even), O (odd), M (mark), or S (space)
[DATA=]*d*	Sets the number of data bits to 7 or 8
[STOP=]*s*	Sets the number of stop bits to 1, 1.5, or 2
[RETRY=]*p*	Causes continuous retrying of the printer, preventing some printer-error messages

MODE *display*

Establishes a display mode for monitors capable of more than one mode or switches between a pair of monitors using different modes. If your display seems to disappear, entering an appropriate MODE command may cure the problem. (See your DOS manual for other uses of MODE.)

Parameter	Function
BW40	40 text columns in black and white.
BW80	80 text columns in black and white.
CO40	40 text columns in color.
CO80	80 text columns in color.
MONO	Monochrome; use to switch from a color monitor to a monochrome one on systems that have both attached. Switch to the color monitor with one of the CO*nn* commands.

◇ **EXTERNAL**

MORE

MORE < [*d:*][*\path*]*filename.txt*

Displays the specified text file, pausing for a keystroke when the screen becomes full.

***command* | MORE**

Displays the output of the specified command, pausing for a keystroke when the screen becomes full.

◆ **INTERNAL**

PATH

PATH [*d:*]*\path*[;[*d:*]*\path2*][;. . .]

Establishes a list of directories in which DOS should look for a file to execute when a command is entered.

⬡ **BATCH**

PAUSE

PAUSE

Temporarily halts the execution of a batch file, displaying the message Press any key when ready.... Execution continues when a key is pressed.

◇ **EXTERNAL**

🏛 **RESIDENT**

PRINT

PRINT [/D:LPT*n*] [/*switches*]

Establishes a print queue. The following switches are used to control its behavior.

Switch	Effect
/D:LPT*n*	Specifies the printer port for which the queue is established; by default, LPT1.
/B:*nnn*	Determines the size in bytes of the internal buffer in which characters are stored while waiting for the printer. The minimum (and default) is 512, the maximum is 16,384.
/U:*t1*	Tells PRINT to wait *t1* clock ticks (18ths of a second) for the printer.
/M:*t2*	Sets the maximum number of clock ticks permitted for printing a single character to *t2*.
/S:*t3*	Sets the maximum number of characters to be printed in the interval specified by /M:*t2* to *t3*.
/Q:*files*	Sets the maximum number of files the print queue can hold.

**PRINT [*d:*][*path*\]*filename.txt*
[[*d:*][*path*\]*filename.ext*]. . .**

Adds the specified text file(s) to the print queue, to be printed while other tasks continue.

PRINT /T

Deletes all files from the print queue, terminating printing.

**PRINT [*d:*][*path*\]*filename.txt* /C
[*d:*][*path*\]*filename.txt***

Removes from the queue the file preceding the /C switch and all subsequent files up to the one before a /P switch.

**PRINT [*d:*][*path*\]*filename.txt* /P
[*d:*][*path*\]*filename.txt***

Adds to the queue the file preceding the /P switch and all subsequent files up to the one before a /C switch.

PRINT

Displays a list of files in the queue.

The /C, /P, and timing parameters may be combined with other parameters on a single command line.

◆ INTERNAL

PROMPT

PROMPT *text*

Establishes the characters displayed by the prompt. When ANSI.SYS is loaded, can optionally set screen colors. See Table 12.1 in Chapter 12 for special characters that allow you to display characters that otherwise would be interpreted as parts of commands.

PROMPT

Reestablishes the default prompt of the drive letter followed by >.

◆ INTERNAL

RD (RMDIR)

RD [*d:***][***path***\\]. . .[***path***]**

Deletes the specified subdirectory.

RD [*d:***]***path*

Deletes a subdirectory subordinate to the current directory.

◇ EXTERNAL

RECOVER

RECOVER [*d:***][***path***\\]***filename.ext*

Rewrites the specified file as FILE0000.REC in the root directory, skipping over data in bad sectors. Use to recover the readable part of a damaged file. *If you can get a program to read the file after several tries, write it to a different drive, rather than using RECOVER.*

RECOVER [*d:***]**

Rewrites all the files on the specified drive to files with names of the form FILE*nnnn*.REC in the root directory of the disk. Deletes all subdirectories. *Use this command only in the direst of emergencies. Better yet, don't use it at all!*

REM

❖ CONFIGURATION

❍ BATCH

REM *text*

Allows you to enter nonexecuting explanatory remarks in batch files and the CONFIG.SYS file.

REN (RENAME)

◆ INTERNAL

RENAME [*d:*][*\path*]*filename.ext newname.ext*

Renames one or more files without changing their location.

REPLACE

◇ EXTERNAL

REPLACE [*path*]*filename.ext* [*target*] [*/switch*]

If files of the same name exist on both the source and the target, replaces those on the target with those on the source. With the /A switch, copies only files not on the target.

Switch	Effect
/S	Replaces files in subdirectories of the target
/U	Replaces only files that are newer than equivalent files in the target
/A	Adds files that are not in the target
/R	Replaces read-only files as well as read-write files
/P	Prompts you for permission before writing each file, so that you can selectively exclude files
/W	Prompts you to press any key to begin copying files

◆ EXTERNAL

RESTORE

RESTORE *source target* [*/switches*]

Restores files that were backed up with the BACKUP command.

Switch	Effect
/S	Restores files to subdirectories of the target
/A:*mm-dd-yy*	Restores files created or modified on or after the specified date
/B:*mm-dd-yy*	Restores files created or modified on or before the specified date
/E:*hh:mm*a/p	Restores files created or modified at or earlier than the specified time
/L:*hh:mm*a/p	Restores files created or modified at or later than the specified time
/M	Restores only those files that have been modified since the last backup, replacing later versions with earlier ones
/N	Restores files that no longer exist on the target
/P	Prompts you for permission to restore when the target file is read-only

◆ EXTERNAL

SETVER

SETVER [*d:dospath*] *filename n.nn*

Tells DOS to report the specified DOS version number to the specified program. The change takes effect after you reboot the computer. Use the *d:dospath* parameter to tell SETVER what directory SETVER is located in if it's not in the current directory.

SETVER [*d:dospath*]

Displays the version table used by SETVER.

SETVER [*d:dospath*] *filename* /D

Deletes the version-table entry for the specified program, so that DOS reports version 5.0.

SHARE

 EXTERNAL

SHARE [/F:*nnn*] [/L:*nnn*]

 RESIDENT

Monitors the opening of files on your hard disk, preventing access to the same file by more than one user on a network or by more than one program in a multitasking environment.

Switch	Effect
/F:*nnn*	Specifies the number of bytes allocated for file-sharing information
/L:*nnn*	Establishes the maximum number of files that can be locked at once

SHELL

❖ **CONFIGURATION**

SHELL=[*d*:][*path*\]COMMAND.COM /P [*d*:][*path*\] [/E:*nnn*]

Specifies the location of the version of COMMAND.COM you want to use. The second drive and path tell DOS the location from which to reload COMMAND.COM after you exit a program. This should be the same as the first drive and path.

Switch	Effect
/P	Specifies that the copy of COMMAND.COM is permanent. This switch is required if you want AUTOEXEC.BAT to be executed.
/E:*nnn*	Sets the size of the DOS environment space at *nnn* bytes.

⬡ BATCH

SHIFT

SHIFT

In a batch file, discards the first parameter on the command line, so that the next variable encountered in the batch file will take the value of the next parameter on the command line. For example, if the next variable is %2, it will receive the value of the third parameter. This command is generally used preceding a GOTO command to allow a group of commands to act on a series of parameters in sequence.

◆ EXTERNAL

SORT

SORT < [*d*:][*path*\]*filename.txt*[>*target*] [/*switches*]

Sorts the specified text file, displaying the output on the screen or optionally sending it to a file or a logical device.

***command* | SORT [> *target*] [/*switches*]**

Sorts the output of *command,* displaying it on the screen or optionally sending it to a file or a logical device.

Switch	Effect
/R	Sorts the output in reverse order, from Z to A, then from 9 to 0
/+*n*	Sorts the output based on the characters in column *n*, counting the first column in the file or on the screen as column 1

❖ CONFIGURATION

STACKS

STACKS=*frames,size*

Changes the number of hardware stacks available to the microprocessor; the default is 9 frames of 128 bytes. Acceptable values for *frames* range from 8 to 64; for the frame *size* from 32 to 512.

SUBST   ◆ EXTERNAL

SUBST *d1*: *d2*:*path*

Allows you to refer to the drive and path specified in the second parameter by the drive name specified in the first parameter.

SUBST *d1*: /D

Detaches the drive and path attached to logical drive *d1*:.

SUBST

Displays a list of substitutions in effect.

SYS   ◆ EXTERNAL

SYS [*d*:] *d2*:

Copies the hidden system files and COMMAND.COM to the drive specified in the second parameter. If the current drive doesn't have these files on it, specify their location before specifying the target.

TREE   ◆ EXTERNAL

TREE [*d*:][*path*] [/*switches*]

Displays a diagram of the directory tree, starting from the current directory, unless you specify another.

Switch	Effect
/F	Lists the files in every directory displayed.
/A	Uses standard ASCII characters to draw the tree, instead of graphics characters. Use this switch if you want to print the diagram on a printer that won't print graphics characters.

❖ EXTERNAL

UNDELETE

UNDELETE *[d:][\path\][filename.ext]* *[/switches]*

If no file name is specified, displays the names of all files in the current or specified directory, one at a time. Asks if you want to undelete each file.

Switch	Effect
/LIST	Lists the deleted files that can be recovered
/ALL	Recovers all the specified files without requesting permission
/DT	Looks only in the deletion tracking file for names of files to recover
/DOS	Looks only in the specified directory for names of files to recover

❖ EXTERNAL

UNFORMAT

UNFORMAT *d:*

Restores a disk erased by FORMAT or restructured by RECOVER, using the MIRROR files if any are available.

UNFORMAT *d:* **/J**

Determines whether the MIRROR files agree with the system information on the disk.

UNFORMAT *d:* *[/switches]*

Switch	Effect
/U	Proceeds without reference to any MIRROR files that may be present
/L	Lists all file and directory names found
/TEST	Displays information regarding what was found on the disk; makes no changes
/P	Sends all messages to LPT1

UNFORMAT /PARTN

Restores the disk-partition table from a diskette to which you copied it with the MIRROR/PARTN command.

UNFORMAT /PARTN /L

Displays a report on the current partition table.

VER   ◆ INTERNAL

VER

Displays the name and release number of the DOS version currently controlling the computer.

VERIFY   ◆ INTERNAL

VERIFY ON

Specifies that read-after-write verification is performed after any command that copies files or disks. This ensures that the copy is readable but not that it is accurate, and it doubles the time required for copying. Use the /V switch to the COPY, REPLACE, DISKCOPY, and XCOPY commands to turn verification on for the particular command line.

VERIFY OFF

Turns off read-after-write verification.

◆ **INTERNAL**

VOL

VOL [*d:*]

Displays the volume label (if any) and serial number (if any) of the specified drive.

◆ **EXTERNAL**

XCOPY

XCOPY [*d:*][*path*\]*filename.ext* [*target*] [/*switches*]

Copies groups of files, which you select using wild-card patterns and the following switches:

Switch	Effect
/S	Copies all files matching the source specification in any subdirectories of the source, as well as the source. Recreates all relevant subdirectories on the target if they don't already exist.
/W	Prompts you to press any key to begin copying files.
/M	Copies only files with the archive attribute set; clears the archive attribute of the source copy.
/A	Copies only files with the archive attribute set; does not clear the archive attribute.
/D:*mm-dd-yy*	Copies only files created on or after the specified date.
/V	Performs read-after-write verification (*see* VERIFY).
/P	Asks for permission before creating each file on the target.
/E	When used with the /S switch, creates subdirectories on the target to match those on the source even if the criteria you use result in there being no files to copy to those directories.

Shell Commands

In the following entries, the command on the Shell's menu bar appears first, separated from the active command by a vertical bar. Thus, for example, if an entry reads File|Move, you first select the File menu, then select the Move command.

For further information on any Shell command, select the command on the menu and press F1.

File|Associate

When the file window is active, permits you to associate a file extension with a program.

File|Copy

When the file window is active, copies the selected files to a target you specify (*see* COPY, above, for details).

File|Create Directory

When the Directory Tree window is active, creates a new directory (*see* MD, above, for details).

File|Delete

When the file window is active, deletes the selected files (*see* DEL, above, for details).

File|Deselect All

Deselects any files that are currently selected.

File|Exit

Returns from the Shell to a command prompt.

File|Move

When the file window is active, moves the selected files to a target you specify. Selected files are erased from the source.

File|Open

If the selected file is a program, runs it.

File|Print

If a print queue has been established using PRINT, prints the selected files (*see* PRINT, above, for details).

File|Rename

When the file window is active, lets you rename all selected files, one at a time.

File|Run

When the *file* window is active, displays an entry line on which you can enter a command. When the *program group* window is active, runs the selected program.

File|Search

Searches the current drive for the files you specify. Wildcard characters may be used to search for multiple files.

File|Select All

When the file window is active, selects all files in the current directory for further actions.

File|View File Contents

Displays the selected files in ASCII or hexadecimal format.

Help|About Shell

Displays copyright information about the Shell.

Help|Commands

Explains how to use Shell menu commands.

Help|Index

Displays an index of topics about which you can get help.

Help|Keyboard

Displays tables of keys that have special meanings in the Shell, with their effects.

Help|Procedures

Displays an index to help on procedures associated with Shell menus.

Help|Shell Basics

Displays an introduction to using the Shell.

Help|Using Help

Presents an introduction to procedures for using the Help menu.

Options|Colors

Allows you to select a color scheme for the Shell.

Options|Confirmation

Lets you decide whether you will be asked for permission to proceed when deleting a file, overwriting a file, or performing a mouse operation.

Options|Display

Lets you select text or graphics mode for the Shell; with some monitors, lets you select the number of lines of text that will appear on the Shell screen.

Options|Enable Task Swapper

Lets you turn the Task Swapper on and off. When it's on, you can load more than one program at a time and switch among them.

Options|File Display Options

Lets you select whether files in the file window should be sorted, and if so, in what order. Lets you decide whether the names of hidden and system files should appear in the file window.

Options|Select Across Directories

Lets you determine whether files you select remain selected when you change directories.

Options|Show Information

Displays a window containing information about the current file (including its attributes), all selected files, the current directory, and the current drive.

Tree|Collapse Branch

Lets you hide from view all subdirectories of the current directory.

Tree|Expand All

Displays all directories on the current drive.

Tree|Expand Branch

Displays all subdirectories of the current directory.

Tree|Expand One Level

Displays the subdirectories one level below the current directory.

View|All Files

Displays a single file window, with information about the current file, selected files, the current directory, and the current drive.

View|Dual File Lists

Displays two Directory Tree and file windows, and two drive selection bars.

View|Program/File List

Displays a single Directory Tree and file window, with the program group window at the bottom of the screen.

View|Program List

Displays only the program group window.

View|Refresh

Rescans the current drive, to make sure that the information displayed by the Shell is current.

View|Repaint Screen

Refreshes the screen display.

View|Single File List

Displays a single Directory Tree and file window.

Common DOS Error Messages

This appendix discusses many common DOS error messages and explains their cause and cure. While a few error messages indicate that something is seriously wrong, most are simply the result of your entering a command line incorrectly. As someone once said, "Experience teaches you to recognize a mistake when you've made it again."

Many error messages are followed by one of the following prompts:

```
    Press any key to continue...
```

or

```
    Abort, Retry, Fail?
```

The former suggests that you correct the condition mentioned in the error message and press a key to let DOS know you have done so. The latter occurs in somewhat more serious circumstances, known as *device errors,* although the condition will often be easily correctable. When you see the latter message, it means that DOS has been unable to communicate properly with a device referenced in a command. The problem may be as simple as your having specified a diskette drive that has no diskette in it.

When you see the `Abort, Retry, Fail?` message, you are asked to press a key—A, R, or F—to tell DOS what action to take. When you press A for Abort, DOS immediately terminates the command and returns you to a DOS prompt. If you're using some software when you see the message, you will lose any work you haven't saved. When you press R for Retry, DOS tries to carry out the command again. If the problem is as simple as failure to insert a diskette, insert one and press R. When you press F for Fail, DOS tells the program that's running that it was unable to carry out the request—but it allows the program to keep running. This may give you a chance to save your work (possibly to another drive) before trying again.

Occasionally this trio of options is joined by a fourth: Ignore. Pressing I for Ignore tells DOS to proceed as if the error had not occurred; but unlike Fail, DOS doesn't inform the program. This may be dangerous.

```
Access denied
```

You tried to edit or delete a read-only or system file.

Either behave yourself or change the file's attribute using ATTRIB.

```
Bad command or file name
```

You entered a command that DOS doesn't recognize. This can occur when you mistype a command, when you don't give sufficient information (e.g., when a program is neither in the current directory nor on the path, and you failed to specify the path, or when the program is in fact not in the computer).

```
Bad or missing Command Interpreter
```

DOS was unable to read COMMAND.COM from the location where it expected to find the program during the boot process. This is most likely to happen if you boot from a diskette whose CONFIG.SYS contains a SHELL command pointing to a copy of COMMAND.COM on a hard disk when the hard disk has gone bad. Alternatively, the SHELL command on your diskette may point to a directory that no longer contains COMMAND.COM. At worst it means that something has gone wrong with COMMAND.COM, and the program will have to be recopied from your original DOS Startup diskette.

To cure any of the simpler problems, read the active CONFIG.SYS file to make sure that the SHELL command points to a valid copy of COMMAND.COM. Pay special attention to the path *after* the file name. This tells DOS where to find COMMAND.COM once DOS has been loaded.

```
Bad or missing filename.ext
```

Your CONFIG.SYS file contains a command that DOS can't execute.

Most probably either the path specified for the program in CONFIG.SYS is not correct or the program is not on the disk.

```
Batch file missing
```

DOS was executing a batch file that no longer exists.

A command in the batch file erased or renamed the batch file. Edit your batch file to prevent this from occurring again.

```
Cannot load COMMAND.COM, system halted
```

DOS was unable to reload COMMAND.COM into memory from the location specified in the COMSPEC variable (or the path following the file name in the SHELL command in CONFIG.SYS).

This can occur for no apparent reason. Reboot the computer. If it happens again, use a diskette that you know can boot the system, check that your previous boot disk contains a copy of COMMAND.COM with the same date as your other DOS files, and make sure that it's in the location specified in the SHELL command. (See `Bad or missing command interpreter`.)

```
Current drive is no longer valid
```

If you make a diskette drive current; get an error message implying that a diskette is not ready or not there; don't correct the condition; and choose Abort, you'll keep seeing the same message. If you choose Fail, you'll eventually see the above message. This means that there's no diskette—or no readable diskette—in the specified drive. Make a different drive current.

```
Data error reading/writing drive d:
```

DOS is probably attempting to read or write to a bad sector.

If reading, press R for Retry several times; if you're lucky, DOS will successfully read the file once. If it does, save it immediately to another disk. If your file is on diskette, use DISKCOPY to copy the diskette and check all the files on the copy to make sure they are readable. (You can now copy your original file back to the new diskette.) Reformat the original diskette.

If writing, use a different diskette.

If it's a hard drive, run CHKDSK with the /F switch. If that fails to correct the condition, back up the disk, reformat it, and restore it. If the message persists, back up your hard disk (if you haven't already) and call your service technician.

```
 Disk boot failure
```

You attempted to start the system from a disk that doesn't contain the three essential DOS system files.

If it's a diskette, use a different one that you know will start your system.

If it's a hard disk, it may not have DOS on it. See Chapter 2 for instructions on installing DOS.

If it's a hard disk that formerly started your system, something has gone wrong with it. Either you've lost your format or one of the system files is corrupted. Begin by using the SYS command to copy the system files to your hard disk. If that works, everything is OK. If it works for a while and then the message recurs, back up, reformat, and restore the disk. If the problem still recurs, see your dealer or a qualified service technician.

One other possibility is that you've set up your hard disk using FDISK but forgot to set up an active partition. See Appendix A for instructions.

```
 Divide overflow
```

This is most likely caused by an error in a program itself or by a conflict between resident programs.

If you see this message after loading a resident program, try changing the order in which your resident programs are loaded. If the message persists, remove all device drivers and resident programs from your CONFIG.SYS and AUTO-EXEC.BAT files, respectively, and add them back one at a time, starting with the one that produced the message, until the message reappears. Contact the publisher of the two programs that conflict and ask for advice.

```
Drive not ready
```

You forgot to close the door on a diskette drive or you've removed a diskette from a drive that's current. Place a diskette in the drive, close the door, and press R for Retry.

```
Error in EXE file
```

Something has probably gone wrong with a program file.

Try the command again. If the message recurs, reinstall the program from the original source. If it still recurs, contact the software publisher and report your problem.

```
Error writing device PRN
```

The printer is off-line, not turned on, or out of paper. Correct the condition and press R for Retry.

```
File cannot be copied onto itself
```

You entered a command that specified the same source and target for a copy.

This is most likely to happen when you enter only the source, thinking the target is current, when in fact the source is current. Retype the command with the correct information or make the target current.

```
File creation error
```

DOS was unable to create a file by the name you specified. Most probably either the file name contained invalid characters or you specified a file name that was the same as a subdirectory name in the same directory.

```
File not found
```

You asked DOS to act on a file that wasn't in the specified directory.

Most probably you mistyped the file name or the path name or failed to specify enough path information for DOS to find the file. Possibly the file does not exist.

```
General failure reading/writing drive d:
```

The most likely cause of this message is an attempt to read or write to an unformatted disk. If it's a diskette drive, replace the diskette with one that's formatted and press R for Retry. If it's a hard disk, first try rebooting the computer. If that doesn't work, you'll have to format the disk. If it's a hard disk that previously worked, this indicates serious trouble. However, reformatting it and restoring the files may cure the problem. If not, contact your computer dealer or a qualified service technician.

```
Insert disk with batch file
```

You've started a batch file from a diskette that you've since removed.

Replace the original diskette and press a key. If you're going to repeat the procedure, copy the batch file to the diskette that will be in the drive when the message occurs or place the batch file on the path.

```
Insufficient disk space
```

DOS tried to copy a file to a disk that didn't have enough room for it. If there was already a file by the same name on the target, it will have been erased.

Use a different disk or erase some files from the target.

```
Insufficient memory to load filename
```

The program you tried to run requires more memory than is currently available. Possibly you tried to run a program from a secondary prompt while a program is already in memory.

Run MEM with the /C switch, to see if there's something you can remove from memory, and try again.

If you're at a secondary prompt, enter exit, exit from the original program, and try again.

```
Invalid directory
```

Either you mistyped something in the path name (possibly you inserted spaces or omitted a backslash) or the directory doesn't exist.

Try retyping the command. If you see the same message, try to make the directory current or use the TREE command to see a list of all your directories. If you can't, it probably doesn't exist.

```
Invalid drive in search path
```

Your search path contains a reference to a drive that doesn't exist.

Most probably your path contains a reference to a drive created by SUBST, a RAM disk, or a network drive that has not been properly created. Execute the commands that create the virtual disk and try again.

```
Invalid drive specification
```

Your command contained a reference to a drive that doesn't exist, as far as DOS knows.

Check to see that you typed the command correctly. If you did, it may be a virtual drive you forgot to establish. If it's a hard drive that has been valid in the past, one of several things may have happened. If you previously needed a device driver to access the disk, it may be missing. If not, you may be booting from a diskette containing a version of DOS that doesn't know how to read the disk in question. (This might happen, for example, if you have a larger-than-32-megabyte partition and you boot with DOS 3.3). Enter ver to see whether you're using DOS 5. If you are and you don't need a device driver, the disk has gone bad. Try running UNFORMAT /PARTN. If that doesn't work, reformat and restore the disk. If that doesn't work, run FDISK and re-create your partition table.

```
Invalid number of parameters
```

You entered too few or too many parameters for a command.

Most likely you entered a space instead of a period in a file name.

```
Invalid parameter
```

You entered a parameter that DOS doesn't recognize.

See Appendix C for a list of valid parameters for the command.

```
No Paper
```

The printer is off-line or out of paper.

Correct the condition and press R for Retry.

```
Non-DOS disk
```

You'll see this message if the disk was formatted by another operating system or if the file allocation table is damaged or contains invalid information.

If you know it's a DOS-formatted diskette, run CHKDSK on it with the /F switch. You will probably lose some files, but you may be able to salvage the rest.

```
Non-system disk or disk error
```

You attempted to boot from a diskette that doesn't contain the three system files.

Replace the diskette with one you know will start your system and press a key.

```
Packed file corrupt
```

You ran a program that's not accustomed to the large amount of memory DOS 5 makes available.

Enter the command LOADFIX as a prefix to the command that loads the program. If the command was c:\util\runit, enter loadfix c:\util\runit.

```
Path not found
```

DOS couldn't find the path you specified.

Either you made a typing error or the path does not exist. See the error message Invalid Directory for further details.

```
Read fault error reading drive d:
```

DOS was unable to read from the disk; it may be improperly seated in the drive or may have a bad sector.

Open the drive, take out the diskette and reinsert it, and press R for Retry. If the failure repeats, press A for Abort and run CHKDSK with the /F switch.

```
Sector not found
```

The data DOS is trying to read is probably in a bad sector.

Retry several times; if you're lucky, DOS will successfully read the file once. If it does, save it immediately to another disk. If it's a diskette, use DISKCOPY to copy the diskette and check all the files on the copy to make sure they are readable. (You can now copy your original file back to the new diskette.) Reformat the original diskette.

```
Seek error reading/writing drive d:
```

DOS was unable to locate the proper track on a disk.

If it's a diskette, open the drive, take out the diskette and reinsert it, and press R for Retry. If failure recurs, press A for Abort and run CHKDSK with the /F switch. If it's a hard disk, press A for Abort and run CHKDSK. If the message recurs often, back up your hard disk completely and get a new one.

```
Stack overflow, system halted
```

DOS doesn't have enough hardware stacks to contain the information it needs.

If your CONFIG.SYS contains the command stacks=0,0, delete it. If it doesn't, add the command stacks=32,128.

```
Unable to create directory
```

You asked DOS to create a directory that already exists or to create a directory that has the same name as an existing file. You're most likely to see this message when using the installation program for software that normally creates a directory, and you've already created one by the same name.

If you're trying to create the directory, use a different name. If an installation program is trying to create the directory, it won't be able to, since the directory already exists.

```
Unrecognized command in CONFIG.SYS
```

DOS couldn't interpret a command in CONFIG.SYS.

This message has the same causes and cures as a Bad command or file name message at a prompt.

```
Write fault error writing drive d:
```

DOS was unable to write to the disk; it may be improperly seated in the drive or may have a bad sector.

Open the drive, take out the diskette and reinsert it, and press R for Retry. If the failure repeats, press A for Abort and run CHKDSK with the /F switch. See `Read fault error` for further details.

```
Write protect error writing drive d:
```

Your diskette has a write-protection tab over the notch or the write-protection slider is opened.

Take out the diskette and read the label. You probably write-protected the diskette for a good reason. If it's the correct diskette, remove the write-protection tab and press R for Retry. If you're installing a program from an original diskette, it's probably trying to record registration information. If this worries you, copy the diskette and repeat the installation from the copy.

Glossary

Application program   A program used to accomplish specific tasks such as word processing, accounting, looking up data in tables

ASCII   The American Standard Code for Information Interchange; an agreed-upon system of numbering characters and control codes

Attribute byte   A hidden byte in a file's directory entry indicating the file's attributes

Batch file   A file containing a list of DOS commands to be executed sequentially

Bit   A *b*inary dig*it*; the smallest unit of information recognized by the computer; a bit can have a value of either 0 or 1

Boot   *See* Cold boot; Warm boot

Boot record   The first sector of a disk, containing the program that starts the computer and provides information about the disk's structure

Bootstrap program   The program in the boot record that starts the computer

Buffer   Any portion of memory set aside as a temporary storage area for use by a program or a hardware device

Button   A location on the screen that initiates or cancels an action when clicked with a mouse

Byte   A unit of information storage equivalent to one character

Central processing unit (CPU) The computer's master control chip

Chain A series of consecutive clusters or allocation units on a disk; a file may have one or several chains

Character Any letter of the alphabet, a numeral, a mathematical or grammatic symbol, a graphic symbol, or a control code that has an ASCII number

Cluster The smallest unit in which disk space is allocated; its size depends on the type and size of disk

Cold boot Starting the computer by turning it off and on or pressing a reset button

Command line The line on which you enter DOS commands

Command processor The computer's main control program; in DOS it is called COMMAND.COM

Console The keyboard and screen

Control characters The first 32 characters of the ASCII set; generally they act as commands rather than displayable or printable characters

Control files A pair of text files, CONFIG.SYS and AUTOEXEC.BAT, that can be used to tell your computer about peripheral hardware, to set defaults, and to load resident programs

Conventional memory The memory in which programs are executed; PC-compatible computers can have up to 640 kilobytes of conventional memory

CPU *See* Central processing unit

Cylinder One of a number of concentric rings in the magnetic medium of a disk. Cylinders are divided into a specific number of sectors, which depends on the size and type of disk

Data format The factors that determine how a serial port interprets data coming to it. These comprise baud rate, a start bit, a specific number of data bits, an optional parity bit, and stop bits

Default The value assumed by the computer, or by a command, when none is supplied by the user

Delimiter A character that separates parts of a command; generally a space or a semicolon

Device driver   A file that tells the computer how to address a particular piece of hardware

Dialog box   A box on the screen in which you enter choices or information

Directory   A listing of the files on a disk; directory listings contain the file's name, size, and date and time of origin or modification; they also contain hidden information about the file's attributes and starting location

Disk   A medium for permanent storage of programs or data files

Disk cache   A memory buffer for information read from disk; used to speed up disk access

DOS environment space   An area of memory created by COMMAND.COM for storing information on the location of various items; this information is established by the values assigned to environment variables

DOS reserved area   The first part of a disk, containing information DOS needs to find files and directories; it comprises the boot record, file allocation tables, and root directory

Download   To receive information into the computer from a remote computer (*see* Upload)

End-of-file mark   The Ctrl-Z character; when DOS encounters one, it reads no further in a data file

Environment variable   A group of characters placed in the DOS environment space, to which a value is assigned

Expanded memory   Memory managed by a device driver conforming to the Lotus-Intel-Microsoft Expanded Memory Standard (LIM-EMS)

Expansion slots   Slots inside the system unit into which printed-circuit boards are placed, to give the computer additional capabilities

Extended memory   Memory that may be found in computers with an 80286 (or higher) CPU, managed by the device driver HIMEM.SYS

Extension   Three optional characters at the end of a file name, which usually denote the type of file and are separated from the main part of the name by a period

External command   A command included in DOS as a separate program

File   A series of consecutive bytes attached to a specific name; all computer data, including programs, is stored as files

File allocation table (FAT)   A portion of a disk that indicates where files are physically located

File attribute   A file may have one or more attributes: *read-only,* which prevents a file from being changed; *hidden,* which prevents a file from appearing in a directory; *system,* which prevents both; and *archive,* which indicates that the file has not been backed up; other attributes indicate volume labels and directory names; a file that has no attributes is a *normal,* or *read-write,* file

Filter   A program that processes information and passes the result to another program; used in a pipe

Fixed disk   *See* Hard disk

Floppy disk   A removable disk; a diskette

Format   To organize the magnetic patterns on a disk so they can store data

Function keys   Keys indicated by the letter *F* and a number, which execute commands or perform other functions in a program

Gigabyte   A billion bytes; a thousand megabytes

Graphical user interface   An operating environment characterized by icons, buttons, windows, and pull-down menus

Graphics mode   A method of displaying information on the screen as a series of dots, rather than as characters; text may be displayed in graphics mode (*see* Text mode)

Hard disk   A high-capacity disk comprising several rigid platters, generally internal to the system unit

Hardware   The physical parts of a computer

Hexadecimal   A numbering system using base 16, used extensively in computers

Icon   A graphic image on the screen, used to represent a file in a graphical user interface

Input   To give instructions or data to a computer; the instructions or data given

Input device   Any device from which the CPU can receive data; input devices include the keyboard, disks, mice, digitizing tablets, scanners, serial and parallel ports, and light pens

Insert mode   A mode of entering text in which characters to the right of the cursor are pushed further to the right to make room for new characters (*see* Overtype mode)

Interface   A connection between a computer and a peripheral device; a system by which a human interacts with a computer

Internal command   A DOS command built into the command processor; internal commands can be executed even when no other files or disks are present (*see* External command)

Inverse video   Text on the screen highlighted by switching the colors of the background and the text; if normal text is white on a black background, inverse video shows black text on a white background

Keypad   A rectangularly arranged group of keys used to move the cursor or enter numeric data

Kilobyte (K)   1024 bytes

Label   A marker in a batch file to which execution may be directed by a GOTO command

Logical device name   A name used by the computer to refer to any device attached to a particular port or other destination of output

Logical drive   Anything addressed by a drive name. Logical drives include diskette drives; the "phantom" drive B, which coexists with drive A on computers with a single diskette drive; hard disk partitions; drives created by the SUBST command; drives created using DRIVER.SYS; RAM disks; and network drives

Megabyte (Mb)   1,024,000 bytes

Memory   The part of a computer in which information is stored while the computer is actively using it; only when data is in memory is it accessible to the CPU for processing

Memory address   A pair of hexadecimal numbers that the CPU uses to figure out where an item is stored in memory; the first number specifies a 64 kilobyte range; the second indicates the specific byte within that range

Menu   A list from which commands can be selected and entered

Modem   A contraction for *mo*dulator-*dem*odulator—a device that translates computer data into sound pitches for transmission via phone lines, and translates sound pitches into computer data for reception from phone lines

Monitor   The screen; also called CRT, VDT, display

Multitasking   A system whereby more than one program is executed at a time

On-line help   Advice and instructions that a user can access while running a program

Operating environment   A program run in conjunction with DOS to alter the computer's behavior and/or user interface

Output   The information generated by a computer after it has been processed

Output device   Any device to which the CPU can write data. Output devices include the screen, disks, printers, plotters, and serial and parallel ports

Overtype mode   A mode of entering text where new characters replace those at the cursor as it moves (*see* Insert mode)

Parallel   A mode of communication between the CPU and a peripheral device in which data travels eight bits at a time along eight parallel electrical paths (*see* Serial)

Parameter   A part of a command line that tells the command what object—disk, file, or directory—should be acted upon

Partition   A division of a hard disk addressed by a single drive name

Path name   A complete description of a file, which includes the drive name and the names of any subdirectories between the root directory and the directory containing the file

Peripheral device Any device attached to a computer and operated by it; any part of a computer other than the central processing unit

Pipe A command in which the output from one command becomes the input for another

Platter One of the rigid disks composing a hard disk

Port A point at which an external device can be attached to a computer

Print queue A list of files to be printed, managed by a program that automatically sends the files to the printer while other work progresses

Print spooler A memory buffer containing text that will eventually be printed

Program information file (PIF) A file used by Microsoft Windows for the information it needs to run a program

Prompt Text indicating that the computer is ready to accept a command

RAM *See* Random-access memory

RAM disk A portion of the computer's memory treated by the computer as though it were a storage disk

Random-access memory (RAM) Memory actively used by the CPU for information currently being processed; any information in RAM disappears when the computer is turned off

Read-only memory (ROM) Memory in which basic operating instructions for the computer are permanently stored (*see* Random-access memory)

Redirection The process of directing command output to some point other than its normal destination, either a file, a logical device, or another program

Remark A command in a batch file or the CONFIG.SYS file that explains to the programmer what other commands are supposed to do; remarks are ignored by DOS during execution

Resident program A program that leaves part of its code in memory after running; resident programs are generally of two types: those that alter the way the computer works (examples include PRINT and FASTOPEN)

and those that can be popped up by using a hot key—a special key combination—to perform some task for the user (examples include many commercially available programs)

Resolution   The "grain" of the screen or a printer, generally characterized in dots per inch

ROM   *See* Read-only memory

Root directory   The main directory of any disk

Scroll bar   A part of the screen in a graphical user interface used to bring parts of a window into view

Search path   A list of directories to be searched for a program to execute when a command is entered

Sector   The smallest unit of disk storage that DOS can address; generally 512 bytes

Separator   *See* delimiter

Serial   A mode of communication between the CPU and a peripheral device in which data travels one bit at a time along a single electrical path (*see* Parallel; Data format)

Software   The instructions that set up a structure within which a computer processes information and a person enters specific directions

Subdirectory   Any directory but the root directory, when viewed in relation to another directory to which it is subordinate

Switch   A part of a command line that modifies the way the command operates, usually preceded by a virgule

System unit   The main part of a computer, containing the central processing unit, the disk drives, the power supply, the expansion slots, and the ports

Terminate-and-stay-resident program (TSR)   *See* Resident program

Text mode   A method of displaying information on the screen as a series of characters of fixed size (*see* Graphics mode)

Toggle   A command that can be in one of two states (e.g., on or off)

Track   The intersection of the side of a platter and a cylinder

TSR Terminate-and-stay-resident program (*see* Resident program)

Upload To send data to a remote computer (*see* Download)

Upper memory blocks (UMBs) The range of memory addresses between 640K and 1Mb, which can be used to run device drivers and resident programs

Utility software Programs that help manage the computer

Virtual disk *See* Virtual drive

Virtual drive Any disk drive that has no independent physical existence. Diskette drive A and hard disk partitions are *not* virtual drives; virtual drives include diskette drive B, which coexists with drive A in a single physical diskette drive on computers with a single diskette drive; RAM disks; drives created by DRIVER.SYS; drives created by the SUBST command; and network drives that don't coexist with physical drives

Warm boot Starting the computer by pressing Ctrl-Alt-Del, which resets the central processing unit but does not clear memory

Wild-card pattern A group of characters including the * and ? characters, which can stand for any characters in a file name; used to select a group of files

Window An outlined portion of the screen in which a specific process takes place; characteristic of, but not exclusive to, a graphical user interface

Index